TO LIVE IN PEACE

TO LIVE IN PEACE

Biblical Faith and the Changing Inner City

Mark R. Gornik

WILLIAM B. EERDMANS PUBLISHING COMPANY
GRAND RAPIDS, MICHIGAN / CAMBRIDGE, U.K.

© 2002 Wm. B. Eerdmans Publishing Co.
All rights reserved

Wm. B. Eerdmans Publishing Co.
2140 Oak Industrial Drive N.E., Grand Rapids, Michigan 49505 /
P.O. Box 163, Cambridge CB3 9PU U.K.
www.eerdmans.com

Printed in the United States of America

13 12 11 10   10 9 8 7 6 5

Library of Congress Cataloging-in-Publication Data

Gornik, Mark R.
To live in peace: biblical faith and the changing inner city /
Mark R. Gornik.
p.   cm.
Includes bibliographical references.
ISBN 978-0-8028-4685-3 (pbk.: alk. paper)
1. City churches — United States.   I. Title.

BV637.G63   2002
253′.09173′2 — dc21

2002023818

Chapter 5 contains an excerpt from Bruce Cockburn's "Broken Wheel," © 1981 by
Golden Mountain Music Corporation (SOCAN), and is used here by permission.

Unless otherwise indicated, the Scripture quotations in this publication are from the
HOLY BIBLE: NEW INTERNATIONAL VERSION. Copyright © 1973, 1978, 1984 by
the International Bible Society. Used by permission of Zondervan Bible Publishers.

For Rita
Útitárs

Contents

CONTENTS

Hope of the Afflicted

When I visited a Baltimore neighborhood called Sandtown in 1997, my most vivid impression was of a disturbingly jarring contrast. I remember what seemed like a whole neighborhood of abandoned houses — each like an oversize skull, empty darkness peering out of its broken doors and windows and mocking the life that had irretrievably abandoned it. In the midst of these ruins, however, there was a street teeming with life — houses repaired and painted with bright colors, neighbors chatting, and children playing in the street. It was as if in this one place a resurrection of sorts had clothed the dry bones of urban death with the pulsating flesh of life. At the heart of this improbable transformation was a small company of Christians who call themselves New Song Community. *To Live in Peace* tells the story of this community and gives a theological rationale for their mission in the inner city. Its author, Mark Gornik, was among the first to relocate to Sandtown in response to God's call to rebuild its ruins. The book is an eloquent testimony to the capacity of lives modeled on Christ's self-giving love and inspired by the Spirit of life to transform hopeless urban landscapes into sites of God's peace.

To read this book properly, jump ahead about 150 pages and go straight to Chapter 5, entitled "Singing a New Song." This is the book's heart, apart from which important theological and sociological reflections that precede and follow it cannot be properly understood, and it tells the story of Sandtown's gradual "resurrection." Inspired by John Perkins's pioneering work in community development (summed up by his famous "three R's": relocation, reconciliation, and redistribution), Mark Gornik and Allan Tibbels simply moved into the neighborhood armed with no "plans or programs," except for the conviction that "the church is God's reconciled community pursuing justice at the point of greatest suffering in the world." They started by hanging around in the community until, as a testimony to "Sandtown's capacity for grace," they were welcomed. From then on, as Gornik explains, everything was an effort made not so much by the few who relocated to Sandtown but by the many who did not abandon it during hard times. First a community church was established; next vacant housing started to be replaced by homes affordable for everyone; then the local educational system and health care system were dramatically improved; and finally an effective employment strategy was put in place. Achievements are easy to enumerate, but at every step of the way it took a miracle of courage and persistence to make it happen.

I came away from reading this book moved and challenged in many ways. The first challenge is a *personal* one. Gornik and Tibbels chose not to pursue the comforts of ministry in middle-class environments and instead to relocate to a place of desolation and hopelessness. For Tibbels this was a special challenge: he is a quadriplegic, a husband, and a father of two girls. What struck me was not just the sainthood of these individuals but how lightly they wore it, without effort or self-importance.

The second challenge is an *ecclesial* one. Despite the rhetoric of service to the world, churches often succumb to the temptation to live primarily for themselves — to increase numbers, improve programs, add new buildings. For the New Song Community, to be the church means to be for others — indeed, *with* others — especially the neediest. "The ministries of justice and reconciliation are not additions that flow out of the church," says Gornik, but are "constitutive of ecclesial life in union with Christ."

The third challenge concerns the *character of service*. It is all too easy to be helping the needy in such a way that the very service rendered humiliates its recipients. Even the talk about "empowerment" often leaves a bitter taste of condescension. *To Live in Peace* is suffused with deep respect for the dignity of the needy. They are not the "others" for whom something must be done, even less the ignorant and unruly who must be disciplined. They are the family who have fallen on hard times and must be encouraged and helped.

The fourth challenge grows out of the striking way in which the New Song Community goes about *connecting faith with life*. Repeatedly, Gornik argues against approaching the problem of the inner cities with blueprints, either derived from faith or informed by secular reasoning (though in the book he does a great deal of theological and sociological heavy-lifting). Instead, he suggests a twofold strategy: (1) keep focused on the vision toward which the community needs to move (the *shalom* of God's new creation) and on the path on which it needs to walk (Christ's self-giving love), and (2) concentrate "upon faithfully doing thousands of little things right over a period of many years."

Finally, the book is a challenge to how we think about *faith-based initiatives*. Gornik knows well that there are significant and unique resources in churches for addressing the needs of inner cities; his whole book is an explication of these resources. And yet he cautions that the present emphasis on faith-based initiatives overly personalizes poverty and social change and therefore disregards both "the needs for infrastructure and capital" and the structural dimension of poverty. The concern is an expression of Gornik's refusal to be caught in false alternatives — either attention to persons or attention to structures. Both need to be addressed if communities are to live in peace, and therefore both the church and the government have a role to play.

The Christian wisdom, commitment, and courage inscribed in Gornik's book and incarnate in New Song Community are extraordinary. My hope is that we all will catch something of Gornik's vision: "Guided by the conviction that Christ crucified creates room for the embrace of others and that the Spirit of the resurrected Christ brings new life," the churches can and must serve "to advance the *shalom* of American inner cities."

MIROSLAV VOLF

Preface

"Greater love has no one than this, that one lay down his life for his friends."

John 15:13

I grew up in Baltimore in an African-American community called Sand-town. Sandtown was an exciting place for a little girl growing up in the 1950s and early '60s. The streets were teeming with neighbors; the corner stores were run by friendly shopowners; nearby Pennsylvania Avenue was vibrant with jazz clubs, movie houses, and seemingly every variety of shopping; and active churches were packed every Sunday. There were no vacant houses, and jobs, while certainly not high-paying for black workers, were available. I never knew we were "poor." We never had much money or many material possessions, but tight-knit extended families, a strong sense of community, a depth of faith in God, and the joy of life were abundant.

As the sixties wore on, several forces converged to bring decline to Sandtown. The manufacturing base, foundational to decent job opportunities for black workers, continued to decline in Baltimore. Housing legislation opened new opportunities for black families, and thousands began to move elsewhere. And when Dr. Martin Luther King was assassinated in 1968, the ensuing riots further decimated an already deteriorating neighborhood, and many shopowners fled, never to return.

And so a once-proud neighborhood began the struggle to cope with lack of jobs, vacant housing, and the onslaught of more and more drugs. By 1980, Sandtown had a population of fewer than 15,000 — a significant decline from a post–World War II high of nearly 45,000 — and had more than a thousand vacant houses, 25 percent of the entire 72-square-block neighborhood. Like most inner-city neighborhoods at the time, Sandtown had become a forgotten community, and a sense of desolation and hopelessness began to pervade it.

Into this context came a small group of white folks in 1986. Pastor Mark Gornik and Allan and Susan Tibbels and their two daughters moved into our neighborhood. It was the first time we had ever seen white people move in. I wondered what it was they wanted. They rehabbed vacant houses and moved into them, hung out on the streets and attended community meetings, and spent time with the children of Sandtown, including my children. The kids talked about how wonderful they were, and when Pastor Mark and the Tibbels began a church together with families from the neighborhood, my kids asked me to go visit, which I did. One Sunday morning when we were getting ready to go to my old church, my kids said they wanted to go to New Song instead because they "liked learning about Jesus there." It wasn't long before I joined New Song, and I have been a part of it ever since.

Pastor Mark and the Tibbels showed a deep love for the community, *my* community, and became my neighbors. Together we began ministries to love our community and rebuild it, restore it to the health and vibrancy I had experienced as a little girl. This effort included creating programs in housing, education, and health care, as well as programs in job development, economic development, and development of the arts.

In 1989 my sister died, and so I suddenly added her two daughters to my household. A single parent at the time, struggling to make ends meet, I was able to become a homeowner through New Song's Habitat for Humanity program. In my resulting joy, I told God to let me know if there was anything I could ever do for Habitat. Be careful what you pray for! I was invited to join the staff, and since 1994 I have served as the Co-Executive Director, as well as serving on several of the program boards. I am now rebuilding my own community, seeing restored joy and *shalom* every single day. And I was married in 1998 to Al Stokes, who grew up in Sandtown and who is a leader of New Song Community Church. Together we enjoy our home and our family, especially our grandchildren.

Inner-city neighborhoods do not need people to come and tell them what they need; we already *know* what we need. One of the best things about Pastor Mark is that he didn't do that. Instead, he became a neighbor, "one of us," and worked side by side with neighborhood folks as *together* we determined our agenda and carried it out.

We've come a long way. One thing that we have never lost in Sandtown is our sense of community, of loving each other and caring for one another.

We also have a deep faith strengthened by the struggles of many decades. And now that we have the resources needed to rebuild, joy and a sense of hope are returning. The daily struggle and pain of losing our children to the streets and our men to the prisons remain, as do the continuing effects of oppression and injustice upon our community. But the struggle and pain are increasingly accompanied by celebration and joy as homes are completed, as our children graduate from high school and go on to college, and as families for the first time have access to primary health care in the midst of our community. Yes, the rebuilding of inner-city communities is possible.

When Pastor Mark moved with his wife, Rita, to New York in 1998, I was brokenhearted to see them leave yet excited to see another New Song established in New York. But this will always be his home, and he will always be my neighbor. He truly "laid down his life" on behalf of my community.

Reconciliation between blacks and whites in America remains a challenge, but it is possible because of the power of the gospel. Pastor Mark's moving in to Sandtown and our struggling together for more than ten years show what is possible when whites are repentant and blacks are willing to forgive.

Mark Gornik is my friend and brother in Christ. He has labored to bring justice and peace to my community. He loves the city. And he exemplifies the commandment of "loving my neighbor as myself," having been a voice for an oppressed people, having worked to bridge the gap between the haves and the have-nots, and having helped to bring in the resources needed to rebuild my community. Together with our neighbors we have worshipped and prayed and studied the Bible — all things which are, as you will see throughout this book, foundational in working for justice and joy in the inner city, and which undergird community development and sustain ministry.

And so I commend Mark's words to you. May God bless this book so that it may awaken the hearts of all men and women to seek his *shalom* and to work for a better tomorrow.

LaVerne S. Stokes

This Little Light

This is the day that the Lord has made in Sandtown, a neighborhood on Baltimore's hard-pressed west side. It is a day of reversal about which the Hebrew prophets had long ago enthused, a time Jesus had announced. This is the day when the last will truly come first, the gentle will be made strong, and the meek will inherit the earth. Arriving as a gift of the Lord, it is a day for being astounded, for celebrating the impossible transformed into the possible, for seeing what was hoped for come to life. For today is moving day for Russell and Thelma Sampson.

Following thirty-seven years of paying painfully high rents to a string of disinterested and absentee landlords, in effect having bought their house many times over but never having gained the deed, the Sampsons are moving from a tiny two-story alley-street house on School Street into a new home on the 1500 block of North Stricker Street. Just a few steps from their present rental unit, the new house they will own has been renovated by Sandtown Habitat for Humanity, a neighborhood-based home ownership program started by New Song Community Church.

All of their lives the Sampsons worked hard and played by the rules, but you wouldn't know it from the cost or the condition of their housing. Rent consumed nearly half their income. Yet until this day, their tiny home, which they maintained as neatly as possible inside, was little more than a brick-skinned shack with rotting floorboards covered with cheap surplus paint. If you put your foot down too hard, it might go right through to the air below. Rats found it easy to gnaw their way in. The house was plagued with other problems: dangerous electrical wiring; a bathroom that leaked; ceilings that were falling down; windows that only sometimes kept the wind and cold out;

narrow, rickety steps. The other units sat empty, with windows broken and doors gone, hollowed husks staring into the alley laden with trash and broken glass. Thelma and Russell were the last "official" residents in the short row of red brick houses on School Street.

Their new house had come a long way. Longtime neighbors estimated that the two-story brick row house at 1504 North Stricker Street where the Sampsons would be moving had sat vacant for twenty years. Not so long ago, faded plywood boards had covered the doorways and window openings. Water had flowed down from the collapsed roof. The labors of scavengers hunting for salable materials had left the house slowly collapsing from top to bottom. Room by tiny room, trash and debris covered the floors, and one could see where electrical fixtures and their connections had been. The plaster surface of the walls and ceiling was pocked with holes, exposing an inner layer of wooden lath strips. Bathroom fixtures, wrested from their fittings, sat turned over.

Along both sides of the treeless block, the pattern of physical dismemberment was similar. Of the two rows of twenty-three connected dwelling units, over half were vacant. But it was hard to distinguish the vacant from the non-vacant, the result of absentee landlords who had allowed their properties to languish and deteriorate. Among the abandoned houses, break-ins and fires were routine. At night, three leaning streetlights cast illumination that seemed equal to no more than a 40-watt lightbulb. The northern end of the block — where Calhoun, Baker, and Stricker streets meet — had become an active open-air drug market, and one of the neighborhood's most violent parcels of asphalt and brick. It was well known as the source for the local "gang" known as CBS, each initial standing for the first letter of one of the streets.

The brutalized streetscape of 1500 North Stricker Street was emblematic not only of much of Sandtown and West Baltimore, but also of similarly sequestered neighborhoods throughout America's cities. The ordnance of destruction in the neighborhood had come not from the weapons of a war between nations, but from the interconnections of race, place, and economics, which, over time, had brought destruction to the fabric of the community. Here we witness urban life gone awry, the entire fabric of existence opposed to God's good, peaceable, and redemptive intentions for the city.

But by the power of the Spirit, who brings new life and renews all things, something different began taking place. House by house, this block began giving way to the rebirth of community rightly ordered, a transformation from ruin to the space where God's peace and wholeness are more present. Amidst the ruins of this forgotten corner of the city, a resurrection of community began. A "new thing" began coming into being.

*   *   *

Around the corner from the Sampsons' old and new homes, on an open lot the size of a small block, people are arriving early this Friday morning to share in the heavy labors of rebuilding. Coming from every point in the neighborhood and from across the entire metropolitan region of Baltimore, five hundred people have been working together all through the week in Sandtown Habitat's annual "blitz build" effort. Early each morning, volunteers, neighbors, staff, and homeowners gather in the large green-and-white tents set up on the lot. Together they sing, hear the Word reflected on, and welcome one another to the challenges of the shared task. When they are dismissed with prayer, the tents quickly empty. Pushing wheelbarrows and carrying hammers, crowbars, and power tools, people go forth to renovate houses throughout the neighborhood. During this week, nearly twenty houses, all vacant and long abandoned, are under construction to become places of homeownership for long-term Sandtown families. Adoration gives way to the tasks of action.

Today, 1504 North Stricker is swirling with activity, since only a few hours remain before the afternoon dedication of the Sampsons' house. A sudden thunderstorm the day before smeared the freshly painted exterior, so today the scaffolding still sits in place as painters work again, this time with the benefit of newly installed tarp — just in case! Inside, every space of the house seems to have someone working on it. The sounds of drills, hammers, and saws fill the house as the final cabinets are hung, plumbing is hooked up and adjusted, and the last pieces of molding are installed. From top to bottom, the house is cleaned of sawdust and building materials.

The beauty of each completed Sandtown Habitat home — restored out of love for God and neighbor — is found in its particular blend of participatory involvement that includes sweat equity and attention to local architectural patterns. Each house celebrates the neighborhood, an affirmation of its history. The Sampsons' house is a complete "gut rehab" — virtually everything about it is new on the inside, from the floors and carpets to the roof to all the systems (plumbing, electrical, and heating). A reconfigured first-floor layout means more open space for the living room, dining area, and kitchen, which is equipped with shiny new appliances. Upstairs are two bedrooms and a bathroom. Unlike the standard rental units in Sandtown, it even comes with a real shower! Like every Sandtown Habitat home, it is simple, solidly constructed housing that is both beautiful and affordable.

At 3:00 P.M. the joyful rhythms and harmonies of gospel music and singing replace the start-and-stop sounds of hammers and saws. Workers scurry out of the back of the house as a bright ribbon is taped across the front door; the scaffolding is hauled away. The week's volunteers — neighborhood residents, church members, friends, and Habitat homeowners — fill the sidewalk and street together in hope and expectation to celebrate the completion of yet another Sandtown Habitat home.

By now, people are leaning out of their windows, stopping their cars, walking by but staying in the mix of people. With the sidewalk for their stage, the "house band" from New Song Community Church has set up and begun playing. Steve Smallman is laying down soaring amplified piano runs, and Elder Clyde Harris's tambourine and booming voice are beckoning everyone together. The exuberant singing and clapping are filtering up and down the streets and alleys. No question. Rebuilding makes you sing with joy, even if your singing voice doesn't adequately express your heart's gladness!

As the music quiets and pauses for an invocation, Janice Jamison, an enthusiastic and committed Sandtown Habitat homeowner, welcomes everyone to the dedication and house blessing. Next comes a "welcome to the block" speech from William Elliott, the first Sandtown homeowner on 1500 North Stricker Street and a committed member of the board of directors. As Mr. Elliott is talking, the members of New Song's Voices of Hope choir move forward and assemble on and around the front steps. The Voices of Hope include many children of Habitat homeowners, present and future. They are the future of Sandtown, and as they lift their voices together in exuberant praise, there is even more reason for pride and hope on this great day.

Presentations follow: a new Bible from a local pastor; a bouquet of flowers to Thelma from other homeowners; words from Jim Rouse, founder of the Enterprise Foundation; then the keys from Mayor Kurt Schmoke. These are great moments. But it is tears and an embrace that form the grammar of this new story now being written.

LaVerne Stokes, one of the first Sandtown Habitat homeowners and the organization's co–executive director, comes to the microphone to speak. LaVerne is an extraordinary leader, a modern-day Esther, a woman that God has raised up for such a time as this to serve her people and community in a life-giving way. Given the intertwining history of LaVerne and the Sampsons, her words of congratulations offer a glimpse of divine glory.

It was in 1950 that Leonard and Margaret Paige, LaVerne's parents, moved to Baltimore, and later in 1956 to the 1500 block of North Stricker Street in Sandtown. It was a time on the cusp of major social changes. Like thousands of other African Americans, the Paiges moved to Baltimore from Virginia seeking work, relief from racism, and a better life. Growing up on North Stricker, LaVerne remembers "a block with trees where I would play with my three sisters and brother." The code of the block, LaVerne recalls, was "if you did something wrong and a neighbor caught you, you took your punishment right away or you would receive twice when they told your parents." Her parents and their neighbors, Russell and Thelma Sampson, would sit behind the house on cool summer evenings listening to R&B music. Their favorite song was "It Took a Hundred Pounds of Clay."

There were no vacant houses on the 1500 block of North Stricker Street during the 1950s and early 1960s. Reminiscing on another occasion, Anna Lewis, known as Miss Betty, a woman of great strength and sweet caring who had lived on the block for over forty years (thirty-seven as a renter, but from 1995 on as a Sandtown Habitat homeowner), recalled, "It used to be great! There were no vacants or trash." It was a "beautiful block" and had won awards for being one of the cleanest in the city. Corner stores and even a storefront church anchored each end of the block. But it was not a golden time about which to be nostalgic. Sandtown was a community "outside the dream," segregated from opportunity, advancement, and the daily possibilities of life that white city residents took for granted. And then things got worse in the 1970s — much worse. Jobs disappeared and families were deeply hurt. People moved and basic institutions were hollowed out. Landlords abandoned their housing. Drugs and their marketing increasingly filled the void. Banks sped up their disinvestments. Life began to unravel.

These memories and the emotions they evoke are packed into the dedication. Before the crowd of nearly two hundred, LaVerne and Thelma embrace one another in tears, sharing a moment of overwhelming power as years of history now converge to signal a new beginning of community hope and possibility. Thelma Sampson then speaks simple yet profound words into the microphone: "How grateful I am to all of you and God. Thank you!"

Before the benediction is pronounced, Elder Harris and Steve Smallman lead the "congregation" in singing "This Little Light of Mine." "Some people may think we don't know any other songs!" Janice Jamison has remarked. But among Sandtown Habitat and New Song's repertoire of songs, it is this song that is always sung at benchmark neighborhood achievements.

> This little light of mine, I'm gonna to let it shine.
> Shine all over my neighborhood, I'm gonna to let it shine.
> All around the neighborhood, I'm gonna to let it shine.
> Let it shine, let it shine, let it shine.

All have come to know the words, and there is obvious rejoicing in a truth that evokes a deep sense of common calling, purpose, and identity — of moving forward together in the neighborhood. Light divine is shining toward a new way of being community.

*   *   *

The metaphor of light in the Bible speaks of God's creative power and majesty (Gen. 1:3-4), salvation and new beginnings (John 1:9; 1 John 1:10), justice and liberation (Isa. 9:2; 58:8). Light shines the path away from chaos and distorted relationships toward the melodious harmonies that God has intended. In John's Gospel, this light is identified with the person of Christ (1:3-9). He is the one who bears "peace" and "will reign on David's throne and over his kingdom, establishing and upholding it with justice and righteousness from that time on and forever" (Isa. 9:7; Luke 1:33). Jesus is the one who has come in human form to bestow light (John 1:9).

Light is not only a divine gift — it is the image that the prophet Isaiah uses to explain the impact of a faithful community in a world where the poor are crushed: "If you do away with the yoke of oppression, with the pointing finger and malicious talk, and if you spend yourselves on behalf of the hungry and satisfy the needs of the oppressed, then your light will rise in the darkness, and your night will become like the noonday" (58:9b-10). The people of God were to be a light among the nations (Isa. 60:1-3), their way of life a centripetal drawing to the peaceable and beautiful city of God (Isa. 2:1-5).[1] This light is God's glory, refracted through faith as costly discipleship that renounces rivalries and violence while doing what is peaceable and good.

A small light can become magnified for others to see and follow. Jesus presents this image in the Sermon on the Mount:

> You are the light of the world. A city on a hill cannot be hidden. Neither do people light a lamp and put it under a bowl. Instead they put it on its stand, and it gives light to everyone in the house. In the same way, let your light shine before men, that they may see your good deeds and praise your Father in heaven. (Matt. 5:14-16)

"Good deeds" refers to the obedience and caring of God's people, especially the care of the stranger, the sick, and the hungry (Matt. 25:31-46). This is the

---

1. On this thematic interpretation of Isaiah 2 as it belonged to the early church via Origen, Justin, Irenaeus, and Tertullian, see the important discussion in Gerhard Lohfink, *Jesus and Community: The Social Dimension of Christian Faith*, trans. John P. Galvin (Philadelphia: Fortress Press, 1984), pp. 170-76. My gratitude to Steve Fowl for pointing me to this study.

"light" of love in action that shines throughout the community, inviting and welcoming in others (Matt. 25:36, 38; 2 Cor. 4:6; Eph. 5:8-9; Phil. 2:15). "The night is nearly over; the day is almost here. So let us put aside the deeds of darkness and put on the armor of light" (Rom. 13:12). The followers of Jesus are "Isaianic heralds, lights to the world."[2]

*   *   *

Finally, the moment has come for the Sampsons to cut the ribbon. "One thousand three, one thousand two, one thousand one — cut the ribbon!" shouts Elder Harris. To the sounds of clapping and cheering the ribbon is cut, the door is opened, and the Sampsons enter their home! A neighborhood open house follows, and everyone crowds into the Sampsons' house to see and rejoice in this show-and-tell, this sermon of God's righteousness and mercy. God had not forgotten Sandtown. "But the needy will not always be forgotten, nor the hope of the afflicted ever perish" (Ps. 9:18; cf. vv. 8-9).

Behind the dedication were thousands of mostly unheralded human contributions that had combined to make the difference in Sandtown. Neighborhood residents had to determine to rebuild their community and begin the work. A faith-driven partnership of black and white, urban and suburban individuals pulled together public and private resources. Absentee owners had to be found, then houses acquired. The city government had to help with cleaning up past liens. An architect and a structural engineer had to be involved. Volunteers had to come together as partners in support of the community. Materials had to be purchased or donated, then delivered. Habitat staff had to guide and oversee the work. People had to pray and not give up.

In the process, the people of a community gained confidence in themselves and one another, confidence that compounded and expanded for the next task. Barriers of race and social distance were being dismantled. From one of the most rubbled blocks in the city, this block of God's work would go on to become a symbol of urban hope and possibility throughout the city.[3] Where decay and an open-air drug market once thrived, there are now planted committed families who own their homes. They are homeowners such as Gene Atkinson, Sedalia Lewis, Renee Hickman, the Millers, Mary

2. N. T. Wright, *Jesus and the Victory of God,* vol. 2 of Christian Origins and the Question of God (Minneapolis: Fortress Press, 1996), p. 660.

3. Sandtown Habitat's efforts on this block were featured in the book by Mary Ellen Hayward and Charles Belfoure entitled *The Baltimore Rowhouse* (New York: Princeton Architectural Press, 1999), p. 184 and photograph no. 129.

Scott, Sophia Turner, Robert Baul, Lisa Coles, Tannya Hall, Edmond Hopkins, Lucille Kenner, and George and Glenda Mack.

This revival amidst the ruins comes not through the powerful and connected but through the people of a community who are working at the grass roots to activate Isaiah's vision of an urban reconfiguring: "Your people will rebuild the ancient ruins and will raise up the age-old foundations; you will be called Repairer of Broken Walls, Restorer of Streets with Dwellings" (58:12).

*　　*　　*

But for all the good news, the two faces of suffering and possibility constantly shadow one another in Sandtown. A year after the momentous day described here, many of the same people who had gathered to celebrate the dedication of the Sampsons' home shared tears as they attended Mrs. Sampson's "homegoing" service. A woman of great faith who knew much about grace, Thelma Sampson had persevered through a hard life. During her extended illness, her neighbors watched over and helped take care of her. After Thelma died, they watched over her husband Russell and regularly brought him meals. A few years later, people gathered for his homegoing service. But those who mourned the Sampsons could take comfort in knowing that they had spent their last months and years in a safe and decent house, one that they owned and that had provided a daily source of gratitude for them before the Lord. This is the way the city and the community are meant to work.

By faith a people are working together to rebuild their homes and break down divisions, doing so in the knowledge that a new day will come when there will be no more tears or suffering. The story of the Sampsons' home is a sign and symbol of the redemption of the city, a light of urban hope and possibility.

Urban Faith Matters

The purpose of this book is to consider the promise and possibility of God's peace for the changing of the American inner city. Drawing not only on theological resources and biblical studies but also on history, sociology, urban studies, and other disciplines, this project emerges out of the pursuit to answer three basic questions: How are we to think about neighborhoods of relegation and ruin? In what ways does the narrative of Christ incarnate, crucified, and risen shape the church to enact the gospel of peace amidst the daily heartaches and hardships of the inner city? And what does God's new creation mean for the encounter of faith with the inner city?

Believing that theory and practice, church and theology are intertwined, I began with the story of rebuilding and reconciliation on Stricker Street. This story shows, I believe, how the God of the overlooked and downtrodden, the God of Scripture, empowers women and men to make a transformational difference for their families, neighbors, community, and city. In a world that is increasingly urban, this project addresses one facet of the immense challenge facing the church and Christian activity for the kingdom of God.[1]

In this chapter, I begin by introducing the status and condition of the inner city. Next I survey currents in faith-based efforts in the inner city, specifically activities of faith that are grounded in the life of the church, placing them in theological, social, and political context. I then introduce the theo-

---

1. The single best introduction to this challenge is Harvie M. Conn and Manuel Ortiz, *Urban Ministry: The Kingdom, the City, and the People of God* (Downers Grove: InterVarsity, 2001).

logical commitments of the city, the gospel, and discipleship, primary beliefs that will underlie the basic contours of my project. I conclude with a review of the plan of the book. This chapter will be challenging in some ways, but it is important for establishing the context and approach we will follow as we seek a genuinely Christian approach to the changing inner city.

INNER CITIES AND THE NEW AMERICAN CITY

From one perspective, as this new decade and century begin, the urban poor in America are no longer with us. In the 1980s and 1990s the poor — especially single-parent African-American women and young men — were made scapegoats for national decline. But today, thanks to welfare reform and the lingering effects of the economically overheated 1990s, the poor are barely noticed, heard, or mentioned. This is deceiving, for the poor and excluded have not really gone away. National rates for child poverty remain high, food pantry use is rising, housing has become more unaffordable and unavailable, and employment is tentative — frequently temporary and subject to termination. In fact, many African-American communities — and, increasingly, Latino and multi-ethnic communities — find themselves confronted by new forms of economic and political dispossession.

What has happened, to employ Ralph Ellison's metaphor, is that although the inner city is very real, it has been covered by a blanket of invisibility. C. Eric Lincoln observes that invisibility "is most painful when it is preclusive — jobs not offered, invitations not issued, opportunities denied."[2] What explains this "low-grade" form of assault? In remarks on race that apply equally to the inner city, Lincoln comments, "Racial anonymity derives from the presumption of inconsequence — the inconsequence of black persons and of their achievements, actual or potential."[3] Considered as disposable and expendable as any throwaway American product, the inner city is treated as morally and socially inconsequential.

While the assertion of identity and meaning never waits for permission, anonymity and invisibility are refuted by seeing and recognizing, by changing the way in which one looks at and knows the world. Camilo José Vergara's judgment in *The New American Ghetto*, an extraordinary document of history, photography, and social analysis, reminds us that the nation's landscape is de-

2. Lincoln, *Coming Through the Fire: Surviving Race and Place in America* (Durham: Duke University Press, 1996), p. 94.
3. Lincoln, *Coming Through the Fire*, p. 94.

fined by geographies of inconsequence, invisibility, and anonymity. "Ghettos, as intrinsic to the identity of the United States as New England villages, vast national parks, and leafy suburbs, nevertheless remain unique in their social and physical isolation from the nation's mainstream."[4] Our inner cities are both present — integral to the meaning of the world in which we live — and absent. Layers of social distance and denial feed their nonexistence.

Shaped by "revolutions in economy, demography, and space," as historian Michael B. Katz observes, a new American city marked by inequality and poverty has emerged.[5] The economic expansion of the 1990s and the early twenty-first century has left many neighborhoods out of the flow of prosperity. East Brooklyn, many parts of the Bronx, Newark, North Philadelphia, West Baltimore, Anacostia in Washington D.C., East St. Louis, Overtown in Miami, North Lawndale in Chicago, large sections of Detroit, and South Central Los Angeles are among those urban places that still face intense distress.[6] From the Sunbelt cities of Las Vegas and Houston to the South's Atlanta to the Northeast's Camden, few cities do not feel and evidence the presence of division. This follows a pattern from the 1970s in which poverty "has become more urban, more concentrated, and more firmly implanted in large metropolises, particularly in the older industrial cities with immense and highly segregated black and Hispanic residents."[7]

Not all people who are poor and live in the city live in neighborhoods of concentrated and persistent poverty, and not all people who live in the inner city have incomes below the poverty line. This is a given, though social and racial stereotypes die hard. Yet inner-city neighborhoods are a focal point of urban suffering and exclusion, and everyone who lives in the inner city knows firsthand the struggle for survival. In 1972, one-third of the nation's poor lived in central city census tracts of high poverty, but by 1991 that number had risen to 60 percent.[8] According to one researcher, "There are nearly three thousand

4. Vergara, *The New American Ghetto* (New Brunswick: Rutgers University Press, 1995), p. 2.

5. Katz, *The Price of Citizenship: Redefining the American Welfare State* (New York: Metropolitan Books, 2001), p. 33, and pp. 33-56.

6. Statistical data can be found in U.S. Department of Housing and Urban Development, "Now Is the Time: Places Left Behind in the New Economy" (Washington, D.C.: U.S. Department of Housing and Urban Development, 1999).

7. William Julius Wilson, "Studying Inner-City Social Dislocations: The Challenge of Public Agenda Research," *American Sociological Review* 56 (February 1991): 1.

8. John D. Kasarda, "Cities as Places Where People Live and Work: Urban Change and Neighborhood Distress," in *Interwoven Destinies: Cities and the Nation*, ed. Henry G. Cisneros (New York: W. W. Norton, 1993), p. 82.

high-poverty neighborhoods in the United States with about 8.5 million residents."[9] A "high-poverty neighborhood" is typically a geographical area, commonly a census tract, where more than 40 percent of the population live below the poverty line. A persistent, high level of joblessness, as William Julius Wilson has emphasized,[10] is one of its primary features, but according to Katherine Newman's important research, so are the indignities and extreme hardships faced by the majority of people who are working yet poor.[11]

A focus on statistics presents an important but only partial view of both the harshness of life in the inner city and the increasing income disparity in America. For example, in 2001 the federally set poverty threshold for a family of three — a single parent and two children — was $14,629. The harsh truth is that a full-time minimum-wage salary will not lift a family above this threshold. Given the high cost of living, especially in certain cities, people can budget and manage well, yet simply not have enough money for both a small apartment and food.[12] Despite the problems associated with such statistics, they do not press us to fully comprehend either the personal costs or the moral implications of the inner city.[13] More indicative of life in the inner city are the human costs of living in neighborhoods with substandard housing, environmental hazards, failing schools, weak job opportunities, and inadequate essential retail services.

Too often, death comes before its time in the inner city. Public health studies consistently show that with all variables accounted for, low social status and concentrated poverty are associated with decreased longevity, and suggest that social and economic forces linked to neighborhoods are major factors. A 1990 article in the *New England Journal of Medicine* revealed that black men living in Harlem were less likely to reach age 65 than their counterparts in Bangladesh.[14] A more recent study in this same publication reported

9. Paul A. Jargowsky, *Poverty and Place: Ghettos, Barrios, and the American City* (New York: Russell Sage Foundation, 1997), p. 15.

10. Wilson, *When Work Disappears: The World of the New Urban Poor* (New York: Alfred A. Knopf, 1996).

11. Newman, *No Shame in My Game: The Working Poor in the Inner City* (New York: Alfred A. Knopf and The Russell Sage Foundation, 1999).

12. Nina Bernstein, "Family Needs Far Exceed the Official Poverty Line," *New York Times,* 13 September 2000, B-1, 6; Louis Uchitelle, "How to Define Poverty? Let Us Count the Ways," *New York Times,* 26 May 2001, B-7, 9.

13. Loïc J. D. Wacquant, "Three Pernicious Premises in the Study of the American Ghetto," *International Journal of Urban and Regional Research* 21, no. 2 (June 1997): 342-44.

14. Colin McCord and Harold P. Freeman, "Excess Mortality in Harlem," *The New England Journal of Medicine* 322, no. 3 (18 January 1990): 173-77.

that children in Harlem continue to face diminished life-expectancy rates.[15] Funerals take place too often and too early in the inner city.

In a range of ways, the challenge of the American inner city is connected to the global setting. When the previous century began, the world's population was 8 percent urban. Today that figure is close to 50 percent. By the next quarter-century mark, demographers project that a full quarter of the world's population not only will be poor but will live in shantytowns, favelas, and squatter settlements of Southern hemispheric cities such as Addis Ababa, Nairobi, Lagos, São Paulo, Calcutta, and Manila.[16] Put another way, "In 2025, the number of city-dwellers could reach 5 billion individuals (two thirds of them in poor countries)."[17] More and more "non-persons" who live in grinding poverty are being created on a global scale. Reports the World Bank, "In 1998 1.2 billion people worldwide — 24% of the population of the developing world — had consumption levels below $1 a day."[18] The urban world will be increasingly filled with children begging in the streets, uprooted families living in makeshift conditions, and women laboring for a meager existence.

Marked by new divisions of power and poverty, our global cities, as the urban theorist Saskia Sassen has pointed out, have generated new centers and new peripheries.[19] And as Manuel Castells has argued in his multivolume study of the information age, the present dynamic of urban inclusion and exclusion is global in nature.[20] Under such social and economic conditions, increased pressures are visited upon families and local communities, priming ethnic, racial, and social tensions. In his critically important book *Exclusion and Embrace: A Theological Exploration of Identity, Otherness, and Reconciliation*, Miroslav Volf rightly states, "It may not be too much to claim that the future of our world will depend upon how we deal with identity and differ-

---

15. Arline T. Geronimus et al., "Excess Mortality among Blacks and Whites in the United States," *New England Journal of Medicine*, 335, no. 21 (21 November 1997): 1552-58.

16. David B. Barrett and Todd M. Johnson, "Annual Statistical Table on Global Mission: 2000," *International Bulletin on Missionary Research* 24, no. 1 (January 2000): 24-25.

17. Rem Koolhas et al., *Mutations* (Barcelona: ACTAR, n.d.), p. 3.

18. Irene Tinker, "Alleviating Poverty: Investing in Women's Work," *Journal of American Planning Association* 66, no. 3 (Summer 2000): 230.

19. Sassen, *Globalization and Its Discontents: Essays on the New Mobility of People and Money* (New York: The New Press, 1998), chap. 1; Loïc J. D. Wacquant, "The Rise of Advanced Marginality: Notes on Its Nature and Implications," *Acta Sociologica* 39, no. 2 (1996): 121-39.

20. Castells, *The Information Age: Economy, Society, and Culture*, vol. 3: *End of Millennium*, 2d ed. (Oxford: Blackwell, 2000), pp. 68-168.

ence."[21] The central site for this challenge will be our cities, in particular the local communities in our cities.[22]

On my desk sits a .357 magnum shell casing and a jagged piece of shrapnel. The shell casing I picked up off the basketball court across the street from my home in Sandtown; the shrapnel I collected from the ground in Vukovar, a small city in Croatia that had been "cleansed" during the recent war. The shell casing and the piece of shrapnel are about the same size and color. These pieces of metal remind me that the political, social, theological, economic, ecological, and health dilemmas confronting these and the world's other cities share much in common. We must not neglect the shared future the city faces in an interconnected world.

In summary, we do not dwell in a peaceful urban world where every need is met, every community is held in equal respect, and every stranger is welcomed. But there is hope. Both acknowledging what is wrong and and living differently are essential parts of the Christian witness. In Mark's Gospel, Jesus said, "The poor you will always have with you" (14:7). This text is often used to imply that nothing can be done about poverty. But Jesus is not saying that at all, as Ched Myers has pointed out. The text "is a statement not about the poor but about the social location of the discipleship church: You will always be among the poor and can do the right thing for them at any time."[23] The new American city confronts the church with an obligation to recover the biblical tradition of passionate concern for the widow, the orphan, the poor, and the stranger. In the next section we'll look at some of the ways the church is fulfilling the obligations of discipleship — and some of the ways in which it is not.

THE GOSPEL IN ACTION

Describing the work of Dolores Mission, a Catholic parish in the Pico-Union Section of Los Angeles, a church worker summarized their efforts as "trying to put the gospel into practice." We find a similar grassroots commitment not only in other American cities but also in the cities of Asia, Africa, and Latin America where the poor are proclaimers of the gospel. Working its way up

21. Volf, *Exclusion and Embrace* (Nashville: Abingdon, 1996), p. 20.

22. Claire Jean Kim, *Bitter Fruit: The Politics of Black-Korean Conflict in New York City* (New Haven: Yale University Press, 2000).

23. Myers, Marie Dennis, Joseph Nangle, Cynthia Moe-Lobeda, and Stuart Taylor, *"Say to This Mountain": Mark's Story of Discipleship* (Maryknoll: Orbis, 1996), p. 184.

from the grass roots, the saving power of the gospel as heralded by (1 Cor. 1:23; Col. 1:23) and embodied among the poor (1 Cor. 1:26-31) is a powerful ferment for wholeness and reconciliation, justice and peace.

Faith-based initiatives — whether understood as an outgrowth of the power of belief, the practical impact of a local church in action, or "faith" attached to the endeavors of organizing and community development — have become very important.[24] Over the last decade especially, there has been growing public interest in these initiatives and their redemptive potential.[25] A recent study found that when it comes to the public benefits of religion, Americans value the efforts of faith-based organizations.[26] Although the emphasis here is on Christian contributions, we should not neglect other spiritually based initiatives, including the efforts of Muslims, which deserve the attention and admiration of Christians. Especially important in the United States are community development corporations, known as CDCs, local groups that develop housing, create jobs and retail services, provide social services, and enhance community.[27] Though not without their difficulties, CDCs and other community-based organizations make an inestimable contribution to neighborhood development. Yet in a unique way, churches and related institutions of faith have a distinctive social and spiritual impact in the city.[28]

In the last presidential election, both major candidates expressed strong

---

24. On terminology, see Stephen Hart, *Cultural Dilemmas of Progressive Politics: Styles of Engagement among Grassroots Activists* (Chicago: University of Chicago Press, 2001), pp. 255-56n.1.

25. As examples, see Joel Klein, "In God They Trust," *The New Yorker,* 16 June 1997, pp. 40-48; and Robert Worth, "Amazing Grace: Can Churches Save the Inner City?" *Washington Monthly* 30, nos. 1-2 (January/February 1998): 28-31.

26. Public Agenda, "For Goodness' Sake: Why So Many Want Religion to Play a Greater Role in American Life" (New York: Public Agenda, 2001).

27. This movement is well chronicled in Paul S. Grogan and Tony Proscio, *Comeback Cities: A Blueprint for Urban Neighborhood Revival* (Boulder: Westview Press, 2000); and Roberta Brandes Gratz, *The Living City* (New York: Simon & Schuster, 1989). For a survey documenting the efforts of more than 2,500 CDCs, see the report by the National Congress for Community Economic Development, *Coming of Age: Trends and Achievements of Community-Based Development Organizations* (Washington, D.C.: National Congress for Community Economic Development, 1999); and Neil R. Peirce, "Victory in the CDC Regatta?" *The Sun,* 11 April 1999, 3-C.

28. According to the report *Coming of Age,* 14 percent of CDCs are religiously based. Such a statistic is generally taken to support the breadth of church involvement in community development. But it is important to remember that the church's work is much broader than CDC activity. It is also important to remember that not all CDCs are equal in capacity and effectiveness.

interest in increasing support for faith-based ministries. In actuality, this was in keeping with the practice of the Clinton administration. Still, under the presidency of George W. Bush, faith-based initiatives have received increased attention, at least initially; the White House has even established an Office of Faith-Based and Community Initiatives. In this bipartisan recognition, many have found common ground to move beyond traditional labels of liberal and conservative. In his book *Faith Works,* Jim Wallis of the Call to Renewal and *Sojourners* chronicles a myriad of activities that point toward what he believes is a new "third way" of moral and spiritual politics, a movement that is emerging from below.[29] How has such widespread and diversely held recognition of faith as a means of social change come about? What, if anything, is new in claims for its importance in confronting poverty? More importantly, how is faith defined, and who sets the terms of the debate on the role of the church?

The Church as the Community of the Good Samaritan

One of the most familiar stories of Scripture is the parable of the Good Samaritan. Jesus told this parable to explain what it means to truly love God and neighbor. When it is read in light of the inner city, it helps to explain the source and shape of Christian "faith-based" activity. Recounted in Luke's Gospel (10:25-37), the parable tells the story of a man who has been beaten and abandoned for dead on the road to Jericho. Two "religious" people pass by but do nothing; finally a Samaritan stops and tends to the man's needs. Traditionally the story is told in a way that poses the moral or ethical question "Who is my neighbor?" This usually leads to a discussion of the "spatial definition" of a neighbor and the nature of individual obligation: "Who is *my* neighbor?" This reading fits the individualistic interpretative framework of Americans and white evangelicals. However, a different and more demanding way of reading the text is called for if we are to understand the teaching and ministry of Jesus.

Rather than being used to launch an abstract discussion of "Who is my neighbor?" the parable should be read as providing a concrete challenge: "Who *will* be neighbor to the beaten, bruised and left behind" (10:36)?[30] This

---

29. Wallis, *Faith Works: Lessons from the Life of an Activist Preacher* (New York: Random House, 2000).

30. This argument is sharply made by Leonardo Boff in *When Theology Listens to the Poor,* translated by Robert R. Barr (San Francisco: Harper & Row, 1988), pp. 32-33. Support

is a communal question. Instead of being posed to an individual hearer, the challenge should be presented to the community that follows Christ (Luke 10:30). Jesus is inviting people into his mission and way of life. Thus the parable of the Good Samaritan asks us, "What kind of community will cross over social and ethnic boundaries, like the Samaritan, and share in Christ's mission, especially in relationship to the battered and bruised?"[31] We should also keep in mind that this is a parable of reconciliation, a story of a new community anchored in the disclosure of Christ as both the broken one and the one who heals.

From this reading of the biblical text we can gather a number of perspectives on faith and the inner city. First, Jesus continues to call forth communities of women and men to follow him in his mission, people who reflexively practice their faith by serving the beaten down and the brokenhearted. Second, this call is not individualistic but communal. As a call, it is underscored as an invitation of grace extended to all. Finally, the story teaches us that Christian discipleship requires social and geographical connection, not distance. To read the story rightly therefore means not to pass by suffering but to enter into the place of joblessness, institutional violence, alienation, and stigmatization, and to do so ultimately because of the authoritative word of the Lord (Luke 10:37). When read from the vantage point of the streets of the inner city, the parable of the Good Samaritan identifies the church as a people called to concretely love communities that have been wounded and abandoned (Luke 10:36) and to build communities of love across every boundary. Rightly reading this parable means putting the gospel into action in everyday life.

The Ecology of Faith

Meeting in reclaimed theaters, grocery stores, clubs, gas stations, and apartments as well as in the more ornate, tall-steepled houses of worship, the main institutions taking up the challenge to love the harmed and abandoned in

---

for this exegesis can be found in Joel B. Green, *The Gospel of Luke,* NICNT series (Grand Rapids: Eerdmans, 1997), pp. 424-32; and I. Howard Marshall, *Commentary on Luke,* NIGTC series (Grand Rapids: Eerdmans, 1978), pp. 444-50.

31. Boff, *When Theology Listens to the Poor,* p. 33. A further twist to the traditional reading comes about when we ask, "Which character do we identify with when reading the story?" What about the view from the place of the beaten and bruised? In addition to Boff, see J. I. H. McDonald, "The View from the Ditch — And Other Angles," *Scottish Journal of Theology* 49, no. 1 (1996): 28-30.

America's inner cities are African-American and Latino congregations. While not every church serves as a community leader or neighborhood anchor, I agree with Michael Katz's observation that "Perhaps the only viable institutions remaining in inner cities are churches."[32] This should not be reduced to merely a social phenomenon — as important as that is — but interpreted on terms that the churches themselves would make: a theological event that reveals the vitality of the Spirit. Too easily missed in a "functionalist" view of religion, as Harvie Conn and Manuel Ortiz point out, is "the human response to the revelation of God . . . the holistic response of the whole human self, the image of God. It is the voice of the heart (Prov. 4:23; Matt. 12:34)."[33]

In keeping with its history, the African-American church remains at the forefront of urban ministry, binding the wounds of injustice and seeking more just patterns of life.[34] When virtually every other church left the city, the black church remained, its witness irrepressible. Here lies the historical precedent for faith-based ministry in the American city.[35] Due to recent demographic changes (including Latino immigration), a rich diversity of ecclesiastical life can be found in the inner city. Many different traditions and theologies compose the "ecology" of congregational life and activity.[36] Independent, Catholic, Baptist, Pentecostal, Holiness, evangelical, and many other traditions offer a rich, overlapping diversity of language, culture, and styles in Latino, Black, and multi-ethnic bodies of faith.[37]

32. Katz, "Reframing the 'Underclass' Debate," in *The "Underclass" Debate: Views from History*, ed. Michael B. Katz (Princeton: Princeton University Press, 1993), p. 477.

33. Conn and Ortiz, *Urban Ministry*, p. 92.

34. Andrew Billingsley, *Mighty Like a River: The Black Church and Social Reform* (New York: Oxford University Press, 1999); Katherine Day, "The Renaissance of Community Economic Development among African-American Churches in the 1990s," in *The Blackwell Companion to Sociology of Religion*, ed. Richard K. Fenn (Oxford: Blackwell, 2001), pp. 321-35.

35. A historical source of significant influence may well be the evangelical voluntary society. On this development, see Andrew F. Walls, *The Missionary Movement in Christian History: Studies in the Transmission of Faith* (Maryknoll: Orbis, 1996), pp. 241-54.

36. On the use of religious "ecology," see Omar M. McRoberts, "Understanding the 'New' Black Pentecostal Activism: Lessons from Ecumenical Urban Ministries in Boston," *Sociology of Religion* 60, no. 1 (Spring 1999): 47-70; Nancy Tatom Ammerman, *Congregation and Community* (New Brunswick: Rutgers University Press, 1997), pp. 36-40.

37. While the literature is vast, the following texts provide an introduction. Covering these traditions is the collection of essays edited by Clifford J. Green, *Churches, Cities, and Human Community: Urban Ministry in the United States* (Grand Rapids: Eerdmans, 1996). For a history and evaluation of evangelicals in the city, see Harvie M. Conn, *The American City and the Evangelical Church: A Historical Overview* (Grand Rapids: Baker, 1994). Perspective on the Latino/Hispanic church can be found in Ana Maria Diaz-Stevens and Anthony M. Stevens-Arroyo, *Recognizing the Latino Resurgence in U.S. Religion: The Emmaus Paradigm*

Within the ecology of inner-city faith, three trends are increasingly prevalent. First, there is a shift away from mainline and traditional churches to newer evangelical and Pentecostal churches, a movement that is swiftly altering the religious map of the city.[38] Especially important in this regard is the rise of Spanish-speaking Protestant and independent churches.[39] Second, there is a relatively new movement of churches that are combining a multiethnic common life with community development, generating what Charles Marsh has aptly called the next phase of the quest for the "beloved community."[40] Churches associated with the Christian Community Development Association, founded by John Perkins and based at Lawndale Community Church in Chicago, represent this trend. Third, churches that love and care for the city recognize that they have more in common with each other than differences of doctrine or polity might suggest. Growing networks of urban churches that cross over traditional ecclesiastical boundaries to serve spiritual

---

(Boulder: Westview Press, 1998); Manuel Ortiz, *The Hispanic Challenge: Opportunities Confronting the Church* (Downers Grove: InterVarsity, 1993); and Eldin Villafañe, *The Liberating Spirit: Toward an Hispanic American Pentecostal Social Ethic* (Grand Rapids: Eerdmans, 1993), pp. 41-132. Among the expansive literature on the black church experience, recent and important discussions include Albert J. Raboteau, *A Fire in the Bones: Reflections on African American Religious History* (Boston: Beacon Press, 1995); Raboteau, *Canaan Land: A Religious History of African Americans* (Oxford: Oxford University Press, 1999, 2001); and C. Eric Lincoln and Lawrence H. Mamiya, *The Black Church in the African American Experience* (Durham: Duke University Press, 1990). While storefront congregations have received remarkably limited attention, see Frances Kostaleros, *Feeling the Spirit: Faith and Hope in an Evangelical Storefront Church* (Columbia: University of South Carolina Press, 1995). The Catholic contribution to faith in the city is far-reaching and diverse. For some important dimensions of Catholic involvement in the inner city, see Lawrence J. Engel, "The Influence of Saul Alinsky on the Campaign for Human Development," *Theological Studies* 59, no. 4 (1998): 636-61; and J. Bryan Hehir, "Religious Ideas and Social Policy: Subsidiarity and the Catholic Style of Ministry," in *Who Will Provide? The Changing Role of Religion in American Social Welfare*, ed. Mary Jo Bane, Brent Coffin, and Ronald Thiemann (Boulder: Westview Press, 2000), pp. 97-120.

38. This shift was evident to some degree, at least in the early days of the debate in 2001, in the response to President's Bush's faith-based initiative. Grassroots churches were considerably more in favor of it than mainline representatives. See Laurie Goodstein, "A Clerical, and Racial, Gap over Federal Help," *New York Times*, 24 March 2001, A-1, 11.

39. Mike Davis, "L.A.'s Pentecostal Earthquake," *Grand Street* 17, no. 4 (Spring 1999): 97-101; Andrea K. Walker, "It's No Longer *The* Church," *New York Times*, 9 February 1997, 13-1, 12.

40. Marsh, "The Beloved Community: An American Search," in *Religion, Race, and Justice in a Changing America*, ed. Gary Orfield and Holly J. Lebowitz (New York: The Century Foundation Press, 1999), pp. 60-65.

and economic needs are suggestive not simply of a post-denominational future but of a new urban future for the church.

Church and Community

While there is no uniform way that churches engage the inner city, there are common reasons why they can be key actors in the process of holistic change: "Congregational religions, in particular, offer institutional structures, practices, and narratives that help individuals navigate economic difficulties, sickness, and domestic troubles."[41] To better conceptualize the role of the congregations in inner-city neighborhoods, it is useful to distinguish three basic and complementary roles: churches as healing communities, churches as healers of communities, and churches as organizers for more just communities.[42] These are of course not the only ways to think about the ways in which churches seek to influence and interact with inner-city neighborhoods. Much depends on an individual church's internal dynamics, its understanding of its mission and evangelism, and its relationship to the community. Nor am I suggesting that conceptualizing the church in its role of healing represents an individualistic or therapeutic approach to ministry. Rather, I am considering the church as a social body — the body of Christ — that holds forth the potential for personal, social, and political renewal.

Churches as Healing Communities: The church is the community where women, men, and children can come together and find healing. It is a space for laying down burdens and discovering the restorative power of grace. The full life of the church can offer healing through worship, prayer, Bible study, fellowship, and sharing. For children and young people faced with the dangers of the street, the church is a place of literal salvation; for women faced with added burdens of oppression, the church is a shelter from the storm; for people in recovery, the church is a support system. Because of God's salva-

---

41. Anna Peterson, Manuel Vásquez, and Philip Williams, "Christianity and Social Change in the Shadow of Globalization," in *Christianity, Social Change, and Globalization in the Americas,* ed. Anna Peterson, Manuel Vásquez, and Philip Williams (New Brunswick: Rutgers University Press, 2001), p. 7.

42. This typology is slightly modified from John Hatch and Anne Callan, "How Churches Can Function as Healing Communities" (Chapel Hill: School of Public Health, University of North Carolina, n.d.). It is interesting to observe that these categories parallel Christ's offices — priestly (church as healing community), kingly (church as healer of communities), and prophetic (church as organizer for just communities). Might there not be something of the breadth of Christ in this diverse ministry of the urban church (John 20:21)?

tion, the church tells and embodies the healing power of dignity, hope, and new life in Christ. As a healing community of faith, the church lays hands on the wounded and offers its prayers for the sick.

Churches as Healers of Community: The church is a builder of community. Joining a concern for the whole person and a concern for the whole community together into social, economic, and spiritual models of ministries, churches and their affiliated ministries have initiated a wide range of efforts that give practical expression to God's love and justice. Common activities may include operating credit unions and neighborhood banks; creating, retaining, and attracting jobs; developing and managing housing for families and the elderly; educating children in after-school programs and religiously based schools; and providing preventive and primary health care for the uninsured and underserved.[43]

Churches as Organizers for Just Communities: Congregations are key agents in mobilizing people on behalf of schools that educate children, wages that sustain families, housing that stabilizes neighborhoods, and public services that maintain communities. Through four leading national organizations involved in church-based community organizing — the Industrial Areas Foundation (IAF), the Gamaliel Foundation, Direct Access Resource Training (DART), and the Pacific Institute for Community Organization (PICO) — churches have become leaders in social change.[44] So extensive are these church-based organizing initiatives that it can be rightly concluded that such activity "represents one of the largest and most dynamic efforts to build democratic power, promote social justice, and strengthen public life in the United States today."[45]

In summary, the work of the church in the inner city is incredibly di-

43. June Manning Thomas and Reynard N. Blake Jr., "Faith-Based Community Development and African-American Neighborhoods," in *Revitalizing Urban Neighborhoods,* ed. W. Dennis Keating, Norman Krumholz, and Philip Star (Lawrence: University of Kansas Press, 1996), pp. 131-43.

44. The best case studies of church-based community organizing are these: on PICO, Richard L. Wood, "Religious Culture and Political Action," *Sociological Theory* 17, no. 3 (November 1999), 307-33; and "Social Capital and Political Culture: God Meets Politics in the Inner City," *American Behavioral Scientist* 40, no. 5 (March/April 1997): 595-605; on IAF, Mark R. Warren, *Dry Bones Rattling: Community Building to Revitalize American Democracy* (Princeton: Princeton University Press, 2001). Particularly important for the American story of community organizing is Saul Alinsky, the founder of IAF.

45. Mark R. Warren and Richard L. Wood, *Faith-Based Community Organizing: The State of the Field* (Jericho, N.Y.: Interfaith Funders, 2001), p. 13. See further Stephen Hart, *Cultural Dilemmas of Progressive Politics: Styles of Engagement among Grassroots Activists* (Chicago: University of Chicago Press, 2001), pp. 27-120.

verse and differentiated, covering everything from community development and organizing, to social support and social capital, to relief and education, to prayer and worship. The church contributes to social movements and public life through its "tool kit" of religious culture, including rituals, prayer, fellowship, Bible reading, and use of Christian imagery.[46]

However, it is one thing to give recognition and assign value to particular churches and faith-based efforts, but another to consider if the church can impact the fabric of entire cities. Los Angeles and New York, cities widely considered to be urban trendsetters, provide illuminating examples of what the church can accomplish in whole cities.

Politics of the Spirit

In the global and polyglot cities of Los Angeles and New York, the church is engaged in evangelism, reconciliation, community organizing, and community development. But even these categories do not capture the full range of congregational involvement in sustaining and healing urban communities. Church members in these cities are bringing a "politics of the Spirit" to bear on every area of life.

Los Angeles

When major parts of the city of Los Angeles erupted ten years ago following the Rodney King verdict, it was church members, not the police or the politicians, who effectively worked the streets, listening to and talking with people and meeting basic human needs. As researchers at the Center for Religion and Civic Culture at the University of Southern California discovered, the churches were important because they were already in place and involved in the lives of people. The Center's research documented an intricate web of congregations working with gangs and addicted persons, providing health care and other human services, praying for the wholeness of the city, organizing for political empowerment, and seeking to model love and reconciliation.[47] As this incident illustrates, the people of faith in Los Angeles, through

---

46. Mary Pattillo-McCoy, "Church Culture as a Strategy of Action in the Black Community," *American Sociological Review* 63, no. 6 (December 1998): 767-84; Wood, "Religious Culture and Political Action," pp. 307-33.

47. The Center has generated a number of excellent reports. See John B. Orr, Donald E. Miller, Wade Clark Roof, and J. Gordon Melton, *Politics of the Spirit: Religion and*

religiously based civic engagement, are addressing the changing needs of ethnically diverse people, generating a "politics of the Spirit."

New York

A global trendsetter in finance, the arts, fashion, and advertising, New York is also discovering new ways of being the church, especially in its globally connected and multi-ethnic boroughs of Queens, the Bronx, and Brooklyn.[48] Large parts of Brooklyn, Harlem, and the South Bronx, once so battered as to be national symbols of urban ruin, have been rebuilt. The involvement of local government was essential (especially in land disposition and financing), but vital catalysts in many instances were local community groups, especially congregations, who prayed, organized, and invested their resources and lives in renewing their neighborhoods.[49] Today, as people herald a "renaissance" in neighborhoods such as the South Bronx and Harlem, it is important to remember that the commitment of the churches often made the initial and most substantial differences.

Can the church significantly impact the city? If we try to imagine the civic fabric of New York and Los Angeles without the presence of its churches, we will recognize that they are making profound contributions. In both these cities and elsewhere, churches are making a difference because they have several key characteristics:

- History and presence
- Institutional capacity
- Concrete commitment to meeting human needs
- Vision for personal, social, and spiritual transformation

As functional as this list is, in some way and in every church setting, these characteristics emerge out of theological beliefs and stories.

Multiethnicity in Los Angeles (Los Angeles: University of Southern California, 1994); *Politics of the Spirit: Portraits of Faith and Community in Los Angeles* (Los Angeles: Center for Religion and Civic Culture, University of Southern California, 1997); and John Orr, *Los Angeles Religion: A Civic Profile* (Los Angeles: Center for Religion and Civic Culture, University of Southern California, 1998).

48. *Signs of Hope in the City: Ministries of Community Renewal,* ed. Robert D. Carle and Louis A. DeCaro Jr. (Valley Forge: Judson Press, 1997).

49. Samuel G. Freedman, *Upon This Rock: The Miracles of a Black Church* (New York: HarperCollins, 1993); Jim Rooney, *Organizing the South Bronx* (New York: State University of New York Press, 1995).

Having examined the lived effects of faith in the inner city, we now turn to some of the broader political, social, and cultural reasons for faith-based community development and organizing in the inner city.

Picking Up the Pieces

A major reason for the present interest in faith-based efforts is the movement away from a centralized social safety net and toward a new reliance on local government and partnership with nonprofit organizations. As a result of government "decentralizing," "downsizing," and "reinventing" at the federal, state, and municipal levels, political commitment to the poor — from housing investment to health care to public assistance — has become more limited and reluctant. The conventional wisdom is that these changes are building personal responsibility in a market economy, and that, in fact, helping the poor is not government's responsibility. Others conclude that these changes are at best short-sighted because they do not account for the real job market or the complexity of many family situations, and because cuts in social programs punish the poor. Moreover, many also hold that the government's advocacy of faith-based efforts is a smokescreen for priorities that favor corporate interests and the well-off. Whatever the correct reading of the situation is, the changes seem here to stay for the foreseeable future, and they have altered the social-service landscape.[50]

Another reason why faith-based initiatives have become so important in the city is the deconstruction of the Enlightenment model of knowledge, progress, and development. Whether "postmodernity" or "advanced modernity" is the best terminology to characterize this shift is not important for our discussion. Rather, it is critical to observe that as the grand narrative of Enlightenment "progress" shows increasing signs of social, economic, and intellectual collapse, it is the words and works of faith that are tending to the wounds of its failure. Overall, as David Bosch argues in his major study *Transforming Mission: Paradigm Shifts in Theology of Mission*, the post-Enlightenment change brings with it significant challenges to the church's paradigm of mission.[51] Not least among these challenges are the demands of the poor.

---

50. See the well-documented volume by Ron A. Cnaan, with Robert J. Winberg and Stephanie C. Boddie, *The Newer Deal: Social Work and Religion in Partnership* (New York: Columbia University Press, 1999).

51. Bosch, *Transforming Mission: Paradigm Shifts in Theology of Mission* (Maryknoll: Orbis, 1991).

Instead of rendering religion irrelevant, the failures of "advanced modernity" fueled the "resurgence" of religion in the city, argues Meredith Ramsay.[52] The growth in faith-based activism, Ramsay suggests, is in fact a reply to individualistic market forces.[53] According to Ramsay, who is writing in an urban policy journal, the "forces of modernity have so emptied the public sphere of its normative and transcendent dimensions that the church alone is left with enough moral standing to rise to the demand for a return to a formative project."[54] At the same time, the postmodern recognition and celebration of particularities (among them ethnicity, culture, and gender), which in part comes out of a rejection of grand stories and meta-narratives, has provided an important opening for grassroots movements, spiritual ones included.[55]

The lingering tenets of modernity would have us believe that sound and right development "techniques" are all inner cities need to be "fixed." These techniques include rational planning, a reliance on experts, consensus-building between all stakeholders, a strategy for all the social systems, and a knowledge base of best practices. Such techniques were ostensibly applied in "comprehensive community development," a major emphasis of foundation-directed community revitalization activity in the 1990s.[56] Everything in a community's social system, of course, is interconnected.[57] The problem is that such an approach remains an incomplete and technical fix for something that is much more deeply broken. Under this model, community iself is reduced in value to simply one of many "stakeholders."

52. Ramsay, "Redeeming the City: Exploring the Relationship between Church and Metropolis," *Urban Affairs Review* 33, no. 5 (May 1998): 600-601.

53. Ramsay, "Redeeming the City," pp. 599-601.

54. Ramsay, "Redeeming the City," p. 621.

55. Patricia A. Wilson, "Empowerment: Community Economic Development from the Inside Out," *Urban Studies* 33, vols. 4-5 (1996): 622-24. What I read as a response to this is the work of J. Richard Middleton and and Brian J. Walsh, *Truth Is Stranger than It Used to Be: Biblical Faith in a Post-Modern Age* (Downers Grove: InterVarsity Press, 1995).

56. Prudence Brown, "Comprehensive Neighborhood-Based Initiatives," *Cityscape: A Journal of Policy Research and Development* 2, no. 2 (May 1996): 161-76. Given the intended scope of comprehensive community-development initiatives, it can be argued that they are secular imitations of faith-based initiatives and the church.

57. One perspective on the need for a more comprehensive approach is James Traub, "What No School Can Do," *New York Times Magazine,* 16 January 2000, pp. 52-57, 68, 81, 90-91.

Civil Society and Faith

Understanding the place and role of "civil society" is also important for framing current interest in faith-based ministry. The extension of market valuation into all of life has, along with other forces, been devastating to the associational shape of civil society in the inner city.[58] Cornel West has described the toll it has taken on the African-American community: "The recent market-driven shattering of black civil society — black families, neighborhoods, schools, churches, mosques — leaves more and more black people vulnerable to daily lives endured with little sense of self and fragile existential moorings."[59]

This "shattering" of civil society makes a compelling case — often prescribed on communitarian grounds of shared rights and responsibilities, with frequent reference to Alexis de Tocqueville's observations on America's story and its associational life — for the renewal of local organizations, cultural institutions, and voluntary associations and congregations.[60] Mark R. Warren's study entitled *Dry Bones Rattling: Community Building to Revitalize American Democracy*[61] does an excellent job of demonstrating the connection of faith to social and political renewal through revitalizing local institutional life. When civil society is strengthened at the grass roots, especially through organizing via congregations as associational bodies, the democratic values of participation, contribution, and social justice are advanced, and disenfranchisement is reversed.

A structural change in how we think about civil society is required, especially in its relationship to the church. This change is necessary because civil-society advocates typically count on the "intermediary" or "mediating" role of churches to accomplish a structural and more lasting impact on people's lives.[62] Although the concept of "mediating institutions" may seem quite

---

58. Richard Sennett, "The New Capitalism," *Social Research* 64, no. 2 (Summer 1997): 176-77; Cornel West, *Race Matters* (Boston: Beacon, 1993), pp. 15, 17.

59. West, *Race Matters*, p. 16.

60. Representative of this interest is Jean Bethke Elshtain, *Democracy on Trial* (New York: Basic Books, 1995). For a review of the issues, see John A. Coleman, S. J., "A Limited and a Vibrant Society: Christianity and Civil Society," in *Civil Society and Government*, ed. Nancy L. Rosenblum and Robert C. Post (Princeton: Princeton University Press, 2002), pp. 223-54.

61. Warren, *Dry Bones Rattling*.

62. Peter L. Berger and Richard John Neuhaus, *To Empower People: The Role of Mediating Structures in Public Policy* (Washington, D.C.: American Enterprise Institute for Public Policy Research, 1977). This publication very much helped to set the terms of the current debate. A Trinitarian rationale for the existence of mediating institutions is presented by

reasonable on its own terms, it can be a dubious label for the church and other local groups to accept. If all that congregations and other local groups do is stand between the market and the state, in effect acting as a buffer, they will become co-opted and consumed by them.[63] "Civil society" then becomes an instrument of the ubiquitous market and the coercive power of the nation-state. While on creational grounds institutional life and by extension civil society is to be affirmed, distortions joined to the fallen urban order must be rejected.

Churches are not just institutions that help comprise civil society. Churches are also living communities of truth, grace, and reconciliation. As a result of Jesus' victory over death, Paul's confessional summary of Christian identity cuts across every dividing line: "There is neither Jew nor Greek, slave nor free, male nor female, for you are all one in Christ Jesus" (Gal. 3:28; 1 Cor. 10:17; Col. 3:11). As the body of Christ, congregations advance a politics of mutuality and justice, one that begins with the subversive conviction that Jesus Christ is Lord over all (Phil. 2:11). It is through the church that "the manifold wisdom of God is made known to the rulers and authorities in heavenly realms" (Eph. 3:10; cf. 1 Cor. 10:11). Such descriptions of the church do not enable it to fit comfortably within the confines of the label "mediating institution" and the liberal claims concerning the social order in which the concept is embedded.

Renewing civil society is a very important overarching contribution of Christianity to urban life, not as justification of the status quo but in service of the transformation of community and the public sphere. The development and affirmation of alternative institutional life can have a reformational effect on the status quo. If, ultimately, communitarian theory is moralistic, it does not necessarily help and may in fact harm the inner city.[64] The commitment to a more free, just, and participatory society — those elements that underpin "civil society," John de Gruchy shows — finds its origin in the "prophetic vision" of justice, righteousness, and solidarity set out in the Hebrew tradi-

---

Todd H. Speidell, "A Trinitarian Ontology of Persons in Society," *Scottish Journal of Theology* 47, no. 3 (1994): 283-300.

63. Daniel M. Bell Jr., "Men of Stone and Struggle: Latin American Liberationists at the End of History," *Modern Theology* 14, no. 1 (January 1998): 113-39. A less critical assessment of the future of church and civil society for Christian mission is provided by Stanley H. Skreslet, "Networking, Civil Society, and the NGO: A New Model for Ecumenical Mission," *Missiology* 25, no. 3 (July 1997): 307-19.

64. Larry Bennett, "Do We Really Wish to Live in a Communitarian City? Communitarian Thinking and the Redevelopment of Chicago's Cabrini-Green Public Housing Complex," *Journal of Urban Affairs* 20, no. 2 (1998): 99-116.

tion.[65] Behind this is the God of the widow, the orphan, and the stranger. Churches can be leaders in the renewal of communities by being committed to a moral vision of the city, supporting families, being passionate about the biblical call to do justice, and witnessing to the hope and peace of God's reign. Kingdom values, perspectives, and practices have great leavening potential for society. In the midst of a wide search for the meaning of needs and shared responsibility, this is not an insignificant contribution.[66]

Changing Direction

From our brief survey of currents in faith and the city, it is abundantly clear that many churches are doing important things in the city and are not simply "religious consumers." This should be celebrated. But around every corner from new housing and signs of recovery there remain vacant buildings, trash-strewn lots, abandoned businesses, and boarded storefronts.[67] Urban schools are still widely failing, the health care system is not open or working for the poor and uninsured, and most young people still face a future of jobs flipping hamburgers or stocking shelves. Much more remains to be done, and though a number of churches are involved in their communities, too many are disengaged. This is the other side of the parable of the Good Samaritan, the passing by (Luke 10:31-32).

Studies have found that a smaller number of churches are actually involved in social service delivery and development than is commonly perceived.[68] Studies that tend to give a favorable impression of the church in the inner city look principally at what services and programs churches are offering, not at how conditions in neighborhoods are or are not changing.[69] A

65. De Gruchy, *Christianity and Democracy: A Theology for a Just World Order* (Cambridge: Cambridge University Press, 1995).

66. On this search, see Michael Ignatieff, *The Needs of Strangers* (New York: Picador, 1984).

67. Jim Yardley, "Second Opinion on South Bronx Revival," *New York Times,* 13 December 1997, B-1, 5.

68. Arthur E. Farnsley II, "Urban Congregations as Local Actors," *Research Notes from Faith and Community,* The Polis Center, Indianapolis Religion Briefing Paper No. 3, August 1997; Farnsley, "Can Churches Save the City? A Look at Resources," *Christian Century,* 9 December 1998, pp. 1182-84; "Assessing the Roles of Faith-Based Organizations in Community Development," *Recent Research Results,* November 2001, pp. 1-2.

69. Ron Cnaan, "Our Hidden Safety Net," *Brookings Review* 17, no. 2 (Spring 1999): 50-53; Ron A. Cnaan with Robert J. Winberg and Stephanie C. Boddie, *The Newer Deal,* pp. 229-76.

good case can be made that the emphasis in such studies should be reversed. A church with an inner-city address and a myriad of programs but minimal community involvement and proportionately little local membership may be more of a mixed blessing to the community than anecdotal accounts and program surveys of congregations have suggested.

For example, the recent comprehensive research of churches in a Boston neighborhood by Omar McRoberts, a sociologist at the University of Chicago, suggests a negative economic impact from the high density of its population of largely commuter churches: they may take up hard-to-find space for commercial development. This follows from their often ambivalent or disconnected relationship to the community. Mission, McRoberts found, is not as neighborhood-focused as might be imagined, and church membership is rarely drawn from the community. This study, as yet unpublished, may well prove to be the most important ground-level study of the church in relationship to the inner city that we have.[70] But each neighborhood will require its own analysis.

The connection between disconnected churches and health status is also troubling. In a careful statistical mapping project of the health status of infants in Baltimore inner-city neighborhoods, researchers found that adverse pregnancy outcomes (pre-term delivery, low birth weight, and very low birth weight) were not significantly different in areas with more churches.[71] Although this study of statistical association does not allow for conclusions of cause and effect, it encourages closer scrutiny of the quality of interaction between church and community. Together, these studies indicate that if the church is not to be a barrier to a community's holistic development, it must look very closely at the nature of its presence in relationship to community social and economic development.

Why are so many churches disengaged from their surrounding communities? The possibilities are many, including the rise of the commuter church, increased class stratification, physical fear, and the overwhelming effects of macro economic and social forces on older pastoral strategies, theological perspectives, and models of the church. According to C. Eric Lincoln and Lawrence H. Mamiya, the black church has historically experienced a dialectic tension between the other-worldly and the this-worldly, communal and

70. McRoberts, "Saving Four Corners: Religion and Revitalization in a Depressed Neighborhood," Ph.D. diss., Harvard University, 2000.

71. Robert E. Aronson, "The Influence of Residential Context on Pregnancy Outcome: A Multi-Method and Multi-Level Study," Ph.D. thesis, The Johns Hopkins School of Hygiene and Public Health (Department of International Health), 1997, pp. 66, 156-57.

privatistic dimensions of the purpose of the church,[72] differences that surface in other ways in most ecclesial traditions. It takes little effort to document that most white congregations left both the city and the inner city long ago, which suggests that they have given primary emphasis to a privatistic account of faith. In summary, what can easily be forgotten in celebratory discussions is that the church is a fallen and imperfect institution, always in need of change and reform.

How can a church change direction? First, repentance and conversion are in order (2 Cor. 7:10). Such reformation comes about when the church recognizes its weakness and failures, its susceptibility to spiritual idols and powers, and therefore listens to the corrective voices of Scripture and the community. For if it is true that "judgment begins with the family of God" (1 Pet. 4:17), then listening to critical and dissenting voices is crucial for revitalizing the church's life and witness. In Sandtown it was not atypical for me to hear a neighbor wonder aloud about church involvement. In fact, a leading community activist once said to me, "Tell me, what are the churches really doing around here? I don't see anything." She also commented, "That church is just interested in improving their building." There must be more of a place for negative assessments of the church's lack of grassroots ministry practices.[73] We must especially hear the anger of youth who have been denied a place in society and do not find a home in the church. Such stories need to be heard as a call for humility and change. Finally, pastors and their churches, wherever they are located, need to make a choice to be either part of the solution or part of the problem.[74]

Drawing attention to the church's shortcomings and failures is not meant to undercut the fact that many churches are doing vital redemptive work in the inner city. Indeed, given the presence of so many vital urban churches, especially African-American and Latino congregations, there is good reason to anticipate that the churches will continue to play important roles in community revitalization.[75] But the challenge continues to be that of being reformed by the Word in response to the cries of the people in the inner city.

---

72. Lincoln and Mamiya, *The Black Church in the African American Experience*, pp. 12-13.

73. Cathy J. Cohen, "The Church?" *Boston Review* 26, no. 2 (April/May 2001): 11-12.

74. One tool is a "hermeneutics of suspicion," contextualized to the city. See the proposals of Merold Westphal, *Suspicion and Faith: The Religious Uses of Modern Atheism* (New York: Fordham University Press, 1998). This work influenced the approach of this paragraph.

75. See the argument of Cheryl Townsend Gilkes, "Plenty Good Room. . . . In a Changing Black Church," in *One Nation under God? Religion and American Culture*, ed. Marjorie Garber and Rebecca L. Walkowitz (New York: Routledge, 1999), pp. 161-83.

THE CITY, THE GOSPEL, AND DISCIPLESHIP

At this point I want to situate the overall arguments of this book in a series of theological commitments relating to the city, the gospel, and discipleship.[76] When it came to the extraordinary advance of the early church in the city, sociologist Rodney Stark observed, "[The] central doctrines of Christianity prompted and sustained attractive, liberating, and effective social relations and organizations."[77] As I hope to show, the following commitments to the city, the gospel, and discipleship "prompt" and "sustain" what it means to live in Christ in the city. It is my contention that theological vision and beliefs do not exist alongside the responsibilities of reflection and action but are central to them.

The City and the New Creation

"The city in the American imagination has played roughly the role of hell in Christian theology,"[78] writes historian Garry Wills. For Americans, the density and diversity of the city are enemies of the suburban ideal. The result is devastating, according to Camilo José Vergara: "Lacking a shared vision of the value of our cities, we accept their destruction and fragmentation as inevitable."[79] Will political models, planning theory, or economic concepts provide an alternative urban imagination? I will propose that nothing provides greater nourishment and challenge to the imagination than the biblical story of the new city. The biblical language and imagery of God's new urban world, a world that has as its end the glorification of the Triune God, provides the strongest basis upon which to develop healing visions, new attitudes, and pastoral strategies in the inner city.

There is perhaps no more important place to start than with Augustine (354-430), who as the North African Bishop of Hippo embarked upon arguably the most intense theological reflection on the city that has ever been

---

76. On the role of basic commitments, see Volf, *Exclusion and Embrace*, p. 210.

77. Stark, *The Rise of Christianity: A Sociologist Reconsiders History* (Princeton: Princeton University Press, 1996), p. 211. The author's original emphasis is not reproduced in the quotation.

78. Wills, *John Wayne's America: The Politics of Celebrity* (New York: Simon & Schuster, 1997), p. 303. For a historical statement on the causes, see Daniel Lazare, *America's Undeclared War: What's Killing Our Cities and How We Can Stop It* (New York: Harcourt, Brace, 2001).

79. Vergara, *The New American Ghetto*, p. 200.

done. In his expansively conceived work *The City of God*,[80] Augustine characterized the world as an urban story, culminating in its final chapter as God's new city of peace.[81] For Augustine, the story line of history follows the trajectory of two cities, the city of the earth and the city of God, Babylon and Jerusalem. The former is a city of violence, the latter a city of perfect peace, as John Milbank has stressed.[82] For Augustine, the future peace of the city is social and anticipatory: "In its pilgrim state the heavenly city possesses this peace by faith; and by this faith it lives righteously when it refers to the attainment of that peace every good action toward God and man; for the life of the city is a social life."[83]

Some interpreters have argued that in Augustine's telling of the world's story, the Christian community pilgrimages too quickly through the present city and in the process overvalorizes the role of the church.[84] Augustine may have given the world too incidental a role in God's redemptive purposes and the church too central a role, particularly if he is taken to conflate the church with the city of God.[85] But however one reads Augustine on these matters, it is important for the church to appreciate and recover his biblical optic of the city that, though now fallen and filled with suffering, will be redeemed as the peaceable city of God.[86]

To elaborate: I propose that we locate the future of the inner city in a theology of the new creation (2 Cor. 5:17-21; Eph. 1:9-10; Col. 1:20; Rev. 21:1–22:5). According to Gordon D. Fee, the Apostle Paul uses the language

---

80. Augustine, *The City of God*, translated by Marcus Dods (New York: The Modern Library, 1993), XVI:2.

81. On the biblical grammar of the city for the development of Augustine's argumentation, see the recent argument of Harry O. Maier, "The End of the City and the City without End: *The City of God* as Revelation," *Augustinian Studies* 30, no. 2 (1999): 153-64.

82. Augustine, *The City of God*, XV:5-7; XIX:11. John Milbank, *Theology and Social Theory: Beyond Secular Reason* (Oxford: Blackwell, 1990), pp. 389-92.

83. Augustine, *The City of God*, XIX:17.

84. Augustine, *The City of God*, XV:1. See further Nicholas Wolterstorff, "Christian Political Reflection: Diognetian or Augustinian," *Princeton Seminary Bulletin* 20, no. 2 (New Series 1999): 150-68.

85. Harvie M. Conn, "The Kingdom of God and the City of Man: A History of the City/Church Dialogue," in *Discipling the City: A Comprehensive Approach to Urban Ministry*, 2d ed., ed. Roger S. Greenway (Grand Rapids: Baker, 1992), p. 252.

86. In *The Desire of the Nations: Rediscovering the Roots of Political Theology* (Cambridge: Cambridge University Press, 1996), Oliver O'Donovan observes, "As the church performs its eucharist for the life now ended, it keeps before its eyes the civic character of its destiny. For no destiny can possibly be conceived in the world, or even out of it, other than that of a city" (285).

of the "new creation" to describe "the coming of God's eschatological rule inaugurated by Christ — especially through his death and resurrection — and the gift of the Spirit."[87] This situates the city, community ministry, and the church in the larger redemptive historical framework of creation, fall, redemption, and new creation. These connections are vital for a theology of the city. They allow us to speak not only of the transformation that comes to individuals as a result of the death, resurrection, and ascension of Christ, but also of the transformation of the entire fallen creation, including the city (2 Cor. 5:17-21; cf. Gal. 6:15; Eph. 1:10; 3:9). A new urban world is part of God's holistic salvation of the fallen creation and cosmos (2 Cor. 6:2).

When Scripture paints a picture of the new creation, its most comprehensive image is the new city of God. According to Isaiah 65:17-25, the new city forms the peaceable home that fulfills God's promised justice for the poor, salvation for the humble, and the renewal of creation:

> "Behold, I will create new heavens and a new earth. The former things
>   will not be remembered, nor will they come to mind.
> But be glad and rejoice forever in what I will create, for I will create
>   Jerusalem to be a delight and its people a joy.
> I will rejoice over Jerusalem and take delight in my people; the sound
>   of weeping and of crying will be heard in it no more.
> Never again will there be in it an infant that lives but a few days, or an
>   old man who does not live out his years; he who dies at a hundred
>   will be thought a mere youth; he who fails to reach a hundred will
>   be considered accursed.
> They will build houses and dwell in them; they will plant vineyards
>   and eat their fruit.
> No longer will they build houses and others live in them, or plant and
>   others eat. For as the days of a tree, so will be the days of my
>   people; my chosen ones will long enjoy the works of their hands.
> They will not toil in vain or bear children doomed to misfortune; for
>   they will be a people blessed by the LORD, they and their
>   descendants with them.
> Before they call I will answer; while they are still speaking I will hear.
> The wolf and the lamb will feed together, and the lion will eat straw
>   like the ox, but dust will be the serpent's food. They will neither
>   harm nor destroy in all my holy mountain," says the LORD.

---

87. Fee, *Listening to the Spirit in the Text* (Grand Rapids: Eerdmans, 2000), p. 57.

When the city is redeemed, Isaiah's vision announced, no infant or aged woman or man dies before their time, dignity and integrity are restored to work, ownership returns to the one who labors, trust and safety unite diverse neighbors, and communion with God flourishes. It is a vision of reconciliation.

John's portrait at the end of the New Testament indicates the importance of this story for understanding the world. Here the seer of Patmos declares in Revelation 21:1-5 that the new city of the Lamb will be absent of sorrow, violence, death, and exploitation (cf. Isa. 25:8):

> Then I saw a new heaven and a new earth, for the first heaven and the first earth had passed away, and there was no longer any sea. I saw the Holy City, the new Jerusalem, coming down out of heaven from God, prepared as a bride beautifully dressed for her husband. And I heard a loud voice from the throne saying, "Now the dwelling of God is with men, and he will live with them. They will be his people, and God himself will be with them and be their God. He will wipe every tear from their eyes. There will be no more death or mourning or crying or pain, for the old order of things has passed away."

Coming down from heaven (Rev. 21:2), the city is God's gift, not the product of human hands.

God's new city, the world to come, is a world of reconciliation, not homogenization. For God's new creation does not isolate or separate people but joins them together, celebrating unity in diversity.[88] The nations will gather in worship, bringing together their various cultures, languages, and ethnicity (Rev. 7:9). In this gathering, identity will be neither erased nor privileged but celebrated in God's wondrous new community (Rev. 22:3). To this city the nations will bring their works to be redeemed (Rev. 21:26). For as a place of cultural activity, the new city is marked by the experience of the transformation of "all things" (Rev. 21:5).

With his emphasis on biblical hope and the future of God in light of the Western world's exhausted project, the German theologian Jürgen Moltmann is an important resource for building a theology of the city from a new-creation perspective. As he expresses it in his important study *The Coming of God*, "The end is still to come *and* the new world is present."[89] And of the end

---

88. For a helpful discussion, see Richard Bauckham, *The Theology of the Book of Revelation* (Cambridge: Cambridge University Press, 1993), pp. 132-40.

89. Moltmann, *The Coming of God: Christian Eschatology*, trans. Margaret Kohl (Minneapolis: Fortress, 1996), p. 232.

he says, "The city of God is the center of the new creation."[90] What is new about the new creation, says Moltmann, is the mutual indwelling of God and Christ: "The innermost heart of the vision of the new Jerusalem and the new creation of heaven and earth is nothing other than the immediate, omnipresent and eternal indwelling of God and of Christ."[91] The future of the city is not to be essentialized, for neither the future nor the city is the center of the biblical story. Rather, the center of the future and the city is the eternal presence of God.[92]

Urban hope is based not on any notion of human progress but on the Lamb that was slain, the one who in self-giving life and death redeemed the world (Rev. 5:6, 12; cf. 1:1). Because the conditions of the city are so brutal — what the seer understood to be the realities of unholy Babylon — the very end of the biblical witness is a prayer and cry of hope: "Come, Lord Jesus" (Rev. 22:20; cf. 22:17).[93] Christ is "the hope of glory" (Col. 1:27), the promise of the new creation. For this reason, the hopes and cries in the face of urban oppression are hopes and cries for Christ, the coming of God who will make all things urban all new.

The Gospel as Good News for the Poor

To speak of Jesus as the Savior of the world is to speak of him as Redeemer of the city and bearer of good news for the poor. In his inaugural and programmatic sermon of Luke 4:16-21, Jesus announces the gospel, bound up with his person, as a new beginning for the poor, the oppressed, and the city. Citing passages from Isaiah 58 and 61, Jesus proclaims,

> The Spirit of the Lord is on me,
>   because he has anointed me
>   to preach good news to the poor.
> He has sent me to proclaim freedom for the prisoners

90. Moltmann, *The Coming of God,* p. 308.
91. Moltmann, *The Coming of God,* p. 315.
92. In his essay entitled "Eschatology in *The Coming of God,*" in *God Will Be All in All: The Eschatology of Jürgen Moltmann,* ed. Richard Bauckham (Edinburgh: T. & T. Clark, 1999), Bauckham characterizes Moltmann's eschatology as Christological, integrative, redemptive, processive, theocentric, contextual, and politically and pastorally responsible (pp. 1-34).
93. Jürgen Moltmann, *The Source of Life: The Holy Spirit and the Theology of Life,* trans. Margaret Kohl (Minneapolis: Fortress, 1997), p. 11.

and recovery of sight for the blind,
to release the oppressed,
to proclaim the year of the Lord's favor. (Luke 4:18-19)

Jesus is *the* good news for the poor, the incarcerated, the sick, and the oppressed. Three connections are made here that explain further the meaning of the gospel in Luke: Jesus announces the reign of God by way of the Jubilee, he comes to restore the city, and he comes in the power of the Spirit.[94]

Jesus proclaims that he has come to bring "good news" to the poor, and he makes the announcement in the language and imagery of the Jubilee, "the year of the Lord's favor."[95] In the Old Testament, the year of Jubilee brought release of the land and the return of people to it (Lev. 25; Deut. 15). The background is the central biblical theme of God's presence with and commitment to the poor (Exod. 3; Deut. 15; Pss. 103; 146; Isa. 58; 61). God is the one who defends the poor, the widow, the orphan, and the alien. Jesus is the one who has fulfilled all of these expectations (Luke 1:46-55; 7:20-22). Under the Jubilee reign of God, the gospel means all things are made right — the poor are lifted up, the prisoners are released, sins are forgiven, and the curse of sin is reversed. We should not forget that in the time of Jesus, "gospel" bore political and social meaning. It was a salvation much different from the world's political order[96] and was not interiorized or spiritualized. Christ's proclamation of the gospel was both personally and socially transforming.

Jesus is also interpreting the Jubilee in terms of the city. This is evident in the immediate interpretation of his calling provided a few verses later, when Jesus proclaims, "I must proclaim the good news of the kingdom of God to the other cities also; for I was sent for this purpose" (Luke 4:43, NRSV; cf. 14:21). The "good news" is the Jubilee message of 4:18-19, a citation of Isaiah 61:1-2. In this text, Isaiah links God's new day for the poor with the promise of urban recovery: "They will rebuild the ancient ruins and restore the places long devastated; they will renew the ruined cities that have been devastated for generations" (61:4). Against this background, Jesus understands his ministry, life, and redemptive work as ushering in good news for the city and the oppressed (Luke 9:51). In his suffering on the cross, Jesus identified with the forsakenness of the poor and socially outcast, and called them to live

94. I am indebted here to Harvie M. Conn, "Lucan Perspectives and the City," *Missiology: An International Review* 13, no. 4 (October 1985): 409-28; and Conn and Ortiz, *Urban Ministry*, pp. 116-37.

95. For a discussion of the background of Jubilee, see John Howard Yoder, *The Politics of Jesus: Vicit Agnus Noster*, 2d ed. (Grand Rapids: Eerdmans, 1994), pp. 28-33.

96. Myers et al., *"Say to This Mountain,"* pp. 5-6.

anew in the community of his reign. All of Jesus' Jubilee work takes place in the power of the Spirit (Luke 3:16; 4:18; Acts 10:38).[97] This story of salvation empowers the poor, the outcast, and the forgotten to share in God's redemption of the city.

Discipleship as World Formation and Reconciliation

What are the implications of a new-creation understanding of the city and the gospel for the tasks and obligations of urban discipleship? Two activities attract our attention: Christians working as agents of the kingdom and as ministers of reconciliation. Both activities have an all-embracing and public shape — which is absolutely necessary to address the structures of racism and exclusion that impinge on everyday life in the inner city.

Annunciating the kingdom will mean that instead of accepting the inner city as it is and offering words of future consolation, Christians will work to reverse the misery, suffering, and injustice that too often grip it. Such kingdom-focused work includes establishing alternative institutions, advancing holistic initiatives, and advancing the cause of urban reform. Reflected in the urban visions of Isaiah and Revelation and manifest in the life and gospel of Jesus of Nazareth is God's promise for the renewal and restoration of the city, not its abandonment, exploitation, annihilation, or demolition (Matt. 5:5; Rom. 8:21; Rev. 21:5). The hope of the kingdom and the life of the world to come make a claim on us to work for more just and joyful communities.

Such discipleship is characterized by Nicholas Wolterstorff in *Until Justice and Peace Embrace* as "world formative" Christianity.[98] In Wolterstorff's description, a world-formative Christianity involves "the re-formation of the *social* world."[99] Because sin has impacted the world in its totality, including its social institutions, and because Christ's salvation has come to all of life, Christians are called to struggle for the healing and wholeness of the world. Thus a spirituality of world-formative Christianity stands in contrast to a piety of inwardness and aversion to the world.[100]

What must also be taken up is that which the Apostle Paul called the

97. On the subject of the Spirit and Christ's mission in Luke, see Matthias Wenk, *Community-Forming Power: The Socio-Ethical Role of the Spirit in Luke–Acts* (Sheffield: Sheffield Academic Press, 2000).

98. Wolterstorff, *Until Justice and Peace Embrace* (Grand Rapids: Eerdmans, 1983).

99. Wolterstorff, *Until Justice and Peace Embrace*, p. 10.

100. Wolterstorff, *Until Justice and Peace Embrace*, p. 5.

"ministry of reconciliation" (2 Cor. 5:17-21).[101] Biblically rooted reconciliation is not just personal, but encompasses, as Miroslav Volf proposes, the interpersonal, the spiritual, and the social.[102] Within the scope of this ministry is a broad range of formal and informal activities intended to overcome division and all forms and consequences of violence. Volf's biblical theology of reconciliation was forged in the sorrows of conflict surrounding the former Yugoslavia, and the thrust of it is this: the will to embrace others follows the cross and mirrors the life of the Triune God.[103] Realizing the overarching end for which the world is being redeemed — love and reconciliation — guides the work of seeing relationships rightly ordered.

The life of God in Trinitarian relationship, a life as mutual indwelling, grounds the aims of urban discipleship.[104] A communion of sharing (Luke 4:16; John 10:38; 16:12-15; 17:20-26), the Triune life models for the church and the world the loving and rightly formed social relationships of a new city. Through the Spirit, the Triune God engenders the life of urban discipleship as acts of gratitude, worship, and celebration, giving faith a doxological shape. As the face of God revealed on the cross, the Trinity calls forth in a hurting world the proclamation of grace and reconciliation in Jesus Christ.

When Jesus taught the disciples what it meant to follow him, to join in his story, he told them that the journey required taking up the cross (Mark 10:43-44). As Paul wrote to the church in Corinth, "I resolved to know nothing while I was with you except Jesus Christ and him crucified" (1 Cor. 2:2). Orlando Costas insists on the primacy of the cross in his important missiological reflections on the church. "Worship, evangelism, and service have Christian value if they are done 'outside,' in solidarity with the crucified Jesus and his permanent commitment to the outcast," Costas

101. Robert Schreiter, *Reconciliation: Mission and Ministry in a Changing Social Order* (Maryknoll: Orbis, 1992); and *The Ministry of Reconciliation: Spirituality and Strategies* (Maryknoll: Orbis, 1998). See also William R. Burrows, "Reconciling All in Christ: An Old New Paradigm for Mission," *Mission Studies* 15-1, no. 29 (1998): 79-98.

102. Volf, "The Social Meaning of Reconciliation," *Interpretation* 54, no. 2 (April 2000): 158-72.

103. Volf, *Exclusion and Embrace*, p. 25.

104. This section is indebted to Miroslav Volf, "The Trinity Is Our Social Program: The Doctrine of the Trinity and the Shape of Social Engagement," *Modern Theology* 14, no. 3 (July 1998): 403-23; Orlando E. Costas, *Liberating News: A Theology of Contextual Evangelization* (Grand Rapids: Eerdmans, 1989), pp. 71-87, 149; Anthony C. Thiselton, *Interpreting God and the Postmodern Self: On Meaning, Manipulation, and Promise* (Grand Rapids: Eerdmans, 1995), pp. 153-58; and Jürgen Moltmann, *Experiences in Theology: Ways and Forms of Christian Theology*, trans. Margaret Kohl (Minneapolis: Fortress, 2000), pp. 303-33.

writes.[105] The image of "outside" is that of "outside the gate," taken from the Epistle to the Hebrews, where Christ's disciples are those who, in following him, went "outside the city gate" (13:12). Going outside the gate was not exiting the city but moving outside the privileged space to the place of marginality, crucifixion, and death for the sake of redemption (Heb. 13:13). This is the pattern for the church.

Throughout this book I will be drawing on these basic commitments to the city, the gospel, and discipleship. In summary, the commitments are these: God's new city calls for an alternative vision of the urban world; the gospel is the announcement of the good news manifest in Jesus; and discipleship is the work of world formation and reconciliation. By them, I will argue, the church is able to live faithfully in a hurting and changing urban world.

LOOKING AHEAD

Guided by the conviction that Christ crucified creates room for the embrace of others and that the Spirit of the resurrected Christ brings new life, I believe that local congregations can envision and work toward more just, joyful, and whole communities. However, a focus on the life and calling of the church is not sufficient, either for the church or for the city. Because of God's kingdom, Christian reflection on the inner city, both its present condition and its future, must also envision more peaceable neighborhoods and cities.[106] Putting faith into action requires specific practices and institution-building, tactics and strategies, prophetic words and healing deeds.

As I understand ministry and faith in the city, they cannot be abstracted from particular communities and the narratives they embody.[107] Community

---

105. Costas, *Christ Outside the Gate: Mission Beyond Christendom* (Maryknoll: Orbis, 1982), p. 193.

106. In Moltmann's words, "Theology springs out of a passion for God's kingdom and its righteousness and justice, and this passion grows up in the community of Christ. In that passion, theology becomes imagination for the kingdom of God in the world, and for the world in God's kingdom." See Moltmann, *Experiences in Theology*, p. xx. See also Jürgen Moltmann, Nicholas Wolterstorff, and Ellen T. Charry, *A Passion for God's Reign: Theology, Christian Learning, and the Christian Self,* ed. Miroslav Volf (Grand Rapids: Eerdmans, 1998).

107. This connection between community, narrative, and divine grace I take to be one of the important themes emphasized by Stanley Hauerwas. See his *In Good Company: The Church as Polis* (Notre Dame: University of Notre Dame Press, 1995); and *The Hauerwas Reader,* ed. John Berkman and Michael Cartwright (Durham: Duke University Press, 2001). These themes are particularly important in the African-American Christian tradition, which provides us with perhaps the best model of narrative theology.

change always involves the construction and identification of a new journey and history. So I see little point or possibility in separating church-based community development and organizing from theological and lived narratives.[108] For this reason I begin and end this book with stories about the work of New Song Community Church in Sandtown. As a lived parable of sorts, New Song has the power to illustrate a counter-narrative for the inner city. But I am also interested in seeing through New Song the narrative shape of the habits, skills, and practice of gospel faith.

Although I turn to New Song and Sandtown at significant points in this book, to frame and center our project, this is not primarily an account of either. The story of New Song in Sandtown is best told by letting the people of the community speak for themselves, and this book makes no claim to be that kind of record.[109] While I think that New Song is an extraordinary community of faith, I do not intend to lift it up as a "model" of urban rebuilding or reconciliation. While New Song is a sample of what faithfulness can look like, there is simply no single "model" that is sufficient in and of itself. Moreover, as a community that lives by faith, New Song not only gives powerful testimony to urban possibility but is also fragile and frail. Like all churches, it is not everything it should be. Every day is a gift, a trial, a responsibility, and part of a process. Where will New Song go with the gift of its calling? This remains an open question, a part of the daily risk of faith that every church community must face.

The reading of the inner city and of the Triune God's story for the city that I propose has been most prominently formed by my experiences in Sandtown as a neighbor and pastor. As Stephen E. Fowl and L. Gregory Jones have elucidated in their important book *Reading in Communion,* our practice of reading Scripture is to take place "in communion."[110] Specifically, it is the friendships, ecclesial experiences, and practices of transformational development related to New Song and Sandtown that have showed me how to read Scripture and the inner city with new eyes. I cannot say strongly enough how my neighbors in Sandtown have shaped my faith, my questions, my thinking, and my life. A sister congregation has found a beginning in New York's central Harlem and struggles with what it means to follow Christ in the global

---

108. A working example of bringing narrative and urban theology together is *God So Loves the City: Seeking a Theology of Urban Mission,* ed. Charles Van Engen and Jude Tiersma (Monrovia: MARC, 1994).

109. Such a project is planned in Sandtown.

110. Fowl and Jones, *Reading in Communion: Scripture and Ethics in Christian Life* (Grand Rapids: Eerdmans, 1991).

city. Because my wife and I moved to New York City to be a part of its beginning, it too has been important in my formation.

A brief review of the following chapters will indicate the shape of my discussion. Chapter One, "Excluded Neighborhoods," is a study of the meaning of the inner city and the many faces that have shaped it. Here I argue that inner-city dislocations are caused not by the people of the community but by structural forces that have a history. To make this case, I examine the history of Sandtown. But I seek to go further than social and historical description, presenting a theological analysis of the inner city that draws on the biblical categories of systemic sin and the powers that be. This overall analysis is foundational. In Chapter Two, "A Church of the Streets," I seek to explicate what it means to be a grassroots Christian congregation that, by its very distinctive kingdom focus, social practices, and witness, is a source of gospel joy, hope, and strength to its neighborhood. The model that I propose is a church that is good news incarnated on the streets, not limited to what goes on in the sanctuary.

In Chapter Three, "The Things That Make for Peace," I attempt to develop a framework for living for God's peace in the inner city. Drawing on the vision of Jeremiah in particular, I seek to show ways in which the biblical text provides resources for the church facing the challenges of the global inner city. In Chapter Four, "Out of the Ruins," I offer an analysis of the process of how a people can re-create their neighborhood. A reading of Nehemiah, a theology of the Spirit, and a consideration of the improvisational dynamics that constitute community organizing and development form this chapter. In Chapter Five, "Singing a New Song," I tell the story of New Song Community Church in Sandtown. As I have noted, this is a story in process, and what I say here is hardly to be considered the last or the only word. In the final chapter, "The Future of the Inner City," I seek to account for the trends and developments that confront the inner city, looking at them from the horizon of God's promised urban future.

I cannot escape my background as a white male born into a world of options and privileges. But I can and should struggle with my obligation as a Christian to view the city in all of its forms and conditions through the eyes of the stranger, the excluded, and the poor. Christian reflection on the inner city must emerge out of relationships: the bonds of commitment to Christ and his peace for the poor. In Christ's fellowship with the poor (Matt. 25:45), in his identification with the depths of suffering through the cross, the cries from the depths of the inner city are also his, and the plea that all things might be made right a yearning in the Spirit for God's reign of peace (Rev. 22:17).[111] Our out-

---

111. On the theme of Christ's solidarity as a starting point for ecclesiology and mis-

look on the inner city must grow out of the experience of God and the experience of life in community. While there can be genuine and honest disagreements about urban history and social policy, considerably more is at stake for the Christian community than having the correct view on such matters.

This book represents theological and missiological reflection on the way, situated between the realities of urban brokenness and the hopes for urban wholeness. It is offered as a reason for the hope I believe we need to have in the inner city. As the subtitle is intended to indicate, I have written with the conviction that Scripture provides the essential foundation and resource we need to understand and creatively engage the changing inner city. There is no shortage of historical precedent to support the claim that biblical faith has immense power for generating and sustaining alternative and compelling social visions (Acts 17:6).[112] Knowing that the church faces the complex challenges of urbanization around the world, I hope this book may have some wider service. But I will be most grateful if, by clarifying something of the direction and purpose of Christian identity and agency, *To Live in Peace* serves to advance the *shalom* of the American inner city.

---

sion, one should begin with the lived theology found in the Black and Hispanic/Latino church. Note especially Samuel Solivan, *The Spirit, Pathos, and Liberation: Toward an Hispanic Pentecostal Theology* (Sheffield: Sheffield Academic Press, 1998). See also Jürgen Moltmann, *The Spirit of Life: A Universal Affirmation*, trans. Margaret Kohl (Minneapolis: Fortress, 1992), p. 130; and Moltmann, *The Way of Jesus Christ: Christology in Messianic Dimensions*, trans. Margaret Kohl (Minneapolis: Fortress, 1993), pp. 178-81.

112. For a historical survey, see *Radical Christian Writings: A Reader*, ed. Andrew Bradstock and Christopher Rowland (Oxford: Blackwell, 2002).

CHAPTER 1

Excluded Neighborhoods

O n the day in 1980 when Baltimore's acclaimed Inner Harbor development opened with speeches and festivities, the *Washington Post* turned
west two miles to the neighborhood of Sandtown for urban contrast. The stal-
wart and locally respected community leader Ella Johnson told the paper that
Sandtown "is just an inner city neighborhood. . . . It's buried. A good block is
where there are less than five vacant houses."[1] Two decades later, many parts of
Sandtown still look this way. Such differences in a city can be assigned social,
economic, and political meaning. But as Augustine reminds us, ultimately
such differences in a city reflect a struggle between two competing spiritual visions of urban life, and with it the nature of social arrangements.

Lots of good things are happening in Baltimore. There is a resurgence in
neighborhoods such as Canton, Federal Hill, and Locust Point, a new emphasis on high-tech development in the Inner Harbor area, a strong and expanding non-profit sector. And Baltimore has also had a succession of mayors who
are passionate about the city. It is a unique city that is seeking a better future.
But we need to keep things in perspective.

As David Rusk documents in his study *Baltimore Unbound*, the changes
in the city are related to as yet unchanging patterns of flight and abandonment.[2] Since 1950, the population has dropped from nearly one million to

---

1. Saundra Saperstein, "Sandtown Typical of Urban Blight," *Washington Post*, 2 July
1980, pp. B1, 2. Throughout this chapter, I use the shortened name "Sandtown" rather than
its longer official name, Sandtown-Winchester.

2. Rusk, *Baltimore Unbound: A Strategy for Regional Renewal* (Baltimore: The Abell
Foundation, 1996).

around 630,000, the middle and upper classes having packed up and moved to the suburbs. About a thousand people a month are still leaving the city. By most counts, over 40,000 houses are abandoned, with scores of empty lots being added as demolition crews tear their way across the city's row-house fabric. Baltimore is the nineteenth largest city in the United States, but in 1999 it had the second highest per-capita homicide rate. It made sense that the acclaimed television series *Homicide: Life on the Streets* was set in Baltimore. Only recently has that high rate started (tentatively) to decline.[3] A Johns Hopkins researcher found that, in terms of psychological damage, the children living in Baltimore's inner city were more adversely affected than children living in war-torn Bosnia.[4] Observes the geographer David Harvey, "Baltimore is, for the most part, a mess. Not the kind of enchanting mess that makes cities interesting places to explore, but an awful mess."[5] Harvey is substantially right — which I say with great regret because of how much I love the city.

Like other cities, Baltimore is really two cities, and they relate to one another in surreal juxtaposition. The Baltimore most people know is filled with shiny office towers, new sports stadiums, luxury condominiums, and the Inner Harbor development, which is packed with theme restaurants and has a carnival-like atmosphere. The "other Baltimore" is off the tourist maps. It is the Baltimore represented by Sandtown, just two miles west of the Inner Harbor. This Baltimore has substandard houses, lots filled with trash, greasy carry-outs, liquor stores, and corner markets where sheets of cloudy bullet-proof glass separate customer and merchant. Its visible economy includes the shopping cart filled with reclaimed cans. Here it is far easier to buy illegal drugs than it is to purchase fresh produce and reasonably priced groceries, far simpler to rent a substandard row house than to obtain a mortgage for a simple and decent one.

Underneath the brick, concrete, and steel skin of these two worlds, the trajectories of social and economic inequalities run even deeper. When it comes to education, health care, employment networks, housing conditions, municipal services, and political influence in Baltimore, Sandtown's distance from the center is far — and growing. Private schools serve the one Baltimore, failing schools the other. World-class hospitals treat one population, a shrinking number of clinics and overworked emergency rooms the other.

---

3. Peter Hermann, "Fewer Than 300 Homicides at Last," *Sun Spot* (on-line *Baltimore Sun*), 1 January 2001.

4. Marego Athans, "Psychological Poverty," *The Sun,* 29 June 1999, E-1, 7.

5. Harvey, *Spaces of Hope* (Berkeley: University of California Press, 2000), p. 133.

Connection and opportunity abound in the one Baltimore, disconnection and adversity in the other.[6]

In this chapter I will seek to examine and understand how the 72-square-block community of Winchester, commonly referred to as Sandtown, came into being. I will do this first through a historical analysis. Following the historical analysis, I will propose a theological interpretation of the inner city.[7] I will conclude with a proposal for the inner city that emphasizes the story of salvation and the gracious reign of God.

Sandtown is unique, as is every city and urban community. Each individual neighborhood has its own history, cultural identity, geographical relationships, and connections to larger spatial and social forces. Studies of specific neighborhoods are an important way to learn about cities and urban processes. By drawing on a wider body of literature, however, I hope to show that Sandtown is also emblematic of the changing inner city. Moreover, for all the differences between neighborhoods and cities, there are common threads of suffering and shared patterns of development.[8]

Let me also say that I have certain strong reservations about presenting Sandtown as a representative inner-city neighborhood. Sandtown is much

---

6. There are limits, of course, to the helpfulness of the dual-city metaphor; for one thing, it reduces the complexity of the situation. Yet it is helpful in viewing the urban landscape in moral, economic, political, and spatial terms.

7. Nicholas Wolterstorff has stressed the importance of "theologically faithful economics" rather than a "theology of economics" in "Public Theology or Christian Learning?" in *A Passion for God's Reign: Theology, Christian Learning, and the Christian Self,* ed. Miroslav Volf (Grand Rapids: Eerdmans, 1998), pp. 76-77. I am in full agreement with this view of Christian learning, and share Wolterstorff's concern about "theologians" stepping in where others should tread. However, too few economists, Christian or otherwise, have taken up the cause of faithful economics in service of the poor. The poor cannot wait for Christian economists to produce work that will adequately serve them. It is also the case that essential "learning" about the inner city comes only through the experience and the viewpoint of the community. The issue is one of epistemology. The history of the subject in the social sciences, as Alice O'Connor shows in *Poverty Knowledge: Social Science, Social Policy, and the Poor in Twentieth-Century U.S. History* (Princeton: Princeton University Press, 2001), has produced little more than problematic results.

8. Camilo José Vergara has spent twenty years examining "ghettos" across the nation, and has gathered his findings in *The New American Ghetto* (New Brunswick: Rutgers University Press, 1995). He identifies three contemporary types of ghettos: "green ghettos," characterized by depopulation, vacant land overgrown by nature, and ruins; "institutional ghettos," which are publicly financed places of confinement designed mainly for the native born; and the "new immigrant ghettos," which derive their character from an influx of immigrants, mainly Latino and West Indian. Vergara finds all three types to be interconnected, "channeling people and land to one another" (pp. 14-20).

more than a neighborhood on the margins — it is a community that people call home, where they form loving relationships, break bread together, create traditions, generate memories, and find shared meaning. It is a community where people share the same dreams as the rest of America — good jobs, decent schools, safe streets, and affordable housing. People not only share these dreams; they work hard to achieve them in both individual and collective ways. Sandtown is a place of life and hope, not just suffering and struggle. As Harold McDougall has pointed out, it is, like other African-American neighborhoods in Baltimore, a place where people are tenaciously building community.[9] Drawing attention to institutional forces that have historically caused oppression and harm to Sandtown (or any distressed urban community) does not take away from the humanity of people for whom it is home; it does not reduce the community to the status of victim. Sandtown is not "the problem," but the site where broader forces are at work constructing exclusion and distance.

How the story of the inner city is seen and told affects everything from a vision for ministry to public policy. The Hebrew prophets began their vocation with seeing the city through the eyes of the poor and the ways of justice. From this viewpoint, and its underlying assumptions about God, the prophets followed with analysis and critique. But accompanying the "tearing down" was also the creative and energizing "building and planting," as we find it in Jeremiah's call (Jer. 1:10).[10] Put another way, there cannot be an appreciation for what God's redemption means for the inner city without understanding what has gone wrong, nor can the gospel be announced with integrity without the identification and denunciation of social sin and injustice. Nor can we study the inner city without being challenged to engage in the reversal of its condition. Because I take it that an analysis of social arrangements influences the shape of faithful social and political activity, I order my reflection accordingly.

THE MAKING OF AN INNER-CITY NEIGHBORHOOD

The pre-history of the African-American inner city can be traced to America's "original sin" of slavery and the violent European quest to create a "New

9. McDougall, *Black Baltimore: A New Theory of Community* (Philadelphia: Temple University Press, 1993).

10. Brian J. Walsh, *Subversive Christianity: Imaging God in a Dangerous Time* (Bristol: Regius Press, 1992), p. 36; Walter Brueggemann, *The Prophetic Imagination* (Minneapolis: Fortress, 1978).

World." Often baptized in Christian ideology, this history set in motion subsequent manifestations of racial injustice and economic oppression that remain codified in various forms to this day.[11] Marking Sandtown's specific struggle is a history of three distinct yet overlapping periods of development. The first period begins at the start of the century and goes through World War II, the second corresponds to the postwar years of de-industrialization, and the third follows the inner city into the present era of globalization. Each period retains continuities with the past, especially that of racial and economic inequality, but does so in changing forms.

Period One: The Segregated Inner City

Sandtown has its earliest beginnings in national demographic changes. Given the push of unemployment in the South and the pull of jobs in northern cities, more than "five million blacks . . . moved North during the seven decades starting in 1910."[12] For all that the city would mean negatively, it positively provided blacks with the room to be free in a manner that the South had not. The city was viewed as the "promised land,"[13] though it would not turn out to be a city on a hill.

The Sandtown that we know today has its origins in the public decisions of this era. According to historian Roderick N. Ryon, whose research on West Baltimore I am indebted to, "Segregationist values, notions that blacks should be separated and subordinate, prevailed throughout the country in these turn-of-the-century years, and Baltimore whites deemed the emerging black community of Old West Baltimore a tolerable, even useful city neighborhood."[14] This is what guided the development of Sandtown, in the heart of Old West Baltimore, as an African-American community. According to Ryon, Sandtown was first developed as a white, middle-class neighborhood, and it functioned that way from 1870 to 1900, when it attracted European immigrants. As the nineteenth century turned to the twentieth, the city's population growth and the mobility afforded whites by the streetcar led to the first in a series of demo-

11. For a history of the African-American experience, see *To Make Our World Anew: A History of African Americans*, ed. Robin D. G. Kelley and Earl Lewis (New York: Oxford University Press, 2000).

12. Vergara, *The New American Ghetto*, p. 4.

13. Milton C. Sernett, *Bound for the Promised Land: African American Religion and the Great Migration* (Durham: Duke University Press, 1997).

14. Ryon, "Old West Baltimore," *Maryland Historical Magazine* 77, no. 1 (Spring 1982): 55.

graphic changes on Baltimore's western side.[15] When whites moved socially upward and thus moved to outlying communities, the neighborhoods they left behind became designated for the increasing number of southern blacks migrating to the city. By the end of World War II, Sandtown had become almost exclusively black, Fulton Avenue on the western boundary being perhaps the last major street to undergo a racial transition.

The pattern of residential segregation that created Sandtown was joined to the city's growth and development. With neighborhoods near the industrial jobs in the center of the city reserved for white immigrants only, black Baltimoreans were limited in neighborhood choices, and West Baltimore became a principal place to find housing.[16] This was to the advantage of many urban, affluent whites in nearby neighborhoods such as Bolton Hill, who then had easy access to low-wage black domestic workers.[17] With African Americans cordoned off in one part of the city, they could be, as Ryon points out, "restricted, controlled, watched over,"[18] while still able to contribute to the rise of the privileged and prosperous in other select parts of the city. Sandtown's families lived in overcrowded and substandard rental housing, sharing apartments, while the new white immigrants had more available options. At its peak in the 1940s, the population in Sandtown soared to an estimated 35,000 to 40,000 people.[19]

While poverty was extensive, employment opportunities existed, though they were largely unequal in pay and advancement possibilities when compared to that of their white counterparts. For many, low pay meant long hours, as Ryon points out: "Work, the sheer volume of it, dominated most people's lives."[20] Typically it took a combination of jobs to make ends meet, and blacks were still "last hired and first fired" in the low-paying and menial service sector and in industrial-related work. Local white-owned businesses would hire African Americans only for the most menial tasks.[21] This combination of circumstances usually led to a subsistence existence. However, during the Depression, finding a job was considerably more difficult. Even do-

---

15. This theme of the streetcar and urban transportation is important for Ryon's history of West Baltimore.

16. Ryon, "Old West Baltimore," p. 55.

17. Ryon, "Old West Baltimore," p. 55.

18. Ryon, "Old West Baltimore," p. 55.

19. Ryon, "Old West Baltimore," p. 62; and Ryon, *West Baltimore Neighborhoods: Sketches of Their History, 1840-1960* (Baltimore: The Institute for Publications Design of the University of Baltimore, 1993), p. 124.

20. Ryon, "Old West Baltimore," p. 61.

21. Ryon, "Old West Baltimore," pp. 60-61.

mestic workers found themselves laid off. Predictably, the effects of an economic downturn became magnified among the most vulnerable.

But racial and social oppression never meant surrender and subordination. West Baltimore's durable black churches were the centerpiece of civic leadership, mutual aid, and political protest.[22] Community pressure led to, for example, the construction of a new building for Frederick Douglass High School. (From 1925 until 1954, the school was located in the heart of Sandtown, serving as the only "colored high school" in the city. Among the prominent alumni of old Douglass are Thurgood Marshall and Cab Calloway.) In the 1930s, Sandtown residents joined together and successfully picketed nearby white businesses in the "Don't Buy Where You Can't Work" campaign, considered a prelude to the civil rights movement.[23] Care and concern for one another, virtues of resistance to the dehumanizing pressures of segregation, were forged in suffering and a common task of building community.[24]

Period Two: The Post-Industrial Inner City

When Martin Luther King Jr. was assassinated in 1968, it marked a social and psychological breaking point for many inner-city neighborhoods, and this was certainly true in Sandtown. Until King's death, there had been a growing sense of optimism in the community — and throughout black America — that the nation would achieve a greater level of justice and inclusion. But with

22. Ryon, "Old West Baltimore," p. 63.

23. Ryon, "Old West Baltimore," p. 63. For a history, see Karen Olson, "Old West Baltimore: Segregation, African-American Culture, and the Struggle for Equality," in *The Baltimore Book: New Views of Local History*, ed. Elizabeth Fee, Linda Shopes, and Linda Zeidman (Philadelphia: Temple University Press, 1991), pp. 57-78.

24. Studies that address the interrelated processes that led to this phase of inner-city development include Gregory D. Squires, *Capital and Communities in Black and White: The Intersections of Race, Class, and Uneven Development* (Albany: State University of New York Press, 1994); Thomas J. Sugrue, "The Structures of Urban Poverty: The Reorganization of Space and Work in Three Periods of American History," in *The Underclass Debate: Views from History*, ed. Michael B. Katz (Princeton: Princeton University Press, 1993), pp. 85-117, and more expansively, *The Origins of the Urban Crisis: Race and Inequality in Postwar Detroit* (Princeton: Princeton University Press, 1996); Michael B. Katz, *Improving the Poor: The Welfare State, The "Underclass," and Urban Schools as History* (Princeton: Princeton University Press, 1993), pp. 77-82; Leonard Wallock, "The Myth of the Master Builder: Robert Moses, New York, and the Dynamics of Metropolitan Development Since World War II," *Journal of Urban History* 17, no. 4 (August 1991): 339-62. Perhaps most important has been the work of William Julius Wilson, which I explore below.

King's death, such hopes seemed to die and be buried. The unrest that ensued in cities like Baltimore reflected a feeling of great loss and bitter frustration, a sense that change would be halted. Indeed, King's death provides a marker for the beginning of the second period of inner-city development, a set of circumstances and forces that had been growing since World War II and that would change life in the city profoundly.

In this period Sandtown entered a new zone of urban wreckage, and the accelerants were multiple in origin. More than ever, poverty was concentrated and opportunities were constricted.

During the decade that followed King's death, Sandtown lost nearly a quarter of its population. Those with more resources headed the trend of evacuation, taking with them social and job networks essential to the health of the community. By 1980, nearly one in every six buildings in Sandtown stood vacant.[25] Businesses closed, and churches became commuter congregations. The once-vibrant and bustling Pennsylvania Avenue, where the great theaters of old like the Royal once proudly stood, became a mix of small businesses, vacant buildings, and empty lots.

By 1990, Sandtown's official population had fallen below 11,000, and the count of vacant row houses hovered near the one-thousand mark, about one in every four houses. At the time, the median income was approximately $10,000.[26] The three elementary schools were in such chronic failure that a state takeover was a regular rumor.[27] The rates for both infant mortality and low birth weight were high enough for the federal government to fund an intensive intervention program. Over half the adult population that could work was unemployed, and perhaps only one in five of the young people between the ages of eighteen and twenty-one had a full-time job. As severe as the problems had been in the 1950s and 1960s, joblessness and struggle in Sandtown seemed to have increased by 1990.

These changes in Sandtown were directly related to wider developments in Baltimore. By the 1970s, the industrial and manufacturing job base of the city, critical to the economic health of neighborhoods such as Sandtown and the city as a whole, was in a free fall. Between 1970 and 1985, manufacturing jobs in Baltimore declined by 45 percent, and entry-level positions not re-

25. These statistics come from the report "Sandtown-Winchester," Planning Division: Baltimore City Department of Housing and Community Development, 27 August 1982.

26. "1990 Community Profiles, Baltimore City: Demographic, Housing, Health, Educational, Income, Public Assistance and Crime Data by Census Tracts," Baltimore City Department of Planning, March 1992.

27. This finally came true in 2000, when one of the schools was taken over by a for-profit educational company.

quiring a high-school diploma by 46 percent; knowledge-based jobs requiring at least two years of college increased by 56 percent.[28] The virtual collapse of Baltimore's industrial base hemorrhaged the jobs that had once provided a foundation, no matter how modest and tenuous, for families in Sandtown. People in the neighborhood began giving up on finding formal work, and many left or never entered the formal labor market.

With the enactment of fair and open housing legislation in the 1960s, leaving Sandtown had become a viable option. Many parents, hoping that their children would take the step that they themselves could never have taken, urged them to move out of the neighborhood. It wasn't that the inside of the neighborhood as a community was considered "bad," lifetime resident LaVerne Stokes recalled, but rather that staying "seemed to mean missing out on progress." After all, this was what all citizens of America wanted — the dream of basic rights, opportunities, and responsibilities. Although Sandtown was home, it held bitter memories of the indignities and assaults of segregation.

As the neighborhood's population declined, landlords abandoned their properties. Various forms of redlining (withholding home-loan funds or insurance because the neighborhood was considered an economic risk) increased. Simultaneously, "blockbusting," a real-estate practice that artificially induced the fear of black relocations into white neighborhoods, created panicked selling in nearby areas. The flight of whites opened up adjacent city neighborhoods such as Edmondson Village to the newly mobile black population, quickening the pace of change.[29] Evidence of these population shifts were seen not only in the vacant houses but also in the large churches on Sunday morning. Once neighborhood churches, they became filled with commuter worshipers, the streets packed with their cars.

Along with the economic and demographic changes overtaking Baltimore, Sandtown was significantly impacted by local, regional, and national politics. It is frequently observed that if America had a real urban policy in the postwar years, it was to subsidize the suburbs.[30] Underwritten by government mortgage programs, infrastructure investment, and transportation programs, each wave of suburban sprawl played a heavy role in accelerating the downward turn of conditions in America's cities, Baltimore included. All around the city

28. Marc E. Levine, "Economic Development to Help the Underclass," *The Sun,* 10 January 1988, pp. E-1, 3.

29. A comprehensive accounting of this can be found in W. Edward Orser, *Blockbusting in Baltimore: The Edmondson Village Story* (Lexington: University Press of Kentucky, 1994).

30. On this wider history, see Kenneth T. Jackson, *Crabgrass Frontier: The Suburbanization of the United States* (New York: Oxford University Press, 1985).

suburbs grew. New housing demanded new roads. So highway construction was undertaken to ease suburban commuting back to the center of the city for the high-paying jobs. In fact, it cut a hole through West Baltimore. And as the suburbs drained out the urban population, the tax base followed. Political influence and power shifted to the suburbs as well. Following the population patterns, hospitals and businesses closed in the city to reopen in the suburbs.

One does not have to look hard to see serious shortcomings, failures, and even tragedies in government-driven "urban renewal" and social programs born in the 1960s.[31] But while social policies did not end urban poverty, they hardly caused the crisis facing the inner city, and in many cases they significantly helped people. Head Start, for example, is widely regarded as a positive accomplishment. But such accomplishments were undercut by the war in Vietnam, which drew attention and resources away from inner cities. Later, when support from Washington for cities began to dry up under the "New Federalism" of the 1980s, American cities in general had almost disappeared from the national agenda.[32] What made matters worse in the 1980s was the crack epidemic, with its personal destruction and accompanying violence, which joined the list of crises confronting cities.

The broader story of how Sandtown faced new structural obstacles to the flourishing of life has been well and perhaps best told by William Julius Wilson, a sociologist now at Harvard University. Wilson is perhaps the leading theorist on inner-city dislocations, and his analysis has significantly influenced how scholars and policymakers understand neighborhoods of concentrated poverty. In *The Truly Disadvantaged* (1987)[33] and *When Work Disappears: The World of the New Urban Poor* (1996),[34] Wilson traces the course of major economic and demographic forces that generated the postindustrial inner city, particularly in the "Rust Belt," the northeastern and

---

31. Fred Siegel makes this argument in *The Future Once Happened Here: New York, D.C., L.A., and the Fate of America's Big Cities* (New York: The Free Press, 1997). For an important account of the period's dilemmas, see Vincent J. Cannato, *The Ungovernable City: John Lindsay and His Struggle to Save New York* (New York: Basic Books, 2001).

32. For an overview, see Demetrios Caraley, "Washington Abandons the Cities," *Political Science Quarterly* 107 (Spring 1992): 1-30.

33. See Wilson, *The Truly Disadvantaged: The Inner City, the Underclass, and Public Policy* (Chicago: University of Chicago Press, 1987), especially chapters 2-4. These themes are also discussed in Loïc J. D. Wacquant and William Julius Wilson, "The Cost of Racial and Class Exclusion in the Inner City," *The Annals of the American Academy of Political and Social Science* 501 (January 1989): 8-25.

34. Wilson, *When Work Disappears: The World of the New Urban Poor* (New York: Alfred A. Knopf, 1996).

midwestern regions of the country where heavy industry has declined. Because Wilson's analysis helps illuminate the issues facing Sandtown in very significant ways, I will summarize his main arguments.[35]

As the title *When Work Disappears* suggests, the most substantial factor for Wilson in understanding the inner city is the post-industrial disappearance of work.[36] Drawing on data from Chicago as well as other cities, Wilson identifies a "new urban poverty." He defines the stricken areas as "poor, segregated neighborhoods in which a substantial majority of individual adults are either unemployed or have dropped out of the labor force altogether."[37] Due to post-industrial economic restructuring, scores of factories closed, and many of the remaining manufacturing operations moved overseas. New jobs were being created in suburban neighborhoods, but the potential inner-city worker had few reliable ways to get there. Hence, what labor economists called a "mis-match" developed between the location of workers and the location of employers.[38] The jobs that were being created in cities and that paid well increasingly required advanced degrees and training, leaving out the vast majority of inner-city residents, who had been limited by the failing educational system. Service-sector jobs remained, but actual wages were declining, and the work was typically occasional. Perhaps even more importantly, the informal networks that generate employment leads and placement faded away, creating a growing disconnection from the formal labor market.

Why is the absence of work so destructive to a community? Following Pierre Bourdieu, Wilson concludes that work "is not simply a way to make a living and support one's family. It also constitutes a framework for daily behavior and patterns of interaction because it imposes disciplines and regularities."[39] Employment sets goals and helps give structure to life, family, and community.[40] Especially in our capitalistic society, where identity is mea-

---

35. For developments in Wilson's views, see Wilson, *The Bridge over the Racial Divide: Rising Inequality and Coalition Politics* (Berkeley: University of California Press, 1999); and Teodros Kiros, "Class, Race, and Social Stratification: An Interview with William Julius Wilson," *New Political Science* 21, no. 3 (September 1999): 405-15.

36. Wilson, *When Work Disappears,* pp. 3-50.

37. Wilson, *When Work Disappears,* p. 19.

38. For a review of the literature, see John Kain, "The Spatial Mismatch: Three Decades Later," *Housing Policy Debate* 3, no. 2 (1992): 371-460.

39. Wilson, *When Work Disappears,* p. 73.

40. It seems to me that Wilson is recognizing one interpretive strand of a secularized Puritan view of calling and vocation. At the very least, Wilson suggests how having work that meets certain cultural definitions can become a means of achieving "salvation."

sured by economic and individual success, the absence of work brings shame and discouragement. Since our society also defines identity by individual success, the absence of meaningful employment corrodes a sense of self and, by extension, family and community. To feel unable to support a family and the wider community — which is what occurs with the structural absence of work in the inner city — can severely constrain the manner in which one thinks, feels, and acts with respect to the future. The effects of this in Sandtown have been severe.

With the closure of "the opportunity structure," as Wilson calls it, came a cascade of social changes to neighborhoods.[41] As the number of men who were "eligible" to marry — or could even view the future in optimistic terms — declined, the family structure in the inner city was shattered. Welfare rolls expanded, poverty increased, and crime rose. Identifying problems in the inner city as "related" but not "specific" to the context, Wilson assigns them to larger cultural practices, yet with more painful consequences in jobless neighborhoods.[42] As Wilson points out, social and familial breakdown in the inner city "ought not to be analyzed as if it were unrelated to the broader structure of opportunities and constraints that have evolved over time."[43] This does not mean that Wilson grants no place to the role of race.[44] His research in Chicago points to the prevalence of stereotypes in hiring practices, especially related to black males.[45] However, while race played a continuing factor in inner-city poverty, Wilson stresses that it is the macro-economic forces that had become most significant.

Wilson's view on inner-city poverty is not without its difficulties. These arise from implicit assumptions he made, at least in his earlier work, concerning the role of culture and morality in relationship to poverty and the meaning of human behavior. Another issue of dispute, as Brett Williams has pointed out, is Wilson's choice to center his argument on the employment

---

41. Wilson, *When Work Disappears*, pp. 51-110.

42. Wilson, *When Work Disappears*, p. 56.

43. Wilson, *When Work Disappears*, p. 55.

44. Wilson, *When Work Disappears*, pp. 111-46. Some suggested that Wilson was saying this when he published *The Declining Significance of Race: Blacks and Changing American Institutions*, 2d ed. (Chicago: University of Chicago Press, 1980). For his response, see Wilson, *The Truly Disadvantaged*.

45. Wilson, *When Work Disappears*, pp. 111-46. See further Joleen Kirschenman and Kathryn M. Neckerman, "'We'd Love to Hire Them, But . . .': The Meaning of Race for Employers," in *The Urban Underclass*, ed. Christopher Jencks and Paul E. Peterson (Washington, D.C.: The Brookings Institution, 1991), pp. 203-32; and Philip Moss and Chris Tilly, *Stories Employers Tell: Race, Skill, and Hiring in America* (New York: Russell Sage Foundation, 2001).

history of men, thus gendering work and family.[46] Additionally, Wilson's focus on the unemployed may have had the unintended effect of relegating to a minor role the working residents of the inner city who have found jobs, although they may be low-paying and tenuous.[47]

While such criticisms need to be taken seriously and modifications made where needed, Wilson's central narration on the process of post-industrial inner-city development is accurate and extraordinarily helpful in comprehending the challenges confronting Sandtown and other communities like it in this period. The post-segregation outflow of residents with resources to less distressed (but no less segregated) urban and suburban neighborhoods, the abandonment of the inner city by all levels of government, the disappearance of meaningful employment for men and women — all combined to send Sandtown into a new spiral of agony. The result was brokenness in family structures and in the world of employment, and serious damage to the fabric of community.

In summary, the inner city in the post-industrial period was not created by the character flaws of the people who live there or by the welfare system, but by the searing dynamics of economy, place, and race.[48] The result was a community in economic depression, isolated and excluded from opportunity. Life in its fullness was more deeply diminished.

Period Three: The Global Inner City

What happens around the world impacts the inner city. Beyond post-industrialism and what Wilson terms "the end of work," Sandtown now has joined every other American inner city and barrio in being drawn into a third phase of development, what can be called the "global inner city."[49] Globaliza-

---

46. Williams, "Poverty Among African Americans in the Urban United States," *Human Organization* 51, no. 2 (1992): 164-74.

47. See Katherine S. Newman, *No Shame in My Game: The Working Poor in the Inner City* (New York: Alfred A. Knopf, 1999).

48. Wilson's work, especially *The Truly Disadvantaged,* can be understood, in part at least, as a response to Charles Murray's *Losing Ground: American Social Policy, 1950-1980* (New York: Basic Books, 1984). Murray conjured up a picture of inner-city dislocations causally linked to the rise of welfare, a position embraced by then-president Ronald Reagan. Clearly I think that Wilson is right and Murray is very wrong.

49. Carl Husemoller Nightingale, "The Global Inner City: Toward a Historical Analysis," in *W. E. B. DuBois, Race, and the City: The Philadelphia Negro and Its Legacy,* ed. Michael B. Katz and Thomas Sugrue (Philadelphia: University of Pennsylvania Press, 1998), pp.

tion has come to mean many things. Here I am using it to describe a market economy and cultural forms that move with incredible power and speed throughout the world. On a global scale, this economy produces new winners and losers. Either you are connected to the wired world or you are not. Globalization does not merely impact cities but takes place through them, as Saskia Sassen persuasively argues. Globalization is based in cities, and particularly in the world-class cities such as London, New York, and Tokyo, where the highly specialized tasks of the new economy have become centered.[50] Such cities form the "circuits" of the new economy, Sassen contends, the physical sites that are essential for the complex of its activities.

Globalization has produced not only changes in cities but new differences between cities. Baltimore has not benefitted from the global economy in the way certain other cities have. As a result, Sandtown's present and future increasingly reflect some of the most negative social realities of globalization. In Baltimore, like every other city, most good jobs in the new economy require a highly developed set of knowledge-based skills for which Sandtown residents have not been trained. Current public policies and resources do not suggest this will become a priority. So the jobs being created for the poor are low-wage jobs in areas such as cleaning, food service, and maintenance. The city needs these jobs to keep the sectors producing higher wages operating. A new class division is therefore becoming deeply embedded in the urban landscape. This means a steady stream of low-paying jobs for the "right kind of person" from Sandtown, but usually without health benefits, retirement plans, job security, or potential for long-term advancement. Mixed in with these factors is the reality of the end of welfare and a decreasing social safety net. The new economy has "demanded" this.

Global changes have reinvented the business sector in another way. Major corporations, which had often demanded and received subsidies to stay in the city, have shrunk through mergers and consolidation. In Baltimore, the consequences have been dire: the city has lost almost all of its corporate headquarters in the past few years. Such corporate consolidations are already adding to the tears in the fabric of neighborhoods. Banking provides just one of many examples. Banking mergers have reduced not only the number of employees in a city but also the presence of "redundant" bank branches. And so

---

217-58; Manuel Castells, *The Information Age: Economy, Society, and Culture*, vol. 3: *End of Millennium*, 2d ed. (Oxford: Blackwell, 2000), pp. 128-52.

50. Sassen has provided a powerful accounting of this in *The Global City: New York, London, Tokyo* (Princeton: Princeton University Press, 1991), and *Globalization and Its Discontents: Essays on the New Mobility of People and Money* (New York: The New Press, 1998).

scores of area neighborhoods have no local banks or access to their financial services. Sandtown shares one tiny branch with other neighborhoods. Climbing transaction fees have left many in the inner city feeling unwanted by the banks, anyway. Fringe banking institutions such as check-cashing outlets are filling the void, but users face exploitative prices and limited services. More critically, credit for housing and business development is hard to find, and will be nearly nonexistent in a credit crunch. Additionally, since corporations have fewer community roots, corporate giving and civic leadership have declined significantly.

As Baltimore becomes faced with its new future, the city is turning to the expansion of an already important tourist trade for economic security.[51] Numerous new hotels are underway or planned for construction along the once-industrial waterfront. The Walt Disney Corporation, Barnes and Noble, ESPN, and Planet Hollywood are among the recent players in downtown development. This is not the first time Baltimore has turned in this direction; the city helped pioneer downtown revitalization in the 1980s.[52] But as with the past spurts of downtown redevelopment, any translation of current projects to living-wage employment for Sandtown residents is modest.[53]

William Julius Wilson identifies three key problem areas for the inner city associated with the global economy: employment, training, and wages.[54] The dictum of "last hired and first fired" will be lethal to the community when the global monetary system convulses, as it did in 1997 and 1998. Low-wage and temporary jobs disappear just as easily as they appear. It is also unlikely that necessary training will take place to give inner-city workers access to a higher level of opportunity and occupation. Nor have wages kept up with the cost of living. Community institutions, hollowed out during the post-industrial transformation between the 1970s and the 1990s, face new vulnerability even as their importance has grown under the architectonic forces of global capitalism. All of this negatively impacts upon family and community stability.

In the end, far too many young men in Sandtown have found the period of the new economy to be only a growth era of incarceration. It is a shattering

---

51. *The Tourist City*, ed. Dennis R. Judd and Susan S. Fainstein (New Haven: Yale University Press, 1999).

52. For a view of Baltimore's first downtown renewal through the eyes of one of its primary leaders, see C. Fraser Smith, *William Donald Schaefer: A Political Biography* (Baltimore: The Johns Hopkins University Press, 1999).

53. Marc V. Levine, "Downtown Redevelopment as an Urban Growth Strategy: A Critical Appraisal of the Baltimore Renaissance," *Journal of Urban Affairs* 9, no. 2 (1987): 103-23.

54. Wilson, *When Work Disappears*, pp. 152-55.

reality that so many African-American men are caught up in the criminal justice system. Economic redundancy married to globalization has resulted in social control as the dominant urban policy. When "peace" really means order, not public safety, then the global inner city becomes the incarcerating inner city. This is not the final word on the global inner city, on Baltimore or Sandtown. But it returns the neighborhood to where it started — working hard with a constricted horizon and being, in Roderick Ryon's words, "restricted, controlled, watched over."

THEOLOGICAL REFLECTIONS ON THE CREATION OF URBAN SPACE

What accounts for the high rates of joblessness, the concentrated poverty, the racial segregation, and the discouragement that form the inner city? No one should doubt that there is profound brokenness in many families, homes, and lives. Yet, by the power of the gospel, women, men, children, and families can, on an everyday basis, begin again in their lives and their relationships. Following Jesus, walking in the Spirit, and being transformed from the inside out does renew and restore people. That such a process is, by the word of the gospel, both progressive in nature and universal in requirement is typically overlooked. Equally neglected is the understanding that such change is, on Christian terms, a matter of grace, not moral determination.

Having said this, I also want to point out that the source of collective inner-city struggle is not due in any way to personal failings, the force of nature, a lack of collective activity by the community, the presence of neighborhood "pathology," a lifestyle of sin, or any deficiencies in character or moral behavior. A lack of personal responsibility did not build the inner city. Instead, a historically accurate understanding of the inner city requires us to see inner-city neighborhoods as created by institutionalized racism, economic exclusion, and adverse political determinations. A theologically serious approach to the inner city requires us also to draw on the biblical categories of injustice, structural sin, and the powers that be.[55]

---

55. Jayakumar Christian, *God of the Empty Handed: Poverty, Power, and the Kingdom of God* (Monrovia: MARC, 1999).

Structures of Sin and Injustice

Because urban exclusion, poverty, and misery are bound up with larger and perverse social, economic, and political actions and priorities, a coalition of "institutions and intentions,"[56] one of the requirements of biblical faith is to name such wronging as injustice and in so doing to take account of its urban character. Iris Marion Young analyzes injustice as "oppression, the institutional constraint on self-development, and domination, the institutional constraint on self determination."[57] At stake is not merely the distribution of goods but all of life, and in focus is not only the individual but also groups.[58] Oppression, Young says, reveals itself in five faces: exploitation, marginalization, powerlessness, cultural imperialism, and violence.[59] The presence of any of these results in oppression, and of course they can exist all at once or in various combinations.[60] In Sandtown, and in the inner city generally, all five faces of oppression can be seen at work in the racial and economic construction of space and the burdens of existence.

Examining the biblical witness, we see that injustice is not randomly pronounced but is referenced to the harm that is inflicted upon society's most vulnerable, especially the widow, the orphan, and the stranger (Exod. 3:9; Pss. 94:5-6; 103:6; Prov. 14:31; Mic. 3:1-3). For example, the prophet Amos pronounced in the city streets that sin was found in the legal system that sold "the needy for a pair of sandals" (2:6; cf. 5:12). Injustice as the cause of social sorrow and the restriction of life is a basic biblical category, and is essential for comprehending our urban world.

God's concern with injustice, Nicholas Wolterstorff explains, is bound up with God's love: "God's love for justice is grounded in his love for the victims of injustice. And his love for the victims of injustice belongs to his love for the little ones of the world: for the weak, defenseless ones, the ones at the bottom, the excluded ones, the miscasts, the outcasts, the outsiders. . . . God's love for justice, I suggest, is grounded in his special concern for the hundredth one."[61] For, as

---

56. Sharon Zukin, "How 'Bad' Is It? Institutions and Intentions in the Study of the American Ghetto," *International Journal of Urban and Regional Research* 22, no. 3 (1998): 512.

57. Young, *Justice and the Politics of Difference* (Princeton: Princeton University Press, 1990), p. 37.

58. Young, *Justice and the Politics of Difference*, pp. 42-48.

59. Young, *Justice and the Politics of Difference*, pp. 48-63.

60. Young, *Justice and the Politics of Difference*, p. 64.

61. Wolterstorff, "Why Care About Justice?" *The Reformed Journal* 36, no. 8 (August 1986): 9.

Wolterstorff continues, "God's command to do justice is grounded in his suffering love for the little ones of the world and in his longing to have a people which reflects and celebrates his own holiness."[62] Because human persons are created in God's image, God is harmed whenever any of them are denied standing, sustenance, and dignity (Gen. 1:26-27; 5:1-3; 9:6; 1 Cor. 11:7; James 3:9). Thus the wounding of the poor and vulnerable through oppression is not merely wrong, but is, as Wolterstorff argues (showing that this is the position of Calvin) an assault on God (Prov. 14:31; Matt. 25:31-46).[63] On this basis, God and the inner city have a claim on the city and other human beings, a claim for right relationships.

Because injustice is related to the social world, it cannot be reduced to the actions of individuals. "The structures of our social world are fallen," argues Wolterstorff. "They are alienated from the will of God. Instead of providing authentic fulfillment to those of us who live within them, they spread misery and injustice, squelching the realization of what human life was meant to be."[64] As people in inner-city neighborhoods know, feel, and say in different ways, "The system is against us." Instead of bringing forth human flourishing, the city reproduces various forms of racial, cultural, environmental, and gender-based oppressions.

But does the category of "injustice" enable us to get as far underneath the oppressive conditions of the inner city as we need to go? A review of some recent definitions of the inner city as "ghetto" pushes us further and illuminates the seriousness of the situation. The first definition of "ghetto" comes from Camilo José Vergara. He writes, "Although I respect others' reservations about the term 'ghetto,' I use it to highlight the exclusion of so many poor, minority people from mainstream society. I want to describe the size and strength of the barriers we have built to separate citizens."[65] While I differ with Vergara in that I believe "ghettos" remain *communities*, places people call home and in which they forge a meaningful communal existence, I agree with him that the inner city is exclusionary by design, and as a political and physical construct does all it can to undermine human dignity, purpose, and community.[66]

---

62. Wolterstorff, "Why Care About Justice?" p. 12.

63. Wolterstorff, "The Wounds of God: Calvin's Theology of Social Injustice," *The Reformed Journal* 37, no. 6 (June 1987): 14-22.

64. Wolterstorff, "Why Care About Justice?" p. 23.

65. Vergara, *The New American Ghetto*, p. 9.

66. Vergara, *The New American Ghetto*, p. 9. For a view that recognizes the harshness of inner-city life and also accounts for the presence of community resilience and community building, see Sudhir Alladi Venkatesh, *American Project: The Rise and Fall of a Modern Ghetto* (Cambridge: Harvard University Press, 2000).

For the sociologist Loïc Wacquant, "ghetto" is not "simply a topograph-ical entity or an aggregation of poor families and individuals but an *institu-tional form*, a historically determinate, spatially-based concatenation of mechanisms of *ethnoracial closure and control*."[67] In this dense sentence, Wacquant presents a multidimensional understanding of the "ghetto" that in-volves history, race, and social reality. This is not a morally simple judgment. For Wacquant, the ghetto is more than a place where many poor people re-side; it is a racialized structural form that has come about through a punitive history. For the historian Craig Steven Wilder, an analysis of the construction of the "ghetto" brings to the fore the maldistributions of power.[68] Any study of the inner city must therefore take account of the role of power in the for-mation of racial and social inequality.

Without denying that the use of "ghetto" brings with it potentially neg-ative connotations of the community, it can be a helpful term in naming the inner city as more than a place where a large percentage of people are persis-tently poor. "Ghetto" helps us see the inner city as a space where the people who inhabit it are socially consigned and forgotten, the very essence of *exclu-sion*.[69] Urban exclusion takes place through the construction of walls that di-vide, control, and ultimately injure the poor and the vulnerable. These "walls" may actually be a street, a river, or a railroad track, but their mortar is the power of exclusion. As Douglas Massey and Nancy Denton have argued, it is appropriate to speak of such residential segregation, with its attendant conse-quences, as a form of apartheid.[70]

---

67. Wacquant, "Three Pernicious Premises in the Study of the American Ghetto," *In-ternational Journal of Urban and Regional Research* 21, no. 2 (June 1997): 343.

68. In *A Covenant with Color: Race and Social Power in Brooklyn* (New York: Columbia University Press, 2000), Wilder writes, "The ghetto is not so much a place as it is a relation-ship — the physical manifestation of a perverse imbalance in social power. The ghetto is not the cause of social pathology, it is its destination. It is not the set of ever-changing, ever-negotiated disparities that dominate it but the financial, physical, and legal coercion that give rise to them. It cannot be defined by the people who occupy it but by the struggles that place them there. It is not social inequality but the attempt to predetermine the burden of social inequality. Thus, ghettos are different sizes, have different demographics, and suffer different conditions. They have in common only the lack of power that allows their residents to be physically concentrated and socially targeted" (p. 234).

69. Vergara, *The New American Ghetto*, pp. 20-22.

70. Massey and Denton, *American Apartheid: Segregation and the Making of the Underclass* (Cambridge: Harvard University Press, 1993).

The Powers of Exclusion

Limiting exclusion to only the racial, gender, economic, political, or social dimensions of oppression does not fully account for the ferocity and inner workings of racial hatred, economic rejection, and moral indifference that have built and maintain the walls of the inner city. Is not a spiritual dimension of some kind required for interpretation? In large measure this requires breaking free of an Enlightenment conceptualization of the world that limits the spiritual dimension of social reality.

In *Exclusion and Embrace,* Miroslav Volf has provided an incisive theological analysis of "exclusion," reflections intended to come to grips with ethnic cleansing in the former Yugoslavia.[71] I want to build on his proposal, which in part adapts the important work of Walter Wink[72] that finds in exclusion a system with both an interior and an exterior life. What Volf identifies as an "Exclusion System" and relates to identity and otherness, I will apply to the identity of the inner city in its spatial and social relationship to the dominant control centers of the city. Volf takes care to distinguish exclusion from differentiation: "Exclusion takes place when the violence of expulsion, assimilation, or subjugation and the indifference of abandonment replace the dynamics of taking in and keeping out as well as the mutuality of giving and receiving."[73] Accordingly, "what is exclusionary are the impenetrable barriers that prevent a creative encounter with the other. They are the result either of expulsion or indifference."[74] This process operates as a system embedded in structures and institutions, but it also bears a spiritual identity.

The Apostle Paul identifies the forces that reproduce exclusion with the work of the "principalities and powers" (Rom. 8:38; 1 Cor. 15:24; Eph. 1:20-21; 2:1-2; 6:12; Col. 1:16-20; 2:10).[75] According to Herman Ridderbos, "It is

---

71. Volf, *Exclusion and Embrace: A Theological Exploration of Identity, Otherness, and Reconciliation* (Nashville: Abingdon, 1996), pp. 57-98.

72. See Walter Wink, *Naming the Powers: The Language of Power in the New Testament* (Philadelphia: Fortress, 1984); *Unmasking the Powers: The Invisible Forces That Determine Human Existence* (Philadelphia: Fortress, 1986); and *Engaging the Powers: Discernment and Resistance in a World of Domination* (Minneapolis: Fortress, 1992).

73. Volf, *Exclusion and Embrace,* p. 67.

74. Volf, *Exclusion and Embrace,* p. 67.

75. Two very helpful overviews of the issues involved are Thomas McAlpine, *Facing the Powers: What Are the Options?* (Monrovia: MARC, 1991); and Andrew T. Lincoln, "Liberation from the Powers: Supernatural Spirits or Societal Structures?" in *The Bible in Human Society: Essays in Honor of John Rogerson,* ed. M. Daniel et al. (Sheffield: Sheffield Academic Press, 1995), pp. 335-54.

the dominion of these powers that determines Paul's outlook on the present world. It is they who represent the 'vanity,' the worthlessness and senselessness to which the whole creation, groaning and looking for redemption, has been subjected (cf. Rom. 8:19-23 and 8:38, 39)."[76]

If the purpose of the reign of God is to reconcile all things (2 Cor. 5:19; Eph. 1:10; Col. 1:20), then the primary objective of the powers is to oppose all that supports, advances, and constitutes reconciliation. The "rulers of this age" are servitors of injustice, transpersonal expressions of exploitation, and agents of oppression. Mortally wounded by the cross, they still try to mawl people and communities through "exclusion" and "domination" (1 Cor. 2:8; Gal. 4:1-3; Rev. 2:12-13). Exclusionary in aim and intention, the "principalities and powers" can be embedded in political, social, and economic institutions of the inner city.

Further accounting for the existence of the inner city is "the world" as Scripture describes it. In Ephesians 2:2, the values of the sin-dominated social world ("the ways of this world") and the hostile supernatural powers ("the ruler of the kingdom of the air") are drawn together (cf. 1 Cor. 1:13). Here "the world" is not the created order, which is repeatedly deemed good according to the account of creation in Genesis 1, but the fallen order we read about in Genesis 3, which expresses itself in institutions, practices, and historical narratives.[77] "World" used in this manner is parallel to, but not identical with, the powers.

William Stringfellow, a lawyer and theologian who devoted significant attention to the powers, came to emphasize their role while living and working in East Harlem during the 1960s. He saw little way to understand the injustice and struggles of Harlem apart from talking about the powers. Stringfellow "demythologized" the powers into three primary categories: ideologies, institutions, and images.[78] Without denying my general agreement with Stringfellow, I think he creates a dichotomy between creation and redemption that seems to assume that all creation is fallen to such depths that substantial redemption is impossible. The price of not seeing the full picture can be spiritual disengagement, and no inner-city community can afford to

76. Ridderbos, *Paul: An Outline of His Theology*, trans. John Richard De Witt (Grand Rapids: Eerdmans, 1975), p. 92.

77. For further exegetical elaboration, see Luke T. Johnson, "Friendship with the World/Friendship with God: A Study of Discipleship in James," in *Discipleship in the New Testament*, ed. Fernando F. Segovia (Philadelphia: Fortress, 1985), pp. 166-83.

78. For Stringfellow's writings on the powers and the city, *A Keeper of the Word: Selected Writings of William Stringfellow*, ed. Bill Wylie Kellermann (Grand Rapids: Eerdmans, 1994), pp. 192-222.

pay such a price. Certainly institutions are fallen — but they were created by God for good, and thus their redemption is possible. Notwithstanding this criticism, Stringfellow's writing demands continued attention as a resource for understanding and engaging the inner city.

How are we to name the work of the powers in the inner city? We need a contextual approach, one that does not overrate their abilities or deny that there is a spiritual dimension to exclusion. The interconnected array of overarching negative factors — systemic racism, economic abandonment, gun marketers and dealers who saturate cities with their wares, a legal system that never seems to uphold the cause of the poor, and racially driven incarceration policies — may be thought of as macro-level kinds of exclusion. I also think the ideology of the underclass, so prominent in the past two decades, is a significant part of this exclusion. "Underclass" is a label of moral deficiency rooted in a discourse of Otherness. Specifically, "underclass" refers to lazy and immoral individuals whose sorrows of extreme poverty are self-inflicted. It means the poor are poor in the inner city because of social pathology.[79] By the ideology of the underclass, women — especially single mothers — are demonized, and men are criminalized. Our study of Sandtown's development finds more than sufficient reason to reject this ideology,[80] and gives great reason to be concerned when it is used to develop public policy or shape public opinion.[81] Moreover, the ethics of the kingdom shifts the issues of what counts as right living rather dramatically.[82]

At the local level, the presence of the powers can be seen in the exploit-

---

79. An extended historical interpretation of inner-city poverty that strongly connects it with "underclass" behavior is Nicholas Lemann, *The Promised Land: The Great Black Migration and How It Changed America* (New York: Alfred A. Knopf, 1991), especially pp. 281-91.

80. Important critiques of the underclass thesis are offered by Adolph L. Reed Jr., *Stirrings in the Jug: Black Politics in the Post-Segregation Era* (Minneapolis: University of Minnesota Press, 1999), pp. 179-96; and Herbert J. Gans, "Deconstructing the Underclass Thesis: The Term's Danger as a Planning Concept," *APA Journal* 56, no. 3 (Summer 1990): 271-77. Their targets are both "liberal" and "conservative" schools of thought. Theologically, a critique of underclass ideology has at least three strands of argumentation: the universality of sin (Acts 10:34-35; Rom. 3:23), Jesus' rejection of elitist moral reasoning (Matt. 19:23-24; 23:23-27), and Jesus' identification with and honoring of the "underclass"/outcast of his day (Matt. 5:3, 5). Additionally, one can hardly hold that "violence" and "self-destructive behavior," traits attributed to the whole of the inner city as "underclass," are not wholly part of American culture.

81. Herbert J. Gans, *The War Against the Poor: The Underclass and Antipoverty Policy* (New York: Basic Books, 1995).

82. N. T. Wright, *Jesus and the Victory of God* (Minneapolis: Fortess, 1996), pp. 274-97.

iveness of check-cashing centers, proliferating liquor stores and their corporate suppliers, slum-housing "investors" who deal properties like playing cards, and lottery games that drain precious resources from those who have the least in the false hope of instant redemption.[83] In the grasp of the powers, people and communities can turn against themselves, bringing hurt and even destruction to their world. We can thus speak of the work of the powers in the inner city by naming all that keeps children, adults, and families from enjoying the wholeness that God intends for all of creation. The powers are not "out there" as much as they are at work in the here and now, creating "from the top down" barriers to wholeness.[84]

THE CORNER AND THE STORY OF SALVATION

Following Vergara and Wacquant, among others, I have argued that a main theme of the inner city that requires our attention is its status as a community excluded on the basis of race, ethnicity, and economic status. As a result of such exclusion, there has been a disintegration of community institutions and the ability to meet the basic needs of life. As Wilson and others have argued, this situation came about through profound changes in the macroeconomy and the larger world where people live. Expanding on this presentation, I also concluded that the biblical witness requires that injustice, structural sin, and the powers be factored in to how we understand the complex of ways in which the post-industrial and now global inner city operates. In this final section, I want to look at the spiritual point at which the inner city has arrived, presenting a response in light of the redemptive mission of God in Christ.

The Closure of Horizons

We have come to the end of the narrative of the inner city and the arrival of disenchantment, a time when the horizons of the future have been closed. In his highly discussed essay "Nihilism in Black America," the philosopher

---

83. Liala Beukema, "The Powers and Urban Land Use," *The Gospel and Our Culture* 11, no. 4 (December 1999): 5-6, 8.

84. See the remarks of John Howard Yoder on the "literalness" of "top down" and the powers in "Is There Such a Thing as Being Ready for Another Millennium?" in *The Future of Theology: Essays in Honor of Jürgen Moltmann*, ed. Miroslav Volf, Carmen Krieg, and Thomas Kucharz (Grand Rapids: Eerdmans, 1996), p. 66.

Cornel West wrote that to comprehend the inner city, one must also account for the presence of nihilism and meaninglessness:

> Nihilism is to be understood here not as a philosophic doctrine that there are no rational grounds for legitimate standards or authority; it is, far more, the lived experience of coping with a life of horrifying meaninglessness, hopelessness, and (most important) lovelessness. This usually results in a numbing detachment from others and a self-destructive disposition toward the world. Life without meaning, hope, and love breeds a coldhearted, mean-spirited outlook that destroys both the individual and others.[85]

What is important about West's conclusion is that it joins the changes in social, economic, and political forces to the status of functional community life.[86]

Put in philosophical terms, the Enlightenment or modern project no longer provides coherent meaning and cannot honestly promise inclusion. In many inner-city African-American communities, the historic protection afforded by a sacred cosmos, a belief system that gave meaning and sustenance to life in a racist world, is now nearly eviscerated.[87] Ecclesiastes describes a similar condition of frustration due to the absurdity of life and daily confrontation of the loss of meaning. It tells the story of how reality feels when the future horizon is closed (3:16; 5:8).[88] Accepting nihilism is not necessarily the norm, but it is an existentially honest possibility. Certainly absurdity describes a central facet of the dilemma that confronts neighborhoods such as Sandtown.

It is on Sandtown's corners where the evidence of the nihilistic option is clearest. Here you will find many young men trying to establish identity and meaning through selling drugs, one of the few job markets dependably open and hiring.[89] Yet there is not even much money for an entry-level worker in the corner drug trade. "Do or die" is the motto on the corner in Sandtown.

---

85. Cornel West, *Race Matters* (Boston: Beacon, 1993), pp. 14-15.

86. West, *Race Matters*, p. 16.

87. On the sacred cosmos, see C. Eric Lincoln and Lawrence H. Mamiya, *The Black Church in the African American Experience* (Durham: Duke University Press, 1990), pp. 3-7.

88. See the reading of Elsa Tamez, *When the Horizons Close: Rereading Ecclesiastes,* translated by Margaret Wilde (Maryknoll: Orbis, 2000).

89. David Simon and Edward Burns, *The Corner: A Year in the Life of an Inner City Neighborhood* (New York: Broadway Books, 1997); Elijah Anderson, *Code of the Streets: Decency, Violence, and the Moral Life of the Inner City* (New York: W. W. Norton, 1999).

This means that these young men will do whatever it takes to get what they want, and it comes down to their very survival. Take a life or lose your life, "do or die." These young and gifted men are well aware that in today's new urban economy, they are superfluous, and this may be where they work for life, however few those years add up to be. It is a world that offers no breaks — only drug sweeps, incarceration, and likely early death. The horizons of the corner are closed.

The Opening of the Future

One of the marks of a Christian response to the inner city must therefore be its direct and meaningful response to the closure of everyday opportunities and the closure of future horizons. This involves understanding the story of God's saving work in the world, a feature built into the conclusion of Ecclesiastes.[90] Luke-Acts is a particularly important way of telling the story of salvation for our work in the inner city.[91] As I indicated in the introduction, Luke's Gospel has as its organizing theme the good news of Jesus for the excluded and redemption for the fallen urban order (4:16-21). Throughout the story, the gospel overcomes political and religious obstacles and delivers on its promise of being good news.[92] As part of the fuller story of Luke-Acts, it invites readers to enter into a drama of following Jesus (Acts 7:2-53).[93]

Joel Green has explored the place of the overall plot in Luke, drawing attention to themes that speak to the need for an alternative story to the corner: "The Gospel of Luke narrates the long-awaited intervention and determined activity of God to accomplish his historical purpose."[94] The challenge Luke

90. Ecclesiastes has important apologetic purposes for the church in the inner city. See Tremper Longman III, *The Book of Ecclesiastes*, NICOT series (Grand Rapids: Eerdmans, 1998), for his genre argument of a narrator of faith who provides an alternative worldview.

91. I am adapting a proposal for the postmodern context made by William J. Larkin Jr. in "The Recovery of Luke-Acts as 'Grand Narrative' for the Church's Evangelistic and Edification Tasks in a Postmodern Era," *Journal of the Evangelical Theological Society* 43, no. 3 (September 2000): 405-15. For an approach that takes similar questions seriously, see J. Richard Middleton and Brian J. Walsh, *Truth Is Stranger Than It Used to Be: Biblical Faith in a Postmodern Age* (Downers Grove: InterVarsity, 1995).

92. Larkin, "The Recovery of Luke-Acts as 'Grand Narrative' for the Church's Evangelistic and Edification Tasks in a Postmodern Era," p. 410.

93. Anthony C. Thiselton, *Interpreting God and the Postmodern Self: On Meaning, Manipulation, and Promise* (Grand Rapids: Eerdmans, 1995), p. 147.

94. Green, *The Theology of the Gospel of Luke* (Cambridge: Cambridge University Press, 1995), p. 22.

presents is an invitation to all to respond to God's saving aims, taking up the way of discipleship.[95] Hearers of Jesus' redemptive message are invited to share in the story of God's saving purpose.[96] The invitation remains open.

Another important place where the story of God's saving purposes for the world is told is the letter to the Ephesians, where its overarching theme can be summarized as reconciliation. Paul writes in Ephesians 1:10, a passage that can be taken as a key to the letter, that the purpose of Christ is "to bring all things in heaven and on earth together under one head, even Christ." Reconciliation is making all things right, putting back together the pieces of a broken humanity and a broken world. "For he himself is our peace, who has made the two one and has destroyed the barrier, the dividing wall of hostility" (Eph. 2:14; cf. 2:15-16). The death of Christ, David Ford asserts, has resulted in the "transformation of boundaries."[97] Ephesians emphasizes the glorious truth that Christ has come to break down barriers and walls between Jews and Gentiles, a category inclusive of all ethnic and cultural differences.

Reconciliation is intrinsic to God's central purpose for the world, not just the church (1:9-10). God is creating a world where the barriers to wholeness, barriers both symbolic and real, are taken down. Paul's Christology announces that a new humanity, a restored community, and a redeemed world are replacing present divisions. A socially, economically, and racially divided world is contradicted by the gospel of reconciliation. The future of the inner city is open to new levels of identity and meaning because of Christ crucified, risen, and ascended.

Justification and Justice

For the Apostle Paul, the basis of a new community is established not by achievement or status, but by grace through the death of Christ. This is made clear in Ephesians 2:8-9, where we read, "For it is by grace you have been saved, through faith — and this not from yourselves, it is the gift of God — not by works, so that no one can boast" (cf. Eph. 2:10; 2:5; Rom. 1:17; Gal. 2:16; Phil. 3:9). While the message of the world is that all who dwell in the inner city are unworthy, unwanted, and unneeded, the gospel is a message of acceptance based on divine mercy and love, not on success, social status, or po-

95. Green, *The Theology of the Gospel of Luke*, pp. 35-37, 102-21.
96. Green, *The Theology of the Gospel of Luke*, p. 35.
97. Ford, *Self and Salvation: Being Transformed* (Cambridge: Cambridge University Press, 1999), p. 118.

sition. In profoundly redemptive ways, the grace of the cross is deconstructive of a world based on such markers. As we read in Romans 1:17, "For in the gospel a righteousness from God is revealed, a righteousness that is by faith from first to last, just as it is written: 'The righteous will live by faith.'" Grace deconstructs the hierarchies of status and geography that have destroyed not only individual senses of self-worth and identity but also community.

Translated into classical theological terminology, this is the message of justification by grace alone, and it bears great importance for the "ghetto." The message of the gospel involves not only the dismantling of false markers but also the construction of a new identity, community, and world based on God's work in Christ. God's free justification is subversive to exclusion and constructive of life.[98]

Conversion and spiritual rebirth are central to the transformation of the inner city, not because the sins of the poor caused the sorrows of the inner city (they did not), but because these transformative experiences free all who have been "captive" for participation in God's liberating order.[99] A change of heart is necessary because it is the way to enter the kingdom which Jesus proclaimed and through which he is changing the world (Mark 1:14-15; Gal. 1:4). And without discipleship in line with God's new order through faith in Christ, liberation will not be enough to stay free of every form of oppression (Luke 11:14-28; cf. Gal. 5:1, 13). Christ crucified brings personal and social healing and release from the powers, facets of God's pardon and grace in the midst of the twisted structures of sin and death.

God's justification by grace through the death of Christ calls attention to the neglected but vital link in Scripture between God's justice and the doing of justice, between freedom and empowerment.[100] According to Ephesians 5:8-9, grace invokes a call to do justice and live righteously: "Live as children of light (for the fruit of the light consists in all goodness, righteousness and truth) and find out what pleases the Lord." Doing justice is part of the holistic vocation of Christ's followers in the world (Eph. 6:1, 14). Here we

98. For reflections on the importance of the doctrine of justification by faith for the inner city, see Volf, "Shopkeepers' Gold," *Christian Century*, 12 November 1997, p. 1045.

99. The following discussion is indebted to Volf, *Exclusion and Embrace*, pp. 111-19. For a supporting argument from Galatians, see Beverly Roberts Gaventa, "Is Galatians Just a 'Guy Thing'? A Theological Reflection," *Interpretation* 54, no. 3 (July 2000): 267-78.

100. See Elsa Tamez, *The Amnesty of Grace: Justification by Faith from a Latin American Perspective*, trans. Sharon H. Ringe (Nashville: Abingdon, 1993); James D. G. Dunn, "The Justice of God: A Renewed Perspective on Justification by Faith," *Journal of Theological Studies* 43, no. 1 (April 1992): 1-22; Jürgen Moltmann, *The Spirit of Life: A Universal Affirmation* (Minneapolis: Fortress, 1992), pp. 123-43.

should recall the strong Old Testament imperatives to do justice (Pss. 74:1-4; 112:5; Amos 5:24; Mic. 6:8), which have their standing in the God who "with justice . . . will give decisions for the poor of the earth" (Isa. 11:4). To be liberated from the definitions of the powers and law (race, class, and status) frees one up to participate in a new community of love and grace that serves God's peace and righteousness in the world. Framed rightly, justification enables the recovery of true humanity, community, and service to God. It can be a liberating and world-changing doctrine.

One finds a close relationship between grace and justice in the epistle of James. After reciting the importance of meeting the basic human needs of shelter and sustenance (2:14-17; cf. 1:27), James concludes, "You see that a person is justified by what he does and not by faith alone" (2:24). If God's truth is truly known, then it is concretely practiced (1:22). First John uses different language to say also that knowing God's saving love requires evidence in right social relationships (2:29; 3:7, 10; 4:7-8). By Christ's mercy the oppressed are set free to work for a community of love based on justice for all who have been left out. "Blessed are those who hunger and thirst for justice, for they will be filled" (Matt. 5:6), Jesus pronounced upon those who follow in his steps. Is this not because the deeds of justice serve to bring the world and its structures more into line with God's reign?[101] God in Christ, Paul said, gave himself "so that in him we might become the righteousness of God" (2 Cor. 5:21).

Based on our analysis of the inner city and the biblical writers, Christian commitment to community development, organizing, and holistic ministry in the American inner city should be animated by the biblical demands to do justice, not the modern rhetoric of charity or compassion (Deut. 10:18-19; Deut. 15; Isa. 61:8; Amos 5:7, 24; Mic. 6:8; 2 Cor. 9:9-10).[102] For doing justice in Scripture is not the abstract balancing of "rights," as Stephen Charles Mott reminds us, but the "restoration of that community as originally established by the justice of God; it is a community of equality and freedom from oppression."[103] As Christopher J. H. Wright's work in Old Testament ethics and Israelite society has shown with insight, God has a great interest in stronger families and communities.[104] Urban realities challenge the church to cre-

---

101. Moltmann, *The Spirit of Life*, pp. 138-42.

102. For the importance of justice for Israel and the church, see Walter Brueggemann, *Theology of the Old Testament: Testimony, Dispute, Advocacy* (Minneapolis: Fortress, 1997), pp. 188-90, 460-67, 737-38.

103. Mott, *Biblical Ethics and Social Change* (New York: Oxford University Press, 1982), p. 67.

104. Wright, *An Eye for an Eye: The Place of Old Testament Ethics Today* (Downers

atively pursue building stronger families and communities today in very practical ways and at multiple levels.

An active commitment to right relationships in the inner city comes from our confession of the Triune God, because God's love draws out a love set on God and neighbor in which every need is rightly satisfied.[105] To work for justice and against exclusion does not lock us into a polarity of oppressor and oppressed, rich and poor, for we follow the Christ who looked at the rich young man "and loved him" (Mark 10:21). The Christian witness to the reign of God must include an invitation to the rich and powerful to accept and share in God's saving way. Ultimately, just relationships are to be pursued by way of the cross — in love and self-giving — with the end being reconciliation and embrace.[106]

And where does this movement of grace and love and righteousness begin? Can it really alter the dynamics of the city when the ledger is so set against the poor? In a prophetic presentation of the gospel, Orlando Costas asserts,

> If evangelization starts on the periphery of society, if it works from the bottom up, the good news of God's kingdom is visibly demonstrated and credibly announced as a message of liberating love, justice, and peace. When the gospel makes "somebody" out of the "nobodies" of society, when it restores the self-worth of the marginalized, when it enables the oppressed to have reason for hope, when it empowers the poor to struggle and suffer for justice and peace, then it is truly good news of a new order of life — the saving power of God (Rom. 1:16).[107]

For Costas, this requires evangelizing communities of faith, born of the Spirit and from among the "marginalized and rejected, the sick and uneducated, lit-

---

Grove: InterVarsity, 1983); and *God's People in God's Land: Family, Land, and Property in the Old Testament* (Grand Rapids: Eerdmans, 1990).

105. Rowan Williams writes, "Ultimately, all that can be said by the Christian about justice rests on the doctrine of God, not simply as the God whose truthful love is directed towards us, but as the God whose very life is 'justice,' in the sense that Father, Son and Holy Spirit reflect back to each other perfectly and fully the reality that each one is, 'give glory' to each other." See Williams, *Open to Judgment* (London: Darton, Longman & Todd, 1994), 245-46, quoted by Stanley Hauerwas in *Sanctify Them in the Truth: Holiness Exemplified* (Nashville: Abingdon, 1998), p. 36.

106. Volf, *Exclusion and Embrace*, pp. 224-25.

107. Costas, *Liberating News: A Theology of Contextual Evangelization* (Grand Rapids: Eerdmans, 1989), p. 62.

tle children and alienated women, publicans and sinners, who will be transformed by the saving power of the gospel into a prophetic witnessing movement."[108] We speak of a community of believers whose very existence is a confrontation with the powers (Eph. 3:10-11). To a description of this community, the church, we now turn.

---

108. Costas, *Liberating News,* p. 63.

CHAPTER 2

A Church of the Streets

I will never forget my visit in the late 1980s to the Cathedral of San Salvador in the country of El Salvador. Everywhere one looked outside, the cathedral showed significant signs of decay and structural damage. Inside its walls, faded colors, gaps in the plaster, and peeling paint were just the most obvious indications of decline. Beaten and disheveled, the building was not in the condition that one expects of a "cathedral." Though the need for renovation was great, the construction scaffolding sat idle, collecting dust. Why was no work being done? The answer had to do with one pastor's understanding of the mission of the church. No work was being done on the building because years earlier, the church's leader, Archbishop Oscar Romero, had announced that focusing on the people in his parish was more important than repairing a church building.[1] Archbishop Romero had stopped renovation and redirected the resources to meet the basic needs of a suffering people, placing the church as a people ahead of the church as an outward symbol of authority and power.

Taking the historical setting into account is important. A horrible civil war was going on, and the poor lived in great misery and constant fear of notorious death squads. In a response shaped by the gospel, Romero made the cathedral a place of resistance and hope, a pastoral statement that the church was a community of the poor and vulnerable and that, ultimately, because of Christ crucified, the people would overcome death and find life. It was a belief that shaped the lives, laments, and hopes of many Salvadorians. When I visited the cathedral, people were kneeling and praying quietly in rickety

1. I am grateful to the late Guillermo Cook for relating this story to me during my visit to Central America in 1988.

65

wooden pews, while outside young soldiers nervously paced the square. The contrast was vivid. Inside the church there was a remarkable sense of Christ's presence. The church of Romero belonged to the poor, and therefore to God's future of peace. The weak were strong, while outside the powerful were weak. Not surprisingly, the Archbishop's making the cathedral into such a statement resulted in his martyrdom in 1980. But to this day, the memory of Romero and the way of being church that he believed in remain powerful signs of truth and hope.[2]

Part of what this story reminds us of as we think about the American inner city is that the church is called to be a community of the excluded, the forgotten, and the outcast. Following Christ, the church is to be a space of tears, grace, and hope that bears witness to God's new order.

This chapter is about the church in the inner city. The church I have in mind is a grassroots body of faith that has as its mission God's peace for the city. Called into being by the gospel, prayer and praise, evangelism and actions for justice are woven into its everyday life. This church is not simply a proclaimer of good news; it *is* good news.[3] Models of how to build and nurture such a church are provided by African-American and Latino congregations. In every city they offer profound understandings of God enacted in social ecclesiologies and in worship that is a blend of jubilation and lament. These models form a deep and wide river, to adopt the image of the Psalmist, from which to draw strength for the life of faith.

In what follows, we will examine something of the framework for being a grassroots church in the inner city from three perspectives: (1) the perspective of the kingdom life, (2) the perspective of the common life, and (3) the perspective of the witnessing life. These are categories of formation and development that are essential for ecclesial renewal and mission. While this chapter is but a partial study in ecclesiology, its goal is to bring us to a better understanding of what it means to be a worshipping community of good news in the changing inner city, a church that does not simply have a mission but understands itself as part of God's mission of redeeming the world.

---

2. For an introduction to Romero's spirituality, see *The Violence of Love: The Pastoral Vision of Archbishop Oscar Romero,* compiled and translated by James R. Brockman, S.J. (San Francisco: Harper & Row, 1988). For a moving account of Romero's continuing influence in El Salvador, see Carolyn Forche, "Present among Us," *DoubleTake* 2, no. 3 (Summer 1996): 20-31. On his challenge to the church beyond El Salvador, see William T. Cavanaugh, "Dying for the Eucharist or Being Killed by It? Romero's Challenge to First-World Christians," *Theology Today* 58, no. 2 (July 2001): 177-89.

3. For a powerful account of the history of grassroots Christianity, see Eduardo Hoornaert, *The Memory of the Christian People,* trans. Robert R. Barr (Maryknoll: Orbis, 1988).

THE KINGDOM LIFE OF THE CHURCH

Our first area of focus is the church as a community that is called into being by and serves the reign or kingdom of God. What is the kingdom of God like? According to Herman Ridderbos, the kingdom (or the reign) of God is "the great divine work of salvation in its fulfillment and consummation in Christ."[4] And what does it mean for the inner city? One of the ways in which Jesus described the kingdom was by telling a story about a feast. It might very well be the great feast or fiesta of the kingdom of God — the open table of the Lord for the humble, the pushed aside, the poor, and the forgotten — that is the image or symbol that best expresses the *charism* or unique calling of the church in the inner city. Although it is not commonly read this way, the parable of the great banquet in Luke 14:16-23 opens up vistas on new ways of being church that serve as a sign of God's reign. Embodying the feast of the kingdom in a local setting enables the church to name the story of Jesus and the kingdom that has called it into being.

The Feast of the Kingdom

As the parable opens, a banquet table has been set. However, the expected guests do not arrive (14:16-20). In response to this rejection, the host opens the table for the left out, and the outcast become privileged guests (14:21-23). It would be too simple to say that extra guests are invited. Rather, a completely new gathering is created. After the command to "Go out quickly into the streets and alleys of the town and bring in the poor, the crippled, the blind and the lame" (14:21) is accomplished, a second command to search for still more guests pushes the focus even further outward from the center: "Go out to the roads and lanes and compel people to come in, so that my house will be filled" (14:23, NRSV). Although historically this verse has been horribly misused to justify coercive and even violent "ingathering" tactics,[5] it is meant to be read as a message about the *noncoercive* openness of the abundant table of God.[6] In

4. Ridderbos, *The Coming of the Kingdom,* trans. H. de Jongste (Philadelphia: The Presbyterian and Reformed Publishing Company, 1976), p. 354. For a helpful overview of the kingdom, see Mortimer Arias, *Announcing the Reign of God: Evangelization and the Subversive Memory of Jesus* (Philadelphia: Fortress, 1984).

5. David J. Bosch, *Transforming Mission: Paradigm Shifts in Theology of Mission* (Maryknoll: Orbis, 1991), pp. 219, 236-37.

6. Klyne Snodgrass, "Common Life with Jesus: The Parable of the Banquet in Luke

the context of the Gospels and the actions and words of Jesus, it is a nonviolent invitation of grace.

We can imagine that when the rich and powerful heard this parable proclaimed, they interpreted it as a bracing challenge to discipleship.[7] However, the underlying question of the parable is, "Who will be present at the banquet?"[8] Earlier in Luke, Jesus presented an expansive portrait of the social geography established by the kingdom: "People will come from east and west and north and south, and will take their places at the feast in the kingdom of God. Indeed there are those who are last who will be first, and first who will be last" (13:29-30; cf. 1:53). The parable is rightly understood as an expanded commentary on Jesus' practice and teaching that "when you give a banquet, invite the poor, the crippled, the lame, the blind, and you will be blessed" (Luke 14:13-14).

Jesus received attention because he ate with sinners and outcasts (Luke 7:34). Whom you serve with food and drink, Jesus taught, reveals your understanding of faith (Matt. 25:31-46). Addressing issues of table fellowship in both Galatians and 1 Corinthians, Paul was clear that who gets invited to the common meals of the church is an indicator of fidelity to the gospel. And just as the coming of God came down to a meal, so does the future of all creation look forward to a glorious feast of the nations that knows no end (Isa. 25:6; Luke 13:29; Rev. 19:7, 9). When linked with the table practices of Jesus, the one who ate with women (Luke 7:36-50) and "tax collectors and sinners" (Luke 15:1-2), the radical nature of the parable becomes even clearer. According to John Dominic Crossan, "What Jesus' parable advocates, therefore, is an open commensality, an eating together without using table as a miniature map of society's vertical discriminations and lateral separations."[9] It is a tangible demonstration of the gospel as good news for the poor and of the community of Christ as the gathering of broken bodies, with Jesus as the Eucharistic and healing center.

Today, as then, it is in the alleys "where they hide the truth of cities," as Bruce Cockburn puts it in his brilliant song "Strange Waters."[10] The rarely

---

14:16-24," in *Common Life in the Early Church: Essays Honoring Graydon F. Snyder,* ed. Julian V. Hills (Harrisburg: Trinity Press International, 1998), p. 200.

7. Willi Braun, *Feasting and Social Rhetoric in Luke 14* (Cambridge: Cambridge University Press, 1995).

8. Snodgrass, "Common Life with Jesus," p. 196.

9. Crossan, *Jesus: A Revolutionary Biography* (San Francisco: HarperSanFrancisco, 1994), p. 69.

10. Cockburn, "Strange Waters," from *The Charity of Night,* Golden Mountain Music Corporation, 1996.

seen or traveled alleys have a way of symbolizing what most deeply characterizes a city. Through the eyes of this text, the church is invited to reflect on
what it means to be good news in the alleys of the city. "As he [Jesus] invites
his hearers to enter into the stories of his parables, he is inviting them to enter
into that world and so to join him in the new kingdom and its vision," contends Sylvia Keesmaat.[11]

When we place ourselves in the text, we are invited to enact ways of
Christian community that demonstrate the "anticipation" of God's eternal
feast. In his reflections on the church and God's future, Jürgen Moltmann
gives significant emphasis to the Messianic feast.[12] "It is," he says, "the feast of
the assembled community, which proclaims the gospel, responds to the liberation experienced, baptizes with the token of the new beginning and, at the
table of the Lord, anticipates the fellowship of God's kingdom."[13] By creatively continuing God's feast — by being a community that faithfully proclaims forgiveness, lives in joy, reverses status roles, and opens the table more
and more to the least of these — the church is a foretaste of the fullness of
God and the redemption of all of creation.

Sharing food is a central communal practice of the African-American
church, an ethical practice that creates a space of grace, love, and acceptance,
according to Jualynne E. Dodson and Cheryl Townsend Gilkes.[14] They observe, "The love ethic that pervades the ideology of African American
churches is constantly underscored and reaffirmed in the exchanges of food
and the celebration of church events with grand meals. This love and this
hospitality remind the congregation that they are pilgrims and strangers and
that as they feed somebody one day, they may stand in need on another."[15]
One example of the social power of this image comes from the life of the civil
rights leader Fannie Lou Hamer. In his essential book *God's Long Summer:
Stories of Faith and Civil Rights,* Charles Marsh shows how the story of God's

---

11. Keesmaat, "Strange Neighbors and Risky Care," in *The Challenge of Jesus' Parables,*
ed. Richard N. Longenecker (Grand Rapids: Eerdmans, 2000), p. 265.

12. On the importance of "anticipation" for the eternal feast, see Moltmann, *The
Church in the Power of the Spirit,* trans. Margaret Kohl (Minneapolis: Fortress, 1993), pp. 108-
14; and *The Coming of God: Christian Eschatology,* trans. Margaret Kohl (Minneapolis: Fortress, 1996), pp. 336-39.

13. Moltmann, *The Church in the Power of the Spirit,* p. 261.

14. Jualynne E. Dodson and Cheryl Townsend Gilkes, "There's Nothing Like Church
Food: Food and the U.S. Afro-Christian Tradition: Re-Membering Community and Feeding
the Embodied S/spirit(s)," *Journal of the American Academy of Religion* 63, no. 3 (Fall 1995):
519-38.

15. Dodson and Gilkes, "There's Nothing Like Church Food," p. 535.

"welcoming table" empowered and shaped Hamer's life. Guided by her theology of God's new table, Hamer reached out to people and worked for justice, embodying reconciliation and the gospel.[16] Making room for all expresses the vision that Christ is present and invites us to God's table and God's future.[17]

In the story of the new feast, we have a vision of the kingdom or reign of God, which summarizes the work of God's great saving and healing of the world. In the Gospel of Mark, Jesus announces his ministry with this declaration: "The time has come. . . . The kingdom of God is near. Repent and believe the good news!" (1:14; cf. Matt. 4:23; Luke 4:43; Rev. 1:6; 5:10). As the parable of God's new banquet table demonstrates, the kingdom is both a present experience ("has come") and an empowering hope for the future ("is near"). The church performs the story of the kingdom when it anticipates its future in hope and understands the central place of the gospel of the kingdom for the least of these. By discovering ecclesial life as kingdom life that gives itself away rather than seeks to receive things for itself, the church opens itself up to the Spirit and the future of God.[18] Indeed, this is part of the work of the Spirit. God's feast is to be a living reality, not merely a past story.

The Church and the Story of the Kingdom

Ecclesiology involves something like singing and living "People Get Ready." God's train is coming, and the church needs to get on board and move in God's way and direction. The church is part of a movement in the world, a song with verses still to sing and new ones to compose.

In *The New Testament and the People of God,* N. T. Wright locates the church in the drama of God's redemption.[19] In Wright's telling of the biblical story, there are five acts. Act 1 is creation; Act 2 is the Fall; Act 3 is the story of

---

16. Marsh, *God's Long Summer: Stories of Faith and Civil Rights* (Princeton: Princeton University Press, 1997), pp. 44-48.

17. For a picture of how this material is important for ministry among the homeless, see Stanley P. Saunders and Charles L. Campbell, *The Word on the Street: Performing the Scriptures in the Urban Context* (Grand Rapids: Eerdmans, 2000), pp. 156-75.

18. Miroslav Volf and Maurice Lee, "The Spirit and the Church," *The Conrad Grebel Review,* 18, no. 3 (Fall 2000): 20-45.

19. Wright, *The New Testament and the People of God,* vol. 1 of Christian Origins and the Question of God (Minneapolis: Fortress, 1992), pp. 141-43. On this aspect of Wright's work, I am following the reference and suggestion of J. Richard Middleton and Brian J. Walsh, *Truth Is Stranger Than It Used to Be: Biblical Faith in a Postmodern Age* (Downers Grove: InterVarsity, 1995), p. 182.

Israel; Act 4 is the story of Jesus; and Act 5 (including the New Testament) tells how the story comes to an end.[20] The church not only lives between the final acts, between the life of Jesus and the reconciliation of all things; it is, in Wright's construal, a part of Act 5 itself: "The church is designed, according to this model, as a stage in the creator's work of art. . . . As Paul says in Ephesians 2:10 . . . we are his artwork."[21] Between the climactic work of Christ and the end of the story, the church is responsible for faithfully "improvising" the story.[22] In this, the church should follow Jesus' example, who focused on the kingdom, an emphasis Wright develops more substantially in *Jesus and the Victory of God*. Through his actions and the stories he told, Jesus made known that in him was the coming of the kingdom, which meant God's return to Zion, Israel's return from exile, and a defeat of evil and the powers.[23]

In New Testament times, this broader vision of the kingdom called into being a new community, "a network of cells loyal to him and his kingdom-vision."[24] As Wright sees it, the early church was committed not only to the divinity of Jesus but also to ". . . a new sort of movement . . . a new category . . . a new way of construing what it meant to be human."[25] In this, the church's development and growth are linked to its faithfulness to God's mission in the world.[26] And specifically, as Wright urges us to see, part of this witness to the true King was a response to the powers.[27]

These perspectives help us see the church in the inner city as part of the drama of God, a community that is a part of the artwork of God's peaceable reign. Movement, drama, and mobility are built into the church.

The Anticipation of the Kingdom

In particular, the final act of God's drama, the new creation, is to orient the church's indwelling of God's story. Rightly anticipating God's reign comes to the church as a gift of the Spirit (Rom. 8:23; 2 Cor. 1:22; Eph. 1:14). Indeed, the church's entire life and witness are to be marked, as Miroslav Volf asserts,

---

20. Wright, *The New Testament and the People of God*, pp. 141-43.

21. Wright, *The New Testament and the People of God*, p. 142.

22. Wright, *The New Testament and the People of God*, p. 143.

23. Wright, *Jesus and the Victory of God*, vol. 2 of Christian Origins and the Question of God (Minneapolis: Fortress, 1996).

24. Wright, *Jesus and the Victory of God*, p. 317; cf. pp. 275-79.

25. Wright, *The New Testament and the People of God*, pp. 365; cf. 450-51.

26. Wright, *The New Testament and the People of God*, pp. 359-61.

27. Wright, *The New Testament and the People of God*, p. 370.

by *anticipation*.[28] According to Volf, "The church is not first of all a realm of moral purposes; it is the anticipation, constituted by the presence of the Spirit of God, of the eschatological gathering of the entire people of God in the communion of the triune God."[29] Moltmann makes a similar point. "Converted" to God's future and kingdom, the church is a community called not only to turn away from sin but to awaken to the present possibility of new beginnings.[30] Centrally, it is the Spirit who gives birth to the church as God's anticipatory community, a people who look forward in hope to the transformation of the world. Absent a theological focus on God's reign and new creation, the church will find it most difficult not to reduce the gospel to a private message. When the church reduces the gospel in this way, it severely compromises its ability to faithfully proclaim the good news in the inner city.

The Location of the Kingdom

While the church is a particular community that "gathers" for prayer and proclamation, celebration and fellowship (Matt. 18:20; 1 Cor. 14:23), it is also a people alive to Christ on the pavement of the streets (Luke 13:26; 24:13-16). The wider community of neighbors and neighborhood, in all of its pain, struggle, joy, and identity, is also the "place" where the church is to have its presence and practice service and love.[31] The community is not someplace that is fled or avoided or condemned; it is the site of Christian incarnation. It is where the church's faith is lived and seen by others, its life formed in such a way that Christ humiliated and exalted can be seen.

As the parable of the feast suggests, God's new community is closely identified with the poor. "Blessed are you who are poor, for yours is the kingdom of God," Jesus proclaimed (Luke 6:20; cf. Matt. 5:3; Luke 1:52-53; 7:22-23). These themes are very clear in Jesus' story of the banquet. Even more striking is that God has brought about this new emphasis through Jesus as the despised Galilean, the one without a home, the poor one, the king who comes as a servant (Isa. 42:1-9; Matt. 12:17-21; 25:35; Luke 2:24; 2 Cor. 8:9; Phil. 2:6-8). An ecclesiology of the kingdom must begin not simply with God's concern in Christ for the poor but with Jesus the poor one.

---

28. Volf, *After Our Likeness: The Church as the Image of the Trinity* (Grand Rapids: Eerdmans, 1998), p. 129.

29. Volf, *After Our Likeness*, p. 257.

30. Moltmann, *The Church in the Power of the Spirit*, p. 80.

31. Here I am building on Volf, *After Our Likeness*, p. 137.

Consider further the following description of the church in the epistle of James: "Has not God chosen those who are poor in the eyes of the world to be rich in faith and to inherit the kingdom he promised those who love him?" (2:5). This is not an isolated text in James. Throughout the epistle, God's peace for the poor as the basis for Christian fellowship is developed very clearly.[32] To be the church, James writes, is to be a community that privileges the "poor man in shabby clothes" (2:2). In 1 Corinthians 1:26-29, the Apostle Paul makes a similar statement:

> Not many of you were wise by human standards; not many were influential; not many were of noble birth. But God chose the foolish things of the world to shame the wise; God chose the weak things of the world to shame the strong. He chose the lowly things of this world and the despised things — and the things that are not — to nullify the things that are, so that no one may boast before him.

Here then from both James and Paul is a central witness drawn from all of Scripture: God has sovereignly chosen to work in the world by beginning with the weak who are on the "outside," not the powerful who are on the "inside."

When we speak of the church of the poor and suffering, one that is evangelical in the gospel sense, it is important to emphasize that we do not mean a church that has a unique concern or special ministry to the poor, a mission from the outside. Rather, a church of the poor is a fellowship amidst the hurting and harmed, the excluded and the suffering. As Moltmann concludes in *The Church in the Power of the Spirit,* "The church loses its fellowship with the messianic mission of Jesus if it is not 'the people of the beatitudes' and does not consist of the poor, the mourners, the meek, those who hunger for righteousness, the pure in heart and the persecuted."[33]

God's reign draws the church into a new story, a drama that moves forward in light of its ending with the new creation, demonstrated by the presence of the gospel among the poor. This calls into being communities of faith in Christ that are good news in the inner city. Because of Christ crucified and risen and the gift of the Spirit, life in and for the kingdom of God is the primary orientation of the church. "For the kingdom of God is not a matter of eating and drinking, but of righteousness, peace and joy in the Holy Spirit"

---

32. On how this text and others in James present a "theology of the poor," see Richard Bauckham, *James,* New Testament Readings (London: Routledge, 1999), pp. 185-203.

33. Moltmann, *The Church in the Power of the Spirit,* p. 81.

(Rom. 14:17). The kingdom finds unique expression in a gathered people who testify to its reality in worship and embrace those practices that shape its life in common.

THE COMMON LIFE OF THE CHURCH

The second dimension of the church that is important to stress is the centrality of a vibrant common life. The common life is a means of Christian formation and discipleship for faithful expression of the church's participation in God's story of the renewal of all things in Christ. It is this common life — how people care for one another, generate new patterns of relationship, and take seriously the call to serve their neighbors — that sets the church apart, even more than its building, its programs, its pastor, or its preaching. The significance of the common life is often neglected in traditional and even contemporary discussions of the church — to its great detriment. When people know they are deeply loved, cared for, accepted, and wanted by a community, they are transformed by the experience. And preaching that flows out of community life and serves its formation, rather than being the artificial focus of the church, is similarly transformational.

Biblically defined, the church is not merely a collection of individuals but a social body built around Christ that focuses on God's reign. The many images of the church in Scripture — such as the body of Christ, the people of God, the household of the Spirit — are all pictures of community. Put in terms of the Gospels, when Jesus called women and men to follow him, to join in his mission, he was building a community defined by a festive table with new seating arrangements. N. T. Wright explains it this way: "What we seem to be faced with is the existence of a community which was perceived to be subverting the normal social and cultural life of the empire precisely by its quasi-familial, quasi-ethnic life *as* a community."[34] According to Serene Jones, Calvin describes the church "as a communal context in which people are pulled together and given defining practices and institutional form by a sanctifying grace."[35]

Drawing attention to the communal shape of the church is the work of Stephen Fowl, Richard Hays, and others, who have very helpfully shown that Paul's letters and the rest of the New Testament are to be read not as individu-

---

34. Wright, *The New Testament and the People of God,* p. 450.
35. Jones, *Feminist Theory and Christian Theology: Cartographies of Grace* (Minneapolis: Fortress, 2000), p. 165.

alistic statements but as documents written to and for communities facing various issues in their common life and mission.[36] Hays's translation and explanation of Romans 12:1-2 provide a succinct introduction to a reading of Paul that emphasizes community:

> "Present your bodies [*sōmata,* plural] as a living sacrifice [*thysian,* singular], holy and well-pleasing to God. . . . And do not be conformed to this age, but be transformed by the renewing of your mind" (RH). The community, in its corporate life, is called to embody an alternative order that stands as a sign of God's redemptive purposes in the world. Thus, "community" is not merely a concept; as the term is used here, it points to the concrete social manifestation of the people of God.[37]

Ultimately, the church as a community that rightly relates to God and one another has its life in the fellowship of the triune God.[38] A communion and fellowship of love, the Triune life flows over into the formation of a loving and giving Christian community.

Forming and growing Christian communities in the city means being focused on incarnating the gospel in a manner faithful to the Lord and a particular context (John 1:14; Phil. 2:6-11). Put another way, it means searching to understand what it would mean for Christian communities "to have Christ formed in you" (Gal. 4:19), as the Apostle Paul wrote to believers in Galatia. According to Andrew Walls's account of the transmission of the Christian faith, such a process defines the history of the church.[39] The gospel is always a translation into the vernacular, and not just in its linguistic form but also in its deeper and more complex social and cultural contexts.[40] Pursuing such a witness, Darrell Guder acknowledges, is risky: "Gospel translation is empow-

---

36. See Stephen E. Fowl, *Engaging Scripture: A Model for Theological Interpretation* (Malden: Blackwell, 1998); and Richard B. Hays, *The Moral Vision of the New Testament: Community, Cross, New Creation: A Contemporary Introduction to New Testament Ethics* (San Francisco: HarperSanFrancisco, 1996). Also bringing to light the importance of community for ecclesiology are Robert Banks, *Paul's Idea of Community,* rev. ed (Peabody: Hendrickson, 1994); Gerhard Lohfink, *Jesus and Community: The Social Dimension of the Christian Faith,* trans. John P. Galvin (Philadelphia: Fortress, 1984); and N. T. Wright (various works).

37. Hays, *The Moral Vision of the New Testament,* p. 196; cf. p. 36.

38. Volf, *After Our Likeness: The Church as the Image of the Trinity.*

39. Walls, *The Missionary Movement in Christian History: Studies in the Transmission of Faith* (Maryknoll: Orbis, 1996), pp. 26-42.

40. Lamin Sanneh, *Translating the Message: The Missionary Impact on Culture* (Maryknoll: Orbis, 1989).

ered by the Holy Spirit but takes place in the ambiguity of human frailty and cultural limitations."[41] Both an inherent confidence and an inherent vulnerability are built into Christianity, Walls observes, because the church follows the incarnate Son of God, who took up the cross.

In this section I want to consider four distinctive and interconnected features important in Christian common life. They are as follows:

- The church as a community of grace
- The church as a community of welcome
- The church as a community of reconciliation
- The church as a community of sharing

After examining these, I conclude with a cautionary note about "idealizing" community. My argument is one against dividing the nature of the church from its mission. Mission and common life, word and deed, are a unified whole. As Harvie Conn once said, the church is not a place to go, but a people who go. Everything about the church must serve its kingdom journey.

The Church as a Community of Grace

Everything associated with the inner city as a "ghetto" — rejection, shame, exclusion, cultural rejection, and degradation — is in opposition to divine grace. Defined in classical Christian terms, grace is the alternative of the cross, the unexpected gift of life redeemed from sin that creates the church in all of its brokenness, sinfulness, weakness, pain, and frailty (Eph. 2:8-9). Grace is the healing power of God applied to hearts and lives that have been crushed and have often become hurtful to others. Divine grace knows not moralism but the forgiveness of God. Grace does not overlook suffering; it is the promise of the Lord in the midst of it: "My grace is sufficient for you, for my power is made perfect in weakness" (2 Cor. 12:9). Because of the contrast of grace with the exclusionary ways of the inner city, we can claim that the church as a grace-shaped community is the answer to the inner city in all of its destructive power.

However, both the inward and the outward composition of the inner city works against building and maintaining communities of grace and acceptance. The need for structure and direction amidst the chaos that can en-

41. Guder, *The Continuing Conversion of the Church* (Grand Rapids: Eerdmans, 2000), p. 92.

velop people's lives has led many churches to construct a community based on rules and regulations. Legalism is another term for this, and it creates moralistic churches that often fence out hurting people and keep struggling people discouraged. It confuses biblical faith with cultural standards. Mark Baker is familiar with this problem and writes about it in *Religious No More: Building Communities of Grace and Freedom*,[42] a unique and important study of churches and pastoral practice in Tegucigalpa, Honduras. In his experience, Baker found that many "evangelical" churches were legalistic and moralistic. The challenge, he believes, is to create communities of grace. In response to this challenge, Baker seeks to show how the book of Galatians diagnoses the problem of legalism and provides a model for building communities of grace. Because his concerns converge with ours, we can learn from them and bring them to bear on our context.

According to Baker, "The central question in Galatians is, what is the basis of the united fellowship of Jews and Gentiles — an encounter with Jesus Christ or rather compliance with religious standards?"[43] He is using "religious standards" to refer to the human desire to get on good terms with God. Instead of being "led by the Spirit" (Gal. 5:18), the church has appropriated the structures of a "gospel of bondage" (4:3-11). And it is this religious bondage that has produced the two tables, a racial division of sorts, in Antioch that Paul denounces (2:11-14). One humanly constructed set of standards was being used to exclude others (cf. 6:12-13). Thus the theological center of Galatians is not about individual salvation but about community and boundaries — as Baker expresses it, "Who are the people of God, and what makes them the people of God?"[44]

Paul's refutation, Baker argues, draws in part on the theme of "justification by faith" (Gal. 2:16), which he takes to be "the fact that inclusion in the community of God is based not on religious rules that divide but on God's initiative that brings people together."[45] For Baker and a number of other contemporary biblical scholars who propose a "new perspective" on Paul,

---

42. Baker, *Religious No More: Building Communities of Grace and Freedom* (Downers Grove: InterVarsity, 1999). See also his "Freedom from Legalism and Freedom for Community: A Hermeneutical Case Study on Reading Galatians in a Tegucigalpa Barrio" (Ph.D. dissertation, Duke University, 1996).

43. Baker, *Religious No More*, p. 96. For a further view of reconciliation in Paul and Galatians, see John M. G. Barclay, "'Neither Jew Nor Greek': Multiculturalism and the New Perspective on Paul," in *Ethnicity and the Bible*, ed. Mark G. Brett (Leiden: E. J. Brill, 1996), pp. 197-214.

44. Baker, *Religious No More*, p. 95.

45. Baker, *Religious No More*, p. 108.

God's justifying work in Paul's letters is more about the nature of Christian community than the means of entering the kingdom, as Martin Luther and his Reformation successors had proposed.[46] In fact, Baker's reading of Galatians suggests other themes have precedence in Paul's theologizing. But God's free justification of sinners remains an important Christian doctrine that has wide biblical support.

The Apostle Paul, Baker observes, enlists other images in the theological building of a new community. "Perhaps the most powerful images are 'new creation' and freedom from 'the present evil age' (1:4; 6:15)."[47] As Baker shows, the church is the community delivered by God from "the present evil age" into the reality of the "new creation." In the present reality of the new creation, "There is neither Jew nor Greek, slave nor free, male nor female, for you are all one in Christ Jesus" (Gal. 3:28). Cultural boundaries have been removed by God's liberating action in Christ, and religious observances (whether circumcision or something else) are not to be considered a mark of membership (3:26, 29; 4:5). Because of Christ's faithfulness, the church is a community of freedom that walks in love (6:2). The "freedom" that Paul talks about is not "independence" or "autonomy" as our culture understands it, but life in the era of the Spirit that leads to serving others (5:16, 18, 22, 25). It is the church that emphasizes Christ being "formed in you" as a community that learns to follow in Christ's way (4:19).

What does this mean for building communities of grace in the inner city? When I was a pastor in Sandtown, people — many of whom had the deepest struggles — would regularly tell me, "I'll be in church as soon as I get my life together." This is an illuminating statement. It not only tells us that grace has a hard time finding expression in a commodified culture where results and success are valued above all else. It also reveals something about how the church — and God — are perceived. It is sadly the case that the church is widely viewed as a community for people who fit a certain mold, who have their lives in order. Christianity looks like a "package" that includes more than just Christ, and it all has to be earned. Christian living — even salvation — is equated with a certain lifestyle.

Building communities of grace in the inner city entails creating spiritual and social spaces of freedom and acceptance where relationships of hon-

46. For a discussion of this issue, see Richard B. Gaffin Jr., "Paul the Theologian," *Westminster Theological Journal* 62, no. 1 (Spring 2000): 121-41. See also J. Louis Martyn, *Galatians: A New Translation with Introduction and Commentary* (New York: Doubleday, 1998).

47. Baker, *Religious No More*, p. 108.

esty, support, and encouragement are sustained in the God of grace. Like seasoning in a pot of soup, living grace-fully should permeate *everything* about the pastoral and common life of the church. The freedom of the gospel brings new life, the grace-shaped church a new beginning.

The Church as a Community of Welcome

I well recall the day that a woman in Sandtown asked me if God had forgotten her. She was caring for her grandchildren, right down to paying the electric bill to keep the lights on. It was a nearly impossible task, and she wondered where God was in her world. Home was about to be the street. Like Hagar, she felt abandoned. Certainly one of the most dominant experiences in the inner city is that of dislocation and exile.[48] The Psalmist's cry, "How can we sing the songs of the LORD while in a foreign land?" (137:4), is one often on the hearts and the lips of people in the inner city. Exile is an important biblical theme that reminds all believers that we are strangers and sojourners in the world, but it is especially pertinent to the displaced.[49]

"Homecoming," the social and theological counterpart to exile and being outcast, is a theme also richly developed in the grassroots urban church, and serves as a resource that can generate fresh commitments by the church to families who are "dislocated" in the inner city. According to theologian Cheryl J. Sanders, "An 'exilic' theology would equally obligate the entire community of faith, inclusive of exiles and elites, to offer authentic liturgies of welcome and memory that enable the experience of liberation as homecoming."[50] For all those who need the experience of home, for those who are "outside" (in Paul's language) and "other," and for those who are excluded, the church is to be a welcoming community. In N. T. Wright's reading of the kingdom, a major theme is that Jesus has come to deliver a people from exile.

Romans 15:1-7 puts welcome in a theological and ecclesial perspective: "We who are strong ought to bear with the failings of the weak and not to please ourselves. Each of us should please his neighbor for his good, to build him up" (vv. 1-2). This should be interpreted not so much as an individual command but as a theology for the entire church. Here the model is Christ,

---

48. Justo L. Gonzalez, *Santa Biblia: The Bible Through Hispanic Eyes* (Nashville: Abingdon, 1995), pp. 91-102.

49. Walter Brueggemann, *Theology of the Old Testament: Testimony, Dispute, Advocacy* (Minneapolis: Fortress, 1997), pp. 77-78. See also Gonzalez, *Santa Biblia*, pp. 91-102.

50. Sanders, *Saints in Exile: The Holiness-Pentecostal Experience in African-American Religion and Culture* (Oxford: Oxford University Press, 1999), p. 143.

who "did not please himself" (Rom. 15:3), but suffered for our redemption and hope (15:4) so that the church might be a community of praise (15:5-6). Paul's challenge to be this church in Romans 15:7 is quite direct: "Accept one another, then, just as Christ accepted you, in order to bring praise to God." Christ's life and death are what shape a community of acceptance and embrace, a community that does not please, serve, or justify itself, but welcomes and comes alongside the "weak." The word of welcome privileges and invites the other, the outsider, and the displaced into the body of Christ.

The biblical imperative of hospitality reinforces the church's calling to be a welcoming community, a feature of the church that has been powerfully explored by Christine D. Pohl in *Making Room: Recovering Hospitality as a Christian Tradition*.[51] Earlier in Romans, Paul directed the church to "practice hospitality" (12:13; cf. 1 Pet. 4:9). That this command was not intended to serve only people in the church is suggested by the verse that follows, exhorting the followers of Christ to bless those who harm them (Rom. 12:14). Hospitality, the act of making strangers feel at home and meeting their needs — especially because one knows the experience of social and cultural alienation — takes place through intentional acts.

When "welcome" is set within a theological framework of God's grace in Christ, important implications emerge for the church in the areas of family life, neighborhood youth, and the development of worship space. First, a community of welcome embraces all families. Family life is under intense social, economic, and cultural pressure in the inner city. How is the church to welcome families under such pressure? The church's call to support families is first a call to care for them in whatever form they take. We do well to remember that there are few — if any — examples of "ideal" families in Scripture![52] The church is to be a community where all families are welcomed, loved, and supported. Is this not something of the meaning of the biblical injunction to take special care of the widow and the orphan (Exod. 22:22; James 1:27)? Instead of focusing on negatives, it is better to begin by looking at the strengths of inner-city families, fathers and mothers, building them up from the perspective of their strengths.

By the measure of the reign of God, the church in its common life must give special attention to the needs of children and young people. In his

---

51. Pohl, *Making Room: Recovering Hospitality as a Christian Tradition* (Grand Rapids: Eerdmans, 1999), pp. 104-124. One of the striking features of Pohl's study is the centrality of hospitality by the poor for the poor.

52. Guillermo Cook et al., "The Family in God's Reign: The New Community of Jesus in the Gospel of Mark," *Latin American Pastoral Issues* 18 (1994): 22.

teaching, Jesus gives great significance to children because of their vulnerability; this reflects his commitment to those with little social power.[53] Indeed, Jesus changes the order of the world by putting children first. "The Gospels teach the reign of God *as a children's world,* where small children are the measure, rather than don't measure up to adults, where the small are great and the great must become small," writes Judith Gundry-Volf.[54] The creative re-orientation of congregational structures should revolve around this.

Because of the priority that Jesus gave children and the way in which he welcomed them, a community of welcome in the inner city should have a particular focus on the development of youth. Children and young people are the heart of the community, the way we should measure our church life. Teenagers, who are all "at risk," should be of special concern. Forming children in the ways of God is an essential part of the faith community's call in the city (Prov. 22:6). Demographic trends alone urge this. In Sandtown, for example, approximately one out of three residents is under nineteen, and few are involved in a church. Our inner cities are filled with many Latino and African-American youth searching in the wrong places and the wrong ways for identity and meaning. Alienated from mainstream avenues of opportunity and education, they are at risk for joining a gang, using drugs, and dropping out of school. But in order to reach out to them effectively, the church must understand them. Examining the beliefs and emotions of artists such as the late Tupac Shakur, who was shaped by the violence and deprivation of the inner city, is imperative for working with our youth.[55] The church will often need to seek forgiveness for the ways in which it has excluded young people in the past, and to consider possibilities for new directions.

Youth ministry should be given new priority and focus. Boston's Ten-Point Coalition, a church group that has taken to the streets, has been instrumental in reducing teenage homicide in that city.[56] Indeed, it is only on the

---

53. Judith Gundry-Volf, "To Such as These Belongs the Reign of God: Jesus and Children," *Theology Today* 56 (2000): 469-80.

54. Gundry-Volf, "To Such as These Belongs the Reign of God," p. 480.

55. Along these lines, a study that should be read by urban church youth workers and pastors is Michael Eric Dyson, *Holler If You Hear Me: Searching for Tupac Shakur* (New York: Basic Civitas Books, 2001). For a wider perspective, see Mark Anthony Neal, *What the Music Said: Black Popular Music and Black Popular Culture* (New York: Routledge, 1999).

56. For a convincing account of the reasons why this worked, see Christopher Winship and Jenny Berrien, "Boston Cops and Black Churches," *The Public Interest* 136 (Summer 1999): 52-68. It can be argued that attending and participating in a local church helps young people develop resistance to the difficulties and dangers of inner-city life. The labor econo-

streets that the church can truly meet teenagers and grapple with the complex "codes" of respect, sexuality, and family that shape their lives.[57] How can the church undertake this kind of outreach in concrete ways? Church-based youth workers can reach out to the hip-hop generation, bringing them the good news of the gospel.[58] Every church can develop or collaborate on an after-school center that supports families and the public school system. Those with more resources might even consider helping to start a school or an after-school program that would serve the neighborhood. These efforts must be based on far more than good intentions. Any undertaking that attempts to reach "at-risk" youth without addressing their total community situation and the need for biblical justice is a partial approach at best.

If welcome is about providing a safe spiritual and social home, then careful attention should also be given to church buildings. Ironically, church buildings *can* desacralize the neighborhood and alienate people. Ideally, a church and its building embrace the city, recognizing that all of the city belongs to God. In fact, as a central site of God's passionate concern and presence, the inner city is "holy ground." When ecclesial space is "superior," people of little means often feel it is inappropriate for them to come into such a place. The best "church building" may not be one set apart just for worship, but one designed or adapted for community ministry. Setting aside a room that is always available for prayer and worship is something that should be done if that is at all feasible, and it may be especially important for staff if the building is a site for intense ministry day in and day out. And in general a church building should make families feel comfortable as they enter it and teenagers look forward to "hanging out" in it. A "come-as-you-are" policy for dress supports this friendly feeling. And whether the church is a traditional tall-steepled building or a storefront, it should express beauty in some way; that will also draw people in. Every inner-city church, if it makes the effort, can communicate that it exists to be part of its neighborhood, not beyond or

---

mist Richard B. Freeman tried to quantify the exceptional difference church-going relationships can make in young people's lives in his often-cited study entitled "Who Escapes? The Relation of Church-Going and Other Background Factors to the Socio-Economic Performance of Black Male Youths from Inner City Poverty Tracts," Working Paper No. 1656. Cambridge: National Bureau of Economic Research, 1985.

57. Elijah Anderson, *Code of the Street: Decency, Violence, and the Moral Life of the Inner City* (New York: W. W. Norton, 1999).

58. A helpful summary of successful programs and principles for youth ministry is provided by Harold Dean Trulear, "Faith-Based Initiatives with High-Risk Youth," in *Serving Those in Need: A Handbook for Managing Faith-Based Human Services Organizations*, ed. Edward L. Queen II (San Francisco: Jossey-Bass, 2000), pp. 266-89.

above it.[59] Inner-city neighborhoods need fresh visions of the church as a welcoming community.

The Church as a Community of Reconciliation

Amidst the deep structures of division old and new that have formed our urban world, part of what it must mean to be a community that bears testimony to Christ is to pursue reconciliation across boundaries of culture, race, ethnicity, social class, and gender. For, as Archbishop Desmond Tutu of South Africa reminds the world from his own experience, there really is no future without reconciliation, confession, and forgiveness.[60] Rooted in the loving mutuality of the Trinity (John 17:11), a vision of unity in diversity is drawn from the new city of God, which anticipates a future of embrace and reconciliation for every nation, culture, and language (Rev. 7:9). How should this shape our life with one another in the community of salvation? Reconciliation is something that has been definitively achieved in Christ (Gal. 3:28; Eph. 2:16-18) and yet at the same time is an ongoing process, not simply a one-time event. Living in the narrative of Christ, the church needs to learn not only how to improve its communication skills but also how to exercise the practices of reconciliation, central to which are repentance and forgiveness.[61] A central task of the church in the inner city is to learn how to build communities of reconciliation that express the newness of the kingdom in social, economic, political, and gender relationships.

We gain a picture of both the pain and the possibility of reconciliation in 1 Corinthians, a letter concerned with the life of a particular urban Christian community. A great deal has been written about the social situation in the Corinthian church, and it seems quite clear that there was internal conflict based on differences in social status and power.[62] What was ingrained in

---

59. For a discussion on art in the life of the church, including its role in buildings, see John W. de Gruchy, *Christianity, Art, and Transformation: Theological Aesthetics in the Struggle for Justice* (Cambridge: Cambridge University Press, 2001), pp. 213-54.

60. Tutu, *No Future without Forgiveness* (New York: Doubleday, 1999).

61. For a significant reflection on this subject, see L. Gregory Jones, *Embodying Forgiveness: A Theological Analysis* (Grand Rapids: Eerdmans, 1995).

62. Gerd Theissen, *The Social Setting of Pauline Christianity: Essays on Corinth*, ed. and trans. John H. Schütz (Philadelphia: Fortress, 1982). Among other studies, see Andrew D. Clarke, *Secular and Christian Leadership in Corinth: A Socio-Historical and Exegetical Study of 1 Corinthians 1–6* (Leiden: E. J. Brill, 1993); David G. Horrell, *The Social Ethos of the Corinthian Correspondence: Interests and Ideology from 1 Corinthians to 1 Clement* (Edinburgh:

the hierarchies and divisions of the city of Corinth had found its way into the common life of the church. Paul focused his pastoral work on correcting these problems, his goal being "that there may be no divisions among you" (1:10).[63] It will be helpful for us to look at a few passages to see how Paul went about trying to reshape the habits and practices of the church.

Discussing their assembly, Paul observes, "When you come together, it is not the Lord's Supper you eat, for as you eat, each of you goes ahead without waiting for anybody else. One remains hungry, another gets drunk" (1 Cor. 11:20-21). While it is difficult to know precisely what this means, there are good reasons, as Gerd Theissen has argued, to believe that the division between the "weak" and the "strong" at this common gathering was socially defined (1 Cor. 8:9; cf. 11:17-18).[64] Those with less power and status were left watching or waiting outside as the strong and privileged indulged. One proposal comes from Bruce Winter, who suggests that the observance of the Lord's Supper "had degenerated into a 'private dinner' where the social 'haves' devoured their own meal and drank themselves into stupor with their own wine, while the hungry low-class 'have-nots' were left looking on as slaves did at private dinners. . . . In behaving thus some Christians replicated the dinner 'etiquette' of their secular counterparts."[65] Paul asked the powerful and wealthy some pointed questions about their behavior: "Don't you have homes to eat and drink in? Or do you despise the church of God and humiliate those who have nothing?" (1 Cor. 11:22).

Paul's earlier discussion of the meaning of the Lord's Supper in chapter 10 is certainly relevant here: "Is not the cup of thanksgiving for which we give thanks a participation in the blood of Christ? And is not the bread that we break a participation in the body of Christ? Because there is one loaf, we, who

---

T. & T. Clark, 1996); and Wayne A. Meeks, *The First Urban Christians: The Social World of the Apostle Paul* (New Haven: Yale University Press, 1983). See also Richard A. Horsley, "1 Corinthians: A Case Study of Paul's Assembly as an Alternative Society," in *Paul and Empire: Religion and Power in Roman Imperial Society*, ed. Richard A. Horsley (Harrisburg: Trinity Press, 1997), pp. 242-52. A dissent from the "consensus" position of social heterogeneity represented in these studies is provided by Justin J. Meggitt in *Paul, Poverty, and Survival* (Edinburgh: T. & T. Clark, 1998). One early response to Meggitt is from Dirk Jongkind: "Corinth in the First Century AD: The Search for Another Class," *Tyndale Bulletin* 52, no. 1 (2001): 139-48. For an overview of the issues, see Anthony C. Thiselton, *The First Epistle to the Corinthians*, NIGTC (Grand Rapids: Eerdmans, 2000), pp. 848-53.

63. On reconciliation as a thematic center of 1 Corinthians, see Margaret M. Mitchell, "Paul's 1 Corinthians on Reconciliation in the Church: Promise and Pitfalls," *New Theology Review* 10, no. 2 (May 1997): 39-48.

64. Theissen, *The Social Setting of Pauline Christianity*, pp. 121-43.

65. Winter, *After Paul Left Corinth: The Influence of Secular Ethics and Social Change* (Grand Rapids: Eerdmans, 2001), p. 158.

are many, are one body, for we all partake of the one loaf" (vv. 16-17). It is the cross that confronts the powerful and offers protection to the most vulnerable (1 Cor. 1:23; 2:6-7). The life and death of Jesus had a spiritual and social meaning for the community, especially as a means of deconstructing the privileges and self-understanding of the rich.[66] Unity exists only when no part of the body is devalued (1 Cor. 12:22-23).

Elsewhere in 1 Corinthians, Paul addresses inter-ethnic relationships. He expresses his belief on reconciliation near the beginning of his correspondence when he says, "We preach Christ crucified: a stumbling block to Jews and foolishness to Gentiles, but to those whom God has called, both Jews and Greeks, Christ the power of God and the wisdom of God" (1 Cor. 1:23-24). Incorporated into Christ, Jews and Greeks do not have their identity obliterated; instead, they all have a Christian identity. Dwelling in Christ, who is the wisdom of God, the Corinthian church was to break down the city's dominant cultural, ethnic, and gender boundaries, its actual walls of division.[67] "For we were all baptized by one Spirit into one body — whether Jews or Greeks, slave or free — and we were all given the one Spirit to drink" (1 Cor. 12:13). The dynamic of reconciliation is initiated by the waters of baptism and confirmed in the meal of Christ, a counter-story to the divisive story embedded in the social structure of the city.

Daniel Boyarin has proposed that reconciliation for Paul is motivated by "a Hellenistic desire for the One, which among other things produced an ideal of a universal human essence, beyond difference."[68] But for Paul, a new vision of humanity allows people to celebrate their differences and empower one another in love. Divine newness is expressed not through tolerance or artificial unity, which in the end erases identity, but through relationships remade by the plenitude of the Spirit's multicultural witness, voice, and common life. "Peace no longer depends upon the reduction to the self-identical, but is the sociality of harmonious difference," notes John Milbank.[69]

---

66. Graham Tomlin, *The Power of the Cross: Theology and the Death of Christ in Paul, Luther, and Pascal* (Carlisle: Paternoster, 1998), pp. 98-101.

67. In *The Rise of Christianity: A Sociologist Reconsiders History* (Princeton: Princeton University Press, 1996), Rodney Stark identifies "ethnic precincts" dividing Greco-Roman cities (p. 158).

68. Boyarin, *A Radical Jew: Paul and the Politics of Identity* (Berkeley and Los Angeles: University of California Press, 1994), p. 181. For an analysis of Boyarin's book and a discussion of the issues related to identity, see Judith M. Gundry-Volf and Miroslav Volf, "Paul and the Politics of Identity," *Books and Culture* 3, no. 4 (July/August 1997): 16-18.

69. Milbank, *Theology and Social Theory: Beyond Secular Reason* (Oxford: Blackwell, 1993), p. 5.

Can Paul's theology of community across boundaries, both ethnic and social, address our inner cities, especially as our cities become more diverse? Our discussion of 1 Corinthians suggests numerous ways in which it can, and I want to offer some perspectives on this.

First, in Christ and through the Spirit's gift of redeemed hearts, the church finds that the scope of Christ's embrace does not lead to an end to color, language, and difference, but opens up vistas for celebrating a new community of all persons who love and honor one another.[70] Second, reconciliation depends not on ignoring historic and present injustices but on confronting them through the practices of repentance, forgiveness, and renunciation of status. The reconciliation of people in the church will come about only when new social, economic, and gender patterns that reflect God's alternative community are intentionally worked toward with full awareness of the complexity of the challenge.

Third, those who retain power and status cannot be the arbitrators of unity, especially since giving up power is a sign of reconciliation.[71] Fourth, there can be no genuine reconciliation in the church without equality and right relationships.

Finally, like Paul, I believe that the desire for reconciliation must come from the transformed hearts of all those who recognize that Christ also died for them as ones whose way of life and sins have worked against God's reconciling plan for the world.[72] Convictions concerning the saving work of God provide the passion and the energy to create congregations that demonstrate the community of equals that the kingdom promises and demands. Remembering and trusting in Christ's work make patterns of reconciliation possible.

70. For "whites" especially, there is a need to "read" and "see" racism through the eyes of those who suffer under the gaze of "whiteness" or other power centers. For a reflection that quickly makes clear the continuing role of race in relationships, see Patricia J. Williams, *Seeing a Color-Blind Future: The Paradox of Race* (New York: Noonday Press, 1997). While a "color-blind" society, defined as decentered from whiteness, is an appropriate aim, it is important to remember that the kingdom of God does not erase diversity but celebrates it. Such is the richness of the Triune life for the identity of humanity.

71. James H. Cone has hard but important things to say about such matters in his writings that should be heard in today's climate of easy "reconciliation." See, for example, *God of the Oppressed* (New York: Seabury Press, 1975), pp. 226-46.

72. Seyoon Kim, "2 Cor. 5:11-21 and the Origins of Paul's Concept of Reconciliation," *Novum Testamentum* 39, no. 4 (Oct. 1997): 360-84.

The Church as a Community of Sharing

A church that practices its faith in the inner city should be one that shares "not only the gospel of God but [its] lives as well" (1 Thess. 2:8). In the Spirit, women and men are free to share Scripture and their gifts and ministries for the reign of God (Rom. 12:5-8; 1 Cor. 12:12-27). Such mutual commitment is expressed in the word *koinōnia,* the Greek word for sharing used in the New Testament that refers to both communion with Christ and material resources applied to the common good (Acts 2:42-47; 4:32-35; 2 Cor. 8–9; Gal. 6:6; Phil. 4:5). A community church, therefore, will not "have a ministry" so much as it will be a community of people who read Scripture together, who share in the hope of the gospel, and who share every joy, tragedy, and resource in Christ (Acts 2:42). The body of Christ is not merely a metaphor for the church's relationship to Christ but a real body whose members share both their suffering and their joy (1 Cor. 12:12, 27). "If one part suffers, every part suffers with it; if one part is honored, every part rejoices with it" (1 Cor. 12:26).

Sharing possessions was a particularly important way that the earliest Christian community expressed its life in the kingdom.[73] In an echo of God's directive for the Israelite social order rooted in the Jubilee ("there should be no poor among you"; Deut. 15:4), the early church in Acts 4 is described as a community where "there were no needy persons among them" (Acts 4:34).[74] Elsewhere, Paul argues for sharing through a "collection": "At the present time your plenty will supply what they need, so that in turn their plenty will supply what you need. Then there will be equality" (2 Cor. 8:14). Very intentionally, as Christopher Wright observes, the early church understood itself to be a community of sharing, holiness, and justice in relationship to the poor.[75]

At the same time, we should take note of Justin Meggitt's view that early Christian sharing of economic goods seems to have been a very necessary kind of social survival strategy for impoverished believers.[76] Meggitt calls this strategy of survival "mutualism," defining it as "the implicit or explicit belief that individual and collective well-being is attainable above all by mutual interdependence."[77] Given the context of the American inner city, where

73. Hays, *The Moral Vision of the New Testament,* pp. 464-68; Luke T. Johnson, *Sharing Possessions: Mandate and Symbol of Faith* (Philadelphia: Fortress, 1981).

74. On the relationship between Acts and the Jubilee, see Christopher J. H. Wright, "Jubilee, Year of," in vol. 3 of *The Anchor Bible Dictionary,* ed. David Noel Freedman et al. (New York: Doubleday, 1992), pp. 1025-30.

75. Wright, "Jubilee, Year of," p. 1029.

76. Meggitt, *Paul, Poverty, and Survival,* pp. 155-75.

77. Meggitt, *Paul, Poverty, and Survival,* p. 158 (emphasis deleted).

food, decent housing, and health care can be in short supply, congregations have been developing and will in new ways need to emphasize strategies of "mutualism," formal and informal ways of sharing food, housing, and networks so that people can survive.

Sharing recognizes the peaceable future of God and reflects new life in the Spirit. As Miroslav Volf writes, "Here, then, is the 'justice' of Pentecost that is indistinguishable from embrace: all have their needs met, and the deep desire of people to be themselves, to act in their own right and yet to be understood and affirmed, is satisfied."[78] Noncompetitive giving and receiving is to mark life in the Spirit. Certainly the material sharing in Acts 2 and 4 should not be read without recalling Acts 5, where Ananias and Sapphira claimed to be sharing in full but kept some back from the Apostles, dishonesty that brought about their destruction (vv. 1-11). This passage draws attention to the need for honesty in sharing. In this, remember the witness of the widow who gave two coins "worth only a fraction of a penny." Jesus commended her to his disciples, saying, "I tell you the truth, this poor widow has put more into the treasury than all the others. They all gave out of their wealth; but she, out of her poverty, put in everything — all she had to live on" (Mark 12:43-44).

A common life of sharing should lead to holistic ministry, especially community organization and development. The church shaped by the Spirit must always extend itself in sharing and caring beyond its "membership" (Acts 2:47; Gal. 6:10). In the Reformed tradition, Calvin's commitment to refugees moved him to create entire institutions that focused on economic development and the needs of strangers.[79] When it comes to the social relationship between church and community, the black church experience provides the best example. As Eugenia Eng and her co-authors point out, "In the black community the church serves as both a stable frame of reference and a catalyst for social, political and economic change. . . . The Church as a social unit of identity has also functioned as a unit of solution."[80] Caring for the needs of others, especially those who have been broken at the hands of the powers, is bound up with the church's identity.

---

78. Volf, *Exclusion and Embrace: A Theological Exploration of Identity, Otherness, and Reconciliation* (Nashville: Abingdon, 1996), p. 229.

79. Robert M. Kingdon, "Calvinism and Social Welfare," *Calvin Theological Journal* 17, no. 2 (November 1982): 212-30.

80. Eng, John Hatch, and Anne Callan, "Institutionalizing Social Support through the Church and into the Community," *Health Education Quarterly* 12, no. 1 (Spring 1985): 86. On the church and its natural connections for enhancing the health of community life, see Gary Gunderson, *Deeply Woven Roots: Improving the Quality of Life in Your Community* (Minneapolis: Fortress, 1997).

A Cautionary Note: The Danger of Idealizing Community

When Christ calls a community into being, he does so based on a divine ideal, not a human image or ideal. Though we aspire to Christ's ideal, we are prone to imposing our own visions on the church. Patterns of vulnerability, brokenness, and sinfulness are always present in the life of the church, and the "best" inner-city church is no exception. In fact, it may even be the prime example. Dietrich Bonhoeffer, a German theologian and pastor who was executed for his role in the Resistance near the end of World War II, provides perceptive and relevant comments for the urban church on this matter. In his work *Life Together,* he notes, "On innumerable occasions a whole Christian community has been shattered because it has lived on the basis of a wishful image."[81] There is a constant danger that we will invent or impose our vision of what Christian community should be upon others — a danger that must be faced, Bonhoeffer explains: "Every human idealized image that is brought into the Christian community is a hindrance to genuine community and must be broken up so that genuine community can survive. Those who love their dream of a Christian community more than the Christian community itself become destroyers of that Christian community even though their personal intentions may be ever so honest, earnest, and sacrificial."[82]

How does such a Christian community survive itself? Bonhoeffer's words stir and warn: "By sheer grace, God will not permit us to live in a dream world even for a few weeks and to abandon ourselves to those blissful experiences and exalted moods that sweep over us like a wave of rapture."[83] God's Word of truth, Bonhoeffer stresses, reminds the Christian community of its true foundation in Christ:

> Even when sin and misunderstanding burden the common life, is not the one who sins still a person with whom I stand under the word of Christ? Will not another Christian's sin be an occasion for me ever anew to give thanks that both of us may live in the forgiving love of God in Christ Jesus? Therefore, will not the very moment of great disillusionment with my brother or sister be incomparably wholesome for me because it so thoroughly teaches me that both of us can never live by our own words

81. Dietrich Bonhoeffer, *Life Together,* in vol. 5 of Dietrich Bonhoeffer Works, ed. Geffrey B. Kelly, trans. Daniel Bloesch and James Burtness (Minneapolis: Fortress, 1996), p. 35.
82. Bonhoeffer, *Life Together,* p. 36.
83. Bonhoeffer, *Life Together,* p. 35.

and deeds, but only by that one Word and deed that really binds us together, the forgiveness of sins in Jesus Christ? The bright day of Christian community dawns wherever the early morning mists of dreamy visions are lifting.[84]

Being thankful for one another, with all of our faults, and being thankful for the salvation found in the forgiveness of Christ are two kinds of gratitude that belong together. This is the basis of a life together in Christ in the inner city.

THE WITNESSING LIFE OF THE CHURCH

The third aspect of the church that we will examine is the call to bear witness to Jesus and the hope of the kingdom. Christian witness is about story-telling — the body of Christ bearing witness to the story of God's salvation. Ecclesial life means heeding Christ's call, as its first hearers did: "You will be my witnesses in Jerusalem, and in all Judea and Samaria, and to the ends of the earth" (Acts 1:8; cf. Luke 24:47-49). In *Liberating News* Orlando Costas links the church's announcement of the gospel to the kingdom of God: "Evangelization is . . . a universal invitation to all women and men to become part of the pilgrim people of God in the march toward the new order of life that is the kingdom of God. It is an invitation to become part of a new humanity."[85] Costas puts evangelization forward as a responsibility of the church: "The base of evangelization is the congregation. As a community of love, faith, and hope, the congregation is God's instrument for the transmission of the gospel. Its life should be a continuous perpetual proclamation, 'a fifth gospel,' the incarnation of love, faith, and hope, the reproduction of the good news of salvation in its social context."[86]

The multifaceted *announcement* of the kingdom, with Jesus at the center, is central to the message of the church in the city. According to N. T. Wright, the story of the kingdom was told in four stages:

> It [began] with *invitation:* the kingdom-announcement necessarily included the call to "repent and believe the good news." . . . There was also *welcome:* Jesus' kingdom-stories made it clear that all and sundry were po-

84. Bonhoeffer, *Life Together,* pp. 36-37.

85. Costas, *Liberating News: A Theology of Contextual Evangelization* (Grand Rapids: Eerdmans, 1989), p. 148.

86. Costas, *Liberating News,* p. 133.

tential beneficiaries, with the most striking examples being the poor and the sinners. Invitation and welcome gave birth to *challenge:* those who heard Jesus' call, and understood themselves as characters in his kingdom story, were summoned to live precisely as the renewed-Israel people, personally and corporately. Finally the story generated a *summons.* Some at least of those who made Jesus' story their own were called to go with him on his journey to Jerusalem, to be his companions in mission.[87]

Spreading the news of the kingdom as invitation, welcome, challenge, and summons will draw on the whole expressive life of the church in Christ — its life as a body of believers, its witness in proclamation, and its healing of broken hearts and bodies — that invites and welcomes others to join in God's reign, a feast to which all are invited. If Christianity is to have a vibrant witness in the inner city, then it will need to recover and enact the centrality of the kingdom.

Central to the witnessing life in the inner city is the role of the church. Although it is not to be identified as the kingdom, it is called to be the community here on earth that demonstrates the glories of God's reign. As the body of Christ, the church is called to live for the peace, love, and joy of God's reign. In the book of Acts we read that when the church shared its life and possessions, thus demonstrating that God's Spirit was in their midst, the result was dramatic: "And the Lord added to their number daily those who were being saved" (Acts 2:47). This witnessing aspect of the church is well summarized by Harvie M. Conn:

> We are God's demonstration community of the rule of Christ in the city. On a tract of earth's land purchased with the blood of Christ, Jesus the kingdom developer has begun building new housing. As a sample of what will be, he has erected a model home of what will eventually fill the urban neighborhood. Now he invites the urban world into that model home to take a look at what will be.[88]

At work here is what missiologist Lesslie Newbigin calls the church as the "hermeneutic of the gospel."[89] "Walking your talk" is the translation in urban vernacular. This takes place when incarnation and integrity meet.

---

87. Wright, *Jesus and the Victory of God,* p. 245.

88. *Planting and Growing Urban Churches: From Dream to Reality,* ed. Harvie Conn (Grand Rapids: Baker, 1997), p. 202.

89. Newbigin, *The Gospel in a Pluralist Society* (Grand Rapids: Eerdmans, 1989), pp. 222-33.

Christian witness in the inner city is authentically bearing witness to the truth of the gospel in response to the questions born of suffering, exclusion, and poverty. How do we go about this? The impressive witness of the early church gives us a model. In his book *The First Urban Christians*,[90] Wayne Meeks characterizes the early church movement as attached to cities. And Rodney Stark, author of *The Rise of Christianity: A Sociologist Reconsiders History*,[91] points out that Christians defined themselves by a faith that aligned them with the sick, the hungry, the marginalized, and the afflicted, moving across every ethnic and cultural barrier to bring healing and hope to the city. The costly demands of the gospel were linked to their understanding of a merciful God. Stark summarizes the Christian self-understanding this way: "*Because* God loves humanity, Christians may not please God unless they *love one another*. . . . Perhaps even more revolutionary was the principle that Christian love and charity must extend beyond the boundaries of family and tribe, that it must extend to 'all those who in every place call on the name of our Lord Jesus Christ' (1 Cor. 1:2). Indeed, love and charity must even extend beyond the Christian community."[92] Stark surmises that the early church grew dramatically because its members reached out to others in love and compassion.[93] Commenting on Stark's thesis, Dee Dee Risher observes, "The early church thrived only because it offered a powerful, different vision of how to live and what to live for."[94]

Using Antioch as a case study of Greco-Roman cities, Stark presents a harsh picture of urban life. In this city, densely crowded even by modern standards, people lived in tenement buildings, with the poor making their homes on the top floors. Conditions were cramped and foul, and the buildings themselves frequently collapsed. Poor sanitation meant that filth and disease were rampant. Further complicating these conditions was the population growth driven by newcomers; Antioch and other Greco-Roman cities had fragmented social and ethnic populations. And then there were the challenges

90. Meeks, *The First Urban Christians: The Social World of the Apostle Paul* (New Haven: Yale University Press, 1983).

91. Stark, *The Rise of Christianity: A Sociologist Reconsiders History* (Princeton: Princeton University Press, 1996). For critical analysis of Stark's work, see the *Journal of Early Christian Studies* 6, no. 2 (Summer 1998). An argument similar to the one I am making here is by Dee Dee Risher, "Hope on the Edges," *The Other Side* 35, no. 4 (July/August 1999): 20-23. Risher's piece is superb. My appropriation of Stark is not without qualification of his "rational choice" theory.

92. Stark, *The Rise of Christianity*, p. 212.

93. Stark, *The Rise of Christianity*, pp. 6-7.

94. Risher, "Hope on the Edges," p. 20.

of geography and climate. As a consequence, cities like Antioch were especially vulnerable to "attacks, fires, earthquakes, famines, epidemics, and devastating riots."[95]

Stark draws these details into a harrowing conclusion about the urban conditions of the times:

> Any accurate portrait of Antioch in New Testament times must depict a city filled with misery, danger, fear, despair, and hatred. A city where the average family lived a squalid life in filthy and cramped quarters, where at least half of the children died at birth or during infancy, and where most of the children who lived lost at least one parent before reaching maturity. A city filled with hatred and fear rooted in intense ethnic antagonisms and exacerbated by a constant stream of strangers. A city so lacking in stable networks of attachments that petty incidents could prompt mob violence. A city where crime flourished and the streets were dangerous at night. And, perhaps above all, a city repeatedly smashed by cataclysmic catastrophes: where a resident could expect literally to be homeless from time to time, providing that he or she was among the survivors.[96]

In summary, Antioch was a city plagued by "urban chaos." Stark concludes that in this place and time, people "must often have longed for relief, for hope, indeed for salvation."[97]

At great risk to their own lives, Christians stayed in the city and ministered to fellow city dwellers. This level and form of discipleship was understood to be a universal Christian obligation, born out of confidence in God and faith in Jesus, not something belonging to a few special "heroic" men and women. According to Stark, when an epidemic struck the city, as it often did, Christian men and women were known for staying and nursing the sick when others fled.[98] Christians changed the world in which they lived by being willing to lay down their lives for others. As Risher remarks, "In these conditions of social upheaval, the fresh testimony of the gospel — of a God who loves and heals; of a Messiah who understands and has lived through human suffering, conquering death and opening the promise of new life — was revolutionary. It was a message of salvation that would turn life upside down."[99]

95. Stark, *The Rise of Christianity*, pp. 151, 157, 159.
96. Stark, *The Rise of Christianity*, pp. 160-61.
97. Stark, *The Rise of Christianity*, p. 161.
98. Stark, *The Rise of Christianity*, pp. 73-94.
99. Risher, "Hope on the Edges," p. 21.

In these circumstances, as Stark points out, Christian common life and the hope of the kingdom met together in a powerful urban witness:

> Christianity revitalized life in Greco-Roman cities by providing new norms and new kinds of social relationships able to cope with many urgent urban problems. To cities filled with the homeless and impoverished, Christianity offered charity as well as hope. To cities filled with newcomers and strangers, Christianity offered an immediate basis for attachments. To cities filled with orphans and widows, Christianity provided a new and expanded sense of family. To cities torn by violent ethnic strife, Christianity offered a new basis for social solidarity. . . . And to cities faced with epidemics, fires, and earthquakes, Christianity offered effective nursing services.[100]

While Christianity was a movement of reconciliation between people of all backgrounds, it aligned itself with the hurting and the poor of the city. This was a powerful witness to all strata of society that new life and new forms of community were possible.

When we gather up the themes that Stark identified as characteristic of the early church, there are some significant implications for the witnessing life of the church not only in the inner cities of America but also in the urban centers of Africa, Asia, Eastern Europe, the Middle East, and Latin America, where poverty and inequality are rapidly growing worse. A calling of the church today is to stay in the cities, especially the most seriously abandoned and hurting cities and communities. By keeping faith in the neighborhood, the church resists the disintegration of community. As a basic way of following Christ, the church is especially to love and care for the poor and the sick, the outcast, the unwashed, and the unwanted. Our "unwanted" are men and women with HIV, diabetes, and drug and alcohol addictions. They may be unemployed and hanging out on the corner.

Recognizing the struggle of the household, the church is to be an extended household. For children in neighborhoods where street violence threatens to overcome, the church is to be a sanctuary and a place to learn alternatives. To young men on the corner who have been cut off by society, the church is to extend the invitation to full membership in a new body. To new immigrants, the church is to show hospitality. In communities where ethnic tensions run high, the church is to model love, the discipline of forgiveness, the power of acceptance, and a faith without walls. Willing to love and serve

100. Stark, *The Rise of Christianity,* p. 161.

at great cost, the church and its members are called to put their very lives on the line, even amidst urban suffering and chaos. This means being identified with the body of Christ and all the ways in which it distinguishes itself from the exclusionary groups of our urban age. And in doing all of these things, the church announces the good news of salvation in Christ.

In this chapter I have sought to explore ways of being "a church of the streets," a church truly involved in the inner city. I have done so first by placing the church in kingdom perspective, and then by examining the contours of Christian common life and the nature of urban witness. This witness generates new local visions of church life that are responses to the Word. Being God's people in the city means that new spiritual, social, and material space is created, challenging the structures of the inner city. Through the work of the Spirit, the story of the kingdom generates a new way of life in the city, a central practice of which is the way of peace. To this way of life as a chief characteristic of Christian kingdom activity we now turn.

CHAPTER 3

The Things That Make for Peace

Rodney was smart, outgoing, personable, and great fun to be around. When I first moved to Sandtown in late 1986, Rodney and his brother Frank lived in the house across the street from me, and they were two of the first people I met. We rented our Calhoun Street houses from the same landlord, known for — among other things — using one color of dark reddish-brown paint for the entire block of houses that he owned.

Rodney's life did not work the way it should have. All around Rodney were vacant houses, abandoned shops, warehouses, and open-air drug markets. The fast-food stands, bars, and liquor stores on his row-house street were the full extent of formal economic activity. The school Rodney attended was advancing him nowhere. He lived on a block and in a neighborhood segregated from the social and economic opportunities of the city, a world that had few formal attachments to the labor market. Within the larger story of the world, Rodney was a redundant and disposable person.

It attracted little public attention when, at seventeen, this young man of great potential was found dead in the basement of a vacant house, a gunshot wound to his head. Rarely does the death of young black inner-city males garner attention. Rodney's death was widely assumed to be the result of a drug deal gone awry. Sadly, his life ended in violence like his father's, who had also been murdered. Left behind were people who loved and needed him — a mother and a brother, a girlfriend, and a young daughter. Rodney was not a statistic but part of a family and a community. His funeral was full of intense pain and weeping.

Yet it would be a grievous mistake to treat Rodney's death as just one more heartbreaking tragedy of a young man who went the wrong way in

97

life. Certainly it cannot be denied that he made wrong choices. But there is no escaping the fact that the choices he made had lethal consequences because the violence that took his life was embedded in the brokenness of the city. The powers of exclusion had captured Rodney, holding his world in their thrall, and were not going to let him go without exacting a price. A gunshot to his head was merely the denouement of a system of violence that had built his neighborhood. The place where Rodney lived ended his life. I am convinced of this in part because I know that my life as a teenager would in all likelihood have ended similarly if I had grown up in Sandtown and not the suburbs.

Rodney's death was the first that involved a young person associated with our church. I know that our church made an important difference in his life, especially his friendship with Allan Tibbels, a New Song founder and leader, but our combined efforts fell short. Rodney's death pressed home the seriousness of our challenge and ultimately laid bare our failures as a church. Tragically, the funerals and tears continued as other young people's lives went awry. In the years to come, many of the school-aged "kids" we knew from the early days found themselves in difficult situations, and a majority of the young men ended up shot and wounded, imprisoned, or dead like Rodney.

Our challenge is a significant and comprehensive one. For it is evident that neither moral preachments nor personalized program — no matter how well intentioned — are adequate to counter the deep effects of sin and the bellicose powers that work within the urban system. Christian ministry, discipleship, and witness cannot take place in a social or a historical vacuum. What we need to do is hear the cries of suffering and the word of the Lord as a summons to make the world more right, to know more fully the gospel as good news for the inner city. What is demanded is a spiritual vision for the inner city, a kingdom vision and vocation that responds to the inner city's narrative of violence and exclusion.[1] The biblical witness calls this change and vision *shalom,* the Hebrew word for peace. This how I will speak of faith-shaped urban activity. Peacemaking is the mode of discipleship required for urban transformation in an age of changing cities and multiple forms of exclusions.

Shalom means much more than the absence of conflict. As Nicholas Wolterstorff points out in his book *Until Justice and Peace Embrace,* the con-

---

1. For a creative and important response to the narrative of violence, see J. Richard Middleton and Brian J. Walsh, *Truth Is Stranger Than It Used to Be: Biblical Faith in a Postmodern Age* (Downers Grove: InterVarsity, 1995).

tent of *shalom* is the presence of right and harmonious relationships imbued with delight and flourishing before the Lord.[2] Thus, *shalom* is present not merely when neighborhoods know no violence, but when they work in such a way that young people like Rodney might grow up and flourish. *Shalom* not only reconceptualizes the political and social order of the city; it also reverses the everyday and localized effects of a global market economy and a history of discrimination and exclusion. The gospel of peace is a radical alternative for the city.

In this chapter, by drawing on the biblical image and theme of *shalom*, I want to outline a framework for the multidimensional responsibility of changing neighborhoods, one that focuses on the things that make for peace (Luke 19:41-42). I will begin by clarifying and surveying the concept of God's peace in the biblical witness. Nonviolence is central to this testimony. Then I will offer a reading of Jeremiah 29, a text that may serve as a paradigmatic text on urban ministry. After surveying the biblical material, I will draw some conclusions about the way in which this model of peacemaking can be creatively appropriated for inner-city neighborhoods. Specifically, I will argue that presence, prayer, and public faith are among the things that help make for more peaceable neighborhoods. Finally, I will show how the gentle and intentional ways of peacemaking, a commitment that is guided by nonviolence, can go beyond helping to break the cycles of systemic violence and exclusion in the inner city, how they can offer a strong alternative vision and possibility for the city.

This chapter follows directly from the previous two chapters, taking for granted a social and theological analysis of the inner city and a vision of the church as a peaceable people. Scaled to the neighborhood, my subject explores the perennial inquiry into the relationship between gospel and culture, Christ and incarnation (John 1:14). Because urban peacemaking is about loving our neighbors and exercising discipleship, our subject is also that of Christian mission. To be peacemakers means to take up — with commitment and sacrifice — God's proclamation in Christ of good news to the poor (Luke 4:16-21). Following Christ by faith, urban peacemakers believe that the peace of Christ can transform the self, the community, and the city.

---

2. Wolterstorff, *Until Justice and Peace Embrace* (Grand Rapids: Eerdmans, 1983), pp. 69-72, 124-25.

"SEEK THE PEACE OF THE CITY"

The Old Testament scholar Walter Brueggemann has highlighted the power of biblical images to create alternative and imaginative ways of understanding, living in, and transforming the world.[3] Through the images of Scripture, resistance to oppression can be undertaken, alternatives can be imagined, and new ways of community can be created. *Shalom* is one of the most important images for us to recover if a new situation is to be proposed and developed in the inner city. Appropriating the image of *shalom* can help us break away from conventional urban alternatives (or a perceived lack of alternatives) and generate the energy and vision to forge new beginnings for our families, our communities, and our cities.

Shalom *as Urban Restoration*

At this point it will be helpful to return to a text I emphasized in the Introduction. In Isaiah 65:17-25, the city stands for the peaceable world of God. Isaiah's hope-filled image, a response to very real suffering and injustice (2:1-5), paints an urban picture that includes the health and safety of children, the honoring of every year for older adults, the exercise of work that brings a just return, and the physical world in right relationship to the needs of human beings. Isaiah's message, in short, is that God will redeem the world; the new creation is characterized as the holy city of God. At the end of the passage we read, "Before they call I will answer; while they are still speaking I will hear" (65:24). As Isaiah stresses, God's presence and its recognition occupy a central place in the city as the abode of God's peace.

As Nicholas Wolterstorff expresses it, the horizons of *shalom* are vast:

> Shalom in the first place incorporates right, harmonious relationships to *God* and delight in his service. When the prophets speak of shalom, they speak of a day when human beings will no longer flee God down the corridors of time, a day when they will no longer turn in those corridors to defy their divine pursuer. . . . Secondly, shalom incorporates right harmonious relationships to other *human beings* and delight in human community. Shalom is absent when a society is a collection of individuals all out

3. See Brueggemann, *Texts under Negotiation: The Bible and Postmodern Imagination* (Minneapolis: Fortress, 1993), *The Prophetic Imagination* (Minneapolis: Fortress, 1978), and *The Hopeful Imagination: Prophetic Voices in Exile* (Minneapolis: Fortress, 1986).

to make their own way in the world. . . . Thirdly, shalom incorporates right, harmonious relationships to nature and delight in our physical surroundings. Shalom comes when we, bodily creatures and not disembodied souls, shape the world with our labor and find fulfillment in so doing and delight in its results.[4]

From our covenant relationship with God to our social institutions, *shalom* is God putting back together a broken world. To take another image of peace from Isaiah, *shalom* is not just the wolf and the lamb co-existing but the wolf and the lamb finding their rest in one another (11:6-7; 65:25). *Shalom* is more than physical safety for the child playing near the cobra's nest; it is the child and the cobra successfully playing together. Accordingly, what is called for, Wolterstorff proposes, are commitments and activities that sanctify the world.[5] *Shalom* as sanctification embraces all dimensions of life, for God's holiness is to extend to all of life.

Precisely because *shalom* is about the world made right in holiness and truth, it cannot be detached from right relationships, but is preceded by and dependent upon justice. *Shalom*, Wolterstorff recognizes, exists within an "ethical community."[6] A lack of justice precludes the experience of *shalom*, as this promise of Isaiah indicates: "The fruit of righteousness will be peace; the effect of righteousness will be quietness and confidence forever" (Isa. 32:17; cf. Pss. 72:1-4; 85:10). The pervasive commands of Scripture to do justice presume that the foundation for peace is the restoration of right relationships (Amos 5:24; Mic. 6:8). Turning "swords into plowshares" is the cultural activity of a people committed to God's peaceable city.

In Micah 4:4 we find a wonderful picture of *shalom* that gathers in the themes of justice and security as they are fulfilled in the presence of God:

> Every man will sit under his own vine and under his own fig tree,
>   and no one will make them afraid,
>   for the LORD Almighty has spoken.

According to Micah, peace visits when people live without fear, without want of food or shelter, and therefore are able to be open to others. Thus *shalom* is

---

4. Wolterstorff, *Until Justice and Peace Embrace*, p. 70.

5. According to Wolterstorff, "There is, in Reformed life, a displacement from the emphasis on conversion so characteristic of Anglo-American evangelicals to an emphasis on sanctification, understood holistically." See "Can a Calvinist Be Progressive?" *Gereformeerd Theologisch Tijdschrift* 88 (1998): 251.

6. Wolterstorff, *Until Justice and Peace Embrace*, p. 71.

good news for a world where economic and social practices run counter to God's purposes for creation. As God's promise of a peaceable human existence, of a world that includes economic justice, *shalom* upholds spiritual struggle for a life of wholeness and integrity.

The New Testament continues the theme of God's peace in all of its fullness, applying it with particularity to the person and work of Christ.[7] Christians hear Isaiah's promise of "swords beaten into plowshares" in the cry of a tiny babe, the promised Savior, who comes in peace to restore the fallen urban order. As the climactic verse of Zechariah's song in Luke tells us, this is a child who will "guide our feet into the path of peace" (1:79). Peter summarizes the gospel story as God having inaugurated an urban peace plan for the cities of the world, "telling the good news of peace through Jesus Christ, who is Lord of all" (Acts 10:36; cf. Luke 10:5-6; 19:38). In his life, N. T. Wright explains, "Jesus declared that the way to the kingdom was the way of peace, the way of love, and the way of the cross."[8] The promised *shalom* of the prophets has come in God's Son, who through his wounds is creating a new community of peace that crosses every barrier and dividing line. He is "our peace," making those who have been divided one in the body of Christ (Eph. 2:14-16; Col. 3:15; cf. Matt. 5:9). And in its fullest expression, God's peace culminates in a city, the urban vision of John of Patmos (Rev. 21–22). Here, Isaiah's promise of a world without tears and division has been fulfilled. It is a world based on the Lamb who was slain, a city built on the work of the cross of Christ. And the church is to be a sign of this world.

Because *shalom* is what God intends for the world, sin, as Cornelius Plantinga puts it in his book on the subject, is the vandalism of *shalom*.[9] At its very root, sin is oriented against God. As part of creaturely estrangement from covenant relationship with God, sin is expressed through injustice, racism, structures of exclusion, and a lack of mercy. Sin brings alienation into every area of urban life, from the condition of the human heart to family relationships to economic life, breaking down the integrity that God intended for all of creation. For these reasons, sin is the vandalism of *shalom*. Plantinga's proposal runs parallel to that of Wolterstorff, who writes, "To be impoverished is to fall short of shalom. That is what is wrong with poverty."[10] If

---

7. On peace as a theme in Luke's Gospel that continues the concerns of *shalom*, see Willard M. Swartley, "Politics or Peace *(Eirene)* in Luke's Gospel," in *Political Issues in Luke-Acts*, ed. Richard J. Cassidy and Philip J. Scharper (Maryknoll: Orbis Books, 1983), pp. 18-37.

8. Wright, *Jesus and the Victory of God* (Minneapolis: Fortress, 1996), p. 595.

9. Plantinga, *Not the Way It's Supposed to Be: A Breviary of Sin* (Grand Rapids: Eerdmans, 1995), pp. 7-27.

10. Wolterstorff, *Until Justice and Peace Embrace*, p. 77.

Plantinga and Wolterstorff are right — and I think that they are — then *shalom* is God's urban renovation project, the restoration of a defaced urban existence. It is the reversal of human alienation from God, from creation, and from one another. Because *shalom* is the end of poverty, injustice, and exclusion, to seek the *shalom* of the city is to work to reverse the effects of sin and the Fall on the city and to proclaim the news of One who comes in peace.[11]

Jeremiah's Alternative Way

When Jeremiah wrote a letter to the Israelites exiled in Babylon, he told them to "seek the peace [*shalom*] and prosperity of the city to which I have carried you into exile. Pray to the LORD for it, for if it has peace [*shalom*], you too will have peace [*shalom*]" (29:7, my translation). The contours of peacemaking were to include presence, prayer, and public activity, with an outcome that Daniel L. Smith describes as a "strategic posture for exilic existence . . . best described as 'nonviolent social resistance.'"[12] As we develop a reflection on this passage, we will see that Jeremiah 29 provides continued direction for the church's urban identity and responsibility.

Jeremiah's imperative came to the Israelites as they found themselves exiled and captive in the city of Babylon. Since they were political hostages in a foreign imperial city, the moment was ripe for confusion and concern. On the one hand, as Smith observes, it seems as if a group of prophets was telling the people to rise up and defeat their enemies (29:8-9).[13] On the other hand, Smith argues, it also looks like another group was telling them to stay quiet and survive. Into this setting Jeremiah sent a letter that called for them to reject both these views and instead seek the flourishing of the city. In short, Jeremiah urged them to "settle down" and stay in the city, raise their families, and make long-term plans that commended involvement in the life of the city.

Certainly it was hard for the Israelites to "sing the songs of the LORD while in a foreign land" (Ps. 137:4). Still, they were to "build houses and settle down; plant gardens and eat what they produce. Marry and have sons and

11. An over-realized theology of *shalom* can be problematic. Controlled by the biblical story of creation, fall, and redemption, the gospel demands sharing, stewardship, and justice. Placing blessing, justice, health, and joy in the now-but-not-yet of redemptive history can help us understand the remaining brokenness of our world.

12. Smith, "Jeremiah as Prophet of Nonviolent Resistance," *Journal for the Study of the Old Testament* 43 (1989): 95.

13. Smith, "Jeremiah as Prophet of Nonviolent Resistance," p. 99.

daughters. . . . Increase in number there; do not decrease" (29:5-6). They were to build in the city, grow in the city, and keep faith in the city, in these ways enacting the prophetic witness (1:10). This was a rejection of the call to violence as a means of social and political change.[14] But in its place was a call to redeem the city. There could be no separate peace for God's people apart from the general condition of the city as a whole; the two were bound together. Faithful engagement, not withdrawal, was Jeremiah's way. A peaceable urban presence would not underwrite Babylonian domination. Rather, it would bear witness to the true God of the Israelites.

Such an urban strategy was profoundly counter-intuitive: the Israelites were to practice their faith by blessing their enemies, defying their power by exceeding expectations for civic life. As Smith proposes, Jeremiah is advocating a "nonviolent social resistance" that emphasizes trust in God's sovereignty, hope in God's future, the practices of nonviolence, and the everyday acts of cultural production. "'For I know the plans I have for you,' declares the LORD, 'plans to prosper you and not to harm you, plans to give you hope and a future'" (29:11). What Smith finds here are not "prescriptions for suicide or acceptance of evil, but alternative means of faithfulness and mechanisms for survival."[15] Let us not ignore that this project of God's is the renewal of community. "'I will gather you from all the nations and places where I have banished you,'" declares the LORD, "'and will bring you back to the place from which I carried you into exile'" (29:14).

Consistent with this account but with its own angle of vision is John Howard Yoder's proposal that Jeremiah 29 offers a "Jeremianic model."[16] Yoder's important argument is filled with insights that can help the church navigate its way in the complexity of the global city.[17] Essentially, as I understand Yoder, he sees the Israelites becoming "fluent" in the Babylonian culture, creating a cross-cultural bridge back to the healing elements of a God-centered life.[18] Yoder summarizes the force of Jeremiah's command this way: "Seek the peace of the city" is too weak a translation for Jeremiah's command; it should be translated "Seek the salvation of the culture to which God has

---

14. Smith, "Jeremiah as Prophet of Nonviolent Resistance," p. 102.

15. Smith, "Jeremiah as Prophet of Nonviolent Resistance," p. 104.

16. Yoder, "See How They Go with Their Face to the Sun," in *For the Nations: Essays Public and Evangelical* (Grand Rapids: Eerdmans, 1997), pp. 51-78.

17. To pursue this further, see Yoder, *For the Nations,* pp. 15-78 especially. For an interesting comparative analysis, see Douglas Harink, "For or Against the Nations: Yoder, Hauerwas, What's the Difference?" *Toronto Journal of Theology* 17, no. 1 (Spring 2001): 167-85.

18. Yoder, "See How They Go with Their Face to the Sun," pp. 72-73.

sent you."[19] Perhaps with this translation Yoder over-reads the text, but I would not dismiss this interpretation too quickly. God's peace, as we have seen, is comprehensive and all-embracing, a summary of God's intention of salvation for the city.

The point to be taken from Yoder's remarks is that engagement, not withdrawal, is the witness of faith, and it is salvific because God's peace is salvific. Jeremiah's command, as Yoder recognizes, was not simply a survival strategy for a minority people but also a call to healing the nations that stands in the line of faith-driven public intercessions such as those of Joseph, Esther, and Daniel and his three friends.[20] Regardless of the Israelites' marginal status, healing for the nations would come through their distinctively faith-shaped presence in the city. While avoiding obedience to the empire and its idols and by remaining focused on the worship of the true God, the exiles were to exercise great commitment to the flourishing of the city and its citizenry.

Serving the Welfare of the City

What remains of this call to urban peacemaking in the New Testament? As Bruce W. Winter shows in his impressive study entitled *Seek the Welfare of the City: Christians as Benefactors and Citizens,*[21] Jeremiah's ethic and exilic image of distinctive civic engagement resonates throughout the life of the early church in the New Testament. Though Winter's study seemingly sets up a questionable and unnecessary divide between the church community and individual Christians in ethical address,[22] his proposals can be very helpful to us as we seek to understand the spiritual, social, and civic life of the early church in the city.

Winter sees in Peter's first epistle a key example of the Jeremiah paradigm of seeking the welfare of the city. Peter addresses his epistle to a people

19. Yoder, "See How They Go with Their Face to the Sun," p. 76.
20. Yoder, "See How They Go with Their Face to the Sun," pp. 56-57.
21. Winter, *Seek the Welfare of the City: Christians as Benefactors and Citizens* (Grand Rapids: Eerdmans, 1994). Throughout the rest of this section, this work will be referred to parenthetically in the text. See also Bruce W. Winter, "'Seek the Welfare of the City': Social Ethics According to 1 Peter," *Themelios* 13, no. 3 (April/May 1988): 91-94.
22. In the context of the framework of 1 Peter, Winter writes, "Surprisingly, no mention is made of the church *per se*. This general epistle deals with the difficulty of fulfilling their responsibility as benefactors in the unsettled circumstances in which Christians found themselves" (*Seek the Welfare of the City,* p. 19). However, the church is absolutely the context, assumed from 1:1-2 forward.

who were in a situation analogous to that of the Babylonian exiles, identifying them as "sojourners" or "pilgrims" (1:1), terms which I think underscore *both* the reality of their marginal social status *and* their spiritual identity.[23] As they lived in the cities found in the provinces of Galatia, Asia, and Bithynia, their suffering and minority status were very real (3:8-16). With this experience came attendant questions of identity and calling. There was the risk of assimilation to the dominant culture, and with it the loss of distinctiveness. At the same time, there was the risk of being unnecessarily "other" (2:15; 4:19; see *SWC*, p. 18.)

Drawing a link back to Jeremiah's paradigmatic passage and the Psalms, Winter finds that Peter locates the church's pilgrim identity within the task of seeking the peace of their city (3:11//Ps. 34:14): "He must turn from evil and do good; he must seek peace and pursue it." His hearers were to do good works (1:17), "obviously oriented towards the needs of others in the temporal cities in which they lived" (*SWC*, p. 19). This doing good took place in the "public place" (*politeia*), involving "the whole of life in the public domain of a city, in contrast to private existence in a household" (*SWC*, p. 2). Although pilgrims in orientation, these believers were not to move through the world without faithful engagement.

God's future was the motivation upon which they were to seek the well-being of the city (2:11-12; 4:19). As Winter explains,

> To stand in the "true grace of God" demanded a deep commitment to the welfare of the city within the framework of a living eschatological hope. That enabled the Christian to place personal concerns second to the needs of others in the city. This firm, eschatological hope of a secure inheritance meant that their present or impending suffering would be no ultimate catastrophe for them (4:12). The setting of one's hope on the grace to be revealed at the revelation of Jesus Christ (1:13) provided the perspective for fulfilling the Christian mandate to seek the welfare of the earthly city and not personal aggrandisement. (*SWC*, p. 19)

According to Winter, the church's calling in 1 Peter was (1) "to declare" the mercies of God (2:9-10), (2) "to follow" Christ in suffering (2:21), and (3) "to bless" others, not repaying evil for evil (3:9; 4:19; see *SWC*, pp. 19-20). In 1 Peter 2:13-17, believers are enjoined to do good works for the city's sake be-

---

23. Contra Winter, *Seek the Welfare of the City*, who holds to a theological definition (p. 16). See John H. Elliott, *1 Peter: A New Translation with Introduction and Commentary*, Anchor Bible (New York: Doubleday, 2000), pp. 84-101.

cause it is the will of God (2:17). At the same time, Peter recognizes God's general beneficence to all of the creation as an additional basis for care and concern (*SWC*, p. 23). In summary, Winter observes, "Despite the complex and far from ideal social situations of the Christians addressed in 1 Peter, there were no extenuating circumstances which exempted them from seeking the blessing of the city" (*SWC*, p. 23).

Winter also finds the Jeremiah paradigm at work elsewhere in the New Testament, including Paul's letters. According to Winter, Christians were called to be first-class citizens or benefactors in service to God (Rom. 13:3-4; cf. 1 Pet. 2:14-15), the well-off especially called to provide for the wider public needs (*SWC*, pp. 26-40). Winter cites Erastus the Aedile, mentioned in Romans (16:23), as likely being a well-off and civic-minded benefactor (*SWC*, pp. 180-97).[24] But in a society known for the activities of privileged "benefactors," the gospel broadened the working definition of benefaction to "every Christian . . . in his/her society" (*SWC*, p. 42), moving distinctively beyond the patronage system of the Roman period (1 Thess. 4:11-12; 2 Thess. 3:6-13; see *SWC*, pp. 42-60). Ordinary Christians "did good because good needed to be done, and did so without expectations of reciprocity or repayment" (*SWC*, p. 60). They were to work hard to assist others in greater need, even those "widows" who were able (1 Tim. 5:13-16; see *SWC*, pp. 62-68). In all of this, ordinary believers were to reach outside of their own households.

Another example comes from Paul's interaction with the Corinthian Christians, where Winter locates Paul's interest in the peace of the city in his call to put others first (1 Cor. 10:24, 33; 11:1; see *SWC*, pp. 175-77). "Nobody should seek his own good, but the good of others" (1 Cor. 10:24), Paul instructs them. Using himself as an example, he writes, "For I am not seeking my own good but the good of many, so that they may be saved" (1 Cor. 10:33). Unlike many other first-century social groups, Christians focused not on their own privileges or status but on the benefit of the neighbor and the neighbor's relationship to God (10:32-33; cf. Rom. 15:2; Gal. 6:10). On the basis of a wider calling to serve the city, Paul urges the church in 1 Corinthians 10:23-33 not to yield to pagan self-fulfillment but to undertake the costly care of others — including non-Christian "others." Concludes Winter, "Civic rights must now be evaluated as to the effect they have on one's relationship with Christian and non-Christian alike" (*SWC*, p. 176).

Surveying the biblical material, Winter concludes, "There was no dichotomy in the thinking of the early church between the gospel/church min-

---

24. For a different view, see Justin J. Meggitt, *Paul, Poverty, and Survival* (Edinburgh: T. & T. Clark, 1998), pp. 135-41.

istry and the seeking of the welfare of the city" (*SWC*, p. 196). Seeking that welfare was understood to be the task of every able-bodied Christian. According to Winter, "The Christian social ethic . . . can only be described as an unprecedented social revolution of the ancient benefaction tradition" (*SWC*, p. 209). And, as Markus Bockmuehl has pointed out, giving and receiving, in terms of Christ's story, has a different end than a retooling of the patronage system, one based on the need to obtain or maintain status and control (Luke 22:25).[25] The grace present among believers leads through Christ to a new mutuality. Among Paul's most important changes to the benefactor tradition was an "economy of grace."[26] Based on the gospel, Paul reversed all relationships based on cultural convention, power, and status. In response to the public demands of the gospel, in the name of Jesus, Christians nonviolently and creatively sought the good and wholeness of the city where God had placed them (Phil. 2:4). By the cross (1 Cor. 1:18–2:10), urban believers were agents of God's peace.

By seeking the peace of the city, were Paul and the early church communities compromising their witness to the empire? Did they resist the imperial claims of the empire, claims that conflicted with the claims of Jesus as Lord? That Paul and the early church knew their message and their community were in conflict with the empire is clear.[27] By confessing Jesus as Lord, the church resisted the powers.[28] Even as a small and socially insignificant community, the church was a powerful witness in the city to God's new urban society, one built on the cross. That it was a church of suffering and martyrdom is not to be forgotten. And while the peace of the earthly city would not be pure or complete, it would be real.

25. Bockmuehl, *Jewish Law in Gentile Churches: Halakah and the Beginning of Public Ethics* (Edinburgh: T. & T. Clark, 2000), p. 123.

26. G. W. Peterman, *Paul's Gift from Philippi: Conventions of Gift-Exchange and Christian Giving* (Cambridge: Cambridge University Press, 1997); Stephen E. Fowl, "Know Your Context: Giving and Receiving Money in Philippians," *Interpretation* 56, no. 1 (January 2002): 45-58.

27. For a relevant discussion, see *Paul and Empire: Religion and Power in Roman Imperial Society*, ed. Richard A. Horsley (Harrisburg: Trinity Press International, 1997).

28. In "To Serve God and Rule the World," John Howard Yoder connects the practice of the church in Revelation to reflections on Jeremiah 29 (*The Royal Priesthood: Essays Ecclesiological and Ecumenical*, ed. Michael G. Cartwright [Grand Rapids: Eerdmans, 1994], pp. 128-40).

The Word in the City

Before moving forward, I want to call attention to some of the most direct ways in which the biblical material we have surveyed — and the perspectives of Wolterstorff, Winter, and Yoder — can help guide urban responsibility. How does biblical faith guide the people of God amidst the exile of the inner city?

First, *shalom* is a vision big enough for the city in all of its dimensions. As it guided the life of the exiles in Babylon and shaped the ministry of the early church and their everyday life in the city, so it remains a guiding image in kingdom life in the city today. Urban discipleship is comprehensive and critical for the well-being of the city.

Second, peacemaking forms a continuing way of mission engagement in a hostile and contested urban environment. It is among the ecclesial and public practices of the kingdom. Mission is God's call, inaugurated in Genesis, to be a "multidimensional" blessing to the nations (Gen. 12:1-3).[29] When we come to the New Testament church, we find this theme of seeking the good of the city to be central to God's universal mission of salvation.[30] In specific practices, it includes the exhortation "to do good to all people" (Gal. 6:10) and to "build up" our neighbors (Rom. 15:2). Urban settings are full of different power interests, competing ideas, and conflicting demands. Peacemaking, and in particular loving one's "enemies," not only puts the church in a different light in relationship to its neighbors but is also a means of social change.

Third, the church as a Eucharistic community is the basis for its witness of peacemaking. If Christ is the peace that forms the church and determines its identity, then the church as a peaceable community exists for the city. The church is a body renewed by Christ to represent hope for a broken world. Committed to reconciliation and the practices of repentance and forgiveness, it should not fail to recognize the possibility of peace for the inner city.

Finally, peacemaking enables the church to maintain the integrity of its witness and commitment to the city while operating in a pluralistic civic setting. Even where notions of the civic good are disputed and conflicted, civic participation need not mean a dilution of conviction or faith. Peacemaking is a form of social involvement that can certainly include resistance but also go beyond it. We now turn to the issue of how this relates to the church's calling

29. M. Daniel Carroll, "Blessing the Nations: Toward a Biblical Theology of Mission from Genesis," *Bulletin for Biblical Research* 10, no. 1 (2000): 17-34.

30. Philip H. Towner, "Romans 13:1-7 and Paul's Missiological Perspective: A Call to Political Quietism or Transformation?" in *Romans and the People of God: Essays in Honor of Gordon D. Fee on the Occasion of His 65th Birthday,* ed. Sven K. Soderlund and N. T. Wright (Grand Rapids: Eerdmans, 1999), pp. 149-69.

of servanthood in the inner city, and a refinement of the notion of its identity for urban responsibility in the public place.

CREATING SPACES OF GOD'S PEACE

Shalom is always God's work and a summons to discipleship, both a gift and a command. To cite Nicholas Wolterstorff once again,

> Shalom is both God's cause in the world and our human calling. Even though the full incursion of shalom into our history will be divine gift and not merely human achievement, even though its episodic incursion into our lives now also has a dimension of divine gift, nonetheless it is shalom that we are to work and struggle for. We are not to stand around, hands folded, waiting for shalom to arrive. We are workers in God's cause, his peace-workers. The *missio Dei* is *our* mission.[31]

When Thomas saw the wounds of the risen Christ and was drawn into Christ and his healing, Jesus said to him, "Peace be with you" (John 20:26). Similarly, the church by its gracious relations and activities is to offer God's peace to a hurting world. Sharing the peace is sharing the living and transforming Christ, faith meeting the culture at its points of deepest need. While always a gift of grace, peace will not come about in the Sandtowns of our world unless the church works at it intentionally and more tenaciously than the forces communities are up against. Our efforts have to be commensurate with the challenge.

An Interactive Model

How are specific Christian communities to bring Christ's peace to bear in very concrete social and residential locations? Much will depend upon how we understand the city and its workings. Peter Marcuse and Ronald van Kempen argue that we should not think of "*the* city" as if it were "a whole, organic entity."[32] Rather, we should treat it as a complex form with many differ-

---

31. Wolterstorff, *Until Justice and Peace Embrace*, p. 72.
32. Marcuse and van Kempen, "Conclusion: A Changed Spatial Order," in *Globalizing Cities: A New Spatial Order?* ed. Peter Marcuse and Ronald van Kempen (Oxford: Blackwell, 2000), p. 265.

ent "layers." These layers may include residential spaces, transportation patterns, and commercial areas. Accordingly, "Each layer shows the entire space of the city, but no one layer shows the complete city. Some layers reflect differences in usage, others differences in time, others differences in the components of the built environment. Each one reflects a divided city."[33]

Jane Jacobs identifies three types of "neighborhoods" in her classic study *The Death and Life of Great American Cities.*[34] The first is the city as a whole, the second is the street neighborhood, and the third is the city at the "district" or subcity size.[35] "Each of these kinds of neighborhoods has different functions," she points out, "but the three supplement each other in complex fashion. It is impossible to say which one is more important than the others. For success with staying power at any spot, all three are necessary."[36] While we will want to add the global "neighborhood" to Jacobs's framework, recognizing its all-demanding force, she is right to insist, as were Marcuse and van Kempen in a different way, that to have a positive impact on a city, it is crucial to think, live, and work at multiple levels or layers. Cities and neighborhoods are complex places, and to treat them otherwise can render peacemaking ineffective. At the same time, it is important not to lose sight of the city as a whole — especially its underlying social, political, and economic directions.

While an interactive model is required, it works best to begin with what Jacobs termed the street neighborhood,[37] while always taking into account the larger forces at play in the urban environment. Neighborhoods are the places of

---

33. Marcuse and van Kempen, "Conclusion," pp. 265-66.

34. Jacobs, *The Death and Life of Great American Cities* (New York: The Modern Library, 1993). This is a framework called attention to by Roger Sanjek, *The Future of Us All: Race and Neighborhood Politics in New York City* (Ithaca: Cornell University Press, 1998), pp. 2-4.

35. Jacobs, *The Death and Life of Great American Cities*, pp. 153-82.

36. Jacobs, *The Death and Life of Great American Cities*, p. 153.

37. Whether they spread out or go up, neighborhoods almost always have fuzzy boundaries. A helpful summary of the term "neighborhood" in relationship to community development can be found in Robert J. Chaskin, "Neighborhood as a Unit of Planning and Action," *Journal of Planning Literature* 13, no. 1 (August 1998): 11-30. Generally people identify their neighborhood on multiple levels. They move out concentrically from their immediate block, then to a two-to-three block area, and then to travel corridors. There are the "official" boundaries, drawn for planning purposes and political districting, and then there are the "working boundaries," informal and fluid in shape, that have been determined internally by the people themselves. For more on the importance of neighborhoods, see Ray Suarez, *The Old Neighborhood: What We Lost in the Great Suburban Migration, 1966-1999* (New York: Free Press, 1999); and Howard Hallman, *Neighborhoods: Their Place in Urban Life* (Beverly Hills: Sage Publications, 1984).

double Dutch and hoops, laughing and hanging out on the stoop, debate and friendship, dog-walking and the sounds of hip-hop, faith and struggle. They are geographies of face-to-face relationships and sites where social forces surface and can be identified. Many of the films of Spike Lee, such as *Do the Right Thing*, reveal the neighborhood as a complicated social and political space. In everyday terms, neighborhoods are experienced as both public and private spaces. Here is where life is redlined and the powers are at work. Engaging, understanding, challenging, and reforming the social, economic, and physical characteristics of local communities can bring *shalom* to people's lives. Vibrant neighborhoods are part of the *shalom* that God desires for the city. Beginning at the grass roots and moving upward may also be the most effective means of producing change in institutions and structures. That the public realm may be constructed on a history of violence only underscores the need for a robust Christian approach to urban peacemaking.

Into the Flow and Mix of the City

Christianity has always been, as the mission historian Andrew Walls argues, both a prisoner and a liberator of culture.[38] While the Christian faith is a distinctive tradition, it influences and is influenced by the cultural setting and other settings it inhabits. As Miroslav Volf observes, Christian communities dwell in "overlapping territories."[39] Believers live *in* Christ, yet do so in particular and diverse social settings. Just as the Corinthian believers lived in Christ in the city of Corinth (1 Cor. 1:2), so, for example, Christians live in Christ in New York and its particular communities.[40] Biblical faith promotes an identity that's centered in Christ yet situated in the city which God has called.

In the process of peacemaking, Christians will sometimes bless the social world, at other times denounce and stand in antithesis to it, and many times simply learn and benefit from the city as God's gift. Volf argues — cor-

38. Walls, *The Missionary Movement in Christian History: Studies in the Transmission of Faith* (Maryknoll: Orbis, 1996), pp. 3-15.

39. Miroslav Volf, *Exclusion and Embrace: A Theological Exploration of Identity, Otherness, and Reconciliation* (Nashville: Abingdon, 1996), pp. 207-11.

40. This discussion on difference and rootedness builds on two works of Miroslav Volf: "Theology, Meaning, and Power," in *The Future of Theology: Essays in Honor of Jürgen Moltmann*, ed. Miroslav Volf (Grand Rapids: Eerdmans, 1996), pp. 98-113; and "When Gospel and Culture Intersect: Notes on the Nature of Christian Difference," in *Pentecostalism in Context: Essays in Honor of William W. Menzies*, ed. Wonsuk Ma and Robert P. Menzies (Sheffield: Sheffield Academic Press, 1997), pp. 223-36.

rectly, I think — that faith makes an "internal" difference in a culture: "There is no single correct way to relate to a given culture as a whole, or even to its dominant thrust; there are only numerous ways of accepting, transforming, or replacing various aspects of a culture from within."[41] Volf's point on Christianity and culture relates equally to the city. Certainly there will be dimensions of urban life in need of transformation as well as areas of acceptance. None of this is simple or without risk, for the church is not invulnerable to the city, its systems and its structures. But engaging the city from within is key to renewing communities. There is redemptive energy and direction in the biblical images of salt, leaven, and light (Matt. 5:13-16).

This highlights once again the necessity of the church's having a vital relationship to the community, both theologically and institutionally. As Robert Linthicum expresses it, a church can see itself in relationship to the city in three different ways: as a church in the city, as a church for the city, or as a church with the city.[42] A church *in* a community has no real attachment to its neighborhood. The congregation probably commutes in and simply meets to worship there. This church usually views itself as a fortress and the neighborhood as the world of the forbidden streets. A church *for* a community recognizes its communal responsibility and develops programs and outreach efforts. But because it is not grounded in the experience of the people it is trying to reach, it fails. This church views itself as a savior of the community but engages the world of the street selectively. Both of these relational attitudes treat the community as the other and as helpless, and therefore will fail to promote holistic revitalization.

Linthicum's alternative proposal to these two inherently problematic models is a church *with* the community. This church incarnates itself within the community and becomes one with its neighbors in the struggle. The community defines the church's mission and identity. Weak, tentative, or even inappropriate attachments to the community are replaced by embrace and mutuality. Indeed, rightly framed, the church is not only *with* the community but *of* the community.[43] Here the church and the community work in mutu-

41. Volf, "Theology, Meaning, and Power," p. 101 (italics not replicated).

42. Linthicum, *Empowering the Poor: Community Organizing among the City's "Rag, Tag and Bobtail"* (Monrovia: MARC, 1991), pp. 21-30. For an analysis that uses "the streets" to define the church's relationship to the community, see Omar McRoberts, "Saving Four Corners: Religion and Revitalization in a Depressed Neighborhood," Ph.D. diss., Harvard University, 2000.

43. Jude Tiersma, "What Does It Mean to Be Incarnational When We Are Not the Messiah?" in *God So Loves the City: Seeking a Theology for Urban Mission*, ed. Charles Van Engen and Jude Tiersma (Monrovia: MARC, 1994), p. 24.

ality for reasons that grow out of their common history and their shared future. The church brings its faith commitments both to the questions that are asked and to the actions that are taken. It is involved in the mix, flow, and fray of community life, not isolated and removed. The church discerns its life in the life of the community. Such a church rejects a privileged moral, social, or even epistemological position (1 Cor. 2:1-2). It does not see itself as a savior, for it knows too well its own frailties and weaknesses. Rather, by way of the cross, by way of sharing suffering and hope (Rom. 8:17; Col. 1:24), sorrows and joys (2 Cor. 6:2), a church of the community pours itself out so that God's *shalom* can be more deeply experienced (2 Cor. 4:7-12).

Michel de Certeau's distinction between strategy and tactics is helpful for characterizing peacemaking in the inner city, at least at a comparative level. "Strategies," he argues, are actions that belong to the powerful and articulate a plan for mastering a place. "Tactics" are actions that take place in the absence of power, "maneuvers" that involve different isolated actions.[44] The diasporic shape of urban faith affirms this insight. Bringing peace to the inner city is not a matter of drawing up grand plans, but instead involves the daily improvisational practices of neighboring, prayer, and social commitment that establish signs of God's reign and hints of the pattern of the city to come. For peace to become more present in our most excluded neighborhoods, many things need to happen simultaneously. To this subject we now turn more directly.

PRESENCE, PRAYER, AND PUBLIC ACTIVITY

In this section we will examine the ways in which peacemaking serves the creation of spaces or geographies that more deeply reflect God's *shalom*, delight, and flourishing. To do so, let us return to Jeremiah's proposal to the exiles in 29:5-7. Eldin Villafañe has observed that this passage offers "an overarching, wholistic vision for the city," for it joins together "a theology of context, a theology of mission, and a theology of spirituality."[45] Indeed, this passage gives

---

44. Certeau, *The Practice of Everyday Life,* trans. Steven Rendall (Berkeley: University of California Press, 1984), pp. 34-39. The use of Certeau is suggested by Stanley Hauerwas, *After Christendom: How the Church Is to Behave If Freedom, Justice, and a Christian Nation Are Bad Ideas* (Nashville: Abingdon, 1991, 1999), pp. 15-18.

45. Villafañe, *Seek the Peace of the City: Reflections on Urban Ministry* (Grand Rapids: Eerdmans, 1995), p. 2. My categories also parallel those of Robert C. Linthicum, *City of God, City of Satan: A Biblical Theology of the Urban Church* (Grand Rapids: Zondervan, 1992), pp. 145-92.

us the basis on which to explore presence (context), prayer (spirituality), and public activity (mission). What unites these three things is the practical, spiritual, and material difference they can make in a local community. The results of implementing this paradigm can be transformational for the city as a whole.

Presence: Dwelling as Neighbors and Friends

In *American Ruins,* Camilo José Vergara makes the interesting proposal that members of a religious order might be the best group to occupy a vacant railroad station in Detroit, creating an alternative community that reclaims both the structure and the economic activity within it.[46] Christian history provides precedent for this proposal, not least in parts of the monastic movement. However, this doesn't go far enough. As the doctrine of the priesthood of all believers makes clear, all Christians — not just those in a special order — should find ways to dwell redemptively in the city. That this may also require new orders of lay and ordained religious to point the way does not take away from the principle.

To share as neighbors and friends in the everyday experiences of life, to invest as neighbors and friends in the development of others is both the extension and the foundation of *shalom.* It means to reject — as individuals, families, and churches — withdrawing into privileged social and economic enclaves inside and outside the city.[47] According to the imperative of Jeremiah, the task of faith is quite basic: "Build houses and settle down; plant gardens and eat what they produce. Marry and have sons and daughters. . . . Increase in number there; do not decrease" (29:5-6). People of biblical faith are called to live in the city, to raise their families there, and to share in the struggle for life and the things that make for peace.[48]

Social theory supports this claim. What Robert Putnam and others call social capital has been in recent years a subject of major interest in theories of urban decay and proposals of urban regeneration. The concept of social capital accents the effects of relationships on the well-being of the community.

46. Vergara, *American Ruins* (New York: Monacelli Press, 1999), pp. 56-59.
47. In *The Work of Nations: Preparing Ourselves for 21st-Century Capitalism* (New York: Alfred A. Knopf, 1991), Robert B. Reich warns against the "secession of the successful" into private and protected enclaves.
48. Families — not simply individuals — are key to healthy urban life, as the historian Kenneth T. Jackson notes in his op-ed piece entitled "Once Again, the City Beckons," *New York Times,* 30 March 2001, A-23.

That is, the more people build and remain in relationships of reciprocity, particularly in local institutions and associations, the greater the increase in trust that builds among them. This dynamic of trust, Putnam argues, enables shared economic, political, and civic advancement.[49] Social capital is considered a basis for local activism.[50] Social capital is unique in that the more people use it, the more of it everyone has access to. "The aspect of social capital that makes it a classic public good is its property of nonexcludability; that is, its benefits are available to all living within a particular community, and access to it cannot be restricted."[51] Of course, social capital can be used wrongly to serve the purposes of exclusion and oppression. It must intentionally be directed to serve the flourishing of others.

Typically — and incorrectly — social-capital theorists often picture inner-city neighborhoods as socially atomized, depleted of social capital resources.[52] This is a misleading depiction, because while there is no question that local institutions in the inner city have been harmed and that the social fabric has been torn, every neighborhood also has considerable strengths, capacities, and reserves of mutual responsibility and caring. Indeed, without strong relationships of caring, survival in the inner city would be impossible.

Many observers have also missed the significant role that congregations play in increasing social capital. Because they are based on relationships and social networks, churches are inherently rich in social capital, and are therefore one of the most natural resources for the renewal of community life.[53] Because churches are already organized and already have as their mission at least some expression of concern for the city, Ernesto Cortés Jr. is right when

49. Putnam, *Making Democracy Work: Civic Traditions in Modern Italy* (Princeton: Princeton University Press, 1993); and "The Prosperous Community: Social Capital and Public Life," *The American Prospect* 13 (Spring 1993): 35-42.

50. Marilyn Gittell et al., "Social Capital and Social Change," *Urban Affairs Review* 36, no. 2 (November 2000): 123-47. See also *Social Capital and Poor Communities*, ed. Susan Saegert, J. Philip Thompson, and Mark R. Warren (New York: Russell Sage Foundation, 2001).

51. Ichiro Kawachi, Bruce P. Kennedy, Kimberly Lochner, and Dorothy Prothrow-Stith, "Social Capital, Income Inequality, and Mortality," *American Journal of Public Health* 87, no. 9 (September 1997): 1496.

52. For example, see the report issued by the Committee for Economic Development, *Rebuilding Inner-City Communities: A New Approach to the Nation's Urban Crisis* (New York: Committee for Economic Development, 1995); and Robert Wuthnow, *Loose Connections: Joining Together in America's Fragmented Communities* (Cambridge: Harvard University Press, 1998), pp. 110-34.

53. Nancy Tatom Ammerman, *Congregation and Community* (New Brunswick: Rutgers University Press, 1997), pp. 362-67.

he says that they are considered a strong foundation for community organizing, a subject we will address in the next chapter.[54]

Two important biblical resources for the building of a stronger community life are the practices of neighboring and friendship. Neighborly commitment is central to the faith demands of the Old Testament. In a study of the wisdom book of Proverbs, Ronald Clements shows how neighboring was to be conceptualized and practiced in everyday life so that life in the city might be made better.[55] Throughout Proverbs, attention is paid to the inequalities that can cause fissures between neighbors and damage community life.[56] The sage is not naïve about the human condition. For example, Proverbs 14:20 observes, "The poor are shunned even by their neighbors, but the rich have many friends." The next proverb provides a corrective, a better way: "He who despises his neighbor sins, but blessed is he who is kind to the needy" (v. 21).

Patterns of communication are also an important theme in Proverbs.[57] Communication that promotes trust and respect between neighbors is exemplified in Proverbs 11:2, which reads, "A man who lacks judgment derides his neighbor, but a man of understanding holds his tongue." Neighboring in Proverbs entailed the daily work of building a just and supportive community characterized by trust. "Without such trust," Clements points out, "a healthy social environment could not be established, and where there was no such feeling of interdependence and solidarity *(ḥesed)* the very foundations of morality would be undermined."[58] In *ḥesed*, the mutual commitment to the flourishing of others, we find the glue for community.

According to the biblical material beyond Proverbs, neighboring is not only interpersonal but also social. For, as Walter Brueggemann points out, "The Deuteronomic tradition presents society as a neighborhood and enjoins

54. Cortés, "Reweaving the Fabric: The Iron Rule and the IAF Strategy for Power and Politics," in *Interwoven Destinies: Cities and the Nation,* ed. Henry G. Cisneros (New York: W. W. Norton, 1993), pp. 294-319.

55. Clements, "The Good Neighbour in the Book of Proverbs," in *Of Prophets' Visions and the Wisdom of Sages: Essays in Honour of R. Norman Whybray on His Seventieth Birthday,* ed. Heather A. McKay and David J. A. Clines, Supplement Series 162 (Sheffield: Journal for the Study of the Old Testament, 1992), 209-28. Texts which for Clement introduce the issue of neighboring include 3:27-29; 12:26; 16:29; 17:17; 18:24; and 27:10.

56. Other texts on inequality that Clements cites in "The Good Neighbour in the Book of Proverbs" are 6:1-3; 14:31; 17:5; 17:8; 19:4; 19:6; and 19:7 (pp. 218-22).

57. Additional texts on communication that Clements points to in "The Good Neighbour in the Book of Proverbs" include 11:9; 11:13; 19:5; 20:6; 24:28; 25:9-10; 25:17; and 26:18-19 (pp. 222-27).

58. Clements, "The Good Neighbour in the Book of Proverbs," pp. 223-24.

attitudes and policies that enhance neighborliness. Deuteronomy insists that economic life must be organized to ensure the well being of widows, orphans and immigrants. This response to dislocation insists that maintaining a public economy of compassion and justice is a way to move beyond despair."[59]

With this as background, the emphasis of New Testament passages on neighborly activity comes into sharper relief (i.e., Luke 10:29-37; Rom. 13:9-10; 15:2; Gal. 5:14; Eph. 4:25; James 2:8). A relationship with Christ, as the parable of the Good Samaritan expresses, is defined not by being a neighbor in the passive sense but by finding ways to cross boundaries and to be a neighbor to the afflicted in ways that advance their flourishing. While neighboring is important, Jesus teaches that a deeper goal of relationships is friendship:

> My command is this: Love each other as I have loved you. Greater love has no one than this, that one lay down his life for his friends. You are my friends if you do what I command. I no longer call you servants, because a servant does not know his master's business. Instead, I have called you friends, for everything that I learned from my Father I have made known to you. (John 15:12-15)

Friendship that is in imitation of Christ's friendship with women and men is both something of the peace that God desires and the relational bridge to the peace of the city.

Prayer: The Urban Future Belongs to the Intercessors

True hope for the future of the inner city is grounded in prayer. As Walter Wink reminds us, "History belongs to the intercessors."[60] Intercessory prayer is required if new alternatives are to flow into the "world" (Rev. 11:15) of the inner city. As Wink points out, "Even a small number of people, firmly committed to the new inevitability on which they have fixed their imaginations, can decisively affect the shape the future takes. These shapers of the future are the intercessors, who call out the future, the longed-for new present."[61] For Wink, prayer constitutes resistance against the powers. When Christians pray

---

59. Brueggemann, "Conversations among Exiles," *Christian Century*, 2-9 July 1997, p. 631.

60. Wink, *Engaging the Powers: Discernment and Resistance in a World of Domination* (Minneapolis: Fortress, 1992), p. 298.

61. Wink, *Engaging the Powers*, p. 299.

the Lord's Prayer, which recognizes the authority of God over the powers of the age, the hope of the kingdom over the fallen world, they declare resistance and a counterview of the city.

Prayer as kingdom activity is not the last hope for the inner city; it is the beginning of hope. This at least was the conviction of Jeremiah (Jer. 29:7; cf. Ps. 122). Without a spirituality grounded in biblical faith, which has as its center the life of prayer, it is easy to lose faith and deny that there is hope. The systemic and social forces of the city are simply overwhelming without the life of prayer and faith. Prayer is the cry from the depths to God, a plea that the world be different, that our children not die before their time, that our homes be decent, and that our hearts be made new.

One of the models Jesus gives for praying in a time of injustice is that of the widow in Luke 18:1-8. Jesus tells this story to show the disciples "that they should always pray and not give up" (v. 1). "Grant me justice against my adversary" (v. 3), the widow kept demanding of the judge, who "neither feared God nor cared about men" (v. 2). "No" was never an answer she accepted, and her persistence made all the difference:

> For some time he [the judge] refused. But finally he said to himself, "Even though I don't fear God or care about men, yet because this widow keeps bothering me, I will see that she gets justice, so that she won't eventually wear me out with her coming!" (vv. 4-5)

Jesus finishes the story by comparing the unjust judge to God: "And will not God bring about justice for his chosen ones, who cry out to him day and night? . . . I tell you, he will see that they get justice, and quickly" (vv. 7-8). When justice is required, when the daily struggle for life seems overwhelming, Jesus teaches us to pray and not give up in the face of oppression. Are slum landlords exploiting the neighborhood? Are merchants of death selling their wares? Are uncaring public officials in office? Is there conflict on the street? Jesus teaches us to pray about it.

For all the emphasis we are to place on our prayers in seeking the peace of the city, it is the intercessory prayer life of Jesus the high priest that is most important. Christ, according to the writer of Hebrews, "is able to save completely those who come to God through him, because he always lives to intercede for them" (7:25; cf. 7:26-28; John 17). Because of his own struggles and suffering here on earth, he knows the struggles and suffering of humanity. I think this explains why we have such a rich prayer tradition in communities of faith that are suffering. Christ intercedes on behalf of his people, with real knowledge and solidarity, and this recognition of Christ the high priest gives

119

strength and saving love in the midst of hardship.[62] Here is the basis for praying for our neighbors and one another.

In every circumstance, in every need, prayer is one of the most important ways that the church can serve the cause of God's peace in the city.

Public Activity: Putting Faith into Action

The heart of Jeremiah 29:7 — the command "to seek the peace of the city" — includes working to make practical improvements in the lives of families and the community. Peacemaking is a public responsibility. By this I mean not those things that are narrowly political (although, for example, voting is extremely important for inner-city communities) but faithful engagement with the larger issues that affect daily life, including public health and public services. This involves seeking to enhance life and to change neighborhood outcomes. To seek the peace of the city means that Christians are to be active participants — not spectators — working to bring alternative forms of urban life into being. Seeking the peace of the inner city therefore enjoins activity that enhances the social, physical, aesthetic, and economic world in which we dwell. It is transformational activity that responds to the context.

The diversity of ways that churches can actively seek the peace of their communities includes getting involved in local schools, beginning after-school programs, building reasonably priced houses for potential homeowners, and conducting public health initiatives. To seek the public peace of the city also entails working within the complicated webs of city government, real estate, education, and finance, to name but a few arenas. Public faith requires being in the mix and flow of a neighborhood's associational life, including the myriad of civic associations, improvement groups, community boards, PTAs, and block clubs that are found in the city. It means laboring alongside other churches and religious communities, perhaps forming coalitions with them. And it also means that churches should find ways to work closely with community-based organizations and networks. This is the work of being salt and light.

In seeking the peace of the city, we do well to avoid beginning with complex plans and major proposals. Certainly community plans are important, but they should emerge out of genuine local ownership and responsibility. Responding to real needs, they will have an ad hoc, organic character. This

---

62. James B. Torrance, *Worship, Community, and the Triune God of Grace* (Downers Grove: InterVarsity, 1996), pp. 43-50.

means that what the church is called to do and how it should go about answering that call will not always be clear. The church is to bring its faith into the messy world of the city because it is called to "look . . . to the interests of others" (Phil. 2:4).

Following the Jeremiah paradigm, I have argued that peacemaking is a vocation comprehensive enough to embrace and change the entire city, yet equally able to make a difference in the micro-neighborhood, on a single block. Specifically, the Jeremiah paradigm of presence, prayer, and public activity is to be a naturally interactive paradigm of ministry in the changing inner city.

THE DIFFERENCE OF PEACEMAKING

Abraham Kuyper (1837-1920), the Dutch politician and Reformed theologian, declared, "There is not a square inch [literally, thumb's breadth] in the whole of our human existence over which Christ, who is sovereign over *all,* does not cry: 'Mine.'"[63] Kuyper's assertion that Christ is Lord over every inch of the city is an affirmation of the thoroughly religious character of our calling and the conviction that our calling can potentially involve all aspects of the city. It also helps us recognize that seeking the peace of the inner city is a struggle that takes place literally inch by inch. The social and economic violence that created the inner city is not overcome with the simple announcement of a counter-narrative of peace, but rather requires the hard work of forging concrete new beginnings of *shalom.* Exclusion is too deeply woven into the fabric of the city for any other approach to be workable. The reality of *shalom* in terms of a more just and joyful community is secured only through conviction and agency, and then it awaits the consummation of peace found in the grace of the new city of God.

Christian communities need to learn to work in complex and differentiated urban settings, in the world as it is, while firmly maintaining normative beliefs and convictions. But how are Christians to live the truth of the gospel acceptably (without naiveté, manipulation, or alienation) in a fractured and increasingly market-driven civic setting? How can peacemaking be a noncoercive activity in a pluralistic city?

---

63. Kuyper, cited by Nicholas Wolterstorff in "Christian Political Reflection: Diognetian or Augustinian?" *Princeton Seminary Bulletin* 20, no. 2 (1999): 152.

Peacemaking without Manipulation

John McKnight has made the insightful argument that "serving" others can get in the way of building community. All too often, he argues, human service ends up being about our own needs and desires, not the underlying human fabric of a neighborhood.[64] What has been done in the name of development has regularly produced violence against the poor, the very persons such projects are "intended" to help. Let us also confess that faith as a social movement or a church project can deepen the alienation and marginalizaton of inner-city communities. Not all that is done in the name of peace is peaceable, and not every church is peaceable in its sense of responsibility. Urban ministry runs counter to the *shalom* of God when it begins and ends with "blaming the victim," when "community building," "evangelistic strategies," and "outreach ministry" are competitive and controlling, and when attempts are made to place people into a predefined order.

Whenever a church defines a community and its needs apart from the people of the community, a manipulative process is set in motion, one that often serves only the extension of the church's own interests, goals, and power. Language, agenda-setting, and unconsciously held notions of superiority are common conductors of a manipulative process. Here it is useful for us to recall Robert Linthicum's helpful distinctions between a church *for* the community and a church *with* the community. A church for the community can give in to the temptation to "lord it over others," underwriting and justifying sinful practices in the name of what is seemingly "best," "true," or "right."[65] When this occurs, the transmission of the faith may be curbed, the cultural encounter of the gospel with the city diluted, and the church's complicity in the violence of the city realized.

Inner-city neighborhoods are skilled in discerning between the well-intentioned and the self-serving. By necessity, they know and signal that they know the difference between sincere yet fumbling efforts (made by the church that is honestly attempting to be *with* the community) and insincere yet "professional" attempts of "service" (made by the church claiming to be "for" the community). Inner-city residents are highly gifted in the art of discernment; they have often watched people trying to import their agendas.

---

64. McKnight, *The Careless Society: Community and Its Counterfeits* (New York: Basic Books, 1995).

65. For a discussion of ways in which scriptural interpretation can be used to underwrite sinful practices, see Stephen E. Fowl, *Engaging Scripture: A Model for Theological Interpretation* (Oxford: Blackwell, 1998), pp. 32-61.

The analysis of the sage of Proverbs is relevant here: "A rich man may be wise in his own eyes, but a poor man who has discernment sees through him" (28:11). My experience is that inner-city communities do not judge as harshly the stumbling yet humble. Indeed, they are quite likely to show an amazing grace in response. But to that which is self-serving and manipulative in the name of "service," these communities react in ways that protect their own interests. At times it may seem like a community "buys in" to a development plan or a religious project, but in subtle ways usually invisible to outsiders, resistance to such manipulation is constantly taking place.[66]

First and foremost, every church or ministry undertaking a development project needs to be acutely aware of the power of sin and the potential presence of the powers within its corporate identity.[67] Christian claims for truth, Anthony Thiselton has noted, should be joined to the non-manipulative, servant life of Christ.[68] Truth becomes tainted by the interests of power and prestige when it is not matched with the cross and the doing of truth (1 John 3:21) in love (2 John 6).[69] Only relationships of solidarity and trust will foster healthy communication and provide the ground for genuine transformation.

The Way of Christ Crucified

Peacemaking, if it is truly to bring about peace, must follow in the steps and the way of the crucified Christ as it confronts and deals with its own power. As we have discussed, it is by way of the cross that the church is guided in its interaction with the networks, institutions, and layers that make up the complex fabric of the city. We can take this a step further and say that "cross bearing" is the way of social change.[70] Specifically, the church can learn both to negotiate its way in the city and to curb the problems of abusive power found even in peacemaking by intentionally adopting a model of Christian presence characterized by "gentleness and respect" (1 Pet. 3:15; cf. Eph. 4:2). The goal

---

66. Confirmation of this can be found in James C. Scott, *Domination and the Arts of Resistance: Hidden Transcripts* (New Haven: Yale University Press, 1990).

67. William Stringfellow was quite aware of this. See *A Keeper of the Word: Selected Writings of William Stringfellow*, ed. Bill Wylie Kellerman (Grand Rapids: Eerdmans, 1994), pp. 262-65.

68. Thiselton, *Interpreting God and the Postmodern Self: On Meaning, Manipulation, and Promise* (Grand Rapids: Eerdmans, 1995), pp. 19-26.

69. Thiselton, *Interpreting God and the Postmodern Self*, pp. 19-26, 36-39.

70. Yoder, *For the Nations*, p. 147.

of urban mission or community ministry is not to obtain power or influence, nor can it ever be to "take over" the neighborhood. Rather, the church's goal is to be God's peace in the broken places and to bear witness to the kingdom of God. It sides not with the privileged and powerful but with those the world counts as nothing. This is the politics of Christ and the cross.

Miroslav Volf has called such an approach the "soft difference."[71] Developing this insight in an important reading of 1 Peter, he writes,

> I do not mean a *weak* difference, for in 1 Peter the difference is anything but weak. It is strong, but it is not hard. Fear for oneself and one's identity creates hardness. The difference that joins itself with hardness always presents the other with a choice: either submit or be rejected, either "become like me or get away from me." In the mission to the world, hard difference operates with open or hidden pressures, manipulation, and threats. A decision for a soft difference, on the other hand, presupposes a fearlessness which 1 Peter repeatedly encourages his readers to assume (3:14; 3:6). People who are secure in themselves — more accurately, who are secure in their God — are able to live the soft difference without fear. They have no need either to subordinate or damn others, but can allow others space to be themselves. For people who live the soft difference, mission fundamentally takes the form of witness and invitation. They seek to win others without pressure or manipulation, sometimes even "without a word" (3:1).[72]

If it is true, as argued earlier, that the ethic of 1 Peter is informed by the Jeremiah paradigm, then it enriches Volf's proposal of "soft difference" in at least one respect. The church's witness in the *city* is to be marked by convictions of truth that bear witness to Christ and create new ways of being community (cf. Col. 3:8-17).

Not only should urban faith be soft, gentle, and humble in its witnessing and often non-conforming difference; it must be alive in practice. This has crucial apologetic value for the urban church in the "post-modern" inner city. Christ's command that his followers "let your light shine before men, that that they may see your good deeds and praise your Father in heaven" (Matt. 5:16) centers this call in the Gospels. In a parallel way, the moral and civic focus of 1 Peter "points to an understanding of public moral persuasion

---

71. Volf, "Soft Difference: Theological Reflections on the Relation Between Church and Culture in 1 Peter," *Ex Auditu* 10 (1994): 15-30.

72. Volf, "Soft Difference," p. 24.

as achieved primarily in Christian *praxis,* rather than philosophical or rhetorical argument."[73] Oriented to the plight of the non-persons in the urban world, Christianity is to offer living expressions of its hope founded and centered in Jesus Christ. Upon this basis it will be asked to give reasons for the hope to which it holds fast (1 Pet. 3:16).

Making a Difference

The church gathers, declares, and then proceeds to witness to God's promise of *shalom.* Peacemaking as healing, proclaiming, and reversing injustice is not a utopian project; its labors work together to serve the kingdom of God (Matt. 9:35-36). Because it is grounded in presence, prayer, and public activity, it is work that "makes a difference." It is work that cannot perfect the community but can certainly make it better. Nicholas Wolterstorff makes this point in his reflections on ministry to children: "It is your calling to struggle to make the world a place in which their innocent, vulnerable playfulness is appropriate. . . . Be under no illusion that your efforts will bring about the holy city for children. But likewise, do not despair of making a difference. For it is God's cause; and God will take both your fumbling and your skillful efforts and use them as building stones for God's holy city."[74] Faithfulness toward the advance of more whole communities, not the development or promise of perfect ones, is the measure of peacemaking.

What differences would *shalom* make? Nourished by the guiding image of *shalom,* not the logic of the market, in a neighborhood where God's peace runs like a deep current, weary families would find new strength and joy. Every gift would be appreciated and called into service. Those able to work would have employment that both served the common good and provided a living wage. Miserable housing would be a thing of the past, replaced by homes offering beauty and safety. Vacant land would be turned into gardens filled with flowers and vegetables, reclaimed for local economic development, or designated for affordable housing. Children would attend schools that nurtured the whole person, mind and spirit, enabling them to navigate the world successfully. Streets would be safe, and the innocent would not fear those who protect. No more would the emergency room be a doctor's office, for quality health services would be personal and available when needed. An

---

73. Bockmuehl, *Jewish Law in Gentile Churches,* p. 191.

74. Wolterstorff, "Playing with Snakes: A Word to Seminary Graduates," *Perspectives* 13, no. 5 (May 1998): 11.

atmosphere of neighborly commitment would reinforce bonds of trust. And by virtue of all of these things being signs of *shalom,* at the center of this experience would be the acknowledgment of God as the giver of this gift, the One in whose service human beings are called to live responsibly. This is how the neighborhoods of the city should work.

To be peacemakers in the American inner city is the opposite of giving in to apathy, of razing neighborhoods, of imploding buildings, of excluding the poor, of insulating oneself from risk. To seek the peace of the city is to have a vision of friendship and community and a commitment to justice, joy, forgiveness, and salvation. It is to engage in kingdom work in the city based on a distinctive understanding of what it means to be the people of God, an understanding that expresses itself in love and sacrifice in service to others, especially the most vulnerable. The church is the community that takes as its watchword Paul's injunction to the Colossians: "Let the peace of Christ rule in your hearts, since as members of one body you were called to peace" (3:15). As a model of God's new urban social order, the church signals an alternative to all forms of exclusion.

In the world of the global inner city, the church's practice of peacemaking is central to its calling. Joining in God's story of redemption, Christians are to be active agents of peace, to make serious and thoughtful faith-informed contributions to the city, signaling that something of "eternal consequence" motivates them — "the God who seeks the great spiritual and physical welfare of the city."[75] Living and working on the edges of the city, inspired by the perspective of the new city of peace and following in the way of the cross, Christians are to confess that Jesus not only rules over every square inch of the city but also calls its inhabitants to a life of peaceable activity in his name and in his way (Matt. 5:39-41; 1 Pet. 2:21). Jesus has not abandoned the inner city; he has come to redeem it. Performed in the name of Jesus, the things that make for peace witness to the grace of God and the promise of the new creation. "Blessed are the peacemakers" (Matt. 5:9).

---

75. Bruce D. Winter, "The Public Place for the People of God," *Vox Evangelica* 25 (1995): 15.

CHAPTER 4

Out of the Ruins

"Let's get to work!" the people proclaim in unison. An urban community is in serious distress — its population depleted, its economic life depressed, its buildings reduced to rubble. The trials of daily life are intense, the struggle to keep hope difficult. Amidst this reality, a small group of people, recognizing the spiritual and economic dimensions of their plight, organize themselves to rebuild their city and communal life. To reach this goal, they pool their skills, marshal resources both public and private, hold back opposing forces, watch over their labors, pray without ceasing, and resolve internal conflicts. Others said it couldn't be done, but as they overcome the many obstacles that face them, a new urban community rises up on the old foundation.

How should we read this story? Is it a past event that tells of rebuilding a ruined Jerusalem, a story that we find recounted in the book of Nehemiah? Or is it a story unfolding today amidst the ruins of America's inner-city neighborhoods? Or is it a story of both past and present? Just as Jerusalem came back from "heaps of rubble" (Neh. 4:2), so today we are seeing abandoned neighborhoods find new life. Rebuilding the city was a challenge then, and in ways both similar and different, it is a challenge today. This chapter takes up the commitments, tasks, and values that go into rebuilding inner-city neighborhoods. My aim is to explore our participation in the drama of God's work of urban restoration.

What does rebuilding mean in an age of information and globalization?

Situated between global forces that value communities only as they are important in economic terms, rebuilding must mean new spiritual directions and modes of community creativity. Rebuilding will include naming suffering, recovering the foundations of hope, and strengthening local institutions.

In the literature and in the field, community development is generally defined in rationally planned, technical terms, and is therefore also determined by the presuppositions of the modern project and the imperatives of the market.[1] Thus community development applied to the inner city is focused on such tasks as creating affordable housing, establishing new economic activity, and increasing the vigor of local social connections.[2]

---

1. Thus the conclusion of Herbert J. Rubin in *Renewing Hope within Neighborhoods of Despair: The Community-Based Development Model* (Albany: State University of New York Press, 2000): "Community-based development organizations are not about leading an in-the-streets revolution, but they are about increasing social equity and demonstrating that a market economy can still have a heart. By reshaping the underlying symbols of a capitalist society to serve a social need, community-based development organizations end up renewing hope in neighborhoods of despair" (p. 274). Note further the following representative definitions of community development. In the Introduction to *Urban Problems and Community Development,* ed. Ronald F. Ferguson and William T. Dickens (Washington, D.C.: The Brookings Institution, 1999), the two editors provide an up-to-date definition of community development: "asset building that improves the quality of life among residents of low- to moderate-income communities" (p. 5). In "Reintegrating Disadvantaged Communities into the Fabric of Urban Life: The Role of Community Development," *Housing Policy Debate* 6, no. 1 (1995): 169-230, Avis C. Vidal casts community development as a force to reintegrate "disadvantaged" urban communities into the fabric of urban life. In *Democracy's Discontent: America in Search of a Public Philosophy* (Cambridge: The Belknap Press of Harvard University Press, 1996), Michael J. Sandel finds in community development a source to help remediate the decline in active citizenship (pp. 333-34).

2. For surveys of community development trends, see *Revitalizing Urban Neighborhoods,* ed. W. Dennis Keating, Norman Krumholz, and Philip Star (Lawrence: University of Kansas Press, 1996); Ferguson and Dickens, eds., *Urban Problems and Community Development*; Pierre Clavel, Jessica Pitt, and Jordan Yin, "The Community Option in Urban Policy," *Urban Affairs Review* 32, no. 4 (March 1997): 435-58; Richard C. Hula, Cynthia Y. Jackson, and Marion Orr, "Urban Politics, Governing Nonprofits, and Community Revitalization," *Urban Affairs Review* 32, no. 4 (March 1997): 459-89; Avis C. Vidal, "Can Community Development Re-Invent Itself?: The Challenge of Strengthening Neighborhoods in the 21st Century," *Journal of the American Planning Association* 63, no. 4 (Autumn 1997): 429-38; Herbert J. Rubin, "There Aren't Going to Be Any Bakeries Here If There Is No Money to Afford Jelly Rolls: The Organic Theory of Community Based Development," *Social Problems* 41, no. 3 (August 1994): 401-24; Rubin, *Renewing Hope within Neighborhoods of Despair*; G. Thomas Kingsley, Joseph B. McNeely, and James O. Gibson, *Community Building Comes of Age* (Baltimore: The Development Training Institute; Washington, D.C.: The Urban Institute, 1997); Robert J. Chaskin, "Building Community Capacity: A Definitional Framework and Case

Because all truth is God's truth and because the city belongs to God, Christians will draw ideas, practices, and perspectives from a wide variety of sources, including the perspective just sketched. Re-creating community is part of our shared creational identity. Therefore, Christian theory and practice are not to be isolated from the field, although they must be discerning and at times stand in vivid contrast to it, especially when it comes to practices that support displacement and marginalization.

At this point I want to explain some of my basic understandings. When I talk about *community* development, I am assuming that the people of the community are the primary agents of action. The community is the primary locus of analysis and planning, and community members determine the type and the pace of change that will affect their families, their neighbors, and their economic life. When I emphasize community *development,* I am not referring to charity, relief, or compassion, but to focused activity that establishes a healthier and more just community. The emphasis is not on programs as ends in themselves or on the renewal of place apart from people, but on the development of people and the celebration of their gifts and callings in the context of their social and material world. Because people exist in a world of structures, community development focuses on renewing the basic communal structures through which people live their lives. While the use of "development" is not without significant problems, as post-development theory rightly suggests, it still has value in describing our human responsibility for cultural renewal.

What is it that Christianity brings to inner-city community development? The practice of Christian community development puts the energy and imagination of the kingdom to work for the peace of the city. Put another way, community development is peaceable work that generates practical ways of living toward a healthier, more just, and more joyful life with our neighbors and before God. Here we meet ecclesiology, the importance of the church as an institutional and spiritual base, for it is in the church that we should be able to learn what transformation and holism mean and how they can be sustained, and it is in this social body that worship, common life, witness, prayer, gospel renewal, and the tasks of doing justice and maintaining hope are united.

As I have suggested, community development and neighborhood revital-

---

Studies from a Comprehensive Community Initiative," *Urban Affairs Review* 36, no. 3 (January 2001): 291-323; and Xavier De Souza Briggs and Elizabeth J. Mueller, *From Neighborhood to Community: Evidence on the Social Effects of Community Development* (New York: Community Development Research Center, New School for Social Research, 1997).

ization are part of the broader cultural responsibility and activity of being bearers of God's image that are bound up with the potential of creation (Gen. 1:26-28). Thus, using the words of Harvie M. Conn and Manuel Ortiz, we can speak of an "urban mandate."[3] Because cities are not a divine afterthought but are part of the original potential of creation, urban stewardship that increases flourishing in the urban environment is a covenant responsibility.[4] To continue the creation theme: rebuilding the broken urban habitat, reforming its structures of inequality and exclusion, is part of making right God's creation (Ps. 146; cf. Pss. 58:12; 61:4; cf. Amos 9:11-15); it is responsible activity that addresses the depths of the Fall. The positive identification of the creation should not be used to justify and harden the existing urban social order. Rather, Christian involvement in rebuilding should serve as a witness to the hope of an urban world of love and right relationships to come — a new creation.

Theologies of liberation have sought to remind us, by way of retrieving the Exodus event and the prophetic Christ, that a just world depends on Christ's identification with the marginalized, on dismantling the structures of racism, oppression, and injustice. They are theologies of life that affirm and draw on God as Deliverer and Jesus as Savior, and trust in God's Word that the liberation of the oppressed is an integral hope of the kingdom. However, in the inner city, the image of post-exilic reconstruction may not only be more common, but may also be more constructively appropriate than the liberation motif of the Exodus (Exod. 19:4, 5).[5] In vernacular ways, we see this when the people of a community are taking responsibility and initiative for creating a healthier and more whole world in which to live, work, and raise their families. Social analysis is not unimportant, nor are the sources of injustice, but the practical work of building community is in the foreground here.

The God who delivers through the Exodus is the same God who creates something new out of the ruins in Nehemiah. The one who came as the op-

---

3. Conn and Ortiz, *Urban Ministry: The Kingdom, the City, and the People of God* (Downers Grove: InterVarsity, 2001), p. 87.

4. In "The Garden and the Plaza: Biblical Images of the City" (*Interpretation* 54, no. 1 [January 2000]), William P. Brown and John T. Carroll observe, "The city is deemed a place for people, like saplings, to grow and flourish. . . . The city embodies life in communion, and it requires deliberate and patient cultivation, the fruits of which are justice and peace" (p. 10). Though not directly oriented to the city, an excellent discussion of a theology of culture that emphasizes the physicality of human responsibility is found in William A. Dyrness, *The Earth Is God's: A Theology of American Culture* (Maryknoll: Orbis, 1997), pp. 58-85.

5. For reflections on the relationship between black liberation theology and the ministry of Pentecostal churches, see Cheryl J. Sanders, *Saints in Exile: The Holiness Pentecostal Experience in African American Religion and Culture* (New York: Oxford, 1996), pp. 114-15.

pressed one to set people free is also the one who came as redeemer of the city to create a new community. Therefore, alongside the imperative "Let my people go" is the imperative "Let us rebuild" — and we have a responsibility to reclaim these words. Not only liberation but also cultural activity are Christian mandates for the *shalom* of the inner city.[6]

The challenge of rebuilding is one facing diverse communities around the world. The significance of community rebuilding as an expression of Christian responsibility and witness is also increasingly clear in the Southern hemisphere. For example, we find in African Christian thought "a quest for a 'theology of reconstruction' to address the social and political ills of the continent."[7]

My approach in this chapter is first to present a reading of the Nehemiah story. Nehemiah not only discloses the experience that many urban communities have undergone, but also, perhaps more than any other portion of the biblical text, helps awaken memory and determination for reviving abandoned urban communities.[8] Such a reading of Nehemiah arises from and urges the formation of intentional communities of faith whose everyday life and witness corresponds to the text's call to be agents of urban transformation. This elaboration leads to a discussion of dynamics of community development, followed by a concluding reflection on the Spirit's work in the rebirth of community.

ENGAGING NEHEMIAH

Numerous biblical motifs can serve to support, empower, and mobilize people to engage the social and political realities of their world. But as the story of a spiritual and social movement toward a new urban community, Nehe-

6. For a highly relevant discussion, see Nicholas Wolterstorff, *Until Justice and Peace Embrace* (Grand Rapids: Eerdmans, 1983), pp. 42-68, 72, 124.

7. Kwame Bediako, "African Christian Thought," in *The Oxford Companion to Christian Thought*, ed. Adrian Hastings (Oxford: Oxford University Press, 2000), p. 9 [8-10]. On the global trend, see Robert J. Schreiter, *The New Catholicity: Theology Between the Global and the Local* (Maryknoll: Orbis, 1997), pp. 113-14. For considerations of the South African story, see Charles Villa-Vicencio, *A Theology of Reconstruction: Nation-Building and Human Rights* (Cambridge: Cambridge University Press, 1992); and Noko Frans Kekana, "The Church and the Reconstruction of South Africa," *Exchange* 28, no. 1 (January 1999): 41-59.

8. Perhaps the most prominent example of Nehemiah invoked in name and spirit is the Nehemiah housing program, first developed in East New York. A stirring account of this program and a congregation central to it is found in Samuel G. Freedman, *Upon This Rock: The Miracles of a Black Church* (New York: HarperCollins, 1993), pp. 307-44.

miah is one of the most important. In particular, Nehemiah recounts a community's movement from tears of loss to tears of joy, from displacement to a new world of dignity before God. The guiding vision of the work is *shalom*, the flourishing of the city of Jerusalem. Nehemiah is profoundly a story about a people struggling to make God's peace more present in the city (Neh. 2:10; cf. Ps. 122:6-9).[9] It is a story about the ways in which the convictions and practice of faith can inhabit and redefine the city.

Stories draw us into a drama, and as a narrative text, Nehemiah does this powerfully. In their essay "Nehemiah as Cultural Revitalization: An Anthropological Perspective,"[10] Kenneth G. Tollefson, an anthropologist, and H. G. M. Williamson, an Old Testament specialist, show that when the cultural revitalization theory of Anthony F. C. Wallace[11] is placed alongside the story of Nehemiah, it reveals an identifiable pattern of events that ultimately leads to community revitalization. Similarly, the missiologist and community organizer Robert Linthicum has explored the ways in which Nehemiah unfolds as an account of community revitalization, drawing wonderful applications to the work of urban community transformation.[12] Perhaps most significantly, Nehemiah is important to us because it is Scripture, and therefore the address of God to our world.[13]

A number of different social-movement theories could be useful in this discussion, but I will draw on Wallace's model — though not rigidly. For

---

9. In a recent article entitled "The Songs of Ascents and Nehemiah" (*Journal for the Study of the Old Testament* 75 [1997]: 43-58), M. D. Goulder proposes that there is a close and textually responsive relationship between Nehemiah and the Songs of Ascents (Psalms 120–134). Goulder argues that each one of these psalms is a celebratory response to a part of Nehemiah. One example of the connections that Goulder finds is between Psalm 122 and Nehemiah 2, with both texts emphasizing the peace or good of the city (p. 49). On the basis of these specific texts, I think Goulder's argument has significant merit.

10. Tollefson and Williamson, "Nehemiah as Cultural Revitalization: An Anthropological Perspective," *Journal for the Study of the Old Testament* 56 (1992): 41-68. This essay builds on their previous Nehemiah scholarship. See Kenneth G. Tollefson, "The Nehemiah Model for Christian Missions," *Missiology: An International Review* 15, no. 1 (January 1987): 31-55; and H. G. M. Williamson, *Ezra, Nehemiah*, WBC 16 (Waco: Word, 1985).

11. Anthony F. C. Wallace, "Revitalization Movements," *American Anthropologist* 58, no. 2 (April 1956): 264-81.

12. Linthicum, *Empowering the Poor: Community Organizing among the City's "Rag, Tag, and Bobtail"* (Monrovia: MARC, 1991); and *City of God, City of Satan: A Biblical Theology of the Urban Church* (Grand Rapids: Zondervan, 1991), pp. 193-229.

13. Kevin J. Vanhoozer, "The Voice and the Actor: A Dramatic Proposal about the Ministry and Minstrelsy of Theology," in *Evangelical Futures: A Conversation on Theological Method*, ed. John G. Stackhouse Jr. (Grand Rapids: Baker, 2000), pp. 61-106.

Wallace, revitalization is a "deliberate, organized, conscious effort by members of a society to construct a more satisfying culture."[14] Every individual has a "mazeway,"[15] an image or view of what society and culture should look like. When the "real world" doesn't conform to this view, stress is the inevitable result. When this individual stress builds and becomes a kind of communal stress, collective action is often taken against it. The goal is to change both mazeways and the actual system in such a way that community can be transformed. According to Wallace, "the effort to work a change in mazeway and 'real' system together so as to permit more effective stress reduction is the effort of revitalization; and the collaboration of a number of persons in such an effort is called a revitalization movement."[16]

By Wallace's account, revitalization is marked by six events: (1) the *mazeway [or worldview] reformulation* — usually that of an individual; (2) the *communication* of this vision to others, and their acceptance of it; (3) the *organization* of people around the goal of this vision; (4) the *adaptation* of the vision in response to resistance and in response to the patterns of the community; (5) wide acceptance of this new view of community, resulting in *cultural transformation;* and finally (6) the *routinization* of the transformative changes made.[17] Wallace's theory has certain underlying problems, including his reductionistic assumptions about religion, and his failure to account for the a priori strengths of a culture. Other models that account for networks, social actors, and different tools of social change are in order. Nonetheless, the general outline of his theory can be very helpful in drawing attention to the narrative purposes of the Nehemiah story.

In Tollefson and Williamson's application of Wallace's theory to Nehemiah, the six revitalization phases and their correspondence in the Nehemiah story are as follows: (1) mazeway reformulation in the vision of a covenant society (1:1-10); (2) communication through sharing the vision (1:11–2:20, esp. 2:17-18); (3) organization through leaders and groups (3:1-32); (4) adaptation to opposition and factionalism (4:1–7:4); (5) cultural transformation through the restructuring of society (7:5–10:39); and (6) routinization through the integration of changes into community life (11:1–13:31).[18] When Nehemiah is read this way, it becomes clear that it is a story of community revitalization.

---

14. Wallace, "Revitalization Movements," p. 265.
15. Wallace, "Revitalization Movements," p. 266.
16. Wallace, "Revitalization Movements," p. 267.
17. Wallace, "Revitalization Movements," pp. 270-75.
18. Tollefson and Williamson, "Nehemiah as Cultural Revitalization," pp. 49-61.

A parallel to this reading is found in a literary approach to the text, a strategy that treats Nehemiah as a coherent whole. In her important study, Tamara Cohn Eskenazi puts forward the thesis that Nehemiah (along with Ezra) "weds people, city, and book and sets forth patterns and expectations for its own era and for subsequent generations. The book advocates a vision of reality in which community replaces heroes, the house of God is expanded, and the word of God is accessible to all through documents that the community must follow."[19] These themes — leadership from the grass roots, the sacredness of urban space, and rebuilding as the enactment of Scripture — will be helpful in illuminating the reasons for different actions and points of view within Nehemiah.

Ultimately what I intend to offer is an interpretation of Nehemiah that stands in continuity with God's drama of redeeming the city and the story of the kingdom of God.[20] This reading will seek to connect the biblical story with locally embodied faith and praxis. As Stephen E. Fowl points out, "Christian interpretation of scripture is primarily [seen as] an activity of Christian communities in which they seek to generate and embody their interpretations of scripture so that they may fulfill their ends of worshipping and living faithfully before the triune God."[21] The reading that I offer, one that comes out of a belief in the text as Scripture and is confirmed by communal experience, is intended to serve communities who, under the Spirit, are seeking the peace of the city.

Reading Nehemiah

Hearing a Call

Nehemiah begins with Jerusalem abandoned and virtually destroyed, its stately stature reduced to rubble. As a group of travelers reported to Nehemiah, "The wall of Jerusalem is broken down, and its gates have been burned with fire" (1:3; cf. 2:2). The consequence of a destroyed wall meant the loss of physical safety for the city's remaining inhabitants, as well as the

19. Eskenazi, *In an Age of Prose: A Literary Approach to Ezra-Nehemiah*, SBL Monograph Series 36 (Atlanta: Scholars Press, 1985), p. 185.

20. On this, see the work of N. T. Wright, which emphasizes Israel's exile and restoration. In particular, see *Jesus and the Victory of God*, vol. 2 of Christian Origins and the Question of God (Minneapolis: Fortress, 1996), pp. 126-27.

21. Fowl, *Engaging Scripture: A Model for Theological Interpretation* (Oxford: Blackwell, 1998), p. 161.

loss of the economic and political activity that took place at the gates. In fact, reducing the wall to rubble symbolized the breaking of the bonds of community.[22] The city was becoming an urban desert, the opposite of a city. Disorder had replaced order, and shame, not pride, was the result.[23] Dominated by foreign powers, the people of God were estranged not only from their city but also from their covenant relationship with God and one another.[24]

Nehemiah held the important position of cupbearer to the king; he was a high-ranking official who served the king his wine. When he heard the news, he "sat down and wept . . . mourned and fasted and prayed" (1:4). In the tradition of "tearful prophets" like Jeremiah, Nehemiah was brought to tears by what he learned. Addressing God in prayer, he invoked a past filled with the unfolding of God's covenant faithfulness, a memory that anchored the future (1:5-11). Serving as a prologue for the communal process that lay ahead, Nehemiah's prayer centered the restoration of community on the faithfulness of God to the people and the city:

> "O LORD, God of heaven, the great and awesome God, who keeps his covenant of love with those who love him and obey his commands, let your ear be attentive and your eyes open to hear the prayer your servant is praying before you day and night for your servants, the people of Israel." (1:5-6)

Nehemiah sought a solution to the crisis in the city not through personal industry or technical prowess but in the presence of an engaged and faithful God.

What Nehemiah said next in his prayer is no doubt one of the most perplexing admissions to the Western individualistic mind-set: "I confess the sins we Israelites, including myself and my father's house, have committed against you" (1:6). Nehemiah "repented" over the decline of Jerusalem, situating his life and the lives of his family within a framework of corporate responsibility.[25] Although Nehemiah was not present — not even born — when things went wrong and the exile began, he acknowledged a transgenerational responsibility.

Knowing what you want and when to ask for it can be everything in

22. Tollefson and Williamson, "Nehemiah as Cultural Revitalization."

23. Douglas Green, "Nehemiah," unpublished paper, Westminster Theological Seminary, n.d.

24. Tollefson and Williamson, "Nehemiah as Cultural Revitalization," p. 49.

25. For an exploration of this issue, see Joel S. Kaminsky, *Corporate Responsibility in the Hebrew Bible*, JSOT Supplement Series 196 (Sheffield: Sheffield Academic Press, 1995).

community development. Discerning what God wanted for the city and taking the risks of embodied intercession was even more crucial for Nehemiah. As cupbearer to the king, Nehemiah had access to a person who could open doors, and he waited for the right moment to share his sense of calling for the city's rebuilding. It is quite possible that had Nehemiah spoken up precipitously, had he presented an idea without a basic plan, he would have been faced with rejection before the project could even have gotten off the ground. Instead, Nehemiah waited for just the right moment before the king (2:1). Could it be that the start of a new year, a traditional occasion for the king's generosity, was such a time?[26]

When Nehemiah brought the king his wine, the king wanted to know why Nehemiah looked grim. Setting aside thoughts of self-protection, Nehemiah replied, "Why should my face not look sad when the city where my fathers are buried lies in ruins, and its gates have been destroyed by fire?" (2:3). In reply, the king asked, "What is it you want?" (2:4). Nehemiah then articulated the plight of his people and a vision for community: "If it pleases the king and if your servant has found favor in his sight, let him send me to the city in Judah where my fathers are buried so that I can rebuild it" (2:5).

Gaining commitments of support was critical. So Nehemiah asked for and received "letters to the governors of Trans-Euphrates, so that they will provide me safe conduct until I arrive in Judah" (2:7) and "a letter to Asaph, keeper of the king's forest, so that he will give me timber to make beams for the gates of the citadel by the temple and for the city wall and for the residence I will occupy" (2:8).

Without drawing any attention to his project, Nehemiah arrived in Jerusalem and surveyed the conditions (2:11-16). What he found was a grim situation that only confirmed earlier reports (2:17a; 1:2-3). The physical skin of the city was in ruin, the population had dwindled precipitously, and the realities of economic and spiritual distress were daunting. Still, a small community of faith had held their ground, unwilling to give up on their city.

Beginning to Take On the Odds

The next step Nehemiah took was to call a community-wide meeting, a public forum in which the people could discuss their situation and tell their stories. "You see the trouble we are in," Nehemiah told them. "Come, let us rebuild the wall of Jerusalem" (2:17). Rebuilding the wall would be the catalytic action that would lead to the renewal of the entire city. By inviting the people

26. H. G. M. Williamson, *Ezra, Nehemiah,* WBC 16 (Waco: Word, 1985), p. 178.

to meet together (2:17) and sharing his personal story (2:18), Nehemiah developed a vision for urban rebuilding based not on his individual calling but on an invitation to work together for the greater good — for God, their families, and their community. As H. G. M. Williamson points out, "He does not simply announce what he intends doing, nor force his will on the audience. Rather . . . he invites the people's participation in the fulfillment of God's call."[27]

Thus community storytelling led to collective action so that a new story might be written. In a powerful assumption of community responsibility and public citizenship, the people of the city came to a consensus that now was the time to "arise and build": "'Let us start the rebuilding.' So they began this good work" (2:18).

Once this task of rebuilding the wall and the city had been clearly articulated, a challenging yet achievable project, it created its own energy, enabling people to do more than they thought they could. It would be the catalytic event of their new story.

A Community Becomes Organized

As a narrative, Nehemiah 3 proceeds slowly. Instead of leaving it at "they went to work," the text names many of the individuals and families involved. As a narrative style, such deliberation highlights the breadth and depth of community involvement in the rebuilding of the city. Giving attention to the hands of laborers stood out in a world of credit-takers. As Tollefson and Williamson note, "While most political leaders tend to record the significance of their accomplishments, here it is the work of the people that is highlighted."[28] Public officials had helped to set the stage, but it was the people who worked together to accomplish the objectives, and their names would not be lost.[29]

In his commentary on Nehemiah, Williamson notes that the people were organized into about forty groups that were deployed simultaneously around the public project. Drawn together through geography, family networks, community relationships, and professional guild affiliations, each "association" focused on a particular section of the city wall or gate.[30] There was real "owner-

27. Williamson, *Ezra, Nehemiah*, p. 193.
28. Tollefson and Williamson, "Nehemiah as Cultural Revitalization," p. 51.
29. Perspectival issues involved in ancient city-making are discussed by D. Bruce MacKay, "A View from the Outskirts: Realignments from Modern to Postmodern in the Archaeological Study of Urbanism," in *Urbanism in Antiquity: From Mesopotamia to Crete,* ed. Walter E. Aufrecht, Neil A. Mirau, and Steven W. Gauley, JSOT Supplement Series 244 (Sheffield: Sheffield Academic Press, 1997), pp. 278-85.

ship," not merely a "sense" of ownership, because the people were doing work vital to their homes (3:30) and their businesses (3:31). Help also came from the districts surrounding Jerusalem; indeed, support poured into the city (3:15).[31] Their labors are to be taken, implicitly, as animated by the same Spirit that equipped Bezalel for construction of the Tabernacle (Exod. 31:2; 35:30–36:1) and others for construction of the Temple (1 Chron. 28:11-12).

Attention to the details of physical space works its way particularly into the second half of chapter three (3:16-31). As Williamson points out, "A new course for the wall is carefully defined by reference to local landmarks, familiar no doubt to the writer's contemporaries, but completely unknown to us in nearly every case."[32] Places such as the "artificial pool and the House of the Heroes" (3:16) may mean little to us today, but these were familiar urban landmarks to the people that defined the city as home. Sensitivity to place as part of cultural renewal was critical.[33]

One can almost hear the "hocking and plocking" sounds of hammers in the text:

> The Jeshanah Gate was repaired by Joiada son of Paseah and Meshullam son of Besodeiah. They laid its beams and put its doors and bolts and bars in place. . . . Shallum son of Hallohesh, ruler of a half-district of Jerusalem, repaired the next section with the help of his daughters. (3:6, 12)

Moving in a counter-clockwise direction, beginning and ending at the Sheep Gate (3:1, 32),[34] the rebuilding went forward at a remarkable pace. Combining new resources with their own, the community acted collectively in their own interest and for the honor of God. What was being recreated was more than a city wall. Under construction was the very life of a community — their relationships to one another, their city, and their God.

Overcoming Difficult Obstacles

Success, however, was met with opposition, and in each instance, it not only demanded changes of the people but also gave them the opportunity to clarify and deepen their understanding of and commitment to the project. Three

---

30. Williamson, *Ezra, Nehemiah*, p. 205.

31. Williamson, *Ezra, Nehemiah*, p. 206.

32. Williamson, *Ezra, Nehemiah*, p. 208.

33. On the importance of place renewal for urban history, see Dolores Hayden, *The Power of Place: Urban Landscapes as Public History* (Cambridge: MIT Press, 1995).

34. Williamson, *Ezra, Nehemiah*, p. 198.

challenges that threatened to undo their progress were a military threat (4:1-17), a growing inequality between rich and poor (5:1-19), and outside political pressure (6:1-19). The first and third were external hazards; the second was primarily internal in origin.

Why was a reconstructed Jerusalem a military and political threat? As Tollefson and Williamson explain, "The Jerusalem restoration project threatened both the economic and political hegemony of Samaria as well as the military stability of the surrounding region."[35] The legitimacy of powerful interests was being called into question by a minority. Sanballat and Tobiah of Samaria were beneficiaries of the established regime. Upon hearing of the project's intent, they became angry, heaping insults and ridicule upon Jerusalem's efforts, labeling the people "feeble" (4:2) and vividly describing their inadequacy: "What they are building — if even a fox climbed up on it, he would break down their wall of stones!" (4:3). Sanballat and Tobiah's insults grew into a violent military threat and a political whispering campaign that preyed on the people's legitimate fears. They threatened "to fight against Jerusalem and stir up trouble against it" (4:8). Literally, the opposition loomed from all sides (4:19-20).

Sanballat's harsh mocking of the people's work provides us with a sense of what was at stake: "Can they bring the stones back to life from those heaps of rubble — burned as they are?" (4:2).[36] Underneath his mocking seems to lie the fear that the people would be successful. This fear is understandable, for in the ancient world, as Doug Green explains, "To build or rebuild a structure carried powerful emotive associations. It was more than a mere engineering activity; it was a movement from chaos to order, from death to life."[37] By rebuilding the city, the people of Jerusalem were bringing their city back to life (cf. Ezek. 37).

To counter the moves of Sanballat and others, the people prayed (4:4-5) and took specific action. Under Nehemiah's direction, the community deployed guards and set up a security system (4:9-14). Nehemiah also urged the people to remember God's history of protecting his people (4:14). Refusing to be intimidated, they did what was required to accomplish their task (4:16-18). Over and over, the story tells how a people worked together to accomplish something larger than themselves by trusting in God.

No sooner had the external crisis ended than an internal conflict arose

---

35. Tollefson and Williamson, "Nehemiah as Cultural Revitalization," p. 52.

36. Here "the rebuilding project is interpreted as a 'life-giving' act." See Green, "Nehemiah," p. 2.

37. Green, "Nehemiah," p. 2.

that was at least as destructive. It concerned the inequality of members within the community. The landless (5:2) and the small-scale farmers (5:3), always just a lost job or a failed harvest away from dire poverty, had sunk deeply into debt. The king's tax was harshly felt by the most vulnerable of the city's citizens, and the consequences were grim:

> Although we are of the same flesh and blood as our countrymen and though our sons are as good as theirs, yet we have to subject our sons and daughters to slavery. Some of our daughters have already been enslaved, but we are powerless, because our fields and our vineyards belong to others. (5:5)

Clearly it did not make sense to rebuild the walls of the city but not the economic life of its citizens. Economic relationships could not be compartmentalized, separated from moral and spiritual values. To heal the rupture caused by indebtedness and its consequences, Nehemiah turned to the Jubilee (Neh. 5:1-19; 10:21; cf. Lev. 25; Deut. 15:1-18; 31:9-13).[38] In accord with the Jubilee, he instituted an immediate plan to forgive debts and return property.

Just as God had heard the cry of the children of Israel in Egypt (3:7-8), so he had heard the groans of the people here.[39] The people's cries for justice were also heard by Nehemiah and by the city leaders.[40] As a result, the political and economic systems were held accountable, and the new breach that had been threatening the walls of the city was mended.[41]

It is here in what might be identified as the "adaptive" phase of revitalization that Nehemiah's qualities as a leader are particularly evident.[42] Nehemiah is neither a superhero nor the "great man" of the story, but perhaps can best be described as an organizer who mobilized the people to rebuild their community on the basis of their faith commitments and tradi-

---

38. On this reform, see José Severino Croatto, "The Debt in Nehemiah's Social Reform: A Study of Nehemiah 5:1-19," in *Subversive Scriptures: Revolutionary Readings of the Christian Bible in Latin America*, ed. and trans. Leif E. Vaage (Valley Forge: Trinity Press International, 1997), pp. 39-59.

39. Croatto, "The Debt in Nehemiah's Social Reform," p. 51.

40. Croatto, "The Debt in Nehemiah's Social Reform," p. 50.

41. For a thematic connection, see Ezekiel 22:29-30.

42. Is Nehemiah the leader too good to be true? Is he presented as an iconic figure? Is the real-life Nehemiah different from the heroic Nehemiah of Scripture? David J. A. Clines seems to think so, but his case seems set against Nehemiah from the start. See his essay entitled "The Nehemiah Memoir: The Perils of Autobiography," in *What Does Eve Do to Help? And Other Readerly Questions to the Old Testament* (Sheffield: JSOT Press, 1990), pp. 124-64.

tions. Certainly he exhibited great personal commitment as well as political and social savvy. Although a single individual's leadership skills, access to resources, and vision could not, by themselves, transform a city into a vibrant, thriving community, Nehemiah was certainly important to this transformation. In order to mobilize the people to make changes necessary for their survival, Nehemiah put himself on the line personally (1–2; 4:6, 9), helped people build on their history (4:14), led by the example of sacrificial downward mobility (4:23; 5:18), and helped to craft clear, practical solutions to problems that built on Israel's traditions (5:1-19). Still, it is the people of the city who defined their situation, formulated a common plan to alter reality, and then moved forward with determined purpose and direction. On the whole, as Tamara Cohn Eskenazi has rightly proposed, the narrative is focused not on Nehemiah the person but rather on the community.[43]

After overcoming profound obstacles, the people completed the building of the wall (6:15). God had called their work into being and sustained its cause, as Nehemiah points out: "When all our enemies heard about this and all the surrounding nations saw it, our enemies lost their self-confidence, because they realized that this work had been done with the help of our God" (6:16).

Throughout the story, in fact, God is recognized as the primary rebuilder of community. Israel's God is recognized as the one who will "give . . . success" (2:20), answer prayers (4:4), strengthen the hands of the workers (6:9-10), and frustrate those who work against community (4:15). Following the psalmist, the people believed that "Unless the LORD builds the house, its builders labor in vain. Unless the LORD watches over the city, the watchmen stand guard in vain" (127:1; cf. Heb. 3:4).[44]

Discovering a New Commitment to Community

Restoring the city's physical walls was a major accomplishment. This would not, however, ensure the community's sustainability. In what Tollefson and Williamson identify as the "cultural transformation" phase, the people of Jerusalem learned that bricks and mortar alone do not make a restored and whole community. For the community was still "estranged from its cultural heritage and spiritual roots."[45] No community can be healthy without the re-

---

43. Eskenazi, *In an Age of Prose,* pp. 144-52, 191.

44. Most likely is a reference to the temple ("house") and Jerusalem ("city"), reminding the hearer of both a place and a history. See Daniel E. Fleming, "'House'/'City': An Unrecognized Parallel Word Pair," *Journal of Biblical Literature* 105, no. 4 (1986): 692.

45. Tollefson and Williamson, "Nehemiah as Cultural Revitalization," p. 55.

newal of its sacred story. Where would communal meaning, values, and purpose emanate from?

According to Tollefson and Williamson, genealogies — lists of names and family histories — make a strong connection to place and memory and thus become the link to discovering the future: "Genealogies link people to their lands, their ancestors, their cultures and their gods. . . . [They are] more than sterile lists of progeny; they are cognitive maps of reality."[46] At Nehemiah's urging, the families living in the city were registered; Nehemiah also "found the genealogical record of those who had been the first to return" (7:5). A strong sense of where they had come from helped anchor the people. A restitution of land also helped to reinforce a sense of place and responsibility.

As Tollefson and Williamson see it, Nehemiah 8–10 "tells us when and how the people changed their ethos and became committed to the radical types of changes described in the next section [chs. 11–13]. In other words, *it supplies the 'cultural transformation phase' that occurs in all such revitalization movements.*"[47] Actually, cultural transformation had been taking place from the moment the people decided to rebuild. But the progression of first "unfreezing" an "old ethos" in Nehemiah 8, next moving toward a "new ethos" in Nehemiah 9, and then making a commitment to this "new ethos" in Nehemiah 10 solidifies gains and clarifies what is at stake.[48]

In a form of celebratory address similar to the call-and-response style of the black sermonic tradition, Ezra read the Book of the Law to the gathered people:

> Ezra opened the book. All the people could see him because he was standing above them; and as he opened it, the people all stood up. Ezra praised the LORD, the great God; and all the people lifted their hands and responded, "Amen! Amen!" (8:5-6)

Then the Levites "read from the Book of the Law of God, making it clear and giving the meaning so that the people could understand what was being read" (8:8; cf. 8:9). Renewal took place as the people rediscovered the Word of God for their history and context.

The people's reaction to the realization of God's faithful presence in rebuilding the city was weeping and mourning (8:9). Seeing this, Nehemiah told them to stop their weeping and to celebrate instead:

46. Tollefson and Williamson, "Nehemiah as Cultural Revitalization," p. 55.
47. Tollefson and Williamson, "Nehemiah as Cultural Revitalization," p. 56.
48. Tollefson and Williamson, "Nehemiah as Cultural Revitalization," p. 56.

"Go and enjoy choice food and sweet drinks, and send some to those who have nothing prepared. This day is sacred to our LORD. Do not grieve, for the joy of the LORD is your strength." (8:10)

A close reading of "the joy of the LORD is your strength" suggests that this verse refers to divine joy, not, as usually understood, the joy experienced by the people.[49] Over the struggle for the renewal of the city, it is God who experiences joy, for it is the joy of life. Such joy and celebration nourished the new beginnings and the belief that in God things need not stay the same. This called the people to celebration, to recognize that a new community had been formed.

In Nehemiah 9, another public gathering is called. Speakers read the Law aloud and reviewed their history. The response was a communal confession of sin and a prayer for renewal that reminds the reader of Nehemiah's parallel experience in chapter 1. The journey of Nehemiah becomes the journey of the people as they recognize their need to change their course. As Tollefson and Williamson explain, "Repentance and prayer have changed the history of their people in the past and it can do so again in the present."[50] The people found that their relationship to God was renewed and that they had become empowered for life in community.

The prayer in Nehemiah 9 suggests a people further reflecting on their story of revitalization.[51] Israel's story is applied to their new setting to strengthen them. Starting out by praising God for the creation (v. 6), the prayer moves on to describe God's relationship with Abraham (vv. 7-8), then praises God for guiding their forefathers through the Exodus (vv. 9-12) and through the wilderness (vv. 12-23). The prayer's final passage centers on the Israelites' life in the promised land (vv. 24-31).[52]

---

49. This argument is advanced by G. C. I. Wong, "A Note on 'Joy' in Nehemiah VIII 10," *Vetus Testamentum* 14, no. 3 (July 1995): 383-86.

50. Tollefson and Williamson, "Nehemiah as Cultural Revitalization," p. 58.

51. Mark J. Boda, "Praying the Tradition: The Origin and Use of Tradition in Nehemiah 9," *Tyndale Bulletin* 48, no. 1 (May 1997): 179-82. The larger argument is found in Mark J. Boda, *Praying the Tradition: The Origin and Use of Tradition in Nehemiah 9* (Berlin: Walter de Gruyter, 1999).

52. Mark Boda makes this comment on the prayer: "Although tradition is used for the purposes of praise and confession, ultimately it is shaped by the agenda of request. The tradition is related in such a way as to strengthen the request of the suppliant. This prayer reveals a community which was embracing its documents as Scripture, treating at least the Pentateuch as an authoritative whole and synthesizing its parts through careful exegesis. In this way, we see a community praying the tradition and in so doing revealing their commitment to that

Nehemiah 10 recounts the story of this service of celebration, which marked a new way of being community, a new ethos that informed the habits of the everyday activity of the city. In one response to God's covenant love, the people agreed to honor the Sabbath year (every seventh year), upholding the notion that the city was a community and that all had a significant place in it (10:31).

Taking on New Challenges

Dedicating the wall, the completion of the most important physical component in the rebuilding project, was not the end of the work. To use a physics analogy, critical mass was needed to assure the longevity of the project. In order to sustain itself, Jerusalem needed a critical mass of residents who would share in upholding the civic, economic, and spiritual fabric of the community (7:4). Guided by the tradition of the tithe (Lev. 27:30-33; Deut. 14:22-29), the surrounding community gave 10 percent of its population back to the city: "Now the leaders of the people settled in Jerusalem, and the rest of the people cast lots to bring one out of every ten to live in Jerusalem, the holy city, while the remaining nine were to stay in their own towns. The people commended all the men who volunteered to live in Jerusalem" (11:1-2). Homesteading for the sake of the city became a simple solution to a complex problem. Nehemiah 11:3–12:26 is a public record of the families who relocated in the city.

While everyone was celebrating the wall and the unity and honor that it stood for (12:27-43), the unspoken question was, Could it all keep going? With the rebuilding of the wall completed, Nehemiah left Jerusalem and returned to his position in the king's court. But as the story seems to draw to a conclusion, we find that the community had begun to lose its memory of its history and calling. When he learned this, Nehemiah returned to Jerusalem for a second term as governor (13:6-7), the length of term unspecified.

Hard choices had to be made if the community was to survive. A series of additional reforms, building on the people's earlier agreement (9:38), was necessary (13:7-13). Most important was a re-emphasis on the observance of the Sabbath (13:15-22). For in its observance, Israel remembered that God was their Creator and Deliverer. Nehemiah also put an end to "intermarriage"

---

tradition as Scripture. This commitment to the tradition does not mean tradition has become static. The Persian Jewish community continued to reshape the tradition into an effective tool for gaining the ear of their God. Inscripturated tradition is creatively related to ever new situations of need among the people of Yahweh" ("Praying the Tradition," p. 182).

(13:1-3, 23-27), an action deemed necessary to preserve community and resist further domination.[53]

An inability to keep faith and community in focus had nearly undermined the substantive reforms. But a renewed commitment to a transcendent basis for community prevailed — at least so far as we know. For the story ends uneasily, unfinished, and open-ended about how committed the people were to God's future for them.[54] Indeed, even with the rebuilding of the temple and the city, there remained a belief that the exile was not yet over (Neh. 9:36-37; cf. Ezra 9:8-9),[55] and that more was still to come. Would the spiritual values that brought them together in a way never before seen continue to guide them? Would the next generation be fortified by the story and internalize the same commitments? Would they remember that only God can rebuild and sustain the life of a community? These questions notwithstanding, the walls of the city had been rebuilt, people were dwelling together in safety, businesses were thriving, and children were running freely through the streets. With the walls of the city rebuilt, God's peace for the city had become a greater reality.

"Performing" Nehemiah

While Jerusalem is not the city of today, and leaps between them should be cautious ones, the city remains the site of faithful cultural and peaceable activity. If the drama of rebuilding depends upon the drama of reading Scripture, then Nehemiah most fittingly encourages founding the rebuilding of distressed neighborhoods on Scripture read not as a "textbook" on community development or a story of moral uplift, but as a story with a distinct

53. While holiness may be considered the theological rationale, minority groups often stress the preservation of cultural identity as a form of resistance and survival. Concerning the subject of mixed marriages, see Daniel Smith-Christopher, "The Mixed Marriage Crisis in Ezra 9–10 and Nehemiah 13: A Study of the Sociology of Post-Exilic Judaean Community," in *Second Temple Studies, 2: Temple Community in the Persian Period,* JSOT Supplement Series 175, ed. Tamara C. Eskenazi and Kent H. Richards (Sheffield: JSOT Press, 1994), pp. 243-65. For another way of looking at questions of marriage, purity, and social context, see Mark G. Brett, *Genesis: Procreation and the Politics of Identity* (London: Routledge, 2001).

54. See Douglas Green, "Ezra-Nehemiah," in *A Complete Literary Guide to the Bible,* ed. Leland Ryken and Tremper Longman III (Grand Rapids: Zondervan, 1993), 206-15; and J. G. McConville, "Ezra-Nehemiah and the Fulfillment of Prophecy," *Vetus Testamentum* 36, no. 2 (1986): 205-24.

55. N. T. Wright, *The New Testament and the People of God,* vol. 1 of Christian Origins and the Question of God (Minneapolis: Fortress, 1992), pp. 268-72.

"narrative world" that interacts with the contemporary urban narrative world.[56] By "story" I mean a plot, a drama that has a beginning and an end. By "narrative world" I mean that the setting, characters, hindrances, and dynamics of Nehemiah mirror the setting, characters, hindrances, and dynamics of faith-based community revitalization in the inner city.[57] It is a world that the reading community involved in neighborhood work will recognize as similar. Imaginatively indwelling the drama of Nehemiah enables community members to bring similar perspectives, responsibilities, and visions to the narrative spaces of the inner city. The overarching connection here is that Nehemiah is part of the story of God's redemptive purposes for the world. In all stories of revitalization, God is the rebuilder of community and involved in the drama of transformation. Such an approach helps safeguard the text from being read outside of its context as Israel's history while at the same time enabling it to creatively serve particular communities in the present.

This approach assumes that the church is a community that reads, interprets, and practices Scripture. Because hearing and doing the Word belong together, the best readings of Nehemiah take place in communities where people are seeking to faithfully proclaim and embody it as Scripture (Col. 3:16; 2 Tim. 3:16; James 1:22; cf. Deut. 30:14).[58] Rightly reading Nehemiah, respecting its authority as Scripture, entails in some way its performance.[59] In performing Nehemiah, the priority is in pointing to the God who rebuilds.[60]

---

56. Anthony C. Thiselton, *New Horizons in Hermeneutics* (Grand Rapids: Zondervan, 1992), pp. 566-75; and Kathryn Greene-McCreight, "'We Are Companions of the Patriarchs,' Or 'Scripture Absorbs Calvin's World,'" *Modern Theology* 14, no. 2 (April 1998): 213-24.

57. I believe this claim is borne out by the narratives of other community-based efforts. For one example that exhibits similar patterns, see Robert Guskind and Neal Peirce, *Against the Tide: The New Community Corporation, 1968-1993* (Newark: New Community Corporation, n.d.).

58. Fowl, *Engaging Scripture*, p. 178.

59. An important discussion of the relationship of biblical authority, narrative, and performance is found in Wright, *The New Testament and the People of God*, pp. 139-43. See also Nicholas Lash, *Theology on the Road to Emmaus* (London: SCM Press, 1986), p. 42; Wayne A. Meeks, "A Hermeneutics of Social Embodiment," *Harvard Theological Review* 79, nos. 1-3 (1986); and Nicholas Wolterstorff, *Divine Discourse: Philosophical Reflections on the Claim That God Speaks* (Cambridge: Cambridge University Press, 1995), pp. 171-82. In my view, performance is able to be most free when it is stabilized in the authority and integrity of the text. Then it is possible for the text to continually read and question the performance, putting forward new questions.

60. See the remarks of Volf, "Theology, Meaning, and Power," in *The Future of Theology: Essays in Honor of Jürgen Moltmann*, ed. Miroslav Volf (Grand Rapids: Eerdmans, 1996), p. 108.

Before I say something further about what it might mean to perform Nehemiah, it is also true and critical to recognize, as Stephen Fowl has stressed, that the formation of a healthy Christian common life, especially the practices of repentance, forgiveness, and reconciliation, is necessary to discover and maintain faithful scriptural interpretations.[61] Those in a community of faith must learn to relate to one another in ways that enable them to carry forward vibrant community work.

In the story of Nehemiah there are renewal activities and patterns that are crucial to a community development project. Among them are hearing the call to rebuild, the mobilization of the people of the community, the emphasis on networking, the recognition that conflicts will arise, the power of celebrating victories, and the centrality of faith and its traditions. Emphasizing community leadership, recognizing the city as bearing sacramental meaning, and reading Scripture as a source of community empowerment — themes suggested by Tamara Cohn Eskenazi — continue to be precisely what is needed in community revitalization. When we see ourselves in Nehemiah's world, it can help call us to form a biblically based and kingdom-oriented approach to rebuilding communities.

Although Nehemiah calls attention to issues that are critical in community-building, the practice of "performing" Nehemiah is not to be literalistic or moralistic, or uniform and mechanical. The Nehemiah story cannot be used as some kind of behavioral blueprint that says, in effect, "This is the way to do it." Rather, every community of faith, under the guidance of the Spirit, must thoughtfully discern answers to these questions: How do we faithfully worship and serve God's reign in this concrete setting? How are we to faithfully perform the story of Nehemiah in our context and setting? Vital models of revitalization respond creatively to their location by drawing on a multitude of communal and individual gifts, theological and cultural perspectives, and relevant opportunities. There is no single mechanical pattern of community revitalization, no quick steps that can be taken, only improvisation in the face of opportunities, obstacles, and uncertainty. Because no clear, smooth road can be mapped out at the beginning, there is only the way made by traveling it together — a way of risk, prayer, hard work, and small victories that accumulate. But because the ground beneath these efforts is the presence and historical involvement of God in transforming the world, humility and hope move together in tandem.

---

61. Fowl, *Engaging Scripture*, pp. 179-80. For further discussion on community life, see L. Gregory Jones, "Crafting Communities of Forgiveness," *Interpretation* 54, no. 2 (April 2000): 121-34.

Kenneth Tollefson expresses very well what a textually grounded yet flexible approach to Nehemiah might look like:

> The ultimate value of the Nehemiah model does not rest as much on a rigorous application of it to any specific local community as it does on an inspired application of its comprehensiveness to a new situation. Local variations mitigate against any Nehemiah revitalization facsimiles. The Nehemiah model does provide an invaluable word-picture of what it means to be under mission for our Lord in any society.[62]

"Word picture" is another way of saying "narrative world." Listening to and retelling the story of Nehemiah enables the people of a community to generate a vision of what is possible and then sustain the hard process that will be required. Under Nehemiah's guidance, the people of Jerusalem rebuilt their city; that story helps all their dispersed sons and daughters (Acts 1:8; Gal. 3:29) to see and experience new urban possibilities. In one sense, Nehemiah is an unfinished story, with chapters still to be written as long as our struggling neighborhoods do not know the full resolve of God's peace.

DYNAMICS OF COMMUNITY REBUILDING

Community rebuilding requires a set of distinctive practices, commitments, and skills. It is perhaps best characterized as a craft that is continually learned. As I understand it, faith-based community development is best rooted in the church, yet it also belongs to the expansive work of the kingdom in all areas of urban life. Rebuilding inner-city neighborhoods is the opposite of dissolving, abandoning, and giving up. To speak of urban community development is to bring to light all the efforts that go into recreating place and redeveloping local institutions. Emphasizing the power of a new vision, the process is multifaceted, incorporating spiritual, social, economic, ecological, and aesthetic dimensions of the city. As a spiritual project, rebuilding recognizes God's pledge of urban redemption, and gives witness to the hope of the city and the new creation (Ezek. 37; 1 Cor. 15; Rev. 21). Witness to the God of peace and justice, the God who rebuilds community and calls people to join in the life and work of God's kingdom, is woven into the entire fabric of Christian involvement in community development.

What now follows are some basic dynamics that guide community de-

62. Tollefson, "The Nehemiah Model for Christian Missions," p. 53.

velopment, even though the actual process is always improvisational.[63] That is, community development draws on multiple resources and perspectives rather than following a rigid model of development or social change. In all of this, process and people are central to defining the ends of the undertaking, thus affirming the dignity of the community. To borrow the language of Moltmann, community development in biblical perspective is the applied imagination of the kingdom for the sake of the kingdom in the concrete realities of the inner city. It is thus holistic in word and deed, truly local but also visionary, honest about the nature of change and realities of sin and suffering, yet profoundly expectant and hopeful. Rebuilding seeks to restore the walls — the structures and the institutions — that sustain community life with one another and before God.

One: Neighborhoods Require Care and Stewardship

Neighborhoods are not static entities but living, dynamic communities. Few better understand this truth and its importance for community development than Roberta Brandes Gratz, one of the most thoughtful advocates for preserving and building up neighborhoods and cities. In her book *The Living City,* she writes,

> Cities do not deteriorate overnight and, similarly, are not reborn overnight. Quick-fix responses at best camouflage problems and at worst exacerbate them. Cities respond most durably in the hands of many participants accomplishing gradually smaller bites, making small changes and big differences at the same time.[64]

63. With an eye on international development and non-government organizations (NGOs), Bryant L. Myers has written *Walking with the Poor: Principles and Practices of Transformational Development* (Maryknoll: Orbis, 1999). This is an important Christian interpretation of development that has many applications for the work of church-based community development in the inner city. Myers shows how a number of factors go into the development process undertaken by Christians, including worldview, the role of narrative or story, a biblical theology of poverty and the poor, the nature of social analysis, the life of the community developer, and the place of witness. I place the church more centrally, presume a more structural definition of poverty, and underscore the role of organizing. For an important analysis see the review by Robert C. Linthicum in *Missiology: An International Review* 128, no. 3 (July 2000): 369-70.

64. Gratz, *The Living City* (New York: Simon & Schuster, 1989), p. 148. See also Roberta Brandes Gratz with Norman Mintz, *Cities Back from the Edge: New Life for Downtown* (New York: John Wiley & Sons, 1998).

Out of this conviction Gratz urges the practice of "urban husbandry." "Just as husbandry means the care, management and conservation of animals," she writes, "Urban husbandry means the care, management or conservation of the built environment."[65] Instead of replacing things, Gratz advocates strengthening what is there, allowing an incremental pace and an organic process to emerge from the bottom up, not the top down. Rather than trust in the false promises of large-scale urban projects, urban husbandry celebrates those efforts that are small and more community-grounded and honest.

Such a process looks to the community and recognizes the many ways in which God is already at work. It also seems to me a very good way of describing our creational responsibilities as image-bearers of God and the redemptive energies of the kingdom. Christians are to care about the fabric of the urban environment because it has an impact on our shared public and common life. And instead of trusting in big projects and plans, the way of the kingdom is the mustard seed (Matt. 13:31-32; Mark 4:30-32; Luke 13:18-19), the small and seemingly insignificant growing up to be something of strength and substance.[66] While Gratz does not draw enough attention to the underlying racial and structural dynamics of urban struggle, and thus its spatial and social dimensions, what she has to say about neighborhood dynamics and the built environment is essential for strengthening and rebuilding urban communities.

Whether it is one building, one block, or a larger neighborhood, effective rebuilding depends upon having a well-defined concrete geography or focus area. A focus area enables those involved to set measurable goals and objectives and establish a clear, holistic vision. Just as importantly, a focus area limits the options that can be attempted. It sets the agenda, which means that the unrealistic goal of trying to do "everything everywhere" is eliminated. How is a focus area determined? This requires a process of discernment that looks at both the web of relationships and natural community markers. In this process, the relationship of the church to the community is best described by the word *covenant*. A covenant is a free commitment that says, in effect, "Whatever happens, no matter what, we as the church will stay and deal with it." This means that the church takes a vow of stability, that it is committed to being a church *of* the community. Having a focus area reminds us as well of the importance of small-scale projects and micro-narrative approaches in Christian community development.

---

65. Gratz, *The Living City,* p. 147.

66. On the importance of this theme for the church, see Albert Tizon, "Revisiting the Mustard Seed: The Filipino Evangelical Church in the Age of Globalization," *Phronēsis* 6, no. 1 (1999): 3-26.

Two: Rebuilding Moves Between Lament and Celebration

Just as the urban cry of Lamentations precedes the rebuilding of Jerusalem in
Nehemiah, so tears and shared pain must precede the joys of rebuilding in the
inner city. Put another way, community transformation begins with people
and their struggles as experienced through the grieving of God over the frac-
ture of the city. The psalms and hymns of lament also help us here. Just as
reading the laments of Scripture can enable us to "read" the laments of the inner city, so the laments of the inner city can inform our reading of Scripture.
We should remember that Jesus entered the city of Jerusalem weeping: "As he
approached Jerusalem and saw the city, he wept over it" (Luke 19:41). The urban laments of our day can be seen and heard everywhere: from the graffiti-
painted "rest in peace" murals and the flowers and notes that serve as memori-
als on building walls, light poles, and sidewalks, to the prayers of the suffering,
to the abandoned ruins of our inner cities. And God is there in loving identification with the suffering and wounded (Ps. 91:5; Isa. 63:9; Matt. 25:40).

While rebuilding begins with lament, it ends with rendering thanks to
God. As with all of life, rebuilding can be considered "embodied worship"
(Rom. 12:1; cf. Col. 3:17).[67] Celebration is crucial to fulfill the aims of community redevelopment, for it sustains and keeps in focus the end of community rebuilding, which is the glory of God. Praising God is a gift of grace for
the church and for the city (Ps. 105; 1 Pet. 2:9; Heb. 12:18-24). By definition,
rebuilding is doxological in character, for the city is the site of God's glory (Ps.
87), and God is glorified in the redemption of the city. As a spiritual project,
rebuilding recognizes God's pledge of urban redemption. Sharing in lament
but also joining in celebration is a basic dynamic of the church's role in the
movement of a community from ruin to new life.

Three: Change Percolates from the Bottom Up

Rebuilding must begin with and be determined by the people of the community. It must be from the bottom up. Imposing conceptual categories and language from the outside not only will prove unsuccessful but will be morally
wrong. The community's impetus and ideas for change, its interests, its language, and its sense of pace must lead. Drawing on a community's journey of
survival, courage, self-care, and even anger is a starting point. In other words,

---

67. A discussion of the embodied life of faith as worship is William A. Dyrness, *The
Earth Is God's*, pp. 159-63.

believing in the community is an essential part of community change. For the church, this means passionately loving the community in all its beauty and hurting with it in its brokenness, as well as trusting in the genius and ideas of the community and drawing on its spirituality and depth of commitment, recognizing the community as people created in God's image. For the church, believing in the community also involves a Pentecostal belief in the gifts and capacities of the people of the community. All members of the community — not just a few "leaders" — have an important contribution to make to the re-building effort. Every person has gifts, and every gift is a grace for the common good (Rom. 12:3-8; 1 Cor. 12; Eph. 4:11-13).

Such a counterintuitive conviction that leadership "from below" can transform the world recalls the memory of Moses' mother and the midwives, who set a course that would eventually overcome the great injustice and evil of Pharaoh (Exod. 1:8–2:10).[68] Strength is also drawn from the Magnificat, which announces the reversal of ages through a tiny babe, the divine one who "has brought down rulers from their thrones" and "lifted up the humble" (Luke 1:52, 46-55; cf. 1 Sam. 2:8). Indeed, as history shows, women's experiences and leadership are especially important in the family, the church, the community, and the city.[69] The Christian story also reminds us of the leadership role of children and young people. Was it not a young boy who brought forward loaves and fishes (John 6)? Ultimately, we learn from the cross that what is perceived as "weakness" overcomes all human pretensions of "power" (1 Cor. 1:25). God's chosen way of redeeming the world — working not from the top down but from the bottom up, through Christ — unleashes power from the "edges" of society through women, children, and the poor.[70] Here is where we must look for the lived stories and theologies for the urban future, giving testimony to the way of salvation (1 Cor. 1:19).

Social and community development theory offers numerous confirmations of a locally based approach. As John P. Kretzmann and John McKnight have detailed, *every* community has significant assets or what they also call "building blocks" for reviving a neighborhood. These assets are to orient

---

68. J. Cheryl Exum, "'You Shall Let Every Daughter Live': A Study in Exodus 1:8–2:10," *Semeia* 28 (1983): 63-82.

69. See, for example, Cheryl Townsend Gilkes, *"If It Wasn't for the Women . . .": Black Women's Experience and the Womanist Culture in Church and Community* (Maryknoll: Orbis, 2001); Evelyn Brooks Higginbotham, *Righteous Discontent: The Women's Movement in the Black Baptist Church, 1880-1920* (Cambridge: Harvard University Press, 1993); and Daphne Spain, *How Women Saved the City* (Minneapolis: University of Minnesota Press, 2001).

70. Cheryl J. Sanders, *Ministry at the Margins: The Prophetic Mission of Women, Youth, and the Poor* (Downers Grove: InterVarsity Press, 1997).

community development more than needs or problems, they argue. They say that four main assets can be identified in any neighborhood: (1) the capacities and gifts of local residents, (2) the power of local associations and organizations, (3) the potential of local public institutions, and (4) the diverse streams of local economic activity, including the neighborhood's land and other physical assets.[71] Community change, they argue, really can begin from the inside and move out; it need not be top down. Put another way, local knowledge, gifts, and leadership must be respected and privileged.[72] Moreover, focusing on what God is doing in the community rather than maintaining a consuming focus on "needs" aids in the prevention of burnout, personal and communal.

The history of movements of Christian renewal is that they arise not from the center of power but from the peripheries. However, it is not accurate to say or imply that the church or the community bears the moral burden of correcting injustices they did not create. Macro-factors must not be discounted, and the notion and political discourse of "personal responsibility" should not be used against communities of exclusion. This does not contradict the imperatives of community-based development.[73] Rather, authentic community transformation will not only engage wider economic and political issues but will also provide opportunities for the rich and powerful to be

71. Kretzmann and McKnight, *Building Communities from the Inside Out: A Path toward Finding and Mobilizing a Community's Assets* (Evanston: Center for Urban Affairs and Policy Research, Neighborhood Innovations Network, Northwestern University, 1993).

72. In *Pedagogy of the Oppressed* (New York: Herder & Herder, 1972), Paulo Freire powerfully makes the case for taking the perspective of the poor as the starting point for knowledge. The case for local knowledge in urban development versus the modern liberal sensibility of high modernism is also well argued by James C. Scott, *Seeing Like a State: How Certain Schemes to Improve the Human Condition Have Failed* (New Haven: Yale University Press, 1998), especially pp. 103-46. For expanded comments on the meaning of *metis* or local knowledge, see pp. 309-41. Scott's insights are also applicable to the micro-scale of community renewal.

73. For example, in *Rebuilding the Inner City: A History of Neighborhood Initiatives to Address Poverty in the United States* (New York: Columbia University Press, 1995), Robert Halpern argues that neighborhood efforts have historically been ineffective (219-33). While he makes some important points, his rejection of the local is part of his premise, and his tools of evaluation are incomplete. A similar argument is made by Nicholas Lemann in "The Myth of Community Development" (*New York Times Magazine,* 9 January 1994, pp. 27-31, 50, 54, 60). It is true that both Halpern and Lemann point to aspects of community development that need more critical evaluation and often alteration. However, they misjudge the possibilities of micro-initiatives, not recognizing the significance of a theological description of the world and the way of the mustard seed. Zechariah warns us not to despise "the day of small things" (4:10).

involved and spiritually challenged. Broad and uniquely defined partnerships with business, civic, and political interests will aid urban advance, and should be sought. Anchoring this, of course, must be the community's agenda and aspirations. The community must not be reduced to one "stakeholder" among many, but must instead be the subject of its future. Protecting this primary position requires organizing — which brings us to the next part of our discussion.

Four: Community Organizing Is the Basis of Empowerment

By mobilizing people to unite around what they value and hold most important, community organizing creates the space for the people of the community to define their issues, address shared concerns, confront the principalities and powers, hold public institutions accountable, determine their own future, and create their own institutions.[74] While the scale can vary from a block to a city to a state, the base local or broad, organizing is about creating relationships that enable people to do together what they cannot accomplish by working alone. As the evangelical organization called Christians Supporting Community Organizing proclaims, "Congregation-based community organizing is a process that enlists churches in faith- and value-based action to address the economic, social, and cultural conditions which individuals and families alone lack the power to change."[75]

Community organizing is a discipline that is learned — it demands

---

74. See Ernesto Cortes Jr., "Reweaving the Fabric: The Iron Rule and the IAF Strategy for Power and Politics," in *Interwoven Destinies: Cities and the Nation*, ed. Henry G. Cisneros (New York: W. W. Norton, 1993), pp. 294-319; Stephen Hart, *Cultural Dilemmas of Progressive Politics: Styles of Engagement among Grassroots Activists* (Chicago: University of Chicago Press, 2001), pp. 27-120; Dennis A. Jacobsen, *Doing Justice: Congregations and Community Organizing* (Minneapolis: Fortress, 2001); Mark R. Warren, *Dry Bones Rattling: Community Building to Revitalize American Democracy* (Princeton: Princeton University Press, 2001); Richard L. Wood, "Faith in Action: Religious Resources for Political Success in Three Congregations," *Sociology of Religion* 55, no. 4 (1994): 381-401; and Richard L. Wood, "Social Capital and Political Culture: God Meets Politics in the Inner City," *American Behavioral Scientist* 40, no. 5 (March/April 1997): 595-605.

75. Christians Supporting Community Organizing (CSCO), "Proclamation and Call to Our Churches." The proclamation is available at http://members.aol.com/proc.htm. For an evaluation of the importance of CSCO, see Timothy Sato and Donald E. Miller, *Christians Supporting Community Organizing: A New Voice for Change among Evangelical, Holiness, and Pentecostal Christians* (Los Angeles: University of Southern California, Center for Religion and Civic Culture, 1999).

skills that include dialogue, listening, deliberation, and negotiation.[76] As the Brazilian educator Paulo Freire has underscored, the process of reflection and action by the people of the community, rather than the banking of information, is a core value.[77] Organizing is about learning and applying what is learned. And then its task is the celebration of success. Thus the continual dynamic is reflection — action — celebration.

Because the city is a center of power(s), community organizing always operates with a theory of power. For Christian theology, this touches directly on soteriology, Christology, and the doctrine of sin. Post-modern theorizing that is suspicious of power is more than matched by street-level analysis. Clearly, the nature of power and its use are open to diverse social and theological interpretation, and just as clearly, organizing makes the subject one that must be reckoned with. In facing the powers of the inner city, Christians will draw on Jesus' ministry and confrontation with the powers, the apostolic work of deliverance, and Paul's analysis of the powers. And in Christ crucified, as Paul shows in 1 Corinthians, Christians will find "a revelation of God's power and wisdom . . . a paradigm for God's action in the world . . . a vision of God's use of power through [apparent] powerlessness."[78] The Spirit gives power for this mission (Acts 1:8).

Robert Linthicum has made a major contribution to the Christian conceptualization of community organizing. In numerous articles and books — particularly in *Empowering the Poor: Community Organizing among the City's "Rag, Tag, and Bobtail"*[79] — he has made the case for the church's involvement in community organization. Empowerment, Linthicum stresses, takes place when the people of a community name the hostile forces that are harming them, decide what strategy and steps to take to challenge them, and then organize action that brings about change. A process of continual reflection and action is essential, because it yields new ideas and insights. As Linthicum sees it, the analysis of harmful forces must include social, political, economic, and religious realities. Such analysis, he points out, yields not only physical

---

76. See Stephen T. Hoke, "The Art of Facilitating Change," in *With an Eye on the Future: Development and Mission in the Twenty-First Century* (Monrovia: MARC, 1996), pp. 157-68.

77. Freire, *Pedagogy of the Oppressed*, pp. 57-74. For a relevant dialogue, see Cheryl Bridges Johns, *Pentecostal Formation: A Pedagogy among the Oppressed* (Sheffield: Sheffield Academic Press, 1993).

78. Graham Tomlin, *The Power of the Cross: Theology and the Death of Christ in Paul, Luther, and Pascal* (Carlisle: Paternoster, 1999), pp. 99-100. See also Volf, "Theology, Meaning, and Power," pp. 108-10.

79. Linthicum, *Empowering the Poor*.

and material alterations but also an affirmation of human dignity and the seeds of spiritual renewal in the community. Upon this basis, church and community are able to form the creative and critical partnerships necessary to attain a more just and whole neighborhood. As we have seen, he calls this the church working *with* the community.

The idea of community organizing may seem new to many Christians, yet it has a distinguished and evangelical legacy that extends from the abolitionist movement to the civil rights movement to current community development and living-wage campaigns, efforts that have helped people and communities to create better living conditions and right relationships.[80] The end results of social organization are numerous, including a deeper understanding of the demands of the gospel in the city, a greater appreciation for the value of the individual, and wider civic involvement, all leading to greater community empowerment. The involvement of the church and the power of the gospel enable people to respond to the call to "stand up and lift up your heads, because your redemption is drawing near" (Luke 21:28) and recognize that, united in Christ and one another, they can "live a new life" (Rom. 6:4).

Five: Community Development Is a Vision of Justice and Joy

Community development is about the people of the community engaging in culture-shaping activity for the *shalom* of their neighborhoods. It is cultural activity that makes swords into plowshares. One of the ways in which community development does this is by developing and maintaining community-based housing corporations, health centers, job-creation and job-placement programs, child-care centers, micro-economic enterprises, and food co-ops. The focus of such institution building is the development of people, not programs.

Driven by a vision of community rightly ordered, a vision rooted in the biblical concept of Jubilee, Christ-centered community development is par-

---

80. In their "Proclamation and Call to Our Churches," Christians Supporting Community Organizing focuses on grass-roots organizing as a feature of the evangelical faith tradition. The civil rights movement is but one example: it was an organizing effort that would have been impossible without the church. A wider historical perspective can also be found in Taylor Branch, *Parting the Waters: America in the King Years* (New York: Simon & Schuster, 1989); and *Pillar of Fire: America in the King Years, 1963-1965* (New York: Simon & Schuster, 1998). See also Charles Marsh, "The Civil Rights Movement as Theological Drama: Interpretation and Application," forthcoming in *Modern Theology*.

ticularly committed to the most vulnerable. With a Jubilee perspective, community development offers not charity, relief, or advocacy but the resources for people to achieve healthy families and sustainable community.[81] This vision emphasizes responsibility, accents assets (economic, physical, social, and spiritual), precludes displacement, and does not measure results apart from people. The Jubilee is a vision of justice and joy unmatched in contemporary community development theory and practice. And it is the word of God for the salvation of a broken, misdirected, and sinful world.

In a provocative proposal, Randy Stoecker offers an important critique of the community development corporation model of neighborhood revitalization. In essence, he argues that seldom does a CDC have the capacity to make significant change and that subsequent reliance on outside resources harms organizational accountability to the community. The end result, he believes, is the damaging of community power and social networks. What Stoecker proposes is greater focus on community organizing, local planning, and coalitions of CDCs with greater developmental capacity.[82]

I agree with much of Stoecker's analysis. However, depending on a multitude of local factors, there will often be a significant requirement for local development capacity. The key will be the ability of any effort to enhance a neighborhood's power and social networks.

---

81. For more on the dynamics and implications of the biblical Jubilee, see Christopher J. H. Wright, "Jubilee, Year of," in *The Anchor Bible Dictionary,* ed. David Noel Freedman et al. (New York: Doubleday, 1992), Vol. 3, H-J, pp. 1025-30. Other works that I have found helpful on the Jubilee include Jeffrey A. Fager, *Land Tenure and the Biblical Jubilee: Uncovering Hebrew Ethics through the Sociology of Knowledge,* JSOT Supplement Series 155 (Sheffield: JSOT, 1993); C. René Padilla, "The Relevance of the Jubilee in Today's World (Leviticus 25)," *Mission Studies* 13, nos. 1 and 2, 25 and 26 (1996): 12-31; Sharon H. Ringe, *Jesus, Liberation, and the Biblical Jubilee: Images for Ethics and Christology* (Philadelphia: Fortress, 1985); Robert Bryan Sloan Jr., "Jubilee," *Dictionary of Jesus and the Gospels,* ed. Joel B. Green et al. (Downers Grove: InterVarsity, 1992), pp. 396-97; and John Howard Yoder, *The Politics of Jesus: Vicit Agnus Noster,* 2d ed. (Grand Rapids: Eerdmans, 1994), pp. 60-75.

82. Stoecker, "The CDC Model of Urban Redevelopment: A Critique and Alternative," *Journal of Urban Affairs* 19, no. 1 (1997): 1-22. See as well the subsequent discussion in the same issue of this journal: Rachel G. Bratt, "CDCs: Contributions Outweigh Contradictions: A Reply to Randy Stoecker," *Journal of Urban Affairs* 19, no. 1 (1997): 23-28; W. Dennis Keating, "The CDC Model of Urban Development: A Reply to Randy Stoecker," *Journal of Urban Affairs* 19, no. 1 (1997): 29-33; and Randy Stoecker, "Should We . . . Could We . . . Change the CDC Model? A Rejoinder," *Journal of Urban Affairs* 19, no. 1 (1997): 35-44.

The End Result: The Composition of a New Story

Community development is a storied activity, and the best community developers are storytellers and narrative theologians. Thus it is crucial that the church begins with and holds in great respect a community's stories, both individual and collective. Hearing these stories is a process of discovery that ultimately can lead to forming a new and shared story.[83] One of the primary roles of the church is to draw attention to the larger story of God's presence, salvation, and new creation. In this story, a community moves not just in a different direction but also toward God's future of reconciliation, justice, and joy in the city.[84] Because of grace, Christians know that the human story is always open to new endings. However, a new direction for a community does not result in the removal of the fetters that constrict the community. A new community story does not always erase the subjecting forces of oppression but finds a way through the maze of oppression to begin to establish a new vision and reality of what is possible.[85] Most importantly, the story of the community belongs to the community and is not imposed from outside.

This story, which is about communal transformation, cannot be "written" overnight. "When we talk about community transformation," Robert Linthicum observes, "we are talking about a conversion process in an entire community. It is most often not a sudden conversion. It is a slow, driving process causing an entire community to change their way of understanding themselves."[86] This conversion process occurs on the community's terms. How are we to discern the presence of a new story? Principal evidence is found in testimony, and Pentecost provides the model. Here the change that came upon lives was named in the Spirit as a gift from the Lord. This in turn gave rise to testimonies (Acts 2:4-13). The application to community development is significant. To bear testimony in public settings — to vocalize in word and song how lives, families, and communities have been healed — and to interpret these testimonies as stories of divine power express the encounter

83. In "The Soft Arts of Organizing" (*Social Policy* 26, no. 2 [Winter 1995]), Larry B. McNeil points out, "Organizing is the active unearthing of people's individual stories, the collective examination of the meaning of those stories in light of our shared story, and the opportunity to write new endings to both our individual and collective stories" (p. 19).

84. Myers, *Walking with the Poor*, pp. 20-56, 168-80.

85. For this way of framing the matter, I am indebted to Emmanuel M. Katongole, "Postmodern Illusions and the Challenges of African Theology: The Ecclesial Tactics of Resistance," *Modern Theology* 16, no. 2 (April 2000): 249-50.

86. Linthicum, *Empowering the Poor*, p. 65.

with the Spirit.[87] Recognizing that the Spirit plays a role in bringing forth a new community story is important — indeed, it is central to the Christian witness. But it is when community members hear each other testify to the changes in community life that God's work can be discerned. One cannot just receive the gifts of God; in the Spirit, one must also share and invite others to join. I will now say more about the work of Spirit of God in community transformation.

REBUILDING IN THE SPIRIT

According to Patricia A. Wilson, "Community . . . development starts with its roots in the interior person by touching the heart."[88] What kind of "interior" transformation moves people to pour their hearts into a new vision of a more just and peaceable community? Where will they find the strength to deal with the inevitable failures, contradictions, and tragedies that will occur as they pursue their vision? I have argued that rebuilding is based on a reading and practice of the Word that renews life and community. What is also needed is a theology of rebuilding that takes seriously the experience of the Spirit, which brings about the new birth of persons and communities. Biblical faith is bound up with this. In Ezekiel, God promises, "I will give you a new heart and put a new spirit in you" (36:26; cf. 36:27). And with this promise of God's Spirit also comes God's commitment that "the ruins will be rebuilt. . . . The cities that were lying in ruins, desolate and destroyed, are now fortified and inhabited. . . . [They will be] filled with flocks of people" (36:33, 35, 38).

This invites us to examine more closely the life of the Spirit, especially the creative presence and saving activity of the Spirit. What is required is a theology of the Spirit that is not only personal but is also at home in the sufferings of the inner city and opens up the full horizons of God's salvation.[89] The challenge, then, is to recover from Scripture the Spirit of God who will "renew the face of the earth" (Ps. 104:30; cf. Gen. 1:2; Ezek. 37) and has empowered Christ to bring the good news to the poor (Luke 4:16, 18-19). What I

---

87. Wynand J. de Kock, "Pentecostal Power for a Pentecostal Task: Empowerment through Engagement in South African Context," *Journal of Pentecostal Theology* 16 (2000): 104-5.

88. Wilson, "Empowerment: Community Economic Development from the Inside Out," *Urban Studies* 33, nos. 4-5 (1996): 627.

89. It is the Spirit who undergirds the struggle for life amidst suffering. See D. Lyle Dabney, "*Pneumatologia Crucis:* Reclaiming *Theologia Crucis* for a Theology of the Spirit Today," *Scottish Journal of Theology* 54, no. 4 (2001): 511-24.

am advocating is that all the activities and efforts that go into rebuilding the inner city be understood as taking place in the Spirit.[90]

There is little question that today the Pentecostal church represents Christianity's most important spiritual and social movement among the world's poor.[91] It is a movement of great diversity and ongoing development. Whether or not we identify ourselves as part of a Pentecostal church, we would do well to look here as we consider personal and social transformation in the city. Cheryl J. Sanders, a pastor and a professor at Howard University Divinity School, draws attention in *Saints in Exile* to the African-American Holiness and Pentecostal ecclesial experience as a resource for healing the wounds of "exiles" in the city.[92] Samuel Solivan has provided the church with a significant study in *The Spirit, Pathos, and Liberation: Toward an Hispanic Pentecostal Theology.* Solivan's project is to join the Spirit, theological reflections, and ministry to "a people's suffering, dehumanization, pain, and marginalization."[93] Both Sanders and Solivan connect the life of the Spirit to particular communities of faith, and offer interpretations of the church and the Spirit that are personal and socially transformational for the poor. In fact, listening to the Spirit and being committed to God's peace for the poor are inseparable in their ecclesiologies. Perhaps we are witnessing the emergence of a new "paradigm" that, while not without its issues and questions, is bringing together a concern for salvation and all of life.[94]

We need the Spirit to understand God's future for the city. Here Jürgen Moltmann's interpretation of the Spirit's work as the source of life also speaks to the challenge of developing a theology that responds to the brokenness of the inner city.[95] In Moltmann's account, "The attractive power and inner

90. The argument that follows owes its initial beginnings and reading of the biblical texts to Miroslav Volf, *Work in the Spirit: Toward a Theology of Work* (Oxford: Oxford University Press, 1991), especially pp. 88-119. What I have tried to do is adapt Volf's argument and use of biblical texts to the shape of urban responsibility.

91. Richard Shaull and Waldo Cesar, *Pentecostalism and the Future of the Christian Churches: Promises, Limitations, Challenges* (Grand Rapids: Eerdmans, 2000).

92. Sanders, *Saints in Exile: The Holiness-Pentecostal Experience in African American Religion and Culture* (New York: Oxford University Press, 1996). See further Omar M. McRoberts, "Understanding the 'New' Black Pentecostal Activism: Lessons from Ecumenical Urban Ministries in Boston," *Sociology of Religion* 60, no. 1 (Spring 1999): 47-70.

93. Solivan, *The Spirit, Pathos, and Liberation: Toward an Hispanic Pentecostal Theology* (Sheffield: Sheffield Academic Press, 1998), p. 12.

94. Shaull and Cesar, *Pentecostalism and the Future of the Christian Churches*, pp. 145-47, 150-71.

95. Moltmann, *The Spirit of Life: A Universal Affirmation*, trans. Margaret Kohl (Min-

force of the Spirit of the new creation of all things are not oriented towards the 'the world beyond.' The direction is the future."[96] Instead of fueling resignation toward the world, with its violence and death, the Spirit moves women and men to live toward the new creation of God (2 Cor. 1:22; Eph. 1:14) and everything that this new horizon anticipates (Rom. 8:11; 2 Cor. 5:17; Rev. 21:1-5). For, as Moltmann observes, "The 'Spirit of Christ' effects in us the raising of new energies through the word of the gospel. The 'Spirit of God' opens new possibilities round about us through the circumstances of history."[97] When we receive the Spirit (Gal. 3:2), we see from Scripture that we are thereby equipped for activity in the world (Gal. 5:16-18, 22-26; 6:9-10). God's Spirit unleashes potential and creative energy for new life (1 Cor. 12:6, 11). The gifts of the Spirit are entrusted callings that in love serve the needs of others and the liberation of creation.[98] Called by the Spirit, the church bears the charge of a witnessing community (Acts 1:8; 13:2-4; 20:22).

Accordingly, such a vision of the Spirit empowers the church in its mission in the inner city. For as Moltmann invites us to see, "If the Spirit of God is 'the Spirit of the resurrection,' then we are possessed by a hope which sees unlimited potentialities ahead, because it looks towards God's future."[99] The church is not constrained by what appear to be the limitations imposed by the city, but moves ahead in the abundance of the Spirit's outpouring. This does not contradict the nonutopian, "now-but-not-yet" nature of the kingdom. Redeeming every dimension of an inner-city community is *spiritual work* because it is "the restoration of disrupted community and the communication of life."[100] It is by the Spirit that Jesus brings healing to the sick and hope to the outcast (Luke 4:1, 14, 18; cf. John 14:19; Acts 10:37-38), and it is on the basis of Christ's resurrection that new birth is possible (1 Cor. 15:28). Here we are reminded that the presence of the Spirit in Isaiah is upon the Servant who will bring about knowledge of God, mercy, and justice (Isa. 11, 42, 61).[101] The Spirit who empowered Christ to bring good news to the poor, to proclaim mercy, do justice, and bring healing (Luke 11:20) is the same Spirit who empowers believers in the very per-

---

neapolis: Fortress, 1992); and Moltmann, *The Source of Life: The Holy Spirit and the Theology of Life*, trans. Margaret Kohl (Minneapolis: Fortress, 1997).

96. Moltmann, *The Spirit of Life*, p. 95.

97. Moltmann, *The Spirit of Life*, p. 103.

98. Volf, *Work in the Spirit*, pp. 95-106.

99. Moltmann, *The Spirit of Life*, p. 155.

100. Moltmann, *The Source of Life*, p. 66.

101. Michael Welker, *God the Spirit*, trans. John F. Hoffmeyer (Minneapolis: Fortress, 1994), pp. 108-82.

sonal activity of announcing and living the gospel in the cities of the world (Acts 1:3-12).

Community development is both a set of practices grounded in the image of God and artistry rooted in spirituality. As artistry, it involves, like sculpture, the bringing together and shaping of a variety of materials to create something new. This requires a vision of new possibilities as much as cultivated skills. It is work that requires the fullest expression of our gifts and callings; excellence is its standard. In the joy of its successes and the pain of its shortcomings, the artistry of community work embodies both the now and the not yet of God's reign. As a sign of God's *shalom* to come, it urges the imagination to look in new and creative ways toward the new creation. By bringing forth blessing, wholeness, and joy, community development as artistry of the kingdom is a witness to Christ's healing power in the world.[102]

Throughout this chapter I have sought to reflect on the church's role in rebuilding distressed urban communities. This has led me to examine the interrelationship between our reading of Nehemiah, the craft of community development, and the role of the Spirit in creating new communities. Rebuilding community is never simply a replication of a real or imagined past but the advance of something new and open to the triune God's future for the world. It depends not upon a universal project but upon faithfully doing thousands of little things right over a period of many years. Rooted in the resurrection of Christ and in active hope of God's future, rebuilding is based on the belief that new communities out of the ruins are possible. Revived neighborhoods are possible because of a God who still builds new communities on age-old foundations and raises up what was thought to be dead to new life. Many small versions of the Nehemiah story are still at work, pledges of the kingdom and the city of peace built by God. To one such story we now turn.

102. This paragraph was inspired by seeing neighborhood art projects, viewing a sculpture exhibit at the Guggenheim Museum in New York City, and reading Robert Wuthnow's *Creative Spirituality: The Way of the Artist* (Berkeley and Los Angeles: University of California Press, 2001).

CHAPTER 5

Singing a New Song

I t is a bright spring Sunday morning in Sandtown, a glorious day for New Song Community Church to celebrate its eleventh anniversary.[1] With Bibles tucked under their arms, most people walk from their homes on the surrounding blocks, making their way to the tent that has been raised on the corner of North Gilmor and Presstman streets. The main building just isn't large enough to handle the expected overflow crowd. But whether in a building or on a vacant lot, New Song always begins the week this way. New Song is an interracial community gathered for worship, grounded in the life of a neighborhood, seeking to be formed by the Word into a people who faithfully live for the Triune God.

Sometime after eleven A.M., vibrant music fills the tent and cascades out into the alleys and streets. "Alleluia! We will rejoice! Alleluia! We will rejoice!" the congregation sings with great joy. Mixing and bending chord progressions of traditional gospel music with newer, funkier gospel sounds heard more often on today's city streets, the worship leaders artfully guide in songs of celebration that praise God and call for faithful discipleship. Leading the singing with his strong voice and inviting presence, with his heart and with his head, is Elder C. W. Harris. Behind him and to his left, playing the keyboards, is Steve Smallman, who guides the musicians. To his right, Greg Boone's drumbeats are keeping time, and Wy Plummer is aiding the musical momentum with bass lines. Sonia Street, standing in the front row, adds the

---

1. The service I recount here was held in 1999. The reader should be aware that because New Song is continually growing and responding to its context, some program changes and other changes are not fully reflected in this chapter.

163

percussive texture of the tambourine. Throughout the singing, the church members sway, clap, and raise their hands in worship.

Testifying, giving voice to the struggles and celebrations of faith, is at the heart of New Song's worship.[2] This anniversary Sunday, the history of God's work in the neighborhood is central. "God has been embracing us as a church and a community," Elder Harris observes. Telling this story is a way of keeping the vision and call of New Song alive and growing. The testimonies flow out of this communally shared understanding. Glenda Mack, a Habitat for Humanity homeowner who lives in one of the beautifully renovated homes on North Stricker Street, stands to say, "I used to be living in a rat-infested hole. There were shootings. This neighborhood is blessed. . . . Look at all the families who have been helped." Al Stokes, who grew up in Sandtown and was recently married to LaVerne, a church member and Sandtown leader, praises God for his marriage. "Five months ago, the church came together for my wedding. God has blessed New Song with buildings, doctors, and people. They said nothing good could come out of Sandtown. Someone said nothing good could come out of Nazareth." Looking to the future, Stokes concludes, "By God's grace, we will keep together."

Anniversary Sunday is also Mother's Day, which can be very painful for some. Patrice, who lost both her mother and her father, publicly thanks the Lord for her mother's two sisters, who are there and have become her "mothers," and for the recent changes in her life. "Today I have a family and a job." Patrice then recalls a song that New Song used to sing eleven years ago when it first started. She leads the church in singing it — a rap version of the books of the Bible called "Holy Books."[3] "Mother" Sylvia Simmons also asks the church to sing "Don't Let Hatred Divide You," a soulful song about reconciliation. Janice Jamison, born and raised in Sandtown, remarks that the house her father was born and raised in is now a Sandtown Habitat house. She celebrates how the church keeps "spirits alive . . . and children off the streets." No stranger to the years of hardship in the neighborhood, Janice observes, "Now we have a community that others want to live in."

A sermon is preached, but the voices of the community of faith have been considerably more powerful. People have told stories of faith overcoming trouble and risk, stories that locate them in a new story of community and ultimately place them in the story of God's unrestrained grace and heal-

---

2. For an important discussion on this subject, see Scott A. Ellington, "The Costly Loss of Testimony," *Journal of Pentecostal Theology* 16 (2000): 48-59.

3. This song was written by James Ward, a musician and songwriter who greatly influenced New Song's musical tradition.

ing. The time of prayer that follows the time of testimony reinforces this truth.

Worship is a time of humility and celebration in the presence of God. This is why New Song responds by singing "We've Come This Far by Faith":

We've come this far by faith,
leaning on the Lord.
Trusting in His Holy Word.
He's never failed me yet.
Can't turn around.
We've come this far by faith.

When the past history of the neighborhood is considered, how far the church and community have come is amazing. It hasn't been easy, but it has been an act of faith in a God who authorizes confidence, an act of faith richly rewarded. People, both black and white, are worshipping together in one of the most segregated cities in the nation, a testimony to Christ, who breaks down a world of walls. Around the tent stand new houses where vacant shells stood before. A once-abandoned building is now a school. And on the vacant lot where the people sit, a new community center will soon take shape. All of this has come about, the church confesses, through the resurrecting power of God.

In his closing prayer, Elder Harris says, "And now, church begins after we leave here." Gathering for celebration on Sunday and dispersing to begin the work of doing justice on Monday, a cadence of one and six, forms the essential rhythm of a week in the life of New Song Community Church. Because God's activity in worship is of a piece with God's activity in the world, the worship of the church is of a piece with its life in the neighborhood.[4] The worship of God is flowing out into the streets of Sandtown, where it belongs in order to have integrity and authenticity (Isa. 1:11-17; 58:3-7; Amos 5:21-24; Heb. 13:15-16). For liturgy and justice belong together. Liturgy (or worship), Nicholas Wolterstorff has noted, is not authentic unless the activity of justice is also present.[5] New Song's participatory worship, life of prayer, patterns of testimony, struggle for reconciliation, announcement of pardon and grace, and labors for a more just and joyful community form a single life dedicated to God.

---

4. Nicholas Wolterstorff, "The Reformed Liturgy," in *Major Themes in Reformed Theology*, ed. Donald K. McKim (Grand Rapids: Eerdmans, 1992), p. 291.

5. Nicholas Wolterstorff makes the connection between worship and justice in "Justice as a Condition of Authentic Liturgy," *Theology Today* 48, no. 1 (April 1991): 12.

Monday morning begins the extension of worship with a flurry of activity around the neighborhood. Students begin classes early in the day at New Song Community Learning Center on North Gilmor Street. Along with their teachers, they will be there until late evening throughout the week. Two blocks west, on the 1300 block of North Fulton Avenue, New Song Family Health Center opens its doors, anticipating seeing patients all day. Next door to the health center are the Sandtown Habitat administrative and construction offices, the base of the physical rebuilding effort. The last construction crew will lock up late Saturday evening. Upstairs is EDEN Jobs, where men and women meet with job counselors to find job leads, vocational direction, and encouragement. Throughout the week, in various offices and ministry spaces, parents will hold meetings about their children's education, neighborhood residents will plan and work on more housing, neighbors will find love and mutual encouragement, and in both formal and informal groups, people will study the Bible and pray together. As Elder Harris noted on Sunday, church really begins after the service ends!

The name "New Song" tells a great deal about the church and its hope of God's new creation. In the biblical witness, a "new song" was a response lifted up to God's bringing forth justice and reconciliation (Pss. 40:3; 96:1; 98:1; 144:9; 149:1; Isa. 42:10). Indeed, in John's vision, the "new song" sung by the saints is the chorus of the new city (Rev. 5:9). For a new song is the rhythm of God's future, announcing that the course of the world has changed because of Christ's victory over the powers. Like the meaning of its name, New Song is a community of reconciliation and cultural activity, composing and improvising a "new song" in anticipation of a city where the nations come to worship (Rev. 5:9) and all live in peace (Rev. 21:1-5). A new song is a way of life sung not for itself but for God and the peace of the city, a "counter song" among the rhythms of the city, a voiced theology that anticipates the new creation.

In this chapter I will recount and reflect on the story of New Song Community Church in Sandtown. I will not attempt to tell a comprehensive story or all of its countless stories. Instead I will focus on overall themes in the life of New Song as it has sought to faithfully seek the peace of the city. I will tell the story of New Song to encourage the church in faithful discipleship and to render thanks to God.[6] I hope this story will show how seeking the peace of the city flows out of the heart of a church that is bonded to its community.

---

6. For some early accounts of New Song, see James Bock, "People Find a Voice with New Song," *The Evening Sun*, 17 November 1994, B-1, 2; "Building on Faith," editorial, *The Evening Sun*, 15 July 1994, A-10; and Harold A. McDougall, *Black Baltimore: A New Theory of Community* (Philadelphia: Temple University Press, 1993), pp. 173-79.

THREE R'S PLUS ONE

How did New Song get started? Sandtown has always known the presence of God in many ways: in the creation, in the life of believers, in the Spirit of life, and in its households of faith. But whenever a new church begins, it has a unique story. New Song's history began with the prayers and sacrifice of people in Sandtown; it is a church born of the community. Another part of New Song's beginning belongs to an ongoing conversation about discipleship that Allan Tibbels and I had over a number of years. It is important to say something about our exchange not because of us but because of the theological and moral issues at stake.

Animating our conversation was the question "What would it mean for us to follow Christ in the city of Baltimore, a city racially divided and increasingly home to the region's abandoned poor?" The challenge for Allan was particularly unique. In 1981, while playing basketball with a group of teenagers in a church gym, Allan broke his neck. But even as he and his wife Susan and daughters Jessica and Jennifer faced a considerably more difficult life with him as a quadriplegic, the conviction of being called by the gospel never ceased.

Shaping in every way our understanding of calling was John Perkins, whose pioneering efforts in church-based Christian community development have spanned about four decades.[7] Perkins began his ministry in the 1960s in Mendenhall, Mississippi, where he and his wife, Vera Mae, helped to establish Voice of Calvary.[8] Voice of Calvary was an interracial congregation that initiated cooperative economic ventures, helped develop affordable housing, a health center, and a law office, and undertook numerous civil-rights activities. This same commitment, which was the path of cruciform discipleship in the South during the 1960s, took the Perkins family to Jackson, Mississippi, and then to Pasadena, California, where new churches and ministries were started. Today the Perkinses have come nearly full circle — back to Voice of Calvary in Jackson, Mississippi.

Perkins's message is that if you take the gospel seriously, it means that the church must be serious about justice and reconciliation. It was on this basis that he formulated a strategy that can be summarized as "the three R's":

---

7. In recent years, Perkins's work has led to the formation of the Christian Community Development Association (CCDA). Based at Lawndale Community Church in Chicago, this national alliance of about five hundred groups has committed itself to better understanding how the gospel can be more clearly practiced in struggling communities.

8. This work now goes by the name of Mendenhall Ministries and Church.

relocation, reconciliation, and redistribution. He articulates this basic way of the Christian faith in his book *With Justice for All.*[9]

Relocation begins by asking the question "How did Jesus love?" The Word Incarnate, he began showing his love by living among us. To follow the way of Christ, it is absolutely essential to live in the community where an impact is sought. Incarnational witness is the source of the church's strength.

Reconciliation is the heart of the Christian story, both vertical (with God) and horizontal (with our fellow human beings). Enfolded in the story of a sinful people forgiven and reconciled to a holy God, the church is to embrace, love, forgive, and incorporate people across all barriers of gender, ethnicity, race, culture, and class.

Redistribution speaks to the biblical vision of justice for the poor. Because Christians are to be stewards of God's world and his gifts, they are to work for just relationships in tangible ways, especially through sharing their time, resources, gifts, and skills.

These "three R's" resist and counter-narrate the story of the inner city in at least three ways. Relocation reverses the ongoing demographic decline of the city.[11] Reconciliation responds to the fissures of race, ethnicity, and class

---

9. John Perkins, *With Justice for All* (Ventura: Regal Books, 1982). This remains the best introduction to Perkins's thinking. Essential autobiographical information — which I used in my description of Voice of Calvary — can be found in John Perkins, *Let Justice Roll Down* (Ventura: Regal Books, 1976). Important insights on the ecclesiocentric nature of his work can be found in John Perkins, *A Quiet Revolution* (Waco: Word Books, 1976). Perkins's philosophy on community development can be found in more detail in his book entitled *Beyond Charity: The Call to Christian Community Development* (Grand Rapids: Baker, 1992). See also *Restoring At-Risk Communities: Doing It Right and Doing It Together,* ed. John M. Perkins (Grand Rapids: Baker, 1995).

10. Regrettably, Christians sometimes use "relocation" to assume a sense of moral and intellectual superiority over the people of the community. Instead of being neighbors, they can become exploitative "missionaries." This phenomenon is not limited to cross-cultural situations; it can also be class- or education-based. The people of the community where this occurs are fully aware of what's happening, and they rightly perceive it as just another bid for power. The end result is an inhibiting or blocking of the gospel for all involved. Relocation can also be abused to justify or even enhance the process of gentrification and the displacement of the community. More important are the Christians from the community who made the decision (often a costly one) to stay when it would have been easy to move. For these reasons, relocation is more complex than most of us imagine, and more fraught with danger to Christ's name than has been acknowledged.

11. In "The Enclave, the Citadel, and the Ghetto: What Has Changed in the Post-Fordist U.S. City," Peter Marcuse suggests parts of a similar strategy, though it is unconnected to any church base: "The outcast ghetto, combining race and class in a new form of separation and exclusion, needs to build up its own strength and to break the bondage of that exclu-

that have divided the city. And redistribution refutes the capital depletion and labor-market detachment and exploitation so prevalent in excluded urban neighborhoods.[12]

However, Perkins's "three R's" are not best understood as a strategy for discipleship and witness or even a philosophy of community development. What Perkins is driving at is ecclesiology — or, better, what is driving Perkins is ecclesiology. The church exists for mission, Perkins stresses. With his unique story and conviction, John Perkins directed my friend Allan Tibbels and me to see that the church is God's reconciled community pursuing justice at the point of greatest suffering in the world. As Harvie Conn points out, the ministries of justice and reconciliation are not additions that flow out of the church, deeds tacked on to the "real ministry" of the Word to keep things "balanced."[12] Rather, seeking after justice and reconciliation is constitutive of ecclesial life in union with Christ and in action in the world. This is Perkins's challenge to the church.

Allan and I believed that one more "R" should precede the others — *repentance.* As we talked about why we felt compelled to move to Sandtown, we understood our relocation in the framework of *metanoia,* the Greek word for repentance. Jesus said, "Repent [*metanoia*], for the kingdom of God is at hand." As Peter Price has noted, repentance is not feeling sorry or apologizing, engaging in rituals of regret, but an invitation "to open up a new world view . . . to put an end to business as usual."[13] Repentance means owning sin as an offense against God but also moving forward to a new way of obedience, a turning in a different direction, as its Hebrew counterpart *shub* would suggest. Allan and I took the pain, brokenness, and racial oppression of Sandtown to be our responsibility, the history of Baltimore to be our common history and therefore a call to *metanoia.*

The Canadian singer and songwriter Bruce Cockburn wrestles with the question of corporate responsibility in his song "Broken Wheel":

---

sion. That means *both* strengthening the community, bringing the middle class back and reinforcing cultural ties, *and* breaking down segregation, particularly for the poor, fighting for their integration into the mainstream of economic and political activity and power" (*Urban Affairs Review* 33, no. 2 [November 1997]: 256).

12. Conn, *Evangelism: Doing Justice and Preaching Grace* (Grand Rapids: Zondervan, 1982).

13. Price, "Searching for a Future Waiting to Be Born: Metanoia, Ministry, and Mission into the Third Millennium," *International Review of Mission* 85, no. 39 (October 1996): 541. See also the compelling work by Jim Wallis, *The Call to Conversion: Recovering the Gospel for These Times* (San Francisco: Harper & Row, 1981), esp. pp. 1-17.

Way out on the rim of the galaxy
The gifts of the Lord lie torn
Into whose charge the gifts were given
Have made it a curse for so many to be born
This is my trouble —
These were my fathers

So how am I supposed to feel?
Way out on the rim of the broken wheel

You and me — we are the break in the broken wheel
Bleeding wound that will not heal

As my friend and I saw it, African-American neighborhoods that should be flourishing before God lay torn, and we were part of the break, the reason for this "bleeding wound that will not heal." We might not have been there when Sandtown was constructed, but we were living off the world of myths and privileges on which Sandtown was created, and therefore subject to its judgment. We knew we were complicit in the racism and systemic injustice that led to the brokenness of the neighborhood.

If we really grasped our faith, we had no choice but to repent. As Cockburn points out, "No adult of sound mind/Can be an innocent bystander." Our only hope was (and is) divine grace, as Cockburn knows so well:

Lord, spit on our eyes so we can see
How to wake up from this tragedy.[14]

Because Christ had "spit on our eyes," we believed that we had to deal with the unresolved habits and costs of America's original sin, racism, and to wake up to the tragedy present in our own city. Because of the Gospel, we could no longer remain "innocent bystanders," standing aside as the suffering of Baltimore deepened. Our Christian conversion as an ongoing process required us to take specific steps, unlearning old ways of living and embracing new ways of living. And so we decided to relocate to an inner-city neighborhood — not

14. Bruce Cockburn, "Broken Wheel," *Inner City Front* (Golden Mountain Music Corporation, 1981). For an analysis of this song as a key to Cockburn's theology, see J. Richard Middleton and Brian J. Walsh, "Theology at the Rim of the Broken Wheel: Bruce Cockburn and Christian Faith in a Postmodern World," *Grail* 9, no. 2 (1993): 15-39.

to change it or save it, but to be neighbors and to learn the agenda of the community and to live on the terms set by our neighbors. In the language of the Apostle Paul, we were trying to "work out" our own salvation "with fear and trembling" (Phil. 2:12).

Why did the Tibbels and I move to *Sandtown?* God's leading is the answer. After much prayer and demographic study, we chose Sandtown over other communities because it was a neighborhood of incredibly rich history, character, and internal strength. But, as we have already seen in Chapter 1, Sandtown was also a neighborhood outside "the dream," daily facing the struggle for life. It had one of the highest murder rates in a murderous city, one of the highest infant-mortality rates, one of the highest rates of lead poisoning (from lead-based paint), one of the highest rates of school failure, one of the highest rates of eviction, and seemingly more vacant than occupied housing. We believed that God was calling us to be neighbors. So, following Perkins's challenge to "relocate," that is just what we did. With the blessing of Ella Johnson, the leader of the Sandtown-Winchester Improvement Association, in November of 1986 we began our life in Sandtown with the simple act of renting housing and putting down roots as neighbors.

People asked, "Who are these white people?" It was a fair question! Most white people who come to Sandtown — or, for that matter, any other inner-city neighborhood — want something. They are bill collectors, insurance salesmen, landlords, or drug buyers. When people would ask, "What are you doing here?" our answer was always the same: "We are here to be neighbors." We came to become a part of the neighborhood, to listen, to learn, to build friendships, and to live out our faith. We held tightly to a commitment of God's *shalom* for Sandtown, but we had no plans or programs.[15] Instead of imposing our own agendas, we sought to place our lives in service to the community. We would make the road by traveling it together.

For over two years, when we weren't working to renovate our houses, we were out and around in the community, "hanging out." During this time, the foundational relationships of the church were formed. Allan volunteered at the local Lillian Jones Recreation Center, then run by Pastor Renay Kelley. Kelly Simpkins, who was part of New Song during the first year, got very involved in the center. We also became active in the local community group that Ella Johnson headed, and volunteered to counsel tenants in disputes with landlords. When the center needed fliers delivered to every house in the

15. On suspending all "knowledge" but the cross as a missiological strategy, see 1 Corinthians 2:1-5. This is especially relevant when human knowledge is recognized as having cultural and social elements in its construction.

neighborhood, we volunteered with neighborhood kids we were meeting so that we could learn the streets and meet people. We never drove anywhere in the neighborhood, so we were constantly out and about, meeting new people every day. Yet in every way, we were pretty much useless to the community, other than perhaps as comic relief!

But as people got to know us, they welcomed us, a testimony to Sandtown's capacity for grace and its deep reservoir of spiritual power. This was a much more profoundly social and theological act than anything related to our relocation. My neighbors — including Mac, Shocky, Tick, Raymond, Richard, and Mamie — were among the many in Sandtown who "raised me" as a neighbor and pastor. We realized how blessed we were to be received in this way when we heard about the African-American family that had recently moved into an all-white neighborhood in Baltimore, only to be driven out by threats to their safety. Of course, this is not to say that we had achieved reconciliation, that barriers of race had been broken down, or that many people were not suspicious of us. People should have been suspicious. Still, we were learning about our neighborhood and building trust. While we could never disconnect ourselves from the options that privilege bestowed on us, our future was connected to the future of Sandtown, its struggles and joys becoming ours.

As I have indicated, New Song's roots aren't so much the result of the initial relocation of a few people — that wasn't nearly as important as the staying power of the people who didn't relocate during hard times. New Song's roots are the consequence of God bringing together people of faith from different blocks and backgrounds who shared a love for God, one another, and their neighbors. Beginnings are always important for new churches, and these early days established the foundation for New Song's future.

WHERE JUST TWO OR THREE ARE GATHERED

"Why don't we have our own church right here?" Isaac "Ike" Newman and Antoine Holly asked one Sunday morning as we sat in my living room. Nearly every day, Ike, Antoine, Arteze "Artie" Montgomery, and I played together on the basketball court, went on trips around the city, hung out at my house, or shared a Bible study. Allan was also building many relationships where he and his family now lived — on North Stricker Street, ten blocks from my home. (Originally their relocation had them living in a tiny, wheelchair inaccessible rental house on North Gilmor Street.)

Mother's Day 1988 became the day that New Song began formally meeting regularly for worship and calling itself a church. Our meeting place was my house on North Mount Street, where worshippers sat in a circle on an eclectic collection of donated furniture. On most Sundays, that was a small group — from two to twenty-five of us! Fitt Bennet, Paige Fitz, Frank Ross, Mr. Ulysses Carter, Ike Newman, Antoine Holly, Artie Montgomery, Jermaine Alexander, Reginald "Big Man" Williams, Janita Moore, Shaconda Sullivan, Tyra Sullivan, Paris Sullivan, Mr. Eddie and Esther, and the Tibbels family were among the early neighborhood core group. Soon others like Linda Paige became involved with their families, and many — families and individuals alike — started to consider it their home church and would visit regularly.

People became involved in New Song because it was a community church that, on the basis of the gospel, welcomed and involved them. New Song has a Presbyterian affiliation, but it was accepted and grew because it was a church in and of the community. The wonders of God needed to come alive in the life and thought of the neighborhood (Acts 2:7, 11). We were not concerned with spreading our denominational tradition; we focused on living as neighbors and sharing our Christian faith within this context. In the dynamic movement of the gospel, the experience of Christianity both shapes the context and is shaped by it.

As the church grew by word of mouth among people who did not have a church home in the neighborhood, a borrowed pulpit that sat on wheels and some folding chairs were added. People would be sitting down the hall and up the stairs, and, when the weather was good, outside on the front steps. From the start, we emphasized "come as you are" dress, and services where everyone was welcome and all could participate. We offered prayers for the needs of families and neighbors. Everyone shared and talked about the Word (1 Cor. 14:26). For the first year we didn't take up an offering, though people could give if they wanted to. Later we put an offering plate in the back of the room.

Everything revolved around building community together. So during the summer, for example, at least once a month all of us would pile into a couple of vans and go to a park for a picnic. We would go downtown and sometimes take trips to other cities. Community came through having fun together, sharing our lives, and learning to be followers of Christ together.

Sandtown truly knows something of what Langston Hughes identifies in his poem "Harlem" as "a dream deferred." When the ability to dream a better future dies, the consequences are life-destroying. We knew we needed to articulate our dreams for Sandtown. So one Sunday, with one eye cast on the biblical texts of Nehemiah, Isaiah, and Luke and the other on neighborhood injuries small and large, our small house congregation set out to be urban planners and visionaries. During a series of evening services, we made a list of the problems in the neighborhood: substandard housing, schools that weren't working, massive unemployment, and "health care" that consisted of trips to the emergency room. But then we asked a more important question: "What is God's dream for our community?" To paraphrase Langston Hughes, What would "dreaming a new neighborhood" look like on the blocks where we lived?

Through discussion and dialogue, people shared their views of what the future of their community could look like. Why not a community that provided jobs and developed businesses? Why not a streetscape filled with newly planted trees and no longer marred by vacant houses? Why couldn't the community have a program focusing on middle-school-aged youth that would eventually offer job training or college scholarships? Why couldn't medical help be offered to people with drug addictions? And all of this, the group felt, was part of what it meant to develop spiritually. There were no evident dichotomies or splits between spiritual and material realities. There was never any talk about "social action" or "ministry." The discussion and frame of concern were always about building a better neighborhood for our families and our neighbors, and how our faith made that important.

Putting crayon to paper, hands small and large drew the features of a new community on a large sheet of thin newsprint paper. It was soon filled with the bright, colorful images of a new day. In an upper corner, the sun shone over the neighborhood. The church had a new home, a building that fit in with the architecture of the community. There were community businesses and a church-operated health center. Absent were vacant houses and debris. The streets were renamed "Hope" and "No Drugs." And people were out on the streets, safely enjoying life in Sandtown.

Buildings and figures etched in crayon were evidence of a prayerful and stubborn belief that these city blocks would more fully — and more rightly — experience God's mercy and wholeness. No one in the room was a skilled construction worker, a medical professional, or a potential benefactor with financial means. But there were strengths and assets to build on and a conviction that in our midst, the prophetic Word was coming alive and would empower us to do the work that needed to be done. In Joel 2:28 we read, "I will pour out my Spirit on all people. Your sons and daughters will prophesy, your old men will dream dreams, your young men will see visions." New Song watched this passage come alive in its midst.

NO MORE VACANT HOUSES

Based on our faith, we saw what could happen differently in our neighborhood. Our first common goal was to eliminate vacant housing in our community, not by demolishing current buildings but by creating homes that would be affordable for everyone in Sandtown. Everyone agreed that if this could be accomplished, the direction of the neighborhood would undergo a significant positive change. Many factors called for creating a way for the people of the community to own decent and affordable housing: (1) the vast majority of residents wanted to stay in the community; (2) the average rent/housing cost often exceeded 70 percent of a household's income; (3) virtually all of the available housing was substandard; (4) over 85 percent of the houses being rented were owned by absentee landlords; (5) the rate of home ownership was less than 20 percent; and (6) the growing number of vacant units posed a serious health threat to the neighborhood.

Given these dynamics, we outlined what a truly effective housing program for our neighborhood would have to do: (1) make home ownership a possibility for all residents of Sandtown; (2) rely on the expertise, strengths, and wisdom of the community; (3) eliminate the blight and danger of vacant buildings without destroying the fabric of the neighborhood; (4) enhance the physical fabric of the community; and, in the process, (5) improve the economic base and health status of the community. This was a community-based strategy that would enable the people of the community — who had always been left out of the process and the benefits of urban development — to own, manage, and be stewards of their architectural and economic environment. We didn't start planning by considering the funding or even what funds we thought could be raised. Instead, we began with what was right for Sandtown and faithful to the gospel.

Familiar with Habitat for Humanity International, an organization founded in 1976 by Millard and Linda Fuller, we decided to contextualize the largely rural Habitat model for an inner-city neighborhood.[16] The powerful

16. Millard Fuller has written a number of books on Habitat for Humanity. One that serves as a good introduction is *A Simple, Decent Place to Live: The Building Realization of Habitat for Humanity* (Dallas: Word, 1995). For an evaluation of the present and potential influence of Habitat on U.S. housing policy, see Howard Husock, "It's Time to Take Habitat for Humanity Seriously," *City Journal* 5, no. 3 (Summer 1995): 35-43. However, Husock proposes removing government altogether from the development of affordable housing. This simply isn't reasonable, and Habitat projects should be careful not to give cover to public withdrawal from housing when its own efforts, while important, are quantitatively modest when one looks at the major crisis in affordable housing. For a critical assessment of Habitat's public

Habitat vision that the Fullers have helped bring into being is one that is good news for the world. The ABC's of Habitat are simple but powerful:

1. *Create simple, decent housing.* Habitat builds new homes or renovates vacant housing for home ownership by using a combination of private donations, volunteer labor, donated materials, and sweat equity (hands-on labor) by each prospective homeowner.
2. *Offer no-profit, no-interest mortgages.* The selling of homes in the Habitat program offers a model of community economic development. Each homeowner pays back the entire cost of his/her house. But the mortgage is interest free and sold at no profit, and house payments are reinvested in the community to build more homes.
3. *Offer those who need it most a roof over their head.* Homeowners are chosen on the basis of their financial need, the condition of their present housing, and their willingness to participate in the Habitat program. Most of all, because shelter is a right granted by God, they are folks who simply need a roof over their head.
4. *Stress the importance of sweat equity.* Habitat is a community-built program. Homeowners put in several hundred hours of "sweat equity" working on their own homes as well as other Habitat homes.

Habitat proved to be a powerful vehicle for the practice of hospitality and sharing in Sandtown — although we did depart from the traditional Habitat model in several significant ways. Our effort was locally initiated (in partnership with Ella Johnson and the Sandtown-Winchester Community Association), community led, and part of a holistic approach.

People who were locally involved in housing development viewed the idea with tremendous skepticism, and were candid about that. Among the typical responses were "You're going to use volunteers to build houses?" and "You need lots of money to do housing, but you don't have any." But comments from the neighborhood also included "It can't hurt to try." Generally, a wait-and-see attitude prevailed.

Graciously, Allan Tibbels agreed to focus on organizing the effort. From the beginning of New Song, Allan has provided dedicated, consistent, and remarkable leadership. His patience, passion, spiritual depth, and management

role, see Jerome P. Baggett, *Habitat for Humanity®: Building Private Homes, Building Public Religion* (Philadelphia: Temple University Press, 2001). At the same time, I don't think that Habitat's importance as a theological initiative or its value to local communities is treated with the respect that is deserved.

skills have given New Song its center, and he has provided continuity from the beginning. There simply would be no New Song without his commitment and leadership.

Thus, in 1989, with only a dollar to its name and no housing expertise, New Song initiated Sandtown Habitat for Humanity, starting with a vacant house acquired from the city. Efforts were coordinated with the local community group, Sandtown-Winchester Improvement Association, and its leader, Ella Johnson. During the day, Allan would be out and about in the community, working with Habitat and coordinating construction details. In the evening, he would be on the telephone, calling everyone he knew in an effort to raise money to finish whatever phase that first house was in. The Tibbels's basement served as a storage area, and their living room as a conference room. A local bank provided the first grant for Sandtown Habitat, and it was used to acquire more vacant houses to rehabilitate.

Although Sandtown Habitat was separate from the church, the church provided the energy, vision, values, and resources to make the organization work. Every Sunday we talked about the project, prayed for it, and pledged to put all of our human and financial resources behind it. It was the young men in the church who worked on the first house — Ike, Arteze, Antoine, and Fitt. The following year, Sandtown Habitat completed its first house in partnership with Rosalind Witherspoon and her family. Completing a single house was a challenging but very exciting first step for the church and the community. What increased the excitement was the wider recognition received: the first dedication was attended by Mayor Kurt Schmoke and other local officials, as well as U.S. Senator Paul Sarbanes and then-Congressman Kweisi Mfume.

Is such a housing process too slow? Why not let professional developers do it? Questions like these indicated a misperception of our undertaking. New Song and Sandtown Habitat were building people, leaders, community, an economic base, and capacity, not a product for profit. The highest good was not its profit value as a commodity but its use to the community. And by implementing a community-based housing program that also actively sought the volunteer support of people from the surrounding metropolitan region, Sandtown Habitat became a bridge of communication and human connection between the divides of urban and suburban, rich and poor, black and white. In this way, inner-city isolation began to be broken through as others were invited to share in the work of rebuilding, bringing resources and leaving with firsthand knowledge of the neighborhood and its people, assets, and challenges. Ironically, Habitat did a much better and much less expensive job than traditional developers. Building by a slow-but-sure process, Sandtown

Habitat was evidence that God "chose the lowly things of this world . . . to nullify the things that are" (1 Cor. 1:28).

Expanding its scope of work in the neighborhood, New Song worked and prayed to be able to acquire a building at the corner of Gilmor and Presstman Streets that was known in the neighborhood as "The Mansion." A large abandoned building with an adjacent carriage house and a wildly over-grown yard, the mansion was one of the most popular "playgrounds" in Sandtown. From the start we knew that this building would be the ideal place for worship as well as the perfect base for Habitat and other community ini-tiatives. For three years the church agonized over negotiations to acquire the property. Finally, in 1989, after scraping together every dollar we could find, we were able to purchase the building at an auction. So professionally low-key was the person who handled the auction that even though New Song's bid was the winning one, it was impossible to tell until afterward, when he smiled and congratulated us! With help from the Community Law Center, we ob-tained excellent free legal services that helped us complete the purchase.

The location of the building couldn't have been better: 1385 North Gilmor Street, at the corner of a major intersection in the center of the neigh-borhood. But, having been vacant for over twenty years, the building, once a convent, was in need of extensive rehabilitation. The roof was so badly rotted that, during a rainstorm, water would pour down through the three stories into the first-floor main room. And that was just one of the numerous resto-ration problems we faced. We had spent our last penny to make the purchase — but we were rich in "working capital." Within hours of signing the deed, we began renovation, using a combination of neighborhood "sweat equity" and pro bono professional design services from a local group called the Neighborhood Design Center.

New Song's building renovation was primarily headed up by neighbor-hood youth. Ike, Antoine, Arteze, Fitt, Jermaine, "Big Man," and "Luck" were among the young people in the neighborhood who labored with incredible commitment after school, on weekends, and even on holidays. When a deliv-ery of lumber, drywall, paint, or electrical supplies would arrive, they would interrupt what they were doing to unload and store it. They did almost every-thing: they cleaned the yard, framed new walls, insulated ceilings, set con-crete, painted, built a wheelchair ramp, and boarded up the site at the end of the day. Along the way, help came from others too. Since we had no money for dumpsters to haul away construction debris, Mr. White, who lived in Sandtown, would leave his truck outside the building on Saturdays so we could load it up. On Monday morning he would drive the load to the dump. People from some metropolitan-area churches began to get involved as well.

Mary Ann Bell of McLean Presbyterian Church was among the most dedicated: she never failed to answer a call for assistance.

Significantly for New Song, Baltimore's prestigious Abell Foundation became a key supporter. It all started in 1989 when we met Robert Embry Jr., the president of the foundation, who has a deep love for Baltimore and is committed to efforts that enhance the city. He encouraged New Song to apply for support for the building. A few months later, Sita Culman, the vice president of the foundation, called and said she would like to visit. After unboarding a side entrance with a crowbar, we guided Sita through the first few floors, watching out for rats and broken glass while we shared our dreams to make it a center of community redevelopment. A few months after her visit, we received a grant, the first ever for New Song. And thereafter, at every key juncture of organizational growth, the Abell Foundation provided vital support. Other locally based foundations, including Baltimore Community Foundation and the Harry and Jeanette Weinberg Foundation, as well as the national Annie E. Casey Foundation have played important roles in different facets of New Song's development and growth.

The support of city and state government would also become meaningful. In fact, in 1990, with the help of Mayor Schmoke, John Perkins, and Jack Kemp, then the Housing and Urban Development Secretary, the old convent was dedicated to a new use.

As we continued working to transform our community, still others recognized and supported our efforts. One of the most memorable honors and important events for both Sandtown Habitat and New Song took place in 1992, when President and Mrs. Carter, Habitat's most famous volunteers, came to work in Sandtown. This was the opportunity of a lifetime for Sandtown Habitat, particularly since our respect for President Carter was immense.[17] At the time, Sandtown Habitat had just completed its first five houses. Gary Mitchell was the first and only employee, soon to be joined by John Best as construction manager.

To sustain the impact of the Carters' visit, Sandtown Habitat decided to kick off a five-year, 100-house project. As we continued to grow, so did the support for our venture. A partnership involving technical support and no-interest construction loans from The Enterprise Foundation, founded by James and Patty Rouse, enabled us to double our rate of production. This was truly incredible; it gave the rebuilding process a big push forward. Mayor

---

17. A recent biography by Douglas Brinkley, *The Unfinished Presidency: Jimmy Carter's Journey Beyond the White House* (New York: Viking, 1998), brings together many of the reasons why Carter is such an important person in our world today.

Schmoke and the city of Baltimore provided vacant houses and technical support. Congregations such as the Episcopal Cathedral of the Incarnation began building a house a year. Partnerships with local banking institutions were also important. Bert Hash Jr., a respected local banker, first became involved with Sandtown Habitat, and later became president of its board of directors.

In order to generate public support for the project, President Carter agreed to come to Baltimore in March 1992 for a site visit and an afternoon luncheon. We had only a few months to plan the event, but we managed to secure the banquet room of the downtown Hyatt Hotel, which could hold twelve hundred people. As might be expected, many tickets were sold to a "who's who" of Baltimore's political, social, and business community. But four hundred tickets were reserved for the people of Sandtown. And so on the afternoon of the banquet, cars and buses left en masse from Sandtown for the downtown hotel. After the luncheon, where every seat was filled and the testimonies and talks were moving, the Carters went to Sandtown to visit the work site. Down the 1600 block of North Gilmor Street they walked, stopping to look at the houses underway. A marching band played, and over a thousand people were out to cheer the former President and First Lady. After a brief ceremony, during which they promised to return in a few months to work, a board covering a doorway was symbolically removed from the future home of Sonia Street.

And the Carters did indeed return for an incredible day of rebuilding in Sandtown. Ten houses were started, and Sonia Street's house was completed a few months later. Sonia never tires of saying, "Jimmy Carter and I built my house." And he planted a maple tree in her yard that continues to grow ten years later. Others who worked on their houses and became homeowners were Lillian Armstrong, Debra Burke, LaVerne Stokes, Linda Greene, Darlene McCarter, Sylvia Simmons, and Wanda Smith.

One year later, right on schedule, Sandtown Habitat completed twenty houses. President Carter has often said that when a family becomes owners of a Habitat home, their children begin to talk about where to go to college. How true that is today in Sandtown.

Within five years of the Carters' visit, the hundred houses were completed, and work on a second hundred was begun. (The second hundred would be completed in four years' time.) Festive house dedications took place at a rate of one or two a month. Entire blocks were turned from areas of blight and decay into sites of stability and home ownership. Support from foundations and corporations has been fundamental to this transformation. But also instrumental has been the One Church–One Home program of

Sandtown Habitat, through which congregations have committed funds and volunteers to renovate homes. Episcopal, Catholic, and Presbyterian congregations really engaged this challenge, completing at least half of the houses that Sandtown Habitat has built. Thousands of volunteers a year have also made significant differences. Dr. John Wessner, for example, became involved with the second house that Sandtown completed, bringing a Christmas tree as a housewarming gift. Since then he has volunteered to install the heating system in every home that Sandtown Habitat has completed. Dr. Wessner has given his time, himself, and much more to Sandtown.

On the leadership front, Sandtown Habitat homeowner LaVerne Stokes joined Allan Tibbels as Co–Executive Director. LaVerne's deep faith in God, passionate commitment to the community, and tremendous leadership skills make her a uniquely powerful leader. Together Allan and LaVerne make the best leadership team that I've ever seen.

How did a dream for a renewed and more just community become a reality? Slowly, almost imperceptibly, the Spirit of life brought it about — one person, one family, one house, and one block at a time. It's the story of the loaves and the fishes all over again, the Lord exponentially blessing one house and the commitment of a few to a new life made possible by the widening space for life created by the Spirit.

EXPANDING A HOLISTIC VISION

If Sandtown was to become a healthy, flourishing place where children and families could dwell in peace, then housing was just a beginning. Looking at a neighborhood map and defining the natural boundaries where we lived, we agreed on a fifteen-block focus area in the north-central section out of the seventy-two-block total in Sandtown. New Song's purpose and vision coalesced around seeking the *shalom* — the flourishing of justice, wholeness, and health — of these fifteen blocks, where approximately four thousand people lived. The "map board" that we developed, which showed all of the housing units, became a guide to which houses we had completed and which ones still needed renovation. But this commitment to the *shalom* of a small geographic area would also take the church into the fields of education, health care, and economic development. Our concern was not the delivery of social services. At best, that would address some of the consequences of exclusion; at worst, it would develop dependency. Instead, our goal was to strengthen both families and the community so that they could address their own needs in dignity and in mutuality. This was a task that required institution building, social reform, and spiritual transformation. And at the heart of this needed to be the church, the spiritual center of this calling.

Partnerships and collaboration are important, but if they aren't based on local terms, they can also restrain organizational development and community advancement. So, although genuinely committed to working in collaborative partnership with others to get the job of a better Sandtown done, New Song maintained an independent, single-minded focus on achieving clearly set community goals, raising its own resources, and enhancing community ownership. How a church goes about this — with kindness and gentleness, yet firm resolve — is part of its Christian witness.

Preparing Children for the Future

When we assessed the educational systems in Sandtown, we found them to be severely deficient. By the time children in Sandtown entered the first grade, they were already being set up for failure in a system that largely warehoused them. By the time they reached high-school age, perhaps as many as 70 to 80 percent of them had dropped out. And only a few individuals had gone on to college and stayed in the neighborhood. The voices of parents pleading for changes had gone unheeded for years. Susan Tibbels's first encounter with the local public school was telling. The principal actually refused her two daughters admission to the school, saying, "I don't know why you moved here. You can't make a difference. And I can't help educate your children. They're too far ahead after being in county schools." In effect, he stated that the school had no intention of helping children achieve academic success. Parents later organized to have him removed from his position, but that didn't fix what was wrong with the school. The problems could hardly have been more severe.

Though it was not in her plans when she moved to Sandtown, Susan put her newly acquired education degree to work by starting New Song Community Learning Center at the Gilmor Street building. With no Head Start or other early childhood education program present in the community, Susan enlisted the help of other parents to develop the Center. It began with two preschool classes. Linda Paige was the first staff member, Sonia Street the next. Since New Song preschool was organized as a cooperative, it required parents to be involved on a monthly basis.

As children began graduating from the preschool, parents began thinking that the Learning Center needed to offer even longer-term involvement. They talked about it in regular parents' meetings as well as in informal conversations. And so the after-school program, named the After-Three Club by the participating students, was born. It focused on educational enrichment activities, including tutorial assistance with homework as well as activities in reading, science, language arts, and drama, all with a rich African-American cultural emphasis. And the Center began to flourish. A library and computer lab that were built into the center were used constantly. A wonderful neighborhood gardening program was provided by the Irvine Nature Center. And a vision for a music program and a choir was also realized. Staff member Shelly Harris became choir leader, and Steve Smallman played the piano. This was the beginning of what would become the Voices of Hope choir, later renamed the Sandtown Children of Praise.

If the Center's beginning was modest, its growth was not. A board of parents charted each next step, looking toward their children's future success. Chanel Boone, Renee Hopkins, Jane Johnson, and Mary Lee Williams were involved both as parents and as dedicated staff leaders. After a few years, Jane Johnson became the Assistant Director of the Center. When the first group of students in After-Three reached middle school, it was increasingly clear to students, parents, and teachers alike that these children would be lost if they stayed in the public schools. So in the brief space of the summer of 1995, the parents and staff developed New Song Academy, a full-time school for middle-school students. Basing its academic program on the highly regarded Calvert Curriculum, the academy offered a private-school curriculum stressing educational basics along with a highly creative community-based learning experience. After graduation, students would be placed in private high schools or "magnet" public high schools.

A visit to the classroom on any given day quickly told the story of the school's success. Every visitor received a welcome from the designated greeter of the day as well as the class. "Good afternoon," visitors might hear. "My name is Latoryia Hailey, and welcome to New Song Academy. Class, please stand and welcome our visitors." This showed the increasing confidence and self-respect of the students. And the staff contributed to this success. Corey Barnes, who grew up in the neighborhood, is one example of a teacher who brings a deep commitment to the students and the school.

In 1997, the Academy became part of the public school system's "New Schools Initiative," Maryland's equivalent of a charter school. It began with its core of grades six through eight, then added a grade a year, starting with the first grade. This resulted in a "K-8" program plus a day-care program for children ages three to four. Working with this program of the public school system brought in needed funding yet also enabled the Academy to remain independent and in control of its future. Just two years after joining the program, the Academy was ranked among the top tier of schools in reading and math scores. No longer is it normal for Sandtown students to drop out of school. In fact, grades nine through twelve will soon be added, and a university extension program is projected to be offered on-site.

While there is still a long road ahead, there are numerous factors that contribute to the Center's already being a model of success: the extraordinary and tireless commitment of Susan Tibbels; an atmosphere of unconditional love; parental leadership and involvement; partnerships with area corporations that yield expertise, support, and volunteers; an insititutional commitment to the total achievement of every student; small classroom sizes; and the natural reinforcing links with Habitat and the overall work of New Song. It is about committed leaders like Louise Sutherland, director of the preschool, who grew up two blocks away from the preschool center. She and the preschool staff — Jennie Wood, Norma Jones, and Wanda Smith — are making an incredible contribution to the *shalom* of children in Sandtown. During one of the first years of the center's operation, children drew pictures of what they wanted to be. They showed themselves performing menial jobs. But the following year, when students undertook the same project, they pictured themselves as doctors, ministers, and lawyers. Their view of themselves and the future was changing. Today, after years of hard work, graduates of the Learning Center such as Alesha Clayton, Jana Goodson, Michael Parker, and William Scipio are attending college. Everyone involved in the Learning Center has no doubt that ten years from now — twenty years from now — many students will be returning to Sandtown as college graduates and leaders.

Healthy Families for a Healthy Community

Mr. Ulysses Carter of Mount Street was pivotal in starting the New Song Family Health Center. One day Mr. Carter, one of New Song's first and most committed members, was taken to the hospital because of respiratory problems. Once he was there, his relatively minor health problem was allowed to develop into a different health crisis. During the weeks we visited him, we watched as Mr. Carter slowly died because of negligent care, a fact confirmed for us by a member of the hospital's staff. His death was the first one in our immediate church community.

Every person is created in the image of God, and thus is intended to experience the fullness of life and God's *shalom*. Withholding the basics of life — in Mr. Carter's case, quality health care — prevents a person from rightly experiencing God's *shalom*. This is clearly unjust, a violation of God's sacred image. Regrettably, the scarcity of preventative health services and quality health care is an almost unspeakable reality in America's Sandtowns. The quality of care is not the only critical factor. Many people lack insurance (especially men) and have no access to routine health services. "Health care" in the inner city most often means waiting until a problem is serious enough for the emergency room — and then it becomes even more complex. Dental care is unknown. In the cutthroat world of HMOs, the sickest people are not profitable. So the system cuts corners by making it hard for inner-city HMO patients to get to appointments or see specialists. Even the right medicines can be hard to find at pharmacies in the inner city.[18]

New Song was very concerned to put an end to what was happening to our neighbors and church members like Mr. Carter. So in 1991 New Song founded a primary health care center. With no budget, it operated one evening a week out of the basement of the church. Since this was where the Habitat offices were first located, tools and supplies had to be moved to make room for the patients. The health center's first volunteers were Linda Swallow, a nurse practitioner, and David Thomas, a Johns Hopkins physician and infectious disease specialist who served as the Medical Director. They provided high-quality, loving care to those without insurance or a physician.

Everyone involved wanted the center to expand its hours and services. So in 1996, New Song Family Health Center moved from the basement to a new building the church was able to purchase on Fulton Avenue, making the leap from a one-night-a-week facility to a full-time primary care center. It has six exam rooms, a staff of full-time physicians and nurses, and a community-health outreach worker. At the time of the expansion, Dr. Belinda Chen joined the staff as Medical Director. Lifetime Sandtown residents Torey Reynolds, trained as a neighborhood health worker, started a substance abuse program, and Amelia Harris initially served as the Site Director. Sylvia Simmons, a Habitat homeowner, received training to become a Nursing Assistant.

A partnership with Mercy Medical Center, whose main facility is downtown, ensured not only institutional development but also high-quality resources for necessary tests and referrals.[19] Also critical to growth was a grant from the Robert Wood Johnson Foundation to participate in the Reach Out

---

18. R. Sean Morrison, Sylvan Wallenstein, Dana K. Natale, Richard S. Senzel, and Lo-Li Huang, "'We Don't Carry That' — Failure of Pharmacies in Predominately Nonwhite Neighborhoods to Stock Opioid Analgesics," *The New England Journal of Medicine* 342, no. 14 (April 2000): 1023-26.

19. The hospital is owned and operated by the Sisters of Mercy. This is the same order that once operated a convent in what became New Song's first building on Gilmor Street.

Program,[20] an initiative which enabled the Center to creatively expand and make use of a professional volunteer base. Just two years after opening at Fulton Avenue, the New Song Family Health Center had indeed arrived at a new place, offering comprehensive services to an increasing number of people in Sandtown. What began in a basement as a part-time operation that handled about a thousand patient visits annually had grown to a full-time operation offering multiple services to more than five thousand patients annually. For a number of the people in Sandtown, it meant that they saw a physician for the first time in ten or twenty years.

How does the Health Center sustain its efforts? It takes insurance, of course. But if a patient has no insurance (and more than half do not), a fee is charged based on a sliding scale. No one is ever turned away, and the ability to pay is not a requirement.

Establishing a health center in the community, a place where people know they can go when they need medical attention, has greatly increased Sandtown's sense of community and its potential for health.[21] But the great challenge ahead lies in continuing to build a model of health care that changes the health status of the whole community. This requires not only sustained primary health-care services but also community-based efforts to reduce the underlying social causes of such health challenges as infant mortality, cancer, and environmental poisoning. New Song's Family Health Center can be a tremendous base for this holistic approach.

As the Health Center continues to grow and expand, it is clear that its mission statement is coming true: "As recipients of God's grace, New Song Family Health Center exists to promote health, healing, and hope in partnership with our Sandtown-Winchester community."

Building a Sustainable Economic Life

A sustainable community requires not only good housing, education, and health care, but also jobs and economic security. Having established bases in

20. For an evaluation of this grant program, see H. Denman Scott, Johanna Bell, Stephanie Geller, and Melinda Thomas, "Physicians Helping the Underserved: The Reach Out Program," *JAMA* 283, no. 1 (January 2000): 99-104.

21. Here I am suggesting the importance of Community-Oriented Primary Care, a model that places great importance on local planning, organizing, and evaluation and provider-community collaboration. For an introduction, see A. H. Strelnick, "Community-Oriented Primary Care: The State of an Art," *Archives of Family Medicine* 8 (November/December 1999): 550-52.

other areas, we had to turn our attention to the creation of jobs and economic activity. Even though the Health Center, the Learning Center, and the Habitat effort had created over thirty community jobs, many people were still unemployed, and others were hemmed in by tenuous low-wage work. In 1994, a start-up grant from World Vision U.S. Ministries enabled EDEN (Economic Development Employment Network) to get started and focus directly on job development. Wy Plummer, who then worked for New Song, served as the founding director.

An effective employment strategy would most naturally begin with connecting Sandtown to the regional economy, making connections to employers outside of Sandtown. Wy Plummer helped to organize this process, and Nina Anderson, a lifetime resident of Sandtown and a Habitat homeowner, was hired to help place people in jobs. (Nina and her mother, "Miss Blondie," are two of the most gracious and self-giving people in Sandtown.) By 2000, Nina became the Executive Director of EDEN.

The obstacles confronting this program were enormous. Many people had no record of steady employment, and when EDEN began, the economy was struggling. Some with a felony criminal record couldn't get hired anywhere. EDEN sought to overcome such obstacles through hard work, prayer, and persistence — and it succeeded. In the first five years of operation, EDEN helped over six hundred community residents find work and retain it for more than ninety days. People could come through the doors of EDEN knowing that they would receive assistance in preparing a resume or finding a job lead, or just get encouragement if they needed it. Staff members such as Antoine Bennett made this happen.

In 2000, a Department of Labor grant allowed EDEN to greatly expand. As a regular presence in people's lives, EDEN is now working to provide a "ladder of employment" history. Getting a job is not the ultimate goal; developing a career is. As a faith-based institution, EDEN also strongly encourages people not to move ahead and leave others behind, but to make progress together.

Celebrating the Gifts of Art and Creation

Art and beauty are essential elements in rebuilding a more just and joyful community. Especially important are the musical arts. As C. Eric Lincoln and Lawrence Mamiya observed in their seminal study on the black church, "In our research of the programs and techniques that pastors have found successful in reaching young people, the highest rated answer was music, from youth choirs and concert events to the training of young people in vocal and instrumental forms. The musical heritage of the Black Church has been one of the enduring gems of black culture that has enriched the cultures of the world."[22] It is exciting, then, that the rebuilding effort in Sandtown is crowned by one of the best choirs in the city, the Sandtown Children of Praise. Developed by the Learning Center staff, the choir began to take on its own identity when Steve Smallman followed a call to the ministry of music. Composed of Learning Center students, the choir not only sings at Learning Center graduations and Habitat house dedications but also performs city-wide; it even has recorded two CDs.

An emphasis on the performing arts provides a wonderful alternative to the streets while developing the talents and confidence of children in Sandtown. Parents could not be prouder that their children sing not only at neighborhood events but with the Baltimore Symphony Orchestra. Indeed, the group's renown is so great that they have also sung at the inaugurations of the governor and the mayor and have performed up and down the entire East Coast.

Growing the Church

New Song began as a tiny congregation made up of a few adults and a lot of children and teens. Though our name suggested otherwise, the music initially left a great deal to be desired, to put it kindly. That changed dramatically with Elder Harris's song-leading and Steve Smallman's piano-playing. Steve, who moved to Sandtown with his family in 1992, added tremendously to our worship, later focusing his ministry exclusively on music and the children's choir. Elder Harris is the pastor of Newborn Church, formerly known as Newborn Apostolic Faith Church of the Trinity. A lifetime resident, Elder Harris founded this Pentecostal holiness storefront congregation. As New Song and Newborn recognized that they had a common ministry and witness, the relationship between the two churches began to grow, deeply benefiting both. Elder Harris and some Newborn members are a part of New Song's worship on Sunday morning, but they also maintain their church identity. (Elder Harris's presence and spiritual commitment to the community make him a true community pastor and leader. His passion for the community led him to launch Martha's Place, a transitional residence for neighborhood women recovering from drug addiction.)

22. Lincoln and Mamiya, *The Black Church in the African American Experience* (Durham: Duke University Press, 1990), p. 345.

Because New Song started out with no building, little money, and relatively few members, the church was hardly considered to be a model of a "successful church," especially when judged by contemporary "church growth" standards. But this is not a biblical perspective. As Orlando Costas points out, true church growth is multi-dimensional, involving not only numerical growth but growth in church life and thought as well as growth in community impact.[23] By these criteria, New Song has always been growing in a significant way. Always its growth is joined to the community and ministry. The two have grown together.

New Song's vision was to build a Scripture-based community of children, teenagers, and adults in our neighborhood who were largely uninvolved with the traditional church structures. The vision of the church was to seek the peace of our community, and to define itself not by outside agendas but by an understanding of the reign of God for the community. Costas put it well: "Whatever else we may say about church growth, this much is certain: As a religious entity, the church grows in accordance with its self-understanding — the vision it has of its nature and mission in the world."[24] Over time it became clear that when New Song held to a vision of itself as a community-based and kingdom-driven church, it would flourish.

In the space used for worship hangs a large banner that reads, "Sing to the Lord a New Song."[25] These words, proclaimed on the border, frame a brightly colored scene of women, men, and children from different cultures with hands raised in celebration. This is a visual reminder that the Lord's people are not a monochromatic "club" but a richly textured body of individuals gathered from every culture. For New Song, reconciliation is not something we manufacture but something we receive as a gift of God, the ultimate urban artisan (2 Cor. 5:17-21). As a gift, reconciliation is not simply about strategies but is deeply spiritual.[26] Because forgiveness and grace are not commodities, reconciliation cannot be managed. But reconciliation can and should be patiently nurtured. In a broken and divided city, New Song's recognition of

---

23. Here I am following Costas's definition of church growth in the classic "A Wholistic Concept of Church Growth," in *Exploring Church Growth*, ed. Wilbert R. Shenk (Grand Rapids: Eerdmans, 1983), pp. 95-107. In New Song's growth, the "three C's" — celebration, common life, and community ministry — have been central.

24. Costas, "A Wholistic Concept of Church Growth," p. 99.

25. The banner, designed and constructed by Doreen Kellogg, is a rendering of Revelation 5:9-10.

26. This is a theme in the work of Robert J. Schreiter, *Reconciliation: Mission and Ministry in a Changing Social Order* (Maryknoll: Orbis, 1992); and *The Ministry of Reconciliation: Spirituality and Strategies* (Maryknoll: Orbis, 1998).

"one Lord" and its meaning that we are therefore "one people" celebrates the gospel while refuting the powers.[27]

It is important to stress that without the church and its theological grounding and its belief in God's new world, there would be no community-building activities. The church provides the basis for people to believe that things can change, the support they need to keep going, the conviction that risk-taking is essential to moving forward in life, and the framework through which unity is created.[28] The church is the foundation in which the ministries and the community institutions are rooted and out of which they are able to grow. It is a prophetic sign of God's intentions for human community. New Song is both a community and an ecclesial project that calls forth a transformation of faith and a new way of life in Christ.

Bringing It All Together

Orlando Mobuary and his family provide an example of how New Song can provide a family with the tools they need to build a healthy and whole future. Orlando and his wife, Teresa, were married at New Song. In fact, it was the first wedding celebrated at the church. They became members of the church, and Habitat homeowners on the 1300 block of North Stricker Street in Sandtown, where they began raising their family. A decent, safe, thriving community is what they wanted for their children, a place they could enjoy as they are grew up. And so Orlando, who began work with Sandtown Habitat as a construction intern, has gone on to become an electrician and recently a rehab construction manager. A significant part of the rebuilding of Sandtown depends on him, and Orlando works hard to ensure that each house is the best it can be. He and Teresa send their children to the Learning Center, and they make use of the Health Center. These are the sorts of transforming differences that are occurring for families on every block in the Sandtown focus area.

When I think of the process thus far, there are many stories that bring hope and encouragement. Among the most important to me is the story of Isaac "Ike" Newman. Ike is the young man who first said out loud that we should start a church, and the first individual to work on our church build-

27. N. T. Wright, "One God, One Lord, One People: Incarnational Christology for a Church in a Pagan Environment," *Ex Auditu* 7 (1991): 45-58.

28. Mary Nelson of Bethel New Life in Chicago says that the church is the gas, guts, glue, and grace of community development.

ing. He is not only integrally involved in the overall life of New Song but is also a Habitat employee. For fifteen years he has been rebuilding his community and helping his family and his neighborhood. In December 2000, Ike became a Habitat homeowner. This is what New Song is all about.

THIS FAR, AND MUCH FURTHER TO GO, BY FAITH

During the testimony time of a worship service, Torey Reynolds said, "Our community was down, but there has been a rebirth. Now we are one!" This was a prophetic reminder that while we had far to go, God's Word and Spirit had been active in our midst, building something new (1 Pet. 2:10). Spiritual and social renewal were taking place before our eyes, and when Torey made this proclamation, it was clear that God had been at work in her life and in the life of New Song and Sandtown.

As the life of the church has developed and the work of rebuilding the neighborhood moves forward, it has become clear that a change in direction is taking place in the small area where New Song has focused its spiritual, social, and economic resources. Barriers long in place are being crossed, and a diverse people are no longer strangers but friends. Children are dreaming and achieving new futures filled with hope and possibility. Parents and homeowners are branching out into new areas of leadership. Blocks once vacant and dangerous have become places of beauty, ownership, and safety. In natural and everyday ways, people are sharing their faith with their neighbors and joining in the task of rebuilding their community. People are embracing Christ and his purposes of the reconciliation of all things. In every part of the process, God is being acknowledged as the one who has done "immeasurably more than all we ask or imagine, according to his power that is at work within us" (Eph. 3:20).

How did this transformation come about? What began as a communal reading of Scripture in a house church became a serious commitment to rebuild, house by house. New institutions were defined, born, and cultivated. People took on more and more responsibility. The systems and structures of the city were engaged for the well-being of Sandtown. The small circle of believers that began on Mount Street grew to a larger faith community in the Baltimore metropolitan community. Friends and allies were made. Change came about by the way of leaven, the work of the Spirit leading to a new creation. Ultimately this is understandable only as it represents the great mystery of God's work (Eph. 3:6; 5:32), but it is the way of the gospel and the cross.

By 2002, New Song had indeed flourished: it has more than one hundred full-time staff members, seventy of whom are lifetime Sandtown residents, who work out of six buildings and as many affiliated organizations, with a collective yearly budget of over five million dollars and nearly fifteen million dollars in total assets. The results are both intangible and measurable. Habitat is building at the rate of fifty houses a year, and has committed itself to an amazing goal of a 500-house project. Some five thousand volunteers a year now share in the work, and the labor-intensive week of building begun with the Carters' visit has become an annual event. (Sonia Street continues to work with former President Jimmy Carter in Habitat work sites around the world, most recently South Korea.)

The health center is doubling its size and its number of physicians, the Learning Center is adding grades and new buildings, EDEN is going into new job-development areas, and new people are getting involved in the life of the church. Under the leadership of Jeff White and Johnny Acevedo, growth reached to New York City, where a sister church in Harlem was born in 1998. In 2000, Thurman Williams was called to be the new pastor of New Song in Sandtown. He and his wife, Evie, relocated to Mount Street in 2001. And in another testimony to God's power, a wonderful new community center and day-care facility were dedicated on the vacant lot across from the first building in April 2001. The new community center includes not only a gym but much new classroom and other space for the Learning Center. All of these things are additional signs of God's way of making the impossible possible.

The people of Sandtown have learned never to take any version of "No, you can't do that" for an answer. The process of showing "Yes, we can rebuild, and we will" has created growing confidence, skill, and respect. Overall, the "three R's" of John Perkins set in motion a process of a church and a community growing together. Block by block, it is clear that Sandtown is changing. But to get to this point has been a challenging and sometimes excruciating process, one not always filled with success. Four out of our first five Habitat homeowners decided to move out of Sandtown — though the next 150 have all stayed. Many of the young people in New Song's programs have left before they achieved their full potential, and some have ended up in serious difficulty. Building a large staff has enabled growth in many areas but also led to hard situations. As a young pastor, I made some major mistakes, especially in certain key relationships involving church leadership development. For all involved in New Song, the daily work of keeping funding in place and administrating the components is unrelenting and thus draining. Community development, racial reconciliation, church formation, and life in the neighborhood all bring incredible joys but also unique stresses that can sometimes be overwhelming. Yet in all of this, God continues to sustain and bless.

The overall situation in Baltimore will play a major role in New Song's future. With the city's population still moving out to the suburbs, with capital flying after it, and the murder rate falling but still too high, the neighborhoods around New Song are in deepening crisis. If the New Song focus area becomes an island, it will have to connect to or even create other islands to survive. These hard facts remind us of what we learned from the Nehemiah story — that renewal is a constant process, never a singular event. To stay fresh and in step with God's Spirit, New Song will always have to return to where it began — to its brokenness before God, its vision of peace for the city, its proclamation of the gospel of grace, and its block-by-block, community-based strategy. Strength of any kind is an illusion in the economy of the kingdom; suffering and struggle are much more real in the neighborhood.

With each housing dedication, each choir award, each Learning Center graduation, each job placement, what has become routine is also pregnant with spiritual risk. Will New Song continue to develop its potential or lose its edge? Will the church increase its search for creative economic, educational, social, and health alternatives for the community? Will the five thousand committed to volunteering each year be focused on achieving greater accomplishments for the community and even the city? The future of a church and community ministry is open, always dependent upon more and greater risk-taking and self-giving sacrifice. Three important choices line the road ahead.

First, there is the choice between community and ministry. Will New Song maintain a commitment to grassroots leadership, or will the desire and "need" for growth lead to a reliance on professional pastors, educators, managers, builders, and health workers? Will the need to sustain ministries hold back community empowerment and control? When "ministry" becomes privileged over community, then the people of the community — and their leadership abilities and other gifts, resources, and skills — will always lose. Such a choice is a kingdom choice: will God's reign guide, or will the "needs" of the church and ministry take precedence? In a few years New Song's growth and success could leave the neighborhood behind. A church "of" and "with" the community in its genesis could become just another congregation "in" the neighborhood. The spiritual and pastoral challenge is how to move ahead together, to practice radical *koinonia* in Sandtown.

Second, there is the choice between expanding or contracting the vision. The vision of New Song is a way of being church that seeks to bring the principles of God's liberating reign to all dimensions of urban life and call people to work together for the peace of the neighborhood. Risk, sacrifice, and struggle are the marks of such a discipleship. Here the book of Acts is instructive. The early church was always in tension as mission was put front and center. As the church looked forward (Acts 7), mission bracketed its life and witness, the multicultural Antioch being a case in point (Acts 11:19-30). Although this commitment to mission was tremendously challenging, without it there would have been no church. Will New Song and its leadership entrust its future to the mission of serving the community, the city, and the world, or will it become an ingrown church focused on self-preservation? Will it continue to believe that the gospel is good news for the neighborhood and the city? The charism of New Song is its unique calling, and it needs to be held onto tightly, or the church will die.

Third, there is the choice between cultivating a healthy common life and giving in to destructive patterns. Unity is vital to a church making a difference in the inner city. Much of Ephesians was written to address a distinct lack of unity, expressed in conflicts over the use of gifts and leadership roles. Paul warns of what will happen if the disciplines of confession, forgiveness, and reconciliation are not practiced (Eph. 4:1-13).[29] The same is true in James, which calls the church to live by God's Word in all of their relationships (1:18, 21). New Song's ongoing impact depends upon the health of its common life and the individual growth of its members, a life rooted in the graciousness and forgiveness of Christ.

The challenge of these choices is intensified by the context. Sandtown celebrates its joys, but the pain it experiences on a daily basis is almost overpowering, enough for many to ask, like Hagar and Job, "Where is God?" Far too many people are still hurting and living in conditions that cry out for a taste of *shalom*. But it is important to remember that God is present in Sandtown in the suffering and risen Christ, who dwells in a people. Certainly central to the pastoral task is to attend to the stories that witness to this reality. And it is also essential, as Allan Tibbels often says, to "keep at it." By this Allan means that the church needs to keep its life rooted in the lives of the brokenhearted, building more and more homes, educating more children and providing lifelong learning opportunities, expanding economic activity and starting businesses, providing health care while expanding outreach, supporting families, doing more cooperative and increasingly more complex planning, praying together, and proclaiming the wonders of God's grace. Such practices help the church learn faithfulness and become more agile in negotiating the twists and turns of a changing urban world.

For New Song to continue to be a sign of the new creation, it must remain a movement of the Spirit, not a movement driven by a desire for recog-

---

29. For a particularly illuminating discussion of these issues, see Robert Linthicum, *City of God, City of Satan* (Grand Rapids: Zondervan, 1991), pp. 257-67.

nition. Paul's words to the Galatians are apt for New Song: "Let us not become weary in doing good, for at the proper time we will reap a harvest if we do not give up" (6:9). For no matter how small or fragile the work of community-building is, no matter how fierce the storms of social and economic transition are, New Song stands under the urban promise given to us by God: "I know the plans I have for you . . . plans to prosper you and not to harm you, plans to give you hope and a future" (Jer. 29:11). Therefore New Song must keep at it, knowing that "he who began a good work in you will carry it on to completion until the day of Christ Jesus" (Phil. 1:6). Because God, Immanuel, is with the community, the starting point is the gospel conviction that "God loves Sandtown."

CHAPTER 6

The Future of the Inner City

In 1968, in an act intended to dramatize the problems of poverty and racism in northern cities, Martin Luther King Jr. moved into a slum apartment in Chicago. Just a year earlier, riots had erupted in Watts, and the problems of African-American urban poverty were troubling King immensely. Intent on effecting change, King went to Chicago. As James Cone concludes in his landmark study *Martin and Malcolm and America: A Dream or a Nightmare,* "He was determined to prove that nonviolence could work in the North, dealing with the problems of slums as effectively as it had dealt with segregation in the South."[1] Indeed, we could argue that for King, the pursuit of nonviolence, reconciliation, love, and justice were ways of witnessing to God's world of peace, "the beloved community."

While historians give mixed reviews to the effectiveness of King's Chicago action, it is clear that something bigger was and is at stake. For, as Cone argues, King came to understand that for change to come to the inner city, the underlying structure of American society and the world needed to be changed. As King put it, "We've got to begin to ask questions about the whole society. We are called upon to help the discouraged beggars in life's market place. But one day we must come to see that an edifice which produces beggars needs restructuring."[2] According to Cone, concern for the urban poor and the poor around the world "increasingly became the major preoccupation of his practice and reflections."[3] With a perspective increasingly focused

1. Cone, *Martin and Malcolm and America: A Dream or a Nightmare* (Maryknoll: Orbis, 1991), p. 223.

2. Cone, *Martin and Malcolm and America,* p. 224.

3. Cone, *Martin and Malcolm and America,* p. 225. Here one should turn to the writ-

on both the inner city and the world as a whole, King forged a vision of reconciliation and justice grounded in the church and the gospel.

As new, globally shaped polarities of power and powerlessness and inclusion and exclusion re-create the urban world, King's struggle and Cone's
voice serve as both a reminder and a resource to Christianity, which must understand and engage the whole world. Just as we are to be exegetes of Scripture, so we must also be exegetes of the city, and then by the power and leading of the Spirit, engage the world we live in. Like King, we too need to have as
a moral and Christian preoccupation the future of the poor and all people
who suffer and dwell on the margins of power in the world's cities. We must
care not only about our changing U.S. cities but also about the cities of Asia,
Africa, Eastern Europe, the Middle East, and Latin America. And, as Cone
challenges, the public nature of theology must identify the sources and sins of
racism while also taking the risks of seeking justice.[4]

In this concluding chapter, my goal is to look at the future of the inner
city in a post-welfare, global period, and in light of this future, to examine the
meaning of gospel witness and discipleship. What forces are primed to shape
the inner city in this new century? What will it mean for the church to interpret, proclaim, and embody the gospel in the midst of the social form of the
city now coming into being? How can the gospel of peace make a difference in
urban neighborhoods? What spirituality will serve the multiple tasks shaped
by the kingdom in the city? I will propose that when the question of the future of the inner city is posed in light of God's future of *shalom*, there is a profoundly hopeful basis upon which to build community and seek the flourishing of the city in whatever form it emerges.

SIGNS OF THE CHANGING INNER CITY

If there is one certainty about the city, it is that it will change, and change in
ways we cannot now see or project. The horrific events of September 11 make
this clear. Because a city functions as an intricate web of relationships, systems, and structures, changes in one part of the city can quickly impact the
whole urban fabric. That such change can be hard to foresee does not mean,
however, that we should avoid thinking about the future and the pressures it

---

ings of King. See *A Testament of Hope: The Essential Writings of Martin Luther King, Jr.*, ed.
James M. Washington (San Francisco: Harper & Row, 1986).

4. James H. Cone, *Risks of Faith: The Emergence of a Black Theology of Liberation, 1968-
1998* (Boston: Beacon, 1999).

will visit on grassroots institutions. Those involved in the work of community empowerment, Frances O'Gorman points out, "tend to become so engrossed in today that we look the other way and fail to focus on crucial questions: What are the signs of the future? And what are we going to do about them?"[5] Using *sign* in a way that requires theological and social judgment, the Latin American theologian Jon Sobrino is right in stating that "*the* sign of the times continues to be the crucified people, deprived of life and dignity."[6] As a new century begins, what are the signs of the future of the inner city? Only by naming the signs of the times, present and future, will there be a possibility of pointing in a new direction. And only by attending to the global social and economic forces can we situate the church's ecclesial life and responsibilities for change.

Paul Grogan and Tony Proscio have written the compelling *Comeback Cities: A Blueprint for Neighborhood Revival.*[7] In it they document a series of trends that are turning cities around, making it "more than possible to conclude that an inner-city renaissance in America is eminently achievable, with incalculable benefits to the nation."[8] They argue that the human and social potential of inner-city communities is being brought out by a number of positive forces that have recently coalesced. Citing many examples, they show how retail services are being expanded, capital markets are finally interested in inner-city investment, welfare reform is putting people back to work, crime is being reduced and community policing is allaying tensions, school systems are being changed, and public housing is being reformed. With appropriate political and economic caveats, Grogan and Proscio conclude that when these changes are combined with the accomplishments of the self-help community development corporations, historic and beneficial alterations in the city are possible. Instead of being gloomy and skeptical about the city, they see opportunities developing in ways that leave ideological labels behind: "The reconstruction of cities may be among the first truly postideological issues of the twenty-first century."[9]

5. O'Gorman, "Tomorrow Emerged Yesterday: Are We Facilitators 'Crabbing' the Community Development Process?" in *With an Eye on the Future: Development and Mission in the Twenty-First Century,* ed. Duane H. Elmer and Lois McKinney (Monrovia: MARC, 1996), p. 175.

6. Sobrino, "Theology from Amidst the Victims," in *The Future of Theology: Essays in Honor of Jürgen Moltmann,* ed. Miroslav Volf (Grand Rapids: Eerdmans, 1996), p. 166.

7. Grogan and Proscio, *Comeback Cities: A Blueprint for Neighborhood Revival* (Boulder: Westview Press, 2000).

8. Grogan and Proscio, *Comeback Cities,* p. 49.

9. Grogan and Proscio, *Comeback Cities,* p. 243.

A more pessimistic outlook on the new millennium — one that is more accurate, I think — comes from sociologist Loïc Wacquant, who sees "the rise of a new regime of urban inequality and marginality."[10] Wacquant identifies four intertwining dynamics behind this order. First, there is the overarching social dynamic, the resurgence in social inequality. Second, there is the economic dynamic that involves both the elimination of low-skill jobs and the devaluation of "wage-labour . . . in a manner that . . . no longer grants foolproof protection against the menace of poverty even to those who enter it."[11] Third, there is the political dynamic, the "retrenchment" of the welfare state in advanced societies. Fourth, there is the spatial dynamic, the "concentration and stigmatization" of the poor. For Wacquant, the political is determinative while the effects are social.[12] The end result is a "'new poverty' of which the city is the site and fount."[13] We can fairly conclude that this is also a matter of understanding the failure of the modern project to achieve justice in the city.

The lived reality of the American inner city is caught up in this complex of challenges. First, inequality is increasing in our metropolitan areas. It is an inequality not just of wealth and assets but also of life possibilities. Take health care as an example. From a market approach, the focus is on saving money by putting a cap on spending and therefore on services. As the numbers of uninsured grow among a less-than-healthy population, it is clear that the urban health-care system is not prepared to adequately serve the poor. HMOs have in fact begun to back out of caring for the poor,[14] thus worsening the state of urban health care. Who will step up and provide adequate care for those without insurance? If quality primary care is not available at the community level, the uninsured will continue to rely on the emergency room as a doctor's office, and thus will raise costs for the urban hospitals least able to afford it. As a result, even more hospitals will close, and others will consolidate, lessening both the quality and the accessibility of community-related care.

Wages and employment represent a second challenge to life in the inner city. Perhaps the expansion of the "new economy" has trickled down into the inner city. However, trickle-down job growth is always tentative, awaiting the next economic downturn — as happened in 2001.[15] Service-sector jobs,

10. Wacquant, "Urban Marginality in the Coming Millennium," *Urban Studies* 36, no. 10 (September 1999): 1640.

11. Wacquant, "Urban Marginality in the Coming Millennium," p. 1642.

12. Wacquant, "Urban Marginality in the Coming Millennium," p. 1644.

13. Wacquant, "Urban Marginality in the Coming Millennium," p. 1639.

14. Peter T. Kilborn, "Largest H.M.O.'s Cutting the Poor and Elderly," *New York Times*, 6 July 1998, A-1, 9.

15. Sylvia Nasar with Kirsten B. Mitchell, "Booming Job Market Draws Young Black

which are the jobs most on the rise for those workers outside the knowledge-skills sector, are typically low paying, do not provide health insurance, retirement, or other benefits, and rarely hold open the possibility of advancement. Consequently, this level of employment growth is not helping to end the social and economic isolation of the inner city. With this scenario we face a future where more people work but still cannot afford the essentials of rent, food, and health care. Even with a reduction in unemployment, the social and spatial polarization of America's inner cities from the rest of America may be expected to increase.[16] As larger economic and political changes continue to displace or ignore the poor, I think we must speak of a crisis facing the poor. That public leaders rarely focus on this issue only contributes to the ongoing invisibility of the urban poor.

The ascendancy of neoliberalism has brought a third challenge. Here we find the state changing its role as the traditional provider of a social safety net. The Clinton administration's repeal of welfare and its replacement of that with the Personal Responsibility Act (1996) is perhaps the most important urban-policy development in the last three decades. Certainly one must be grateful for reports of those people once on welfare who have now found work and created new futures for themselves. No one liked the way the old system worked; it needed to be changed. Nevertheless, many saw the change as unmistakably biased against blacks and Hispanic/Latino inner-city residents. Early studies of the change also point to the incredible struggle that many families now face, especially minority households in isolated neighborhoods.[17] In fact, poverty has been increasing for many families who have gotten off welfare. And when the current and very limited public benefits such as Medicaid and food stamps are gone, family resources will be stretched even further. After the new five-year time limits on welfare begin to expire, the ranks of the unskilled, unemployed, and unassisted may increase again in areas of high and chronic unemployment. Early discussions on welfare reform in 2002 don't look good for low-income families. We must not forget that ending poverty is more important than ending welfare.

In the event that the economic run-up of the 1990s turns into a long-

---

Men into Fold," *New York Times*, 23 May 1999, A-1, 24; Richard B. Freeman, "The Rising Tide Lifts . . . ?" in *Understanding Poverty*, ed. Sheldon H. Danziger and Robert Haveman (New York: Russell Sage Foundation/Cambridge: Harvard University Press, 2001), pp. 97-126.

16. Wacquant, "Urban Marginality in the Coming Millennium," p. 1644.

17. Jason DeParle, "Shrinking Welfare Rolls Leave Record Share of Minorities," *New York Times*, 27 July 1998, A-1, 12. For a story that shows the complexity of the challenge facing families, see Lynnell Hancock, *Hands to Work: The Stories of Three Families Racing the Welfare Clock* (New York: William Morrow, 2002).

term downturn, we can expect to see inner-city unemployment rise dispro-
portionately and begin a new cycle of social and familial distress. Because
many of the public systems previously in place have been eliminated, the crisis
could be extensive. Census data from 2000 suggest that while many cities experienced growth in the 1990s, especially Western and Sun Belt cities, during the
same period poorer cities, particularly those in the Northeast and the Rust
Belt, grew poorer.[18] If times continue to be economically stressful, all cities will
be affected, and those furthest behind will face even greater obstacles.

The continued privatization of social services, while often administra-
tively effective, also means that for-profit corporations, including military
contractors, are now competing for the state-by-state contracts that oversee
and manage welfare "reforms."[19] With holes in the safety net growing larger
and more permanent, and political commitment to the most vulnerable di-
minishing, we must ask: What will happen to the families who are not eligible
for social services during periods of economic downturn? Who really cares
about the inner city? Did we miss opportunities for major urban reconstruction in the 1990s? Instead of investment in cities, we have the legacy of the
dotcom bubble, stock-market speculation, and the telecom bust.

A fourth and powerful challenge is posed by "undercrowding," the absence of the population base that fills a thriving neighborhood. This continues to be a significant problem for many neighborhoods, especially in older
cities not strongly affected by immigration. Undercrowding means more than
abandoned houses and vacant lots; it means tears in the fabric of the community. Given the city's critical role in technology, communications, culture, and
finance in this new century, one would think that the city would be getting
stronger for all residents. But gentrification and the displacement of the poor
have reared their ugly heads in a number of major cities. Boston, New York,
Seattle, San Francisco, and Atlanta come immediately to mind, but few cities
are escaping these effects entirely. Feeding this vulnerability of the poor is the
rise in housing costs, government pullbacks from a commitment to affordable housing, a growing reliance on market-driven investment, and a post-
welfare disregard for the poor. "Mixed income" communities, which are a
good idea, have, regrettably, become a euphemism for the displacement of
low-income residents. Yes, it is good and right that the city hold and draw

18. Edward Glaeser and Jesse M. Shapiro, "City Growth and the 2000 Census: Which
Places Grew, and Why" (Washington, D.C.: Center on Urban and Metropolitan Policy, May
2001).

19. Nina Bernstein, "Giant Companies Entering Race to Run State Welfare Programs,"
New York Times, 15 September 1996, A-1, 26; Barbara Ehrenreich, "Spinning the Poor into
Gold," *Harper's*, August 1997, pp. 44-52.

back middle-class residents, but not at the expense of poorer residents. We need livable cities for all citizens, and a right to place and home that transcends income, status, race, and geography.

The physical face of the city is changing as cities such as Chicago, Newark, and Baltimore have been or will be demolishing thousands of the old high-rise project apartments, replacing them with more "community friendly" or "new urbanist" housing. The catalyst for this is the Hope VI Program, sponsored by the Department of Housing and Urban Development. Concerns are mounting that this program has greatly reduced the stock of federal affordable housing units. And history compels us to ask a hard question: Does anything indicate that, for all their advances, these new public housing units will be any different thirty years from now than the buildings they are replacing?[20] Will better ways of renewing communities — ways that effectively integrate the changes into the social fabric of the city and the region — be found? Will there be a public commitment to housing?

Our cities are becoming more and more multi-ethnic as the Latino, Asian, and West Indian populations continue to grow. As Mike Davis observes in *Magical Urbanism: Latinos Reinvent the U.S. City,* the significant growth of the Latino community in major U.S. cities is an "epochal" development in American urban history.[21] These changes bring new opportunities for urban alliances, but also the challenge to find new models of reconciliation in the city. In the city as global circuit, the future will bring new fusions more than ever before. While these exciting new dynamics are reshaping the city, the orderings of power based on race have not been eliminated.

Clearly, we can conclude that the city, like no other geographic entity, is the strategic site for connection to the world, Christian mission and ministry, resistance, and cultural action. Because old patterns and processes are meeting new ones, the future form of the city is still unknown. But we know that we face the challenge of at least two tasks: the search for greater understanding regarding the local impact of complex forces and global changes,[22] and

---

20. Camilo José Vergara, *The New American Ghetto* (New Brunswick: Rutgers University Press, 1995), pp. 56-65, 67-69; Bradford McKee, "Public Housing's Last Hope," *Architecture,* August 1997, pp. 94-105. For a view of the larger historical story, see Lawrence J. Vale, *From the Puritans to the Projects: Public Housing and Public Neighbors* (Cambridge: Harvard University Press, 2000).

21. Davis, *Magical Urbanism: Latinos Reinvent the U.S. City* (London: Verso, 2000). For an important story of diversity, see Roger Sanjek, *The Future of Us All: Race and Neighborhood Politics in New York City* (Ithaca: Cornell University Press, 1998).

22. Thomas Bender, "Describing the World at the End of the Millennium," *Harvard Design Magazine,* Winter/Spring 2000, pp. 68-71.

the obligation to move beyond analysis to specific actions that shape a new direction.

THE RICH MAN, LAZARUS, AND THE DIVIDED CITY

If the church is to faithfully bear witness to the gospel in the global city, it must learn to understand the world and then find ways to creatively respond to it. Doing so will involve looking to the Bible for guidance, for Scripture provides a pathway that can lead to a different future. A text that helps to narrate and critique our time of eviction and abandonment is the parable of the Rich Man and Lazarus in Luke 16:19-31.[23] The gospel teaching dares us to believe that a world divided between the haves and the have-nots, needed people and unneeded communities, an urban world of partitions both high and low, can and will be overcome by heeding the word of the Lord. Such a theological belief enables the church to challenge the underlying religious direction and paradigm of the city.

Jesus begins telling the parable by contrasting two men, an unnamed rich man and a poor man named Lazarus. The rich man is adorned in expensive garments of purple and fine linen. Lazarus, by contrast, is "adorned" only with sores or ulcers, aggravated by the dogs that lick them.[24] The two men are obviously worlds apart in terms of wealth and the basic comforts of life. But when both men die (v. 22), a decisive turn of events takes place. No mention is made of a burial for Lazarus; the text says only that "the angels carried him to Abraham's side" (v. 22). The rich man, according to his social status, receives a proper burial — but finds himself in the torment of hell (vv. 22-24).[25] He moved from "having to longing," while Lazarus moved from "not having and longing" to "not longing and having."[26]

Why are the fortunes of the two men reversed? The answer is found in verse 25, when Abraham speaks to the rich man: "Son, remember that in your lifetime you received your good things, while Lazarus received bad things, but now he is comforted here and you are in agony." The rich man has already received good things; Lazarus has suffered enough and will now be comforted.

23. This exegesis of Luke 16:19-31 follows Richard Bauckham, "The Rich Man and Lazarus: The Parable and the Parallels," *New Testament Studies* 37 (1991): 225-46.

24. I. Howard Marshall, *Commentary on Luke*, NIGTC (Grand Rapids: Eerdmans, 1978), pp. 636, 638.

25. Bauckham, "The Rich Man and Lazarus," p. 231.

26. W. Vogels, "Having or Longing: A Semiotic Analysis of Luke 16:19-31," *Eglise et Theologie* 20 (1989): 43-45.

No moral qualities, details of piety, or good or bad deeds of either man are mentioned. Even the meaning of Lazarus's name, "God helps," tells us more about God than about Lazarus. As Richard Bauckham points out, the two men are used to underscore the situation of inequality portrayed in verses 19-21: "What is wrong with the situation in the world, according to the parable, is the stark inequality in the living conditions of the two men, which is vividly and memorably conveyed simply by the juxtaposition of the rich man's expensive luxury and the poor man's painful beggary (vv. 19-21)."[27]

The second portion of the parable involves the rich man's plea to Abraham that Lazarus be allowed to visit his brothers in order to warn them that unless they change their lives, they too will share in his fate (vv. 28, 30). But his request is refused (vv. 29, 31). Why the refusal? They need only listen to Moses and the prophets, Abraham tells him. They need a witness from beyond the grave, the rich man importunes. Again, the blunt response comes from Abraham: "If they do not listen to Moses and the Prophets, they will not be convinced even if someone rises from the dead" (v. 31). And what did the prophets say? The prophets, compared to urban sentries looking out for the needs of the poor (Isa. 21:11), invoked God's commitment to the weak, the widow, the orphan, and the stranger (Jer. 22:15-16; cf. Isa. 1:16-17; 3:13-15; Jer. 9:23-24; Mic. 6:8). They focused on the way that systems and structures harmed the poor. This emphasis came from the commandments of Moses, in which wholehearted love for God and neighbor are demanded, and especially justice for the vulnerable (Lev. 19:18; Deut. 6:4). If the prophets were asked "whose justice" was at stake, their reply was "God's justice."

Bauckham explains the significance of this context by pointing out that if the rich man's brothers "refuse to see how the situation contradicts God's justice on the evidence of the scriptures, no purported revelation of the fate of the dead will convince them. By refusing an apocalyptic revelation from the world of the dead, the parable throws the emphasis back onto the situation from which it began. . . . It brings us back to the world in which the rich co-exist with the destitute because they do not listen to Moses and the prophets."[28] The suffering and poverty of Lazarus are wrong, according to Jesus, because they contradict the will of God expressed in his Word.

Let me try now to say something about the implications of this parable

27. Bauckham, "The Rich Man and Lazarus," p. 232; see also N. T. Wright, *Jesus and the Victory of God*, vol. 2 of Christian Origins and the Question of God (Minneapolis: Fortress, 1996), p. 255.

28. Bauckham, "The Rich Man and Lazarus," p. 246; Wright, *Jesus and the Victory of God*, p. 256.

for our global and urban time, a period characterized by Zygmunt Bauman as one in which we are moving — not toward each other but away from each other, in alternative worlds of what he calls "tourists" and "vagabonds."[29] Jesus' words are meant today, as they were in his time, to assure the poor. In Christ's message, God makes it clear that he has not abandoned, forsaken, or forgotten the poor. That is the good news of the gospel: nothing can separate us from the love of Jesus, as the Apostle Paul declares (Rom. 8:31-39). Jesus has come as the Poor One for the poor. Jesus is good news, and in the cross and the Resurrection, the reversal of the world has begun. In this parable we find a pastoral message of comfort and hope, an announcement of good news.

Alongside the word of pastoral assurance is the prophetic task of naming the world that excludes the poor and reduces people to their economic value to the global system. Dutch economist Bob Goudzwaard redirects our thoughts, discourse, and actions toward a spiritual interpretation of economic forces and a hopeful alternative:

> Even if people and churches are aware of the spiritual dimensions of what is going on in the world's economy — namely, the evil of exclusion and enslavement as well as the need to choose between God and Mammon — they often forget to speak with the same degree of spirituality about the possible solutions. As a result, elements of despair often enter and reference is made to our lack of power and influence. But if we speak about despair and sin, we need the courage to speak as loudly about hope and redemption.[30]

Because justice is not rolling down, the basic pronouncement of the Hebrew prophets on the city, which Walter Brueggemann summarizes, ought to be applied to the global city: "A city *excessively full* will, under God's demanding surveillance, become a city *starkly empty.*"[31] Living by and for mammon will not just continue to alter the social and physical landscape of the city; it will leave a city empty. A city can consume the world yet lose its soul. This bleak reminder returns us to Augustine's *City of God* and its call to name human pride as the nexus of the human city while bearing faithful witness to the city of the Lamb.

29. Bauman, *Globalization: The Human Consequences* (New York: Columbia University Press, 1998), pp. 77-102.

30. Goudzwaard, "Spiral of Life and Death: The Future of the Global Economy," *Perspectives* 13, no. 3 (March 1998): 17-18.

31. Brueggemann, *Using God's Resources Wisely: Isaiah and Urban Possibility* (Louisville: Westminster/John Knox, 1993), p. 6.

Naming the processes of division and the very partitions themselves enables us to demystify the global city. The material and social processes of the city are hardly abstract: we can see them in real estate, banking, and public practices that characteristically treat the poor as expendable, communities as commodities to be bought and sold. We can see the division in the digital divide and the new exclusions of the information age. Such analysis requires naming economic greed as idolatry, as the Apostle Paul did.[32] "Put to death .. whatever belongs to your earthly nature . . . greed, which is idolatry" (Col. 3:4). Diagnosing and naming the spiritual dimension of the city's direction and form is not the same thing as spiritualizing sin. Nor does it allow for denouncement without a commitment to the grace and peace of the city and all who call it home. The other side of the prophetic "tearing down" is building up; if there is truth-telling, then there must also be tears and compassion.

Thus the parable also draws us back to the biblical writings and worldview on wealth. The biblical portrait is varied, but certainly wealth always carries with it responsibility, because it involves stewardship of God's gifts and his world. Not uncommon is this challenge in Paul's first letter to Timothy:

> Command those who are rich in this present world not to be arrogant nor to put their hope in wealth, which is so uncertain, but to put their hope in God, who richly provides us with everything for our enjoyment. Command them to do good, to be rich in good deeds, and to be generous and willing to share. In this way they will lay up treasure for themselves as a firm foundation for the coming age, so that may take hold of the life that is truly life. (6:17-19)

This reminds us of Jesus' earlier challenge in Luke's Gospel that "a man's life does not consist in the abundance of his possessions" (12:15). This perspective shows us another way of viewing the world, one that speaks of a new order and comes through the words of Hannah (1 Sam. 2:1-10) and of Mary (Luke 1:46-55). We may also draw on the many diverse strands of Christian tradition, including Chrysostom, Aquinas, Calvin, John Wesley, and Saint Francis. Throughout church history, we find strong pastoral challenges to the rich as well as strong pastoral commitment to the poor. I know many gener-

---

32. Pablo Richard, "Biblical Theology in Confrontation with Idols," in Pablo Richard et al., *The Idols of Death and the God of Life: A Theology,* trans. Barbara E. Campbell and Bonnie Shepard (Maryknoll: Orbis, 1983), pp. 3-25; Brian J. Walsh, "Late/Post Modernity and Idolatry: A Contextual Reading of Colossians 2:8–3:4," *Ex Auditu* 15 (1999): 1-17.

ous Christians who are making a difference with their wealth on behalf of the poor and the work of the kingdom. They need to be models and voices for the church at large.

"How do we valorize the evicted components of the economy in a system that values the center?" asks Saskia Sassen, articulating a core interest of her work.[33] It is in the concrete realities of the city that the church is called to give an account of its faith. Telling the story of the Rich Man and Lazarus is one way of changing and then valorizing a new center: the margins. Proclaiming this story renarrates the world in kingdom terms. In living the biblical faith, the church is to take up the strategic practices that make for peace, including empowering community development and local organizing. The parable of the Rich Man and Lazarus reminds the church that the condition of our inner cities requires not only theory but also action that is rooted in the living Word of God. It communicates that the kingdom of God and the ways of God must be a priority in our social relationships and urban development. And it reminds us that economic activity, like all areas of life, is intended to serve the glory of God and the *shalom* of the human community.[34]

CHALLENGES AND OPPORTUNITIES

If it is the church's mission to speak of and witness to hope and redemption, to life against death, and to peace over the violence of the powers, then the following agenda, while partial and preliminary, is important for the church in our cities.[35] Our frame of reference is a vision of God's new city of peace; our practices are rooted in the gracious demands of God's reign; our sense of what is possible is engendered by the Spirit. And our most basic commitment is that any agenda must meet the demands of reality as experienced on the streets.

33. Sassen, "Analytical Borderlands: Race, Gender, and Representation in the New City," in *Re-Presenting the City: Ethnicity, Capital, and Culture in the Twenty-First-Century Metropolis,* ed. Anthony D. King (New York: New York University Press, 1996), p. 184.

34. For further reflections, see M. Douglas Meeks, *God the Economist: The Doctrine of God and Political Economy* (Minneapolis: Fortress, 1989).

35. See further Joan Walsh, "Current Issues; Creative Solutions: A Conference Report on the Civic Work of Congregations," Center for Religion and Civic Culture, University of Southern California, 1998; and Raymond J. Bakke, "The Urban Church in Global Perspective: Reflections on the Past, Challenges for the Future," *Transformation* 9, no. 2 (April/June 1992): 2-5.

New and Renewed Grassroots Churches

At the forefront of an agenda for the urban future must be the development and renewal of grassroots Christian churches and networks.[36] In a changing urban environment, vibrant, healthy, holistically oriented churches with a parish commitment are vital because they are normative institutions that enable families to negotiate a changing world. As such, they are agents of proclaiming the good news and generators of the social and spiritual bonds that contribute to the revitalization of communities. On a daily level, the church clearly can make the difference that allows for survival, given its very personal political, economic, social, and spiritual interest in people's lives. The church fulfills this role not by downplaying its distinctiveness but by recognizing that it is a community "on whom the fulfillment of the ages has come" (1 Cor. 10:11).

When we survey the inner city and the larger world, we realize that the future church is a church of the suffering and the poor. The importance of the church born from below is, at the deepest level, bound up with God's redemption of the world. Jürgen Moltmann's powerful comments speak to the underlying biblical perspective:

> The true fellowship of the poor is of more value than all the alms and development aid of the rich. The problem of poverty in the world is not solved by programmes which mobilize "the church for the poor" or try to win "the poor for the church," but only through the church of the poor itself. Whatever state church and other rich and well-organized churches can do in the way of help, the apostolic charge remains central: to found congregations at the lowest level, congregations which independently discover their powers and potentialities in the liberating history of Christ; for the fellowship of the poor and suffering Christ is the secret of the "holy church" and the "communion of saints."[37]

The future of the church in the city depends on taking up the gospel, the good news of Jesus and the kingdom, for the prisoner, the poor, and the outsider, not as the pretext for a mission strategy, proselytizing, or a programmatic enterprise, but as a living truth and movement that transforms. We see such a

---

36. Essays addressing this subject can be found in *Planting and Growing Urban Churches: From Dream to Reality,* ed. Harvie M. Conn (Grand Rapids: Baker, 1997).

37. Moltmann, *The Church in the Power of the Spirit: A Contribution to Messianic Ecclesiology* (Minneapolis: Fortress, 1993), p. 357.

movement of the gospel in the base Christian communities of Latin America, in the Pentecostal churches of Asia, Africa, and Latin America, and in the African Independent Churches.[38] Born of the Spirit, the church of the poor that impacts the city reads Scripture in communion, practices decentralized leadership, and is committed to holistic ministry.[39]

The planting of grassroots urban churches has its origins in the movement of early Christianity. Harvie Conn has shown that the "Great Commission" of Luke's two-part history, compelled by a view of God's New City (Isa. 60:14; 62:12), accents the urban thrust of the gospel in the world (Luke 24:47-49; Acts 1:8).[40] Both Luke's gospel and Acts stress the growth of the church as the work of the ascended Christ through the Spirit (Luke 17:21; Acts 1:1); they were communities formed by missional callings to move outside sacred territories to every point of the city, particularly where hurt and pain are the greatest. Therefore, according to Conn, the driving reason that the church went to the cities was more theological than methodological (Isa. 54). Still, as Conn has underscored in his body of work, cities are the strategic sites of gospel initiative and presence.

In *The First Urban Christians: The Social World of the Apostle Paul,* Wayne Meeks makes the point that Paul's vocation "was . . . to plant small cells of Christians in scattered households in some of the strategically located cities of the northern Mediterranean basin. . . . The mission of the Pauline circle was conceived from start to finish as an urban movement."[41] By reaching the cities, Paul's missionary impact spread to the surrounding regions (Acts 15:16; Rom. 15:19, 23).[42] Richard Hays provides a similar summary of Paul's church-planting work, locating it in the context of God's broad redemptive purposes for the world:

---

38. Guillermo Cook, *The Expectation of the Poor: Latin American Basic Ecclesial Communities in Protestant Perspective* (Maryknoll: Orbis, 1985); Manuel A. Vásquez, *The Brazilian Popular Church and the Crisis of Modernity* (Cambridge: Cambridge University Press, 1998); Linda Elaine Thomas, *Under the Canopy: Ritual Process and Spiritual Resilience in South Africa* (Columbia: University of South Carolina Press, 1999).

39. C. René Padilla, "The Future of Christianity in Latin America: Missiological Perspectives and Challenges," *International Bulletin of Missionary Research* 23, no. 3 (July 1999): 110.

40. Conn, "Lucan Perspectives and the City," *Missiology: An International Review* 13, no. 4 (October 1985): 425; and Harvie M. Conn and Manuel Ortiz, *Urban Ministry: The Kingdom, the City, and the People of God* (Downers Grove: InterVarsity, 2001), pp. 122-37.

41. Meeks, *The First Urban Christians: The Social World of the Apostle Paul* (New Haven: Yale University Press, 1983), pp. 9-10.

42. Meeks, *The First Urban Christians,* pp. 9-50.

What is God doing in the world in the interval between resurrection and parousia? According to Paul, God is at work through the Spirit to create communities that prefigure and embody the reconciliation and healing of the world. The fruit of God's love is the formation of communities that confess, worship, and pray together in a way that glorifies God (see, e.g., Rom. 15:7-13).[43]

It was in the cities that Paul saw the most biblically important and strategic places to "plant" and "build" (1 Cor. 3:7-10) multi-ethnic communities of the gospel.

Today, as the church finds itself in cities with new social, cultural, and ethnic dynamics,[44] new models of being the church as a "multilingual, multi-cultural, and multiracial" community will be required.[45] What will communities of embrace (to use Miroslav Volf's phrasing) look like in the multi-ethnic neighborhoods of global cities? Based on the Latino/Hispanic cultural and theological experience, Virgilio Elizondo has developed the model of *mestizaje*, a people who understand border crossing and therefore what it means to live in a new land and embrace a new identity.[46] How can this model serve the wider church in its ways of being in the city? How will new church development uphold right relationships in the changing city?

The examples of the early church house and tenement churches suggest possibilities for our urban moment.[47] House churches (Rom. 16:5; 1 Cor. 16:19; Col. 4:15; Philem. 2) were not only models of the reign of God but basic com-

43. Hays, *The Moral Vision of the New Testament: Community, Cross, New Creation: A Contemporary Introduction to New Testament Ethics* (San Francisco: HarperSanFrancisco, 1996), p. 32.

44. Samuel Solivan, *The Spirit, Pathos, and Liberation: Toward an Hispanic Pentecostal Theology* (Sheffield: Sheffield Academic Press, 1998), p. 134.

45. Solivan, *The Spirit, Pathos, and Liberation*, p. 134. For a valuable study, see Manuel Ortiz, *One New People: Models for Developing a Multiethnic Church* (Downers Grove: InterVarsity, 1996).

46. Elizondo, *Galilean Journey: The Mexican American Promise* (Maryknoll: Orbis, 1983).

47. Harvie M. Conn, "Evangelizing the Urban Centers of the World," *Review and Expositor* 90, no. 1 (Winter 1993): 76. On the background of house churches, see Robert Banks, *Paul's Idea of Community*, rev. ed. (Peabody: Hendrickson, 1994); and Bradley Blue, "Acts and the House Church," in *The Book of Acts in Its First-Century Setting*, vol. 2: *Graeco-Roman Setting*, ed. David W. J. Gill and Conrad Gempf (Grand Rapids: Eerdmans, 1994), pp. 119-222. Regarding "tenement churches," see Robert Jewett, "Tenement Churches and Communal Meals in the Early Church: The Implications of a Form-Critical Analysis of 2 Thessalonians 3:10," *Biblical Research* 38 (1993): 23-43.

munities that practiced gospel convictions within their surrounding "neighborhoods" and networks.[48] Experience continues to show that it is in smaller communities that there is a significant possibility that all the people of God will be involved in prayer, gospel sharing, leadership development, social support, and kingdom witness.[49] Smaller communities build on existing infrastructures and require little overhead. Overall, the principle being upheld is that small is significant in the history of the transmission of the Christian faith.[50]

Certainly the development of new churches is important; it is a natural outworking of the gospel. But it is also important for existing congregations that have lost a clear sense of mission and ministry in the community to rediscover it once again, particularly in response to the city's demographic, social, and religious changes. Responding to such changes provides opportunities to rediscover the gospel as good news for the city, not to become "relevant" to the times. A prayerful and painful endeavor that wrestles with both tradition and change, the process of re-founding or re-missioning enables congregations to find new life by better understanding their calling to follow Christ in the city. Church renewal and church planting must both be incorporated into any Christian agenda for the inner city.

Leadership Development

Vital to spiritual and social transformation in the inner city must be a focus on the development of leadership that puts first the liberating hope of the kingdom for the church and the city.[51] Much of the future of the inner city will depend upon the women and men of the community who have the vision, spiritual depth, street smarts, and skills to midwife new ways of being church, of pastoring amidst suffering, and of generating alternative neighborhood visions and narratives (Luke 8:1-3; Rom. 16:1-16; Gal. 5:13-26). It is essential that such leadership emerge most prominently from the community for at least three reasons. First, it is the women and men from the community who know it best. Second, leaders from the community are best able to un-

---

48. Michael H. Crosby, *House of Disciples: Church, Economics, and Justice in Matthew* (Maryknoll: Orbis, 1988).

49. Though it is not directly aimed at urban congregations, a good resource is Robert and Julia Banks, *The Church Comes Home* (Peabody: Hendrickson, 1998).

50. Jonathan J. Bonk, "Thinking Small: Global Missions and American Churches," *Missiology: An International Review* 28, no. 2 (April 2000): 149-61.

51. For a seminal discussion of this subject, see Conn and Ortiz, *Urban Ministry,* pp. 377-469.

derstand what the kingdom of God means for their context. And it is a kingdom-of-God orientation that is most important in terms of content (Acts 20:25, 27). Third, in many circumstances, this will bring the witness of conversion to a new life — but not a life lifted up and out of the community.

It is critical that this leadership not be clerical in the traditional sense of the word or focused on a select few. What we need are non-hierarchical structures that recognize the widest range of gifts, abilities, and callings of the Spirit of women and men.

There are many leadership qualities that we could discuss, but here I want to focus on a single trait: a commitment to a life of self-giving patterned after the life of Christ. Women and men who put the honor of Christ and the needs of their communities first are best able to bring about transformational changes in the inner city. According to Dale B. Martin, Paul modeled this kind of commitment, which was in pointed contrast to what he saw in the society around him. Martin has shown the importance of Paul's soteriological use of the metaphor of slavery to God or Christ in addressing Greco-Roman standards of status and power operative in Corinth.[52] On the one hand, Paul presents himself in 1 Corinthians as a slave of Christ (9:16-18), yet he also says he is a slave to all (9:19-23). What Paul does, Martin argues, is present his leadership (and therefore his authority) as "stepping down to the social level he was to lead."[53] In doing so, he is presenting "an example of the self-lowering leader, the leader who leads from below."[54] In the conflict between those of high status and those considered to be inferior, Paul sided with the poor and non-elite, thereby undermining the position of the wealthy elite. Certainly this interpretation of leadership is subject to abuse and presents real contemporary dangers. Nevertheless, the pattern of servanthood in imitation of Christ remains.

In another study on Corinth, Andrew Clarke observes that when Paul critiques secular leadership patterns in the church, he emphasizes "non-status leadership vocabulary, and . . . urge[s] that they follow specific examples of Christian leadership."[55] In his recent work *Serve the Community of the Church: Christians as Leaders and Ministers,*[56] Clarke develops this theme fur-

---

52. Martin, *Slavery as Salvation: The Metaphor of Slavery in Pauline Christianity* (New Haven: Yale University Press, 1990).

53. Martin, *Slavery as Salvation,* p. 147.

54. Martin, *Slavery as Salvation,* p. 147.

55. Clarke, *Secular and Christian Leadership in Corinth: A Socio-historical and Exegetical Study of 1 Corinthians 1–6* (Leiden: E. J. Brill, 1993), p. 118.

56. Clarke, *Serve the Community of the Church: Christians as Leaders and Ministers* (Grand Rapids: Eerdmans, 2000), pp. 209-52.

ther, expanding on the ways in which Paul presents alternative patterns of leadership for the local church, with himself as an exemplar of one who follows Christ. Renunciation of status, service, love, and ministry are more prominent Pauline themes than "leadership." As in the incarnation of Christ (John 1:4; Phil. 2:6-8), vulnerability and the relinquishment of options mark Paul's example for the church (1 Cor. 9:19-22; 10:31-32; 11:1). Ultimately, it is Christ and the cross which set the standard for the incarnational leadership that is needed for our inner cities (cf. Mark 8:34).

For pastors, the pain of the inner city must be absorbed, not passed by. As Robert Linthicum states in a very compelling way, "Only a man or woman who allows his or her heart to be broken with the pain and the plight of the hurting poor and/or the hurting powerful of the city belongs in ministry there. To be effective in urban ministry, you must have a heart that is as big as the city itself."[57] For one to feel this way, Linthicum also stresses, one must first love the city — its people, communities, streets, markets, parks, architecture, arts, schools, and public life — even its sports teams! If one is to have one's heart split open over the city's wounds, then one must first hold in one's heart the love of Jesus for the city, a love that cries out in pain at its suffering.

New models of grassroots theological and missiological education that occurs in the context of ministry are vital to the ongoing development of urban church leadership. Can and will traditional seminaries with models based on the academy take on this responsibility? Here I want to offer a realistic word. Significant institutional change will take a conversion experience. The most valuable educational approaches for urban ministry will engage the city not as one subject among many but, as Roger Greenway has prophetically advocated, in every area of theological training.[58] Special training for community development and organizing should also be intensified. Mentoring relationships and internships should receive primary focus. Here, the church-based Bible Institute, the single most important urban training model already in operation, is a significant model to celebrate, support, and build upon. Knowing how hard the tasks of urban ministry are, the church must find ways to encourage and support its workers and their families.

---

57. Linthicum, *City of God, City of Satan: A Biblical Theology for the Urban Church* (Grand Rapids: Zondervan, 1990), p. 196.

58. Greenway, "World Urbanization and Missiological Education," in *Missiological Education for the Twenty-first Century: The Book, the Circle, and the Sandals,* ed. J. Dudley Woodberry, Charles Van Engen, and Edgar J. Elliston (Maryknoll: Orbis, 1996), pp. 144-50. See also *Transforming the City: Reframing Education for Urban Ministry,* ed. Eldin Villafañe et al. (Grand Rapids: Eerdmans, 2002).

Community Development and Organizing

Neighborhoods face the challenge of looking out for their own future, and churches face the challenge of being one with their neighbors. This demands renewed commitment to community development and organizing. Reaching youth, developing healthy local economies, confronting environmental racism, creating grassroots labor networks or unions, and maintaining affordable housing are just a few of the challenges facing the church. The biblical demands of justice and reconciliation require us to think afresh, build new relationships, and try new ideas to help raise up our discarded communities. Land trusts, new models of financing for home ownership, asset building, community development banks, charter schools, and health-care partnerships are some of the new approaches that will be required. In terms of health care, it is important not only to focus on primary care and community health but also to address the HIV/AIDS crisis and provide substance-abuse treatment.[59] Most importantly, congregations need the worldview of the mustard seed, a vision of the kingdom that celebrates and privileges local ministry initiatives.

A network society requires new approaches and forms of community organizing. Broadly based movements and place-based initiatives will both be needed. And we must add to the list of old concerns (e.g., bank redlining and public priorities) those of immigration rights, school reform, and livable wages. A variety of biblical stories and images will be important for animating the task of organizing, not least of which is Nehemiah's story of rebuilding the broken walls of community. Also important in this regard is the increasing predominance of evangelical, Pentecostal, and Holiness congregations in the inner city; they have emerged as the prime constituencies for organizing.[60] Longevity will be tied to the centrality of value-based organizing; respect for local theologies, cultures, and churches; and an emphasis on long-term leadership development. Essential will be the creation of new partnerships and strategic relationships with other churches, community institutions, and businesses. Collaboration and creativity are the watchwords for the future.

Supporting, creating, and increasing the capacity for community development initiatives should be a priority. A recent study of community-

---

59. For a moving discussion of faith and health, see David Hilfiker, *Not All of Us Are Saints: A Doctor's Journey with the Poor* (New York: Hill & Wang, 1994).

60. Mike Miller, "Community Organizing: Lost Among Christians?" *Social Policy* 31, no. 1 (Fall 2000): 33-41.

development corporations found four factors to be determinants of success:[61]

- A specific and tangible mission
- Organizational competency, including staff development, financial management, board involvement, and project implementation
- Political capital that enables the group to influence decision-makers
- Funding derived from many sources so as not to be overly vulnerable to cutbacks in a single area

Whether the faith-based initiative is old or new, the task a pioneering one or a secondary phase, these are pressing issues. In light of the increasing demands on church-based endeavors, churches will want to consider new alliances with both other congregations and private and public institutions. The possibility of different churches sharing responsibility for neighborhood CDC should also be looked at closely. Community change will also require partnerships involving public institutions, churches, community groups, businesses, and foundations.

An excellent summary of a practical strategy for community ministry comes from Roberta Brandes Gratz: "Think big, devise a broad strategy, but develop the foundation on small actions and small components. Thinking globally and acting locally really works."[62] Thinking globally will also mean learning globally, drawing on the theologies and lived experiences of Christians from the "Two-thirds World." Starting small and acting locally is the way of the mustard seed, which by cumulative effect *is* changing the world. Holistic ministry does not arise out of ideology but is called forth by biblical faith and community realities.

Economic Alternatives

Economic development and economic investment are two key components of inner-city revitalization. Following the pattern of both Enterprise Zones and Empowerment Zones, the Clinton-Gore administration emphasized a "new markets" program, an approach that remains influential. It mixes a

61. Ross Gittell and Margaret Wilder, "Community Development Corporations: Critical Factors That Influence Success," *Journal of Urban Affairs* 21, no. 3 (1999): 341-62.

62. Roberta Brandes Gratz with Norman Mintz, *Cities Back from the Edge: New Life for Downtown* (New York: John Wiley & Sons, 1998), p. 344.

small amount of government subsidy with for-profit business investment. This was useful, for example, in getting chain stores to open up in underserved markets. Drawing on both public and private resources, it represented a "third way" approach to renewing inner-city neighborhoods. This approach owes much to the influential Harvard economist Michael E. Porter, who has argued for recognition of the "strategic advantages" of inner cities for private-sector business expansion and growth.[63] The advantages Porter points to include the wealth of untapped disposable income and the paucity of retail services. In other words, the assets of the inner city are untapped opportunities for economic investment and profit.

Porter's approach to the economic revitalization of the inner city stresses private enterprise, entrepreneurial initiative by highly qualified business people, and government involvement primarily to clear the regulatory way. He is largely against government subsidy and what he considers to be muddled attempts at economic development by community groups. If this new way of economic development is followed, Porter believes that our inner cities can be revitalized. Porter is right that the inner city has strategic advantages and needs retail as well as job development. Investment in the inner city makes great sense. But the inner city has "strategic advantages" for whom? The presence of flourishing for-profit businesses that operate without subsidies does not necessarily mean more community employment or a change in the real local economy. It does not by itself privilege the most vulnerable of the community, and therefore such an approach can lead from "renewal" to removal. In the face of this new economic environment, communities will need to find ways to leverage their assets, attract investment, and develop relationships with businesses that serve the community, not harm it.

As we have seen in both the Introduction and Chapter 2, the Jubilee is an important theme for the church's common life (Luke 4:16-21; Acts 2:42-47). In Chapter 4, we noted the importance of the Jubilee in Nehemiah's reforms. Focusing as it does on the biblical theme of justice, the practice of community, and the importance of the Sabbath, the Jubilee also serves as a model of community economic development. Leviticus 25 and Deuteronomy 15 are significant examples of this, underlying much of biblical thinking on social justice (cf. Exod. 21:2-6; 23:1-12; Lev. 26, 27; Deut. 15:1-8; 31:9-13; Isa. 58:6; 61:1-4). Instead of a charitable handout, the Jubilee provided households with a release from debts and the return of land lost due to economic hardship. Under this model, the cycle of disenfranchisement was broken, and

63. Porter, "The Competitive Advantage of the Inner City," *Harvard Business Review* 73, no. 3 (May-June 1995): 55-71.

the uneven development of Israelite society was reversed. Based on Sabbath principles, the Jubilee proclaims that the world and the city belong to God: "The land must not be sold permanently, because the land is mine and you are but aliens and my tenants" (Lev. 25:23; cf. Ps. 24:21).

Although we live in a different time and a different world, the underlying worldview of the Jubilee is still relevant and powerful. And as an image, it can help us creatively address issues of investment, structural unemployment, and family brokenness in the inner city — even the crisis facing the global city. The astounding global grassroots movement to pressure wealthy nations to forgive the debts of the Two-thirds World, a movement explicitly grounded in the concept and spirit of Jubilee, speaks to the power of this vision to capture imaginations. Unbinding community from the definitions and limitations of the market, the Jubilee is a beacon of hope. Jubilee economics emphasizes job development, asset creation, local property and land ownership (a primary means of thwarting patterns of eviction and gentrification), community-based economic enterprise and business development, job training, and institution-building. A Jubilee model gives priority to the weakest in the community. It builds community, and it is empowering in the broadest spiritual, political, and economic senses. A Jubilee-based proposal does not cancel out revenue-generating initiatives but directs them to be recycled back into the community, into empowering families.

How might Jubilee-based initiatives be funded? John Howard Yoder's discussion of the Jubilee provides a line of direction. Commenting on Jesus' words on tithing in Luke 11:42, Yoder remarks, "He did not wish to abolish tithes. He wished only to go beyond the level of easy fulfillment and easy moral self-satisfaction which could be had by giving the tithe, and to call people to reach the level of 'righteousness, goodness and good faith.'"[64] Capital redistribution, the kind that goes beyond the tithe, if practiced by churches and Christians, could make a major difference to the future of the inner city. To focus these resources, to be prepared in advance for both opportunities and crisis situations, churches should work to establish community development funds and banks and ties to local financial institutions.[65] It is likely that such strong grassroots efforts would later attract foundation funding and possibly public funding. Will religious and specifically Christian-based foun-

---

64. For a case study, see Larry Foundation, Peter Tufano, and Patricia Walker, "Collaborating with Congregations: Opportunities for Financial Services in the Inner City," *Harvard Business Review* 77, no. 4 (July-August 1999): 57-68.

65. Yoder, *The Politics of Jesus: Vicit Agnus Noster,* 2d ed. (Grand Rapids: Eerdmans, 1994), p. 70.

dations also play a role? This is something that must be strongly encouraged through such means as program-related investment (PRI), start-up funding, and long-term capacity building, perhaps the most neglected area of foundation giving.

At the heart of much of the debate about urban development (and culture) is a conflict over the identity of the city and the community. Is the inner city a commodity or a community? There is no escaping this question in today's world. The Jubilee reminds us that ultimately the community's use of its own resources takes priority over the use of the community as a commodity. Biblical norms of justice require us to hold that a neighborhood is not rightly redeveloped if the people who live there, especially those most excluded and vulnerable, do not have a realistic claim on acquiring the means to sustain their families and maintain or own their homes in the community. Let us not forget that there is a right to *shalom* embedded in Scripture, a vision normative for the world. Recovering the story of Naboth's vineyard (1 Kings 21:1-16; cf. Jer. 22:15-16) and a theology of the land will be important tasks in establishing rights to the city that preserve and build on the important work of community development. Communities are not commodities.

Urban Reform

One lesson we can learn from history is that religious revival that brackets out social reform has little lasting effect on the life of the city.[66] Another lesson is that community work without political empowerment almost certainly faces limitations. Grassroots work can and does bring about local and structural changes. But because neighborhoods are not independent of larger macro-forces, and because self-sufficiency does not truly exist, significant social change and public reform are also needed. A model of urban change that stresses only the local church or neighborhood community development corporations is fundamentally misdirected and insufficient, because it places impossible pressure on them to produce results. Time and resource pressures can be extraordinary on people struggling just to pay the rent. As a consequence, the challenge for the congregations, churches, and parishes of a city is to link local action to justice in the public sphere of institutions. While focus-

66. An important historical case study is Kathryn Teresa Long, *The Revival of 1857-58: Interpreting an American Religious Awakening* (New York: Oxford University Press, 1998). An insightful review is provided by Joel A. Carpenter, "Revivalism Without Social Reform," *Books and Culture* 4, no. 6 (November/December 1998): 26-27.

ing on community residents and the local level is imperative, attention to city, state, and national policies and resource allocation can be equally important. Authorizing the public activity of the church to seek the peace of the city is the Lordship of Christ and his reign over all domains of life.

Finding ways to make *neighborhoods* more whole, peaceable, and just should be our primary policy focus. In this chapter we have already examined the "urban agenda" of Paul Grogan and Tony Proscio, what they call a non-ideological approach to renewing communities and cities. By "urban agenda" they mean "a systemic, concerted application" of four elements: "letting neighborhood groups set and manage their own priorities; enforcing order and safety in public places; freeing market forces to rebuild what was abandoned or destroyed; and deregulating the critical public systems of education, housing, and social welfare."[67] In summary, this represents a formidable approach that emphasizes a hybrid of better government operations and local initiative, not one or the other. It is clear that this approach offers a pragmatic and workable program for bringing back cities and communities, and will have a significant impact on growing cities.

But does this urban agenda go far enough? More is needed, I believe. As Mike Davis writes, "Apart from jobs . . . the vital public resources for the working poor are education, healthcare and transit."[68] Much of the work of improving these resources can take place at the city or state level. And in his study entitled *When Work Disappears,*[69] William Julius Wilson makes a long argument for policy changes at the national level. While Wilson's policy proposals will be interpreted as "liberal" by many, they are very modest proposals when viewed from the day-to-day experience of the inner city.

But before we review Wilson's policy proposals, it will be beneficial for us to take note of two major concepts that underlie his arguments. The first of these is the problem of "the belief structure" that most Americans hold concerning the nature of poverty and welfare.[70] This belief system individualizes the causes of poverty, neglecting the larger structural forces in which they are embedded. When a privatized mind-set prevails, it can deeply influence how people think about race, welfare, and the economy.

Wilson's second concept involves placing his policy proposals in a "race neutral" framework. Instead of targeting certain groups of the "disadvan-

---

67. Grogan and Proscio, *Comeback Cities,* p. 243.

68. Davis, *Magical Urbanism,* p. 134.

69. Wilson, *When Work Disappears: The World of the New Urban Poor* (New York: Alfred A. Knopf, 1996).

70. Wilson, *When Work Disappears,* pp. 149-82.

taged," Wilson universalizes solutions to include the working class and the middle class of every race. As I read him, Wilson does this not because he believes that inner-city poverty is "race neutral" but rather because he does not believe that the public majority will support policies that directly and exclusively aid the inner city. So instead of meeting with that defeat from the outset, Wilson proposes that policy be cast in terms of a wider social vision that includes the working class, which is affected by the same issues.[71] This position is not without its critics — including those who believe in public remedies but also hold that justice will not be attained in American society without addressing race directly in policy.[72] Christian persuasions regarding social justice will make it difficult to "choose" between these visions; our interests will be structural and redemptive.

Wilson's proposals take the form of short-term and long-term solutions. Long-term, Wilson is concerned with addressing two relationships: "the relationship between employment and education and family support systems and, in the metropolitan context, the relationship between the cities and the suburbs."[73] His short-term solutions are "to either revise current programs or create new programs to decrease joblessness among disadvantaged adults."[74] Stressing both public and private involvement, Wilson offers very basic proposals:

> The long-term solutions . . . include the development of a system of national performance standards in public schools, family policies to reinforce the learning systems in the schools, a national system of school-to-work transition, and ways to promote city-suburban integration and cooperation. . . . The short-term solutions . . . range from the development of job information and placement centers and subsidized car pools in the ghetto to the creation of WPA-style jobs.[75]

To this list I would add universal health care. It would help not only inner-city families but also millions of middle-class Americans.

A related issue is wage reform, the importance of which cannot be overestimated. Service-sector jobs, when they can be found, pay the minimum wage or slightly higher, which is not nearly enough to support a family. Rarely

71. Wilson, *When Work Disappears*, pp. 183-206.
72. See *Without Justice for All: The New Liberalism and Our Retreat from Racial Equality*, ed. Adolph Reed Jr. (Boulder: Westview Press, 1999).
73. Wilson, *When Work Disappears*, p. 208.
74. Wilson, *When Work Disappears*, p. 298.
75. Wilson, *When Work Disappears*, p. 237.

do service-sector jobs provide health insurance. Here Katherine Newman's study *No Shame in My Game,* a detailed analysis of low-wage labor in Harlem, serves as a seminal study.[76] Additionally, Kathryn Edin and Laura Lein's important research shows that neither single-parent women who were employed nor those receiving welfare could make ends meet.[77] Therefore, a commitment not only to developing jobs but also to paying laborers a "living wage," a return for work that keeps families out of poverty, is essential.[78]

A living or family wage means a wage-earner would be paid enough to be able to pay for housing, food, transportation, health care, and other basic necessities. Without this kind of wage, work will be a ladder that only goes down, not up. Thanks in great measure to the work of the Industrial Areas Foundation and their campaign for the living wage, initiated in Baltimore by BUILD (Baltimoreans United in Leadership Development), we are beginning to see a positive impact. Labor organizing among the working poor will also likely play a significant role in the future of American cities. As we consider these conditions and challenges, it should remind us that the protection of immigrants and their rights as fellow human beings must be upheld.

With large numbers of structurally unemployed or underemployed individuals in inner cities and Southern hemispheric cities, it is also time for a re-evaluation of the meaning of work that is culturally assumed in the "Protestant tradition." Miroslav Volf has suggested an alternative in *Work in the Spirit.*[79] He argues that work should be defined not by its task but by its use of gifts and purpose in service of others and the new creation. This is the work of the Spirit, and it stands against a globalizing economy that in so many ways is accelerating alienation and division. Volf's definition of work moves toward providing people with social, economic, and spiritual standing and meaning in their work.

Wilson's proposals present a number of challenges for the church. One of the most critical is the opportunity for the church to reconsider individualism, a feature of evangelical traditions that follows in step with the American belief system. As I have tried to demonstrate, individualist thinking is wrong from the standpoint of our analysis of urban poverty and on the basis of a robust theology of sin, injustice, the powers, and exclusion. Christians should be leaders in challenging the inadequacy of individualist assumptions.

76. Newman, *No Shame in My Game: The Working Poor in the Inner City* (New York: Alfred A. Knopf and The Russell Sage Foundation, 1999).

77. Edin and Lein, *Making Ends Meet: How Single Mothers Survive Welfare and Low-Wage Work* (New York: Russell Sage Foundation, 1997).

78. Isaac Martin, "Dawn of the Living Wage: The Diffusion of a Redistributive Municipal Policy," *Urban Affairs Review* 36, no. 4 (March 2001): 470-96.

Faith-based ministries should work especially with their volunteers and their congregational support base to think afresh on these issues, challenging moralistic notions of the "deserving" and "undeserving" poor.

It is not just inner-city residents who face a crisis in health care, wages, education, and housing costs. The middle class and working class of America almost certainly face similar pressures. The ability to draw together wide coalitions around such issues is crucial if a moral and practical politics is to find success. In *The Bridge Over the Racial Divide: Rising Inequality and Coalition Politics,* Wilson continues his advocacy for social rights that create a new vision of race relations but ties it to new networks and coalitions.[80] Instead of heating up the divisions produced by economic inequality, Wilson advocates cross-class, cross-race, and cross-interest coalitions (including churches) that work for the implementation of broader social rights. The end result of such a broad-based coalition would be of great benefit to families in the suburbs as well as the inner city. This would require a great deal of organizing, especially across racial and ethnic lines, but the rewards of such an effort would be great.

Another major area of moral passion for Christians interested in more just cities must involve criminal justice and prison reform, not simply prison ministry. It should break our hearts to see urban policy reduced to locking up the jobless and disenfranchised, especially young African-American males.[81] There are nonabusive ways to uphold public safety and prevent crime, especially violent crime, from happening in the first place, as the Ten-Point Coalition in Boston has shown. But doing so requires a broader strategy of community activity, presence, and organizing. And it requires holding police departments accountable. Local communities will not allow the police to abuse their children or to function like an occupying army.

Clearly, a Christian commitment to cities and urban reform is critically important, and it inescapably joins people of Christian belief to the pluralistic life of the city. Richard Mouw and Sander Griffioen make this insightful point:

79. Volf, *Work in the Spirit: Toward a Theology of Work* (New York: Oxford University Press, 1991).

80. Wilson, *The Bridge Over the Racial Divide: Rising Inequality and Coalition Politics* (Berkeley and Los Angeles: University of California Press, 1999).

81. T. Richard Snyder, *The Protestant Ethic and the Spirit of Punishment* (Grand Rapids: Eerdmans, 2001); Loïc Wacquant, "From Slavery to Mass Incarceration: Rethinking the 'Race Question' in the U.S.," *New Left Review* 13 (January-February 2002): 41-60; and Mark Lewis Taylor, *The Executed God: The Way of the Cross in Lockdown America* (Minneapolis: Fortress, 2001).

Christian conviction is grounded in a particularized yearning for a new kind of public arena, one that will be on display only when the eschaton arrives. The public square as we presently experience it has to be seen against the background of the eternal horizon of the Heavenly City. For those of us who embrace a partially realized eschatology, it is not unrealistic to expect signs of this City here and now. . . .

This yearning, in turn, makes us bold to join others in the larger human quest for a healthy public arena, in the hope that on that journey, too, we will experience those mysterious and surprising inklings of a larger kind of love that can take concrete shape — even in the midst of our highly pluralistic here-and-now — in new forms of citizenship and community.[82]

A biblical vision for urban economic and political life demands hope, perseverance, and a critically minded and enacted faith.

Regional and Global Neighboring

As Martin Luther King Jr. famously observed in the letter he wrote from the Birmingham jail, "We are caught in an inescapable network of mutuality, tied to a single garment of destiny." Wherever we live, in some way we share in the consequences of our culture of prisons and incarceration, social violence, urban abandonment, economic disparity, and racial division. So we must also be bound together in searching for solutions and making constructive connections to neighborhoods. As we noted in our earlier reflections on Jeremiah 29, a strand of the biblical argument is that the well-being of the people of God is joined to the welfare of the city.

Today, a civic-minded *regionalism* recognizes that the city and the larger metropolitan region are interdependent in their economic and social health.[83] This has produced a variety of proposals that run from new models

82. Mouw and Griffioen, *Pluralisms and Horizons: An Essay in Christian Public Philosophy* (Grand Rapids: Eerdmans, 1993), pp. 176-77.

83. Two of the leading advocates for regionalism are Myron Orfield, author of *Metropolitics: A Regional Agenda for Community and Stability* (Washington, D.C.: Brookings Institution Press and Cambridge: The Lincoln Institute of Land Policy, 1997); and Neil Peirce, with Curtis W. Johnson and John Stuart Hall, *Citistates: How Urban America Can Prosper in a Competitive World* (Washington, D.C.: Seven Locks Press, 1993). See also Peter Dreier, John Mollenkopf, and Todd Swanstrom, *Place Matters: Metropolitics for the Twenty-First Century* (Lawrence: University of Kansas Press, 2001).

of governance (and revenue sharing) to planning that works to contain advancing suburban sprawl. Regionalism makes sense even if many of its proposals are not easily adoptable or even always right. It recognizes that a community cannot be divided by deep disparities in basic goods and services without life for all being undermined. As a community that is to have no physical boundaries, as a fellowship of the Spirit, the church should evidence solidarity.

The growing gap between the rich and the poor, the suburb and the city, raises serious ecclesiastical questions. How can there be two churches in the world, one poor and one wealthy? At stake, then, is not just more equal regional development but the unity of the church that confesses one Lord, one faith, one baptism (1 Cor. 12:23; Eph. 4:4-6). Among those who are seeking transformative change is Bishop Anthony Pilla of the archdiocese of Cleveland. In a pastoral letter entitled "The Church in the City," he challenged his church to consider their mission and responsibilities in light of the city's needs. He sought to develop from the gospel a plan of action to address the dwindling population and the abandonment of the city, the social and economic costs of which had deeply affected both the city and the church.

Seeking a "new urban future for Northeast Ohio" based on "the city of God," Bishop Pilla organized a plan of action based on the principles of social justice, the redevelopment of older cities, the interdependence of parishes in their life and mission, a restructuring of parishes to support older urban ones, and, last but certainly not least, God's preferential love for the poor. In his pastoral letter, he addressed church and city alike: "I invite all people of good will to cooperate in the work of creating such a city. I ask our government officials to renew and increase their efforts to assist in the task of developing and redeveloping our urban centers. In a special way, I call on all Catholics in every part of our Cleveland Diocese to join me in this commitment to our cities and the churches in our cities." Here is a commitment and approach that awaits contextual adjustment and replication by other cities and ecclesial bodies.[84]

Joining economics with the gospel in another way, the Apostle Paul worked to reshape the identity of the Corinthians through the "collection" for the poor in Jerusalem that took place "the first day of every week" (1 Cor. 16:1-4; cf. Rom. 15:25-28; 2 Cor. 8–9). Richard Horsley points out that "the network of assemblies had an 'international' political-economic dimension

---

84. Pilla, "The Church in the City," Diocese of Cleveland, n.d.; Neil R. Peirce, "A Bishop Takes on the Suburbs," *The Sun,* 15 May 1995, 7-A.

diametrically opposed to the tributary political economy of the empire."[85] Power relations between patron and client were replaced by the politics of sharing, through which believers looked beyond their immediate horizons to the needs of others and the trans-national reign of God. Through the Spirit, the gospel gives shape to a "theo-cosmopolitics" of sharing characterized by "giving and receiving" (Phil. 4:15). This model of sharing and mutuality that witnesses to the world is much needed for the good of our cities.

While we have focused on local and regional neighboring, it is very important that we take neighboring to the global level. The church must take seriously the transnational dimension of wages, working conditions, health care, and urbanization. Loving our neighbors means responding to demands in the areas of public policy and mission on a global scale. We must also study the broader world context: we can learn vital lessons of urban faith in action from Africa, Asia, and Latin America. Christian communities in the inner city need global interchange that represents the unity of the gospel so that we are truly Christians of the world.

If we take seriously the body of Christ and the demands of sharing the Lord's table, then the recognition of a new narrative that stretches across social, geographical, and ethnic borders is not only possible but theologically necessary. Central to this narrative are the body of Christ and the sharing of the Eucharist, as William Cavanaugh has pointed out in an important essay on the subject: "The Eucharist journeys by telling a story of cosmic proportions within the particular face to face encounter of neighbors and strangers in the Eucharistic gathering. In an economy of hypermobility, we resist not by fleeing, but by abiding."[86] The Eucharistic connection of identity and meaning in Christ is both local and global, free of dichotomy or barriers, says Cavanaugh: "In Eucharistic space . . . we are not juxtaposed, but identified."[87] As such, the body of Christ and the liturgical life of the church read back to the world an alternative.[88]

---

85. Horsley, "1 Corinthians: A Case Study of Paul's Assembly as an Alternative Society," in *Paul and Empire: Religion and Power in Roman Imperial Society*, ed. Richard A. Horsley (Harrisburg: Trinity Press International, 1997), p. 251.

86. Cavanaugh, "The Eucharist as Resistance to Globalization," *Modern Theology* 15, no. 2 (April 1999): 191-92.

87. Cavanaugh, "The Eucharist as Resistance to Globalization," p. 193.

88. Cavanaugh, "The Eucharist as Resistance to Globalization," p. 193.

DEFINING RESPONSIBILITY

If the church is to be a central actor in social change, what is the shape of that calling in relation to public responsibility? What is government's role?[89] The Bush administration's "faith-based initiative" brought to the foreground the question of who is responsible for meeting pressing human needs in the inner city.[90] While the Clinton administration widely supported the efforts of faith communities, and other efforts predated this, President George W. Bush made partnership with faith-based organizations a hallmark of his domestic policy. Under the leadership of John DiIulio, the first director of the Office of Faith-Based and Community Initiatives, he made the commitment that faith-based programs which could show measurable results would be increasingly eligible for support, potentially through vouchers, tax incentives, and Charitable Choice legislation enhancements. By removing the barriers that faith-based groups have traditionally faced in securing federal funding, the administration believes that more will join in as partners in compassion.

Much of the theoretical impetus for this broader political push to provide government assistance to churches came from Marvin Olasky and his book entitled *The Tragedy of American Compassion*.[91] His thesis is that government has usurped the role of private and religious-based compassion, thus harming both the giver and the receiver. What is needed, Olasky believes, is a return to the kind of relational charities that flourished in the nineteenth century, especially those of faith. Morally minded volunteers of compassion are what will most help the poor, he says. I have serious questions about Olasky's historical reconstruction. And it seems to me that he has failed to appreciate the multiple and structural causes of inner-city struggles and has privatized public responsibility for the flourishing of its citizens.

Analysts of America's social-service sector remind us that public fund-

---

89. An excellent discussion of these issues can be found in *Who Will Provide? The Changing Role of Religion in American Social Welfare,* ed. Mary Jo Bane, Brent Coffin, and Ronald Thiemann (Boulder: Westview Press, 2000).

90. For a clarifying view of the interests involved, see Arthur E. Farnsley II, "Faith-based Action," *The Christian Century,* 14 March 2001, pp. 12-15; and *Who Will Provide?* ed. Mary Jo Bane et al. For a vigorous defense of Christian involvement in current faith-based initiatives, see James W. Skillen, "*E Pluribus Unum* and Faith-Based Welfare Reform: A Kuyperian Moment for the Church in God's World," *Princeton Seminary Bulletin* 22, no. 3 (2001): 285-305.

91. Olasky, *The Tragedy of American Compassion* (Washington D.C.: Regnery Publishing Inc., 1992).

ing and private funding have long been meshed.[92] Historians have clearly established that churches and voluntary associations were never exclusively responsible for the care of Americans who are poor, who need medical attention, and who are unable to find work.[93] Government has always played an important role. What must be taken into account is the wide variety of programs that provide support and seek to fight poverty.[94] Will the church really decide to take over the government's role? Thus far the evidence suggests it will not.[95] Can the church do it? The answer is quite clearly no. Should the church do it? While the church should be doing much more, the fact remains that it will take many different sectors to address the challenge of the inner city. Some issues concerning our common polis require the involvement of political institutions.[96]

There are many reasons, therefore, to question Bush's faith-based initiative — even to consider joining in with those Christians whose commitments to peace and justice have led to a call for nonparticipation. There are a number of compelling reasons for such wariness. First, it seems clear from the size of the tax cut for the wealthy that the administration has not made the poor a real priority. For the most part, available money is being shuffled around, not increased. And the nation's military budget and plans look increasingly expansive. Second, the plan takes no account of the needs for infrastructure and capital investment in inner-city neighborhoods. Third, by personalizing poverty and social change, the plan avoids any structural definition of urban poverty. It thus privatizes faith, taking away its role of questioning power. Fourth, the plan does not evaluate critically enough the quality of faith-based groups. Merely adopting the label "faith-based" does not make a program or a ministry effective. Under the label of "faith," some groups have done a disservice to the people they purport to serve.

92. Lester M. Salamon and Helmut K. Anheier, "The Civil Society Sector," *Society* 34, no. 2 (January/February 1997): 60-65.

93. Katz, *The Price of Citizenship: Redefining the American Welfare State* (New York: Metropolitan Books, 2001), pp. 137-70; Heather A. Warren, "Historical Perspectives on Faith-Based Organizations and Community Development," unpublished paper presented to the Project on Lived Theology.

94. See Rebecca Blank, *It Takes a Nation: A New Agenda for Fighting Poverty* (Princeton: Princeton University Press, 1997), pp. 191-219.

95. See Mark Chaves, "Religious Congregations and Welfare Reform: Who Will Take Advantage of 'Charitable Choice'?" *American Sociological Review* 64 (December 1999): 836-46.

96. For a historical case study on the problems and issues, see John Roxborogh, *Thomas Chalmers: Enthusiast for Missions: The Christian Good of Scotland and the Rise of the Missionary Movement* (Edinburgh: Rutherford House, 1999), pp. 99-131.

In all of this, the government's co-option of the language of biblical faith and practice is more than a little problematic. Given this circumstance, the church has a responsibility to provide a critical interpretation and suggest a viable alternative, to "test all things" and discern the "spirit" of the time.

Nevertheless, if community-based groups, churches included, find that a particular government program fits their call and need for funds, most grassroots practitioners likely will become involved in the initiative, making the program work for their communities, seeking to correct injustices of the social and economic system. This kind of selective participation already takes place regularly at the local and state levels. Community developers see it as their job to bring resources into the community, to build common ground wherever possible, not to be political purists in their practice. While dangers always abound, I see here no inherent compromise of the prophetic voice, because, among other reasons, we should not underestimate the power of the prophetic community to witness to the powers and call them to repentance. That new attention to faith-based groups may enable underfunded ministries to do more is potentially — with all the caveats noted above — a very good thing.

In receiving public funding, churches can resolve constitutional questions — as they have for some time — largely by creating separate, nonprofit, tax-exempt organizations to provide for particular needs such as housing, child care, and health care. And while the witness of faith-based groups is certainly important, their primary goal should be results, not conversion. Certainly religion as a motivator and faith as a worldview play essential roles in any endeavor. But the job of faith-based organizations needs to be results-oriented — "building more houses" or "helping children succeed in school." And the work needs to be held to the same standards as those established for "secular" organizations. This in no way suggests that religious motives or the way faith is integrated into life should be downplayed. They remain vital in every context.

This point notwithstanding, churches which believe that their interests and those of the government coalesce in areas such as welfare reform must exercise considerable caution so they do not become instruments of state programs, particularly in coercive ways that jeopardize both individual and communal rights. How can Christians and church- or faith-based organizations participate in any "welfare-to-work" program that may put the poor out on the streets? Pressuring and forcing people to "change," something that government programs require and determine the meaning of, is inconsistent with the practice of being an ecclesial community. Jesus welcomed the homeless and unwanted; he did not discipline them. When the church wears a "tough love" mask for the state, it casts a shadow over the integrity of the gospel.

As any work grows, the choice between integrity and compromise inevitably arises. Does working closely not only with government but also with foundations and corporations mean that the church and its related efforts will become secularized? Will joint ventures with for-profit entities compromise the values of the kingdom? As funding pressures grow, maintaining without compromise the vision and values of the reign of God is never easy. With each funding decision, hard questions must be asked: If we do this, will it compromise the identity of the church? What will the differences be ten years from now? Certainly a key element in any such relationship is the determination of the church or faith-based group to maintain independence of mission and vision. It is essential to be willing to walk away from any funding source, public or private, at any time. The church needs to undertake intensive theological reflection in order to cultivate the right loyalties, commitments, and practices.

While the gospel requires that the church give itself away on behalf of people and the community, at the same time those public figures and institutions that cause misery and sorrow must be held accountable.[97] The body of Christ should have a political shape, voice, and life. In this way we follow the example of Christ's first followers, as N. T. Wright points out: "What we can say for certain is that a summons to risk all in following Jesus places him and his followers firmly on the map of first-century socially and politically subversive movements."[98] There are many times when communities of faith are received as a blessing in the city (Prov. 11:11a). But on other occasions, the critical discourse and engagements of faith will bring about repudiation from institutions of power and social order. The right — or rather, the obligation — of prophetic opposition and exposure of government indifference or injustice has been at the heart of the way in which the African-American and Latino churches have fulfilled their public role.[99] Making the comfortable uneasy will, of course, create dissent. But as history shows, such dissent is vital for upholding the rights of the poor and excluded as well as distinguishing the church from the state. The requirement to act and the requirement to be prophetic will at times exist in great tension (or at least they should), but that

97. See the argument from the German context of Jürgen Moltmann, *God for a Secular Society: The Public Relevance of Theology,* trans. Margaret Kohl (Minneapolis: Fortress, 1999), pp. 60-61.

98. Wright, *Jesus and the Victory of God,* p. 304.

99. Stephen Carter, *God's Name in Vain: The Wrongs and Rights of Religion in Politics* (New York: Basic Books, 2000).

does not mean an attempt should be made to "balance" them out. Rather, prophetic deeds and pastoral actions should strive together equally in the public place.

There are many short-term and intermediate benefits to going along with the new liberal/conservative pragmatic understanding concerning the role of faith-based programs. It may even turn out to be the beginning of a new progressive politics. But in the long term such a pragmatic model may be disastrous for the poor,[100] because it sets up a neo-Constantinian model of patronage that avoids justice and leaves the poor uninvited to the table, leaving out the mutuality of the gospel. Our challenge is to generate social patterns grounded in the giving and receiving of the Triune God.

Can the church "save" the inner city? The answer depends on how the question is defined. By pointing to the kingdom and God's ways of redemption that rise from below, the church does point the city to the way of salvation. In profound social and theological ways, the church of the poor is an agent of God's kingdom in history. But this should not diminish the responsibilities that all sectors of society have in creating a more just and joyful city.

BUILDING ON FAITH, LOVE, AND HOPE

Now that we have set forth a substantial agenda for faith in the city, one bound up with God's mission of *shalom* for the city, it is essential to anchor it in a biblical spirituality. Such a spirituality involves cultivating a passionate love for God and a love for those who are our neighbors, tying together prayer, worship, the Bible, the street, and concrete deeds of *shalom*. It is a life turned toward the God who "exercises kindness, justice and righteousness" (Jer. 9:24) and renews the city (Jer. 29:11-13). For only by living in the life of God, the biblical testimony holds, is it possible to sustain spending ourselves "in behalf of the hungry and satisfy[ing] the needs of the oppressed" (Isa. 58:10; cf. Pss. 111; 112). Only by being rooted in Christ is it possible to complete the long-distance race that is the course of discipleship (Phil. 3:13-14; 2 Tim. 4:6).

Living by the story of Christ, the Christian community is specifically

---

100. For a parallel argument, though one built on a different social analysis and social outcome, see Mark David Wood, *Cornel West and the Politics of Prophetic Pragmatism* (Urbana: University of Illinois Press, 2000). An insightful approach is offered by Ched Myers, "Behold the Treasure of the Church: A Bible Study on the Churches and Welfare Reform," *Sojourners* 28, no. 5 (September-October 1999): 32-34.

called to build on and live by faith, love, and hope. The church is the locus for the practice of spirituality for both practical and biblical reasons. As Paul reminded the Thessalonians, the church as a community is known by "your work produced by faith, your labor prompted by love, and your endurance inspired by hope in our Lord Jesus Christ" (1 Thess. 1:3). Within the community of sisters and brothers, there is a life that sustains, challenges, and, most of all, pushes forward.

Faith, love, and hope practiced in the forsaken inner city draw the church into the "nearness" of the new city and the new creation.[101] Because faith, love, and hope involve an encounter with God, such spirituality does not exhaust; it replenishes. With the mission of the church and God's new world in view, Orlando Costas joins the experience of the Spirit and the Pauline triad together: "The Spirit creates *faith* where there is no faith, making believers participants in God's *love* and heirs to the *hope* for a new world. This activity turns believers into truly spiritual persons, who are nonconformists within history."[102] If believers are to be faithful to Christ, then they must embody faith, love, and hope on the street, amidst all of its pain and sorrow. There is nothing easy about this, but it is a faithful following of God's way.

Faith is not to be used to forget social misery and suffering. Rather, faith is a gift of God, a gift that delivers from the power of sin and redeems for new life in every way. Faith is also a gift of the Spirit that can empower urban transformation, opening up new possibilities of life and peace in the inner city. For, as Jürgen Moltmann has powerfully written, "Faith means crossing the frontiers of the reality which is existent now, and has been determined by the past, and seeking the potentialities for life which have not yet come into being."[103] Exemplified in the life, death, and resurrection of Christ, this faith moves mountains and changes neighborhoods. Jesus commented on the power of this faith when he said, "I tell you the truth, if anyone says to this mountain, 'Go, throw yourself into the sea,' and does not doubt in his heart

101. Writes Jürgen Moltmann, "The 'nearness' of eternal life, the kingdom of God and the new heaven and the new earth must not be pinned down chronologically. It is a *category of intimacy,* and means that which touches believers 'nearly' and is closest to their hearts, so that they live from it and act in accordance with it, just as in the 'nearness' of God's kingdom Jesus himself prayed 'Abba,' dear Father, and out of the 'nearness' of the kingdom healed the sick, received outcasts and raised the dead" (*Experiences in Theology: Ways and Forms of Christian Theology,* trans. Margaret Kohl [Minneapolis: Fortress, 2000], p. 38).

102. Costas, *Christ Outside the Gate: Mission Beyond Christendom* (Maryknoll: Orbis, 1982), p. 90.

103. Moltmann, *The Spirit of Life: A Universal Affirmation,* trans. Margaret Kohl (Minneapolis: Fortress, 1992), p. 115.

but believes that what he says will happen, it will be done for him" (Mark 11:23). Here is Jesus' invitation to confront what appears to be immovable and intransigent, for it will succumb to the power of the kingdom. Faith awakens and enlivens us to the new possibilities inherent in the promise of the kingdom of God. By building communities of faith in the inner city, Christians engage the world with the power of the Word of God.

Love is redemptive. According to Moltmann, "Love is the praxis of God's coming kingdom and his righteousness and justice in this world. . . . It is focused on the others, the weary, the heavy-laden, the humiliated and insulted, the dying and the grieving."[104] Such love answers what Cornel West calls the "nihilistic threat."[105] Nihilism, even as a form of resistance against the sting of exclusion, injustice, racism, and coldness, is a threat to life, especially among young women and men. Can there be any other way but love (1 Cor. 8:1)? As West observes, "Nihilism is not overcome by arguments or analyses; it is tamed by love and care."[106] Love is what we are searching for, bell hooks writes, and when it is truly found, it is love that restores the fabric of community.[107] From God's gracious love springs the labor of Christians for liberation and justice in the world.[108] God's healing love enables love for self and neighbor, subduing the powers of hatred, stigmatization, and exclusion. Christian love does not use force to make economic, political, or spiritual gains (1 Cor. 13); instead, it shares the life of others (John 15:13). As James Olthuis tells us, "Love as excess — love without a why — overflows onto the plains and meadows of life as a celebrating-with. It seeps into life's cracks and fissures as suffering-with."[109] And Paul told the Galatians, "The only thing that counts is faith expressing itself through love" (Gal. 5:6). Will the inner city learn of God's love any other way?

Hope follows love and faith, the outlook of a new future based on God's promise of a redeemed city and world.[110] Hope proclaims — against all the relentless claims that a meaningful future is not possible, and against the constant agonies of suffering — that because of the cross and the resurrection,

104. Moltmann, *Experiences in Theology*, p. 58.

105. West, *Race Matters* (Boston: Beacon, 1993), pp. 11-20.

106. West, *Race Matters*, p. 19.

107. hooks, *Salvation: Black People and Love* (New York: William Morrow, 2001).

108. Gustavo Gutiérrez, *We Drink from Our Own Wells: The Spiritual Journey of a People* (Maryknoll: Orbis, 1984).

109. Olthuis, "Crossing the Threshhold: Sojourning Together in the Wild Spaces of Love," *Toronto Journal of Theology* 11, no. 1 (Spring 1995): 51.

110. Moltmann, *The Coming of God: A Christian Eschatology*, trans. Margaret Kohl (Minneapolis: Augsburg Fortress, 1996).

tomorrow can be different from today. This is the work of the Spirit of life, who draws all of us toward the renewal of life.

Such hope is not a barren word fueled by human optimism that all will "work out." Christian hope is at odds with such optimism, because it ignores the depths of injustice and suffering instead of wrestling with them.[111] Biblical hope is much more. As Paul declares in Romans 5:1-5, Christian hope rests upon the justifying work of Christ, who has been victorious over suffering and death. The result is that "hope does not disappoint us, because God has poured out his love into our hearts by the Holy Spirit, whom he has given us" (5:5). The Spirit gives hope based on the future, Moltmann points out: "The sending-ahead and the fore-taste of God's future bring that future into the present . . . and people are roused to hope."[112] By forming communities of "living hope" that witness to the hope of God in Christ Jesus, Christians stake the future of the city on the living God. "Christian hope dares to live in the power of the mystery of God's not yet," Samuel Solivan declares.[113]

One of the most hopeful passages in Scripture is Jeremiah 32, which has a good deal to do with the city and what it means to anticipate God's future. When the story opens, the prophet Jeremiah finds himself confined in the guards' courtyard and charged with treason as the Babylonians are about to gain power. (Jeremiah has said the right thing at the "wrong" time, which is what prophets did.) His cousin Hanamel, invoking the Jubilee laws of family land redemption, asks Jeremiah to purchase a plot of land that he, Hanamel, owns. According to the laws of Israel, Jeremiah had the right and even the responsibility to buy the land (32:7-8; cf. Lev. 25:25-31). Why would Hanamel not try to sell the land to someone else? Change about to sweep over the city was about to wipe away the land's value. Jeremiah, in response to the voice of God, has already determined to acquire — literally "redeem" — this very public piece of land (32:6, 8). But he does so without a realistic prospect that the title will be honored under the impending Babylonian regime. Nevertheless, he can see the ultimate value of the transaction.

As with any real estate closing, there are witnesses and parties present at the transaction to represent various interests. After the deal is inked, Jeremiah — again at God's direction — puts copies of the deed of purchase in a clay jar, both to ensure their protection and longevity (32:13-14) and to provide a sign of hope for the future: "For this is what the LORD Almighty, the God of

---

111. This concern is taken up in *The Courage to Hope: From Black Suffering to Human Redemption,* ed. Quinton Hosford Dixie and Cornel West (Boston: Beacon, 1999).

112. Moltmann, *Experiences in Theology,* p. 55.

113. Solivan, *The Spirit, Pathos, and Liberation,* p. 92.

Israel, says: Houses, fields, and vineyards will again be bought in this land"
(32:15). Brian Walsh's comments point to some vital implications of this
transaction:

> Essentially, all that is going on here is a normal legal transaction between
> relatives within the context of the covenantal life of Israel. But it is pre-
> cisely the normality of all this that makes it so astounding. These were
> not, remember, normal times. Indeed, this is a normal (or normative!)
> transaction which is intended to maintain covenantal shalom in the land
> in the most abnormal of circumstances. . . . Jeremiah can buy this land
> because he has the vision to look beyond the present calamity, beyond the
> present ending, beyond grief, beyond land loss, defilement, Babylonian
> siege, drought and exile. . . . This field is, as it were, a down payment on
> that hope.[114]

The vacant lot is not just a prosaic physical space but a repository of larger
cultural and theological meaning. It is a symbol that God will renew the land,
the city, and the people.

Jeremiah bases his culture-advancing act upon the hope of God's urban
recovery plans (32:37-41). Unconstrained by the political impossibilities of
the moment, Jeremiah makes public God's vision of a renewed city by buying
a vacant and abandoned lot. This was not just a real estate purchase; it was, as
Walsh puts it, a daring "*act* of hope in the face of *despair.*"[115] The same sort of
creative, imaginative, and committed embodiment of hope — the "normative
shalom-bringing cultural activities"[116] that Jeremiah engaged in — is demanded of Christians today. Locating the future both in the divine narrative
of urban redemption and in the excluded and abandoned neighborhoods of
our cities, we look toward a city to come. By going forward with the everyday
activities of life and faith, we give a steady and living witness to God's promise
of *shalom* for our neighborhoods. And by reclaiming vacant land for housing,
gardens, and community centers, we show our faith in God's future.

To follow Christ is to go to "every city and place" (Luke 10:1, my translation). "Looking for the city that is to come" (Heb. 13:14), Christians are to
abide redemptively in the city (Gal. 4:26; Phil. 1:27; 3:20). For the writer of

---

114. Walsh, *Subversive Christianity: Imaging God in a Dangerous Time* (Great Britain:
Regius, 1992), pp. 87-88. I owe my attention to the hopeful implications of this text to Stephen Fowl.

115. Walsh, *Subversive Christianity,* p. 87.

116. Walsh, *Subversive Christianity,* p. 87.

the Epistle to the Hebrews, this "looking" does not in any way mean disengaging from the city; instead, it leads to worship, prayer, faithful discipleship, sharing, and mission in Christ's way (Heb. 11:10, 16; 12:22; 13:15-16). As John Milbank puts it in his comments on Hebrews 13:13-16, "Christ has abolished the sacrifices of the earthly city, which involved expelling something into a no-man's land; but instead he has inaugurated a new kind of efficacious sacrifice of praise, self-sharing, and probable attendant suffering which unites us with him in the heavenly city."[117]

It is the living memory of Jesus — the rejected, marginal, but ultimately resurrected and ascended one — that opens a new narrative, convicting all who follow him to live vulnerably and passionately for God's reign. This is possible because "we have this hope as an anchor" (Heb. 6:19), which is the promise of God for the redemption of the world realized in the cross. The church lives, risks, and builds on the resurrection love, faith, and hope that it professes and has been given in Christ by the Spirit. By the Spirit of God, the body of Christ knows that even as suffering and violence may grip our cities, a new future of peace for the cities of the world has begun. In faith, in the way of Jesus, and in confidence of God's future, the church in the inner city yearns for, enacts, and tells the story of Jesus, the one who so loved the inner city that he died for it and will come again to reconcile all things.

117. Milbank, *The Word Made Strange: Theology, Language, Culture* (Oxford: Blackwell, 1997), p. 151. Concerning the relationship between Christian comon life, God's city, and witness, see the powerful essay by Stephen E. Fowl, *God's Beautiful City: Christian Mission after Christendom,* The Ekklesia Project, pamphlet no. 4 (Eugene, Ore.: Wipf and Stock Publishers, 2001).

Not in Vain

R ow after row of vacant houses, weed- and trash-covered lots, abandoned factories, and boarded-up stores in the inner city transmit a narrative of loss and ruin. "Urban ruination is serious; it is real; it is not a stage set; it has spiritual authenticity," observes Marshall Berman. "Symbols of modern life have turned into symbols of death. There is nothing like it in the suburbs. Getting down to the bottom of things puts you in touch with some kind of ultimate reality."[1] Camilo José Vergara locates in such urban desolation a demand for interpretation that includes response and engagement: "Ruins stand as witnesses of their own past, not doing what they were built to do, yet possessing an awesome power to stir the soul. As witnesses of the urban condition, they urge us to ask: Is there no choice but to stand by and watch the destruction of our cities?"[2]

There is always a choice, both spiritual and political, to reverse the continuing ruination, depletion, and exploitation of our cities and those who seek its shelter. Our urban ruins and new urban forms invite us to neither the despair of destruction nor the optimism of progress but to the genuine hope of redemption — hope based on renewing our imaginations with the vision and patterns of life that reflect the new creation of God. Christian hope is grounded in the death and resurrection of Christ, not the faded dreams of an age simultaneously winding down and rewinding. The Christian faith thus

1. Berman, cited in Camilo José Vergara, *American Ruins* (New York: Monacelli Press, 1999), p. 8.

2. Vergara, *The New American Ghetto* (New Brunswick: Rutgers University Press, 1995), p. 197.

seeks to grapple honestly with the presence of suffering and the possibility of new beginnings for all of humanity and creation. For in the Crucified and Risen "all things" are transfigured, and the city is an object of divine grace no less than any other aspect of the creation. This is the deep structure upon which hope rests.

The resurrection of Leslie Street points the way to God's future for community and the city. It began, fittingly, with a most improbable sight. In December 1997, eighty people, black and white, young and old, gathered at the corner of Leslie and School streets in Sandtown. With great joy, they prayed, sang "Glory, Glory," and cheered on a giant excavator and rolling dump trucks — which were there to remove about forty vacant houses. After years of praying and planning, people were watching and rejoicing as city workers removed these brick husks. These tiny, alley-street houses had been shoddily designed and constructed, and now they were falling down. They were not architectural gems waiting to be preserved but substandard wrecks collapsing under the weight of their own unjust beginnings. Among the most substandard housing in the neighborhood, the block of houses had once been pictured on the front page of the *New York Times* as an example of "Third World" conditions in the United States.[3] For those in the neighborhood who knew about the story, which was run nationally, it was a painful blow struck at the heart of their dignity and humanity.

In 1994, Sandtown Habitat and the community began working hard on a plan to redevelop the block, and the mayor and the housing department soon approved the proposal. So in December 1997, they were prepared for the demolition and the steps to take after it. Instead of letting the land sit and become another vacant block, Sandtown Habitat moved forward even as the buildings were coming down to set the foundations and raise the roofs of twenty-seven new homes, all intended for ownership by families in the community. Within a month of the demolition, the new foundations were set, masonry work was started, and the framed outline of each house began to take shape.

For over a year, the work went on slowly, with difficulty and expectancy mixing together. Future homeowners spent their weekends laboring at the work site. Volunteers came from as far away as California. After the framing came the interior work. First, heating, plumbing, and electrical systems were installed. Next came the doors, cornices, and windows. And then came the kitchens and the floors. Outside, sewer and water lines were laid, and a new

---

3. Thomas L. Friedman, "Foreign-Aid Agency Shifts to Problems Back Home," *New York Times*, 26 June 1996, A-1, 18.

street was paved. Yards were landscaped. Street trees, mailboxes, and new lighting followed.

Finally, in December 1998, the homes were completed. A day was chosen for the dedication, and a stage was constructed on the south end of the street specifically for the event. On that special day, the front door of each new home was decorated with a bright ribbon. The block was packed with people. The celebration began with the New Song band and children's choir, which set the tone of joy and praise. During a three-hour-long service, each of the home-owner families walked up to the stage and received a set of keys, a Bible, and an embroidered plaque. Those who wanted to speak did so, and many took the opportunity to praise God and celebrate his goodness in their life and community. Partners in the state and city government were recognized and thanked. They were also asked to continue supporting the work, which they publicly agreed to do. Churches that had joined in the effort were celebrated. Finally, everyone raised their hands in a communal blessing over the block. Then, on Elder C. W. Harris's count, the twenty-seven ribbons were cut, and the doors to the homes were opened.

Each house and homeowner family has a remarkable story to tell. For lifetime Sandtown resident Antoine Bennett, owning a home on Leslie Street fulfilled a dream. Jane Johnson moved to Leslie Street with her three children — Alesha, Shawtez, and Chauncy Jr. They had been living in part of the Gilmor Homes public housing, an area besieged by drugs and violence. The difference? "For the first time in years, I slept in peace," Jane said. To live in peace, the plenitude of joy, righteousness, and reconciliation that is the peace of God — this is the meaning of Leslie Street.

Perhaps no individual knew more about the old and the new Leslie Street than Lucky Crosby. He had spent nearly his entire life living on the block, first as a son and later as a father. He knew how bad the conditions were, but he believed they should and could be different. And he was willing to stay and work to achieve that difference. As a member of Sandtown Habitat, Lucky played a major part in rebuilding the block, from start to finish. For years he had rented from an absentee landlord; now he became one of the first homeowners on Leslie Street. His is among the stories that are taken up in the gospel narrative of death and life, reconciliation and renewal.

Isaiah provides visionary words on the urban future: "They will rebuild the ancient ruins and restore the places long devastated; they will renew the ruined cities that have been devastated for generations" (61:4). Here on Leslie Street, this prophetic vision has been "rewritten" by the people of the community. From the day of dedication, when children started up a game of football, to this day, when the street remains filled with children, do we not witness something of the prophet Zechariah's vision being enacted? "The city streets will be filled with boys and girls playing there" (8:5). The promise of *shalom* has claimed a block that knew too little of its touch.

But what about the past, the history that had been shared by so many in Sandtown? Amnesia is impossible. Yet in the sheer glory of dedication day and all that it ushered in, past afflictions have begun to fade. New possibilities have begun to heal painful memories of exclusion, a down payment of what Miroslav Volf calls "the grace of nonremembering"[4] that ultimately is part of the redemption of the world. Indeed, God urges us to "Forget the former things; do not dwell on the past. See, I am doing a new thing! Now it springs up; do you not perceive it?" (Isa. 43:18-19). By looking to the "new thing," it is possible to know that the sins of others, acts that have damaged the community's life, identity, and purpose, do not carry the final day. But without the arduous and costly effort that went into rebuilding the community, an effort offered in response to a God who brings new life, there would be no change.

We are still faced with this question: Do the sweat and struggle that brought a restored block of homes into being have a larger meaning? Nicholas Wolterstorff offers an eloquent answer: "In the eschatological image of the city we have the assurance that our efforts to make these present cities of ours humane places in which to live — efforts which so often are frustrated, efforts which so often yield despair — will, by way of the mysterious patterns of history, eventually provide the tiles and timbers for a city of delight."[5] In the singing, sharing, blessing, and embracing that flowed forth from the rebuilding of Leslie Street, the new city of God is anticipated. While partial and flawed, the rebirth of Leslie Street belongs to the rebirth of all of creation, the continuation of life after the final redemption of the world. The reconciliation of so many things in Sandtown is a sign of the reconciliation of "all things" that is the future of the world (Col. 1:15-20).[6]

Although we still witness the forces of ruin and exclusion at work on the streets and in the city, this is not the end of the story or of our stories. For in 1 Corinthians 15, the Apostle Paul's central statement on the resurrection, he asserts, because of Christ's rising, "Stand firm. Let nothing move you. Always give yourselves fully to the work of the Lord, because you know that your la-

4. Volf, *Exclusion and Embrace: A Theological Exploration of Identity, Otherness, and Reconciliation* (Nashville: Abingdon, 1996), p. 138.

5. Wolterstorff, *Until Justice and Peace Embrace* (Grand Rapids: Eerdmans, 1983), p. 140.

6. Miroslav Volf, "Enter into Joy! Sin, Death, and the Life of the World to Come," in *The End of the World and the Ends of God: Science and Theology on Eschatology*, ed. John Polkinghorne and Michael Welker (Harrisburg: Trinity, 2000), p. 275.

bor in the Lord is not in vain" (15:58; cf. Phil. 3:21). Because of the promissory character of Christ's resurrection, work done in the name of Jesus that redeems the city, block by block, is not in vain. Because of the resurrection of Jesus, every effort mysteriously belongs to the new creation of joy and righteousness.[7] As Paul says elsewhere, "what is mortal" will be "swallowed up by life" (2 Cor. 5:4). When relationships become marked by a new love and mutuality, and when community is rightly restored, here are rumors of *shalom,* suggestions of the life to come breaking through in the city. This is the gift of the Spirit to the transformation of the world: a hope in the eternal presence of God in the city of love.

Bearing witness to Christ, the people of the Lord perform the deeds of *shalom* that witness to the city to come (Rev. 21:1-5). To stay in the community as neighbors, rebuild houses, teach in local schools, open health centers, think long and hard about local urban policy, and proclaim grace on the street corners — this is all part of the rhythm of bearing witness to a city without tears. It is part of the pattern of the work of the Lord. In such a witness we find a new song for the city. LaVerne and Al Stokes, Elder C. W. and Amelia Harris, Isaac Newman, Allan and Susan Tibbels, Janice Jamison, Nina Anderson — they are among those saints who have heard the Lord's call to live out their faith in the city day after day and make a difference. They show that barriers and boundaries can be overcome, that what has been forsaken can be redeemed. By the faithful discipleship that they and others who share their journey exemplify, all are given a reason to sing and not be silent, to hope and not give up, to persevere and not grow faint, and to seek the peace of the city that God has called us to serve.

7. N. T. Wright, *The Challenge of Jesus: Rediscovering Who Jesus Was and Is* (Downers Grove: InterVarsity, 1999), p. 180. For further background, see Anthony C. Thiselton, *The First Epistle to the Corinthians,* NIGTC (Grand Rapids: Eerdmans, 2000), pp. 1228, 1304-6.

Select Bibliography

Anderson, Elijah. *Code of the Streets: Decency, Violence, and the Moral Life of the Inner City.* New York: W. W. Norton, 1999.

Arias, Mortimer. *Announcing the Reign of God: Evangelization and the Subversive Memory of Jesus.* Philadelphia: Fortress, 1984.

Augustine, Saint. *The City of God.* Translated by Marcus Dods. New York: The Modern Library, 1993.

Baker, Mark D. *Religious No More: Building Communities of Grace and Freedom.* Downers Grove: InterVarsity, 1999.

Bakke, Raymond J. "The Urban Church in Global Perspective: Reflections on the Past, Challenges for the Future." *Transformation* 9, no. 2 (April/June 1992): 2-5.

Bane, Mary Jo; Brent Coffin; and Ronald Thiemann, eds. *Who Will Provide? The Changing Role of Religion in American Social Welfare.* Boulder: Westview Press, 2000.

Banks, Robert. *Paul's Idea of Community.* Rev. ed. Peabody: Hendrickson, 1994.

Bauckham, Richard. *James.* New Testament Readings. London: Routledge, 1999.

————. "The Rich Man and Lazarus: The Parable and the Parallels." *New Testament Studies* 37 (1991): 225-46.

————. *The Theology of the Book of Revelation.* Cambridge: Cambridge University Press, 1993.

Bauman, Zygmunt. *Globalization: The Human Consequences.* New York: Columbia, 1998.

Berger, Peter L., and Richard John Neuhaus. *To Empower People: The Role of Mediating Structures in Public Policy.* Washington, D.C.: American Enterprise Institute for Public Policy Research, 1977.

Beukema, Liala. "The Powers and Urban Land Use." *The Gospel and Our Culture* 11, no. 4 (December 1999): 5-6, 8.

Billingsley, Andrew. *Mighty Like a River: The Black Church and Social Reform.* New York: Oxford University Press, 1999.

Blank, Rebecca M. *It Takes a Nation: A New Agenda for Fighting Poverty.* Princeton: Princeton University Press, 1997.

Bockmuehl, Markus. *Jewish Law in Gentile Churches: Halakah and the Beginning of Public Ethics.* Edinburgh: T. & T. Clark, 2000.

Boff, Leonardo. *When Theology Listens to the Poor.* Translated by Robert R. Barr. San Francisco: Harper & Row, 1988.

Bonhoeffer, Dietrich. *Life Together.* In vol. 5 of Dietrich Bonhoeffer Works, edited by Geffrey B. Kelly, translated by Daniel W. Bloesch and James H. Burtness. Minneapolis: Fortress, 1996.

Bonk, Jonathan J. "Thinking Small: Global Missions and American Churches." *Missiology: An International Review* 28, no. 2 (April 2000): 149-61.

Bosch, David J. *Transforming Mission: Paradigm Shifts in Theology of Mission.* Maryknoll: Orbis, 1991.

Brown, Prudence. "Comprehensive Neighborhood-Based Initiatives." *Cityscape: A Journal of Policy Research and Development* 2, no. 2 (May 1996): 161-76.

Burrows, William R. "Reconciling All in Christ: An Old New Paradigm for Mission." *Mission Studies* 15-1, no. 29 (1998): 79-98.

Brueggemann, Walter. *The Prophetic Imagination.* Minneapolis: Fortress, 1978.

———. *Theology of the Old Testament: Testimony, Dispute, Advocacy.* Minneapolis: Fortress, 1997.

———. *Using God's Resources Widely: Isaiah and Urban Possibility.* Louisville: Westminster/John Knox, 1993.

Caraley, Demetrios. "Washington Abandons the Cities." *Political Science Quarterly* 107 (Spring 1992): 1-30.

Carle, Robert D., and Louis A. DeCaro Jr., eds. *Signs of Hope in the City: Ministries of Community Renewal.* Valley Forge: Judson, 1997.

Castells, Manuel. *End of Millennium,* 2d ed. Vol. 3 of *The Information Age: Economy, Society, and Culture.* Oxford: Blackwell, 2000.

Cavanaugh, William. "The Eucharist as Resistance to Globalization." *Modern Theology* 15, no. 2 (April 1999): 181-96.

Chaves, Mark. "Religious Congregations and Welfare Reform: Who Will Take Advantage of 'Charitable Choice'?" *American Sociological Review* 64 (December 1999): 836-46.

Christian, Jayakumar. *God of the Empty Handed: Poverty, Power, and the Kingdom of God.* Monrovia: MARC, 1999.

Clarke, Andrew D. *Secular and Christian Leadership in Corinth: A Socio-Historical and Exegetical Study of 1 Corinthians 1–6.* Leiden: E. J. Brill, 1993.

———. *Serve the Community of the Church: Christians as Leaders and Ministers.* Grand Rapids: Eerdmans, 2000.

Clavel, Pierre; Jessica Pitt; and Jordan Yin. "The Community Option in Urban Policy." *Urban Affairs Review* 32, no. 4 (March 1997): 435-58.

Clements, Ronald E. "The Good Neighbor in the Book of Proverbs." In *Of Prophets' Visions and the Wisdom of Sages: Essays in Honour of R. Norman Whybray on His Seventieth Birthday*, ed. Heather A. McKay and David J. A. Clines, Supplement Series 162, 209-28. Sheffield: Journal for the Study of the Old Testament, 1992.

Cnaan, Ron A., with Robert J. Winberg and Stephanie C. Boddie. *The Newer Deal: Social Work and Religion in Partnership*. New York: Columbia University Press, 1999.

Coleman, John A., S.J. "A Limited and Vibrant Society: Christianity and Civil Society." In *Civil Society and Government*, ed. Nancy L. Rosenblum and Robert C. Post, 223-54. Princeton: Princeton University Press, 2002.

Cone, James H. *Martin and Malcolm in America: A Dream or a Nightmare?* Maryknoll: Orbis, 1991.

————. *Risks of Faith: The Emergence of a Black Theology of Liberation, 1968-1998*. Boston: Beacon, 1999.

Conn, Harvie M. *The American City and the Evangelical Church: A Historical Overview*. Grand Rapids: Baker, 1994.

————. *Evangelism: Doing Justice and Preaching Grace*. Grand Rapids: Zondervan, 1982.

————. "The Kingdom of God and the City of Man: A History of the City/Church Dialogue." In *Discipling the City: A Comprehensive Approach to Urban Ministry*, 2d ed., ed. Roger S. Greenway, 244-77. Grand Rapids: Baker, 1992.

————. "Lucan Perspectives and the City." *Missiology: An International Review* 13, no. 4 (October 1985): 409-28.

————, ed. *Planting and Growing Urban Churches: From Dream to Reality*. Grand Rapids: Baker, 1997.

Conn, Harvie M., and Manuel Ortiz. *Urban Ministry: The Kingdom, the City, and the People of God*. Downers Grove: InterVarsity, 2001.

Cook, Guillermo. *The Expectation of the Poor: Latin American Basic Ecclesial Communities in Protestant Perspective*. Maryknoll: Orbis, 1985.

Cortés, Ernesto, Jr. "Reweaving the Fabric: The Iron Rule and the IAF Strategy for Power and Politics." In *Interwoven Destinies: Cities and the Nation*, ed. Henry G. Cisneros. New York: W. W. Norton, 1993.

Costas, Orlando E. *Christ Outside the Gate: Mission Beyond Christendom*. Maryknoll: Orbis, 1982.

————. *Liberating News: A Theology of Contextual Evangelization*. Grand Rapids: Eerdmans, 1989.

————. "A Wholistic Concept of Church Growth." In *Exploring Church Growth*, ed. Wilbert R. Shenk, 95-107. Grand Rapids: Eerdmans, 1983.

Croatto, José Severino. "The Debt in Nehemiah's Social Reform: A Study of Nehemiah 5:1-19." In *Subversive Scriptures: Revolutionary Readings of the Christian Bible in Latin America*, edited and translated by Leif E. Vaage, 39-59. Valley Forge: Trinity Press Intenational, 1997.

Davis, Mike. *Magical Urbanism: Latinos Reinvent the U.S. City*. London: Verso, 2000.

Day, Katherine. "The Renaissance of Community Economic Development among African-American Churches in the 1990s." In *The Blackwell Companion to Sociology of Religion*, ed. Richard K. Fenn, 321-35. Oxford: Blackwell, 2001.

De Gruchy, John W. *Christianity and Democracy: A Theology for a Just World Order*. Cambridge: Cambridge University Press, 1995.

———. *Christianity, Art, and Transformation: Theological Aesthetics in the Struggle for Justice*. Cambridge: Cambridge University Press, 2001.

Dixie, Quinton Hosford, and Cornel West. *The Courage to Hope: From Black Suffering to Human Redemption*. Boston: Beacon, 1999.

Dodson, Jualynne E., and Cheryl Townsend Gilkes. "There's Nothing Like Church Food: Food and the U.S. Afro-Christian Tradition: Re-Membering Community and Feeding the Embodied S/spirit(s)." *Journal of the American Academy of Religion* 63, no. 3 (Fall 1995): 519-38.

Dunn, James D. G. "The Justice of God: A Renewed Perspective on Justification by Faith." *Journal of Theological Studies* 43 (April 1992): 1-22.

Dyrness, William A. *The Earth Is God's: A Theology of American Culture*. Maryknoll: Orbis, 1997.

Dyson, Michael Eric. *Holler If You Hear Me: Searching for Tupac Shakur*. New York: Basic Civitas Books, 2001.

Edin, Kathryn, and Laura Lein. *Making Ends Meet: How Single Mothers Survive Welfare and Low-Wage Work*. New York: Russell Sage Foundation, 1997.

Ellington, Scott A. "The Costly Loss of Testimony." *Journal of Pentecostal Theology* 16 (2000): 48-59.

Elliott, John H. *1 Peter: A New Translation with Introduction and Commentary*. The Anchor Bible. New York: Doubleday, 2000.

Elizondo, Virgilio. *Galilean Journey: The Mexican-American Promise*. Maryknoll: Orbis, 1983.

Elshtain, Jean Bethke. *Democracy on Trial*. New York: Basic Books, 1995.

Eng, Eugenia; John Hatch; and Anne Callan. "Institutionalizing Social Support through the Church and into the Community." *Health Education Quarterly* 12, no. 1 (Spring 1985): 81-92.

Eskenazi, Tamara Cohn. *In an Age of Prose: A Literary Approach to Ezra–Nehemiah*, SBL Monograph Series 36. Atlanta: Scholars Press, 1985.

Exum, Cheryl J. "'You Shall Let Every Daughter Live': A Study in Exodus 1:8–2:10." *Semeia* 28 (1983): 63-82.

Farnsley, Arthur E, II. "Can Churches Save the City? A Look at Resources." *Christian Century*, 9 December 1998, pp. 1182-84.

———. "Faith-based Action." *Christian Century*, 14 March 2001, pp. 12-15.

Fee, Gordon D. *Listening to the Spirit in the Text*. Grand Rapids: Eerdmans, 2000.

Ferguson, Ronald F., and William T. Dickins, eds. *Urban Problems and Community Development*. Washington, D.C.: The Brookings Institution, 1999.

Forche, Carolyn. "Present among Us." *DoubleTake* 2, no. 3 (Summer 1996): 20-31.

Ford, David F. *Self and Salvation: Being Transformed.* Cambridge: Cambridge University Press, 1999.

Foundation, Larry; Peter Tufano; and Patricia Walker. "Collaborating with Congregations: Opportunities for Financial Services in the Inner City." *Harvard Business Review* 77, no. 4 (July-August 1999): 57-68.

Fowl, Stephen E. *Engaging Scripture: A Model for Theological Interpretation.* Malden: Blackwell, 1998.

————. *God's Beautiful City: Christian Mission after Christendom.* The Ekklesia Project, Pamphlet no. 4. Eugene: Wipf and Stock Publishers, 2001.

————. "Know Your Context: Giving and Receiving Money in Philippians." *Interpretation* 56, no. 1 (January 2002): 45-58.

Fowl, Stephen E., and L. Gregory Jones. *Reading in Communion: Scripture and Ethics in Christian Life.* Grand Rapids: Eerdmans, 1991.

Freedman, Samuel G. *Upon This Rock: The Miracles of a Black Church.* New York: HarperCollins, 1993.

Freeman, Richard B. "The Rising Tide Lifts . . . ?" In *Understanding Poverty,* ed. Sheldon H. Danziger and Robert Haveman, 97-126. New York: Russell Sage Foundation/Cambridge: Harvard University Press, 2001.

Freire, Paulo. *Pedagogy of the Oppressed.* New York: Herder & Herder, 1972.

Gans, Herbert J. *The War against the Poor: The Underclass and Antipoverty Policy.* New York: Basic Books, 1995.

Geronimus, Arline T., et al. "Excess Mortality among Blacks and Whites in the United States." *New England Journal of Medicine* 335, no. 21 (November 1997): 1552-58.

Gilkes, Cheryl Townsend. *"If It Wasn't for the Women . . .": Black Women's Experience and the Womanist Culture in Church and Community.* Maryknoll: Orbis, 2001.

Gittell, Ross, and Margaret Wilder. "Community Development Corporations: Critical Factors That Influence Success." *Journal of Urban Affairs* 21, no. 3 (1999): 341-62.

Glaesser, Edward, and Jesse M. Shapiro. "City Growth and the 2000 Census: Which Places Grew, and Why." Washington, D.C.: Center on Urban and Metropolitan Policy, May 2001.

González, Justo L. *Santa Biblia: The Bible through Hispanic Eyes.* Nashville: Abingdon, 1995.

Goudzwaard, Bob. "Spirals of Life and Death: The Future of the Global Economy." *Perspectives* 13, no. 3 (March 1998): 15-18.

Goulder, M. D. "The Songs of Ascents and Nehemiah." *Journal for the Study of the Old Testament* 75 (1997): 43-58.

Gratz, Roberta Brandes. *The Living City.* New York: Simon & Schuster, 1989.

Gratz, Roberta Brandes, with Norman Mintz. *Cities Back from the Edge: New Life for Downtown.* New York: John Wiley & Sons, 1998.

Green, Clifford J. *Churches, Cities, and Human Community: Urban Ministry in the United States.* Grand Rapids: Eerdmans, 1996.

247

Green, Douglas. "Nehemiah." Unpublished paper. Philadelphia: Westminster Theological Seminary, n.d.

Green, Joel. *The Theology of the Gospel of Luke.* Cambridge: Cambridge University Press, 1995.

Greene-McCreight, Kathryn. "'We Are Companions of the Patriarchs,' or 'Scripture Absorbs Calvin's World.'" *Modern Theology* 14, no. 2 (April 1998): 213-24.

Greenway, Roger S. "World Urbanization and Missiological Education." In *Missiological Education for the Twenty-first Century: The Book, the Circle, and the Sandals,* ed. J. Dudley Woodberry, Charles Van Engen, and Edgar J. Elliston, 144-50. Maryknoll: Orbis, 1996.

Grogan, Paul S., and Tony Proscio. *Comeback Cities: A Blueprint for Urban Neighborhood Revival.* Boulder: Westview Press, 2000.

Gunderson, Gary. *Deeply Woven Roots: Improving the Quality of Life in Your Community.* Minneapolis: Fortess, 1997.

Gundry-Volf, Judith. "To Such as These Belongs the Reign of God." *Theology Today* 56 (2000): 469-80.

Halpern, Robert. *Rebuilding the Inner City: A History of Neighborhood Initiatives to Address Poverty in the United States.* New York: Columbia University Press, 1995.

Hancock, LynNell. *Hands to Work: The Stories of Three Families Racing the Welfare Clock.* New York: William Morrow, 2002.

Hart, Stephen. *Cultural Dilemmas of Progressive Politics: Styles of Engagement among Grassroots Activists.* Chicago: University of Chicago Press, 2001.

Harvey, David. *Spaces of Hope.* Berkeley/Los Angeles: University of California Press, 2000.

Hauerwas, Stanley. *The Hauerwas Reader.* Edited by John Berkman and Michael Cartwright. Durham: Duke University Press, 2001.

Hayden, Dolores. *The Power of Place: Urban Landscapes as Public History.* Cambridge: MIT Press, 1995.

Hays, Richard B. *The Moral Vision of the New Testament: Community, Cross, New Creation: A Contemporary Introduction to New Testament Ethics.* San Francisco: HarperSanFrancisco, 1996.

Hoke, Stephen T. "The Art of Facilitating Change." In *With an Eye on the Future: Development and Mission in the Twenty-First Century,* ed. Duane H. Elmer and Lois McKinney, 157-68. Monrovia: MARC, 1996.

Hoornaert, Eduardo. *The Memory of the Christian People.* Translated by Robert R. Barr. Maryknoll: Orbis, 1988.

Horsley, Richard A., ed. *Paul and Empire: Religion and Power in Roman Imperial Society.* Harrisburg: Trinity Press International, 1997.

Hula, Richard C.; Cynthia Y. Jackson; and Marion Orr. "Urban Politics, Governing Nonprofits, and Community Revitalization." *Urban Affairs Review* 32, no. 4 (March 1997): 459-89.

Ignatieff, Michael. *The Needs of Strangers.* New York: Picador, 1984.

Jackson, Kenneth T. "Once Again, the City Beckons." *New York Times,* 30 March 2001, A-23.

Jacobs, Jane. *The Death and Life of Great American Cities.* New York: The Modern Library, 1993.

Jacobsen, Dennis A. *Doing Justice: Congregations and Community Organizing.* Minneapolis: Fortress, 2001.

Jargowsky, Paul A. *Poverty and Place: Ghettos, Barrios, and the American City.* New York: Russell Sage Foundation, 1997.

Jones, L. Gregory. *Embodying Forgiveness: A Theological Analysis.* Grand Rapids: Eerdmans, 1995.

Jones, Serene. *Feminist Theory and Christian Theology: Cartographies of Grace.* Minneapolis: Fortress, 2000.

Katz, Michael B. *The Price of Citizenship: Redefining the American Welfare State.* New York: Metropolitan Books, 2001.

Keating, W. Dennis; Norman Krumholz; and Philip Star, eds. *Revitalizing Urban Neighborhoods.* Lawrence: University of Kansas Press, 1996.

Keesmaat, Sylvia. "Strange Neighbors and Risky Care." In *The Challenge of Jesus' Parables,* ed. Richard N. Longenecker, 263-85. Grand Rapids: Eerdmans, 2000.

Kim, Claire Jean. *Bitter Fruit: The Politics of Black-Korean Conflict in New York City.* New Haven: Yale University Press, 2000.

Kim, Seyoon. "2 Cor. 5:11-21 and the Origins of Paul's Concept of Reconciliation." *Novum Testamentum* 39, no. 4 (October 1997): 360-84.

King, Martin Luther, Jr. *A Testament of Hope: The Essential Writings of Martin Luther King Jr.* Edited by James M. Washington. San Francisco: Harper & Row, 1986.

Kingsley, G. Thomas; Joseph B. McNeely; and James O. Gibson. *Community-Building Comes of Age.* Baltimore: The Development Training Institute/Washington: The Urban Institute, 1997.

Kiros, Teodros. "Class, Race, and Social Stratification: An Interview with William Julius Wilson." *New Political Science* 21, no. 3 (September 1999): 405-15.

Kretzmann, John P., and John L. McKnight. *Building Communities from the Inside Out: A Path toward Finding and Mobilizing a Community's Assets.* Evanston: Center for Urban Affairs and Policy Research, Neighborhood Innovations Network, Northwestern University, 1993.

Larkin, William J., Jr. "The Recovery of Luke-Acts as 'Grand Narrative' for the Church's Evangelistic and Edification Tasks in a Postmodern Era." *Journal of the Evangelical Theological Society* 43, no. 3 (September 2000): 405-15.

Lazare, Daniel. *America's Undeclared War: What's Killing Our Cities and How We Can Stop It.* New York: Harcourt, 2001.

Lemann, Nicholas. "The Myth of Community Development." *New York Times Magazine.* 9 January 1994, pp. 27-31, 50, 54, 60.

————. *The Promised Land: The Great Black Migration and How It Changed America.* New York: Alfred A. Knopf, 1991.

Levine, Mark V. "Downtown Redevelopment as an Urban Growth Strategy: A Critical

Appraisal of the Baltimore Renaissance." *Journal of Urban Affairs* 9, no. 2 (1987): 103-23.

Lincoln, C. Eric. *Coming through the Fire: Surviving Race and Place in America.* Durham: Duke University Press, 1996.

————, and Lawrence H. Mamiya. *The Black Church in the African American Experience.* Durham: Duke University Press, 1990.

Linthicum, Robert C. *Empowering the Poor: Community Organizing among the City's "Rag, Tag, and Bobtail."* Monrovia: MARC, 1991.

Lohfink, Gerhard. *Jesus and Community: The Social Dimension of Christian Faith.* Translated by John P. Galvin. Philadelphia: Fortress, 1984.

Long, Kathryn Teresa. *The Revival of 1857-58: Interpreting an American Religious Awakening.* New York: Oxford University Press, 1998.

Longman, Tremper, III. *The Book of Ecclesiastes.* NICOT. Grand Rapids: Eerdmans, 1998.

Marcuse, Peter, and Ronald van Kempen. "Conclusion: A Changed Spatial Order." In *Globalizing Cities: A New Spatial Order,* ed. Peter Marcuse and Ronald van Kempen, 249-75. Oxford: Blackwell, 2000.

Marsh, Charles. "The Beloved Community: An American Search." In *Religion, Race, and Justice in a Changing America,* ed. Gary Orfield and Holly J. Lebowitz, 49-66. New York: The Century Foundation Press, 1999.

————. *God's Long Summer: Stories of Faith and Civil Rights.* Princeton: Princeton University Press, 1997.

Martin, Dale B. *Slavery as Salvation: The Metaphor of Slavery in Pauline Christianity.* New Haven: Yale University Press, 1990.

Massey, Douglas S., and Nancy A. Denton. *American Apartheid: Segregation and the Making of the Underclass.* Cambridge: Harvard University Press, 1993.

McAlpine, Thomas H. *Facing the Powers: What Are the Options?* Monrovia: MARC, 1991.

McCord, Colin, and Harold P. Freeman. "Excess Mortality in Harlem." *The New England Journal of Medicine* 322, no. 3 (January 1990): 173-77.

McDougall, Harold A. *Black Baltimore: A New Theory of Community.* Philadelphia: Temple University Press, 1993.

McKnight, John. *The Careless Society: Community and Its Counterfeits.* New York: Basic Books, 1995.

McRoberts, Omar M. "Saving Four Corners: Religion and Revitalization in a Depressed Neighborhood." Ph.D. diss., Harvard University, 2000.

————. "Understanding the 'New' Black Pentecostal Activism: Lessons from Ecumenical Urban Ministries in Boston." *Sociology of Religion* 60, no. 1 (Spring 1999): 47-70.

Meeks, Wayne A. *The First Urban Christians: The Social World of the Apostle Paul.* New Haven: Yale University Press, 1983.

Meggitt, Justin J. *Paul, Poverty, and Survival.* Edinburgh: T. & T. Clark, 1998.

Middleton, J. Richard, and Brian J. Walsh. *Truth Is Stranger Than It Used to Be: Biblical Faith in a Postmodern Age.* Downers Grove: InterVarsity, 1995.

Milbank, John. *Theology and Social Theory: Beyond Secular Reason.* Oxford: Blackwell, 1990.

Miller, Mike. "Community Organizing: Lost among Christians?" *Social Policy* 31, no. 1 (Fall 2000): 33-41.

Mitchell, Margaret M. "Paul's 1 Corinthians on Reconciliation in the Church: Promise and Pitfalls." *New Theology Review* 10, no. 2 (May 1997): 39-48.

Moltmann, Jürgen. *The Church in the Power of the Spirit.* Translated by Margaret Kohl. Minneapolis: Fortress, 1993.

————. *The Coming of God: Christian Eschatology.* Translated by Margaret Kohl. Minneapolis: Fortress, 1996.

————. *Experiences in Theology: Ways and Forms of Christian Theology.* Translated by Margaret Kohl. Minneapolis: Fortress, 2000.

————. *God for a Secular Society: The Public Relevance of Theology.* Translated by Margaret Kohl. Minneapolis: Fortress, 1999.

————. *The Source of Life: The Holy Spirit and the Theology of Life.* Translated by Margaret Kohl. Minneapolis: Fortress, 1997.

————. *The Spirit of Life: A Universal Affirmation.* Translated by Margaret Kohl. Minneapolis: Fortress, 1992.

————. *The Way of Jesus Christ: Christology in Messianic Dimensions.* Translated by Margaret Kohl. Minneapolis: Fortress, 1993.

Moltmann, Jürgen; Nicholas Wolterstorff; and Ellen T. Charry. *A Passion for God's Reign: Theology, Christian Learning, and the Christian Self.* Edited by Miroslav Volf. Grand Rapids: Eerdmans, 1998.

Mott, Stephen Charles. *Biblical Ethics and Social Change.* New York: Oxford University Press, 1982.

Myers, Bryant L. *Walking with the Poor: Principles and Practices of Transformational Development.* Maryknoll: Orbis, 1999.

Myers, Ched. "Behold the Treasure of the Church: A Bible Study on the Churches and Welfare Reform." *Sojourners* 28, no. 5 (September/October 1999): 32-34.

Myers, Ched, et al. *"Say to This Mountain": Mark's Story of Discipleship.* Maryknoll: Orbis, 1996.

Neckerman, Kathryn M. "'We'd Love to Hire Them, But . . .': The Meaning of Race for Employers." In *The Urban Underclass,* ed. Christopher Jencks and Paul E. Peterson, 203-32. Washington, D.C.: The Brookings Institution, 1991.

Newbigin, Lesslie. *The Gospel in a Pluralist Society.* Grand Rapids: Eerdmans, 1989.

Newman, Katherine S. *No Shame in My Game: The Working Poor in the Inner City.* New York: Alfred A. Knopf and The Russell Sage Foundation, 1999.

O'Gorman, Frances. "Tomorrow Emerged Yesterday: Are We Facilitators 'Crabbing' the Community Development Process?" In *With an Eye on the Future: Development and Mission in the Twenty-First Century,* ed. Duane H. Elmer and Lois McKinney, 169-77. Monrovia: MARC, 1996.

251

Olasky, Marvin N. *The Tragedy of American Compassion.* Washington, D.C.: Regnery Publishing, 1992.

Olson, Karen. "Old West Baltimore: Segregation, African-American Culture, and the Struggle for Equality." In *The Baltimore Book: New Perspectives on Local History,* ed. Elizabeth Fee, Linda Shopes, and Linda Zeidman, 57-78. Philadelphia: Temple University Press, 1991.

Orfield, Myron. *Metropolitics: A Regional Agenda for Community and Stability.* Washington, D.C.: The Brookings Institution/Cambridge: The Lincoln Institute of Land Policy, 1997.

Orr, John [B.]. *Los Angeles Religion: A Civic Profile.* Los Angeles: Center for Religion and Civic Culture, University of Southern California, 1998.

Orr, John B.; Donald E. Miller; Wade Clark Roof; and J. Gordon Melton. *Politics of the Spirit: Religion and Multiethnicity in Los Angeles.* Los Angeles: University of Southern California, 1994.

Ortiz, Manuel. *The Hispanic Challenge: Opportunities Confronting the Church.* Downers Grove: InterVarsity, 1993.

―――. *One New People: Models for Developing a Multiethnic Church.* Downers Grove: InterVarsity, 1996.

Pattillo-McCoy, Mary. "Church Culture as a Strategy of Action in the Black Community." *American Sociological Review* 63, no. 6 (December 1998): 767-84.

Peirce, Neil, with Curtis W. Johnson and John Stuart Hall. *Citistates: How Urban America Can Prosper in a Competitive World.* Washington, D.C.: Seven Locks Press, 1993.

Perkins, John M. *Beyond Charity: The Call to Christian Community Development.* Grand Rapids: Baker, 1992.

―――. *Let Justice Roll Down.* Ventura: Regal Books, 1976.

―――. *A Quiet Revolution.* Waco: Word Books, 1976.

―――. *With Justice for All.* Ventura: Regal Books, 1982.

―――, ed. *Restoring At-Risk Communities: Doing It Right and Doing It Together.* Grand Rapids: Baker, 1995.

Plantinga, Cornelius, Jr. *Not the Way It's Supposed to Be: A Breviary of Sin.* Grand Rapids: Eerdmans, 1995.

Pohl, Christine D. *Making Room: Recovering Hospitality as a Christian Tradition.* Grand Rapids: Eerdmans, 1999.

Porter, Michael E. "The Competitive Advantage of the Inner City." *Harvard Business Review* 73, no. 3 (May-June 1995): 55-71.

Putnam, Robert N. *Making Democracy Work: Civic Traditions in Modern Italy.* Princeton: Princeton University Press, 1993.

―――. "The Prosperous Community: Social Capital and Public Life." *The American Prospect* 13 (Spring 1993): 35-42.

Ramsay, Meredith. "Redeeming the City: Exploring the Relationship between Church and Metropolis." *Urban Affairs Review* 33, no. 5 (May 1998): 595-626.

Reed, Adolph L., Jr. *Stirrings in the Jug: Black Politics in the Post-Segregation Era.* Minneapolis: University of Minnesota Press, 1999.

————, ed. *Without Justice for All: The New Liberalism and Our Retreat from Racial Equality.* Boulder: Westview Press, 1999.

Ridderbos, Herman. *The Coming of the Kingdom.* Translated by H. de Jongste. Philadelphia: Presbyterian and Reformed Publishing, 1976.

————. *Paul: An Outline of His Theology.* Translated by John Richard De Witt. Grand Rapids: Eerdmans, 1975.

Risher, Dee Dee. "Hope on the Edges." *The Other Side* 35 (July/August 1999): 20-23.

Rooney, Jim. *Organizing the South Bronx.* New York: State University of New York Press, 1995.

Rubin, Herbert J. *Renewing Hope within Neighborhoods of Despair: The Community-Based Development Model.* Albany: State University of New York Press, 2000.

Rusk, David. *Baltimore Unbound: A Strategy for Regional Renewal.* Baltimore: The Abell Foundation, 1996.

Ryon, Roderick N. "Old West Baltimore." *Maryland Historical Magazine* 77, no. 1 (March 1982): 54-69.

Sanders, Cheryl J. *Ministry at the Margins: The Prophetic Mission of Women, Youth, and the Poor.* Downers Grove: InterVarsity, 1997.

————. *Saints in Exile: The Holiness-Pentecostal Experience in African-American Religion and Culture.* Oxford: Oxford University Press, 1999.

Sanjek, Roger. *The Future of Us All: Race and Neighborhood Politics in New York City.* Ithaca: Cornell University Press, 1998.

Sassen, Saskia. *The Global City: New York, London, Tokyo.* Princeton: Princeton University Press, 1991.

————. *Globalization and Its Discontents: Essays on the New Mobility of People and Money.* New York: Free Press, 1998.

Saunders, Stanley P., and Charles L. Campbell. *The Word on the Street: Performing the Scriptures in the Urban Context.* Grand Rapids: Eerdmans, 2000.

Schreiter, Robert. *The Ministry of Reconciliation: Spirituality and Strategies.* Maryknoll: Orbis, 1998.

————. *Reconciliation: Mission and Ministry in a Changing Social Order.* Maryknoll: Orbis, 1992.

Scott, James C. *Domination and the Arts of Resistance: Hidden Transcripts.* New Haven: Yale University Press, 1990.

————. *Seeing Like a State: How Certain Schemes to Improve the Human Condition Have Failed.* New Haven: Yale University Press, 1998.

Shaull, Richard, and Waldo Cesar. *Pentecostalism and the Future of the Christian Churches: Promises, Limitations, Challenges.* Grand Rapids: Eerdmans, 2000.

Siegel, Fred. *The Future Once Happened Here: New York, D.C., L.A., and the Fate of America's Big Cities.* New York: Free Press, 1997.

Simon, David, and Edward Burns. *The Corner: A Year in the Life of an Inner-City Neighborhood.* New York: Broadway Books, 1997.

Skillen, James W. "*E Pluribus Unum* and Faith-Based Welfare Reform: A Kuyperian Moment for the Church in God's World." *Princeton Seminary Bulletin* 22, no. 3 (2001): 285-305.

Smith, Daniel L. "Jeremiah as Prophet of Nonviolent Resistance." *Journal for the Study of the Old Testament* 43 (1989): 95-107.

Solivan, Samuel. *The Spirit, Pathos, and Liberation: Toward an Hispanic Pentecostal Theology.* Sheffield: Sheffield Academic Press, 1998.

Spain, Daphne. *How Women Saved the City.* Minneapolis: University of Minnesota Press, 2001.

Speidell, Todd H. "A Trinitarian Ontology of Persons in Society." *Scottish Journal of Theology* 47, no. 3 (1994): 283-300.

Stark, Rodney. *The Rise of Christianity: A Sociologist Reconsiders History.* Princeton: Princeton University Press, 1996.

Stoecker, Randy. "The CDC Model of Community Development: A Critique and Alternative." *Journal of Urban Affairs* 19, no. 1 (1997): 1-22.

Stringfellow, William A. *Keeper of the Word: Selected Writings of William Stringfellow.* Edited by Bill Wylie Kellerman. Grand Rapids: Eerdmans, 1994.

Suarez, Ray. *The Old Neighborhood: What We Lost in the Great Suburban Migration, 1966-1999.* New York: Free Press, 1999.

Sugrue, Thomas J. "The Structures of Urban Poverty: The Reorganization of Space and Work in Three Periods of American History." In *The Underclass Debate: Views from History,* ed. Michael B. Katz, 85-177. Princeton: Princeton University Press, 1993.

Tamez, Elsa. *The Amnesty of Grace: Justification by Faith from a Latin American Perspective.* Translated by Sharon H. Ringe. Nashville: Abingdon, 1993.

————. *When the Horizons Close: Rereading Ecclesiastes.* Translated by Margaret Wilde. Maryknoll: Orbis, 2000.

Theissen, Gerd. *The Social Setting of Pauline Christianity: Essays on Corinth.* Translated and edited by John H. Schutz. Philadelphia: Fortress, 1982.

Thiselton, Anthony C. *The First Epistle to the Corinthians.* NIGTC. Grand Rapids: Eerdmans, 2000.

————. *Interpreting God and the Postmodern Self: On Meaning, Manipulation, and Promise.* Grand Rapids: Eerdmans, 1995.

————. *New Horizons in Hermeneutics.* Grand Rapids: Zondervan, 1992.

Tollefson, Kenneth G. "The Nehemiah Model for Christian Missions." *Missiology: An International Review* 15, no. 1 (January 1987): 31-55.

Tollefson, Kenneth G., and H. G. M. Williamson. "Nehemiah as Cultural Revitalization: An Anthropological Perspective." *Journal for the Study of the Old Testament* 56 (1992): 41-68.

Trulear, Harold Dean. "Faith-Based Initiatives with High Risk Youth." In *Serving Those in Need: A Handbook for Managing Faith-Based Human Service Organizations,* ed. Edward L. Queen II, 266-89. San Francisco: Jossey-Bass, 2000.

Vale, Lawrence J. *From the Puritans to the Projects: Public Housing and Public Neighbors.* Cambridge: Harvard University Press, 2000.

Van Engen, Charles, and Jude Tiersma, eds. *God So Loves the City: Seeking a Theology of Urban Mission.* Monrovia: MARC, 1994.

Venkatesh, Sudhir Alladi. *American Project: The Rise and Fall of a Modern Ghetto.* Cambridge: Harvard University Press, 2000.

Vergara, Camilo José. *American Ruins.* New York: Monacelli Press, 1999.

———. *The New American Ghetto.* New Brunswick: Rutgers University Press, 1995.

Vidal, Avis C. "Reintegrating Disadvantaged Communities into the Fabric of Urban Life: The Role of Community Development." *Housing Policy Debate* 6, no. 1 (1995): 169-230.

Villafañe, Eldin. *The Liberating Spirit: Toward an Hispanic American Pentecostal Social Ethic.* Grand Rapids: Eerdmans, 1993.

———. *Seek the Peace of the City: Reflections on Urban Ministry.* Grand Rapids: Eerdmans, 1995.

Villafañe, Eldin, et al., eds. *Transforming the City: Reframing Education for Urban Ministry.* Grand Rapids: Eerdmans, 2002.

Volf, Miroslav. *After Our Likeness: The Church as the Image of the Trinity.* Grand Rapids: Eerdmans, 1998.

———. "Enter into Joy! Sin, Death, and the Life of the World to Come." In *The End of the World and the Ends of God: Science and Theology on Eschatology,* ed. John Polkinghorne and Michael Welker, 256-78. Harrisburg: Trinity Press International.

———. *Exclusion and Embrace: A Theological Exploration of Identity, Otherness, and Reconciliation.* Nashville: Abingdon, 1996.

———. "Shopkeepers' Gold." *Christian Century,* 12 November 1997, p. 1045.

———. "The Social Meaning of Reconciliation." *Interpretation* 54, no. 2 (April 2000): 158-72.

———. "Soft Difference: Theological Reflections on the Relation between Church and Culture in 1 Peter." *Ex Auditu* 10 (1994): 15-30.

———. "Theology, Meaning, and Power." In *The Future of Theology: Essays in Honor of Jürgen Moltmann,* ed. Miroslav Volf, Carmen Krieg, and Thomas Kucharz, 98-113. Grand Rapids: Eerdmans, 1996.

———. "The Trinity Is Our Social Program: The Doctrine of the Trinity and the Shape of Social Engagement." *Modern Theology* 14, no. 3 (July 1998): 403-23.

———. *Work in the Spirit: Toward a Theology of Work.* New York: Oxford University Press, 1991.

Volf, Miroslav, and Maurice Lee. "The Spirit and the Church." *Conrad Grebel Review* 18, no. 3 (Fall 2000): 20-45.

Wacquant, Loïc J. D. "From Slavery to Mass Incarceration: Rethinking the 'Race Question' in the U.S." *New Left Review* 13 (January-February 2002): 41-60.

———. "The Rise of Advanced Marginality: Notes on Its Nature and Implications." *Acta Sociologica* 39, no. 2 (1996): 121-39.

255

————. "Three Pernicious Premises in the Study of the American Ghetto." *International Journal of Urban and Regional Research* 21, no. 2 (June 1997): 341-53.

————. "Urban Marginality in the Coming Millennium." *Urban Studies* 36, no. 10 (September 1999): 1639-47.

Wacquant, Loïc J. D., and William Julius Wilson. "The Cost of Racial and Class Exclusion in the Inner City." *The Annals of the American Academy of Political and Social Science* 501 (January 1989): 8-25.

Wallace, Anthony F. C. "Revitalization Movements." *American Anthropologist* 58, no. 2 (April 1956): 264-81.

Wallis, Jim. *Faith Works: Lessons from the Life of an Activist Preacher.* New York: Random House, 2000.

Walls, Andrew F. *The Missionary Movement in Christian History: Studies in the Transmission of Faith.* Maryknoll: Orbis, 1996.

Walsh, Brian J. *Subversive Christianity: Imaging God in a Dangerous Time.* Bristol, U.K.: Regius, 1992.

Warren, Mark R. *Dry Bones Rattling: Community Building to Revitalize American Democracy.* Princeton: Princeton University Press, 2001.

Warren, Mark R., and Richard L. Wood. *Faith-Based Community Organizing: The State of the Field.* Jericho: Interfaith Funders, 2001.

West, Cornell. *Race Matters.* Boston: Beacon, 1993.

Wilder, Craig Steven. *A Covenant with Color: Race and Social Power in Brooklyn.* New York: Columbia University Press, 2000.

Williams, Brett. "Poverty among African Americans in the Urban United States." *Human Organization* 51, no. 2 (1992): 164-74.

Williamson, H. G. M. *Ezra, Nehemiah.* WBC 16. Waco: Word, 1985.

Wilson, Patricia A. "Empowerment: Community Economic Development from the Inside Out." *Urban Studies* 33, nos. 4-5 (1996): 617-30.

Wilson, William Julius. *The Bridge over the Racial Divide: Rising Inequality and Coalition Politics.* Berkeley/Los Angeles: University of California Press, 1999.

————. *The Truly Disadvantaged: The Inner City, the Underclass, and Public Policy.* Chicago: University of Chicago Press, 1987.

————. *When Work Disappears: The World of the New Urban Poor.* New York: Alfred A. Knopf, 1996.

Wink, Walter. *Engaging the Powers: Discernment and Resistance in a World of Domination.* Minneapolis: Fortress, 1992.

Winship, Christopher, and Jenny Berrien. "Boston Cops and Black Churches." *The Public Interest* 136 (Summer 1999): 52-68.

Winter, Bruce W. *After Paul Left Corinth: The Influence of Secular Ethics and Social Change.* Grand Rapids: Eerdmans, 2001.

————. "The Public Place for the People of God." *Vox Evangelica* 25 (1995): 7-16.

————. *Seek the Welfare of the City: Christians as Benefactors and Citizens.* Grand Rapids: Eerdmans, 1994.

———. "'Seek the Welfare of the City': Social Ethics in 1 Peter." *Themelios* 13, no. 3 (April/May 1988): 91-94.

Wolterstorff, Nicholas. "Christian Political Reflection: Diognetian or Augustinian?" *Princeton Seminary Bulletin* 20, no. 2 (New Series 1999): 150-68.

———. *Divine Discourse: Philosophical Reflections on the Claim That God Speaks.* Cambridge: Cambridge University Press, 1995.

———. "Justice as a Condition of Authentic Liturgy." *Theology Today* 48, no. 1 (April 1991): 6-21.

———. "Playing with Snakes: A Word to Seminary Graduates." *Perspectives* 13, no. 5 (May 1998): 10-11.

———. *Until Justice and Peace Embrace.* Grand Rapids: Eerdmans, 1983.

———. "Why Care about Justice?" *The Reformed Journal* 36, no. 8 (August 1986): 9-14.

———. "The Wounds of God: Calvin's Theology of Social Injustice." *The Reformed Journal* 37, no. 6 (June 1987): 14-22.

Wong, G. C. I. "A Note on 'Joy' in Nehemiah VIII 10." *Vetus Testamentum* 14, no. 3 (July 1995): 383-86.

Wood, Richard L. "Religious Culture and Political Action." *Sociological Theory* 17, no. 3 (November 1999): 307-33.

———. "Social Capital and Political Culture: God Meets Politics in the Inner City." *American Behavioral Scientist* 40, no. 5 (March/April 1997): 595-605.

Worth, Robert. "Amazing Grace: Can Churches Save the Inner City?" *Washington Monthly* 30, nos. 1-2 (January/February 1998): 28-31.

Wright, Christopher J. H. *An Eye for an Eye: The Place of Old Testament Ethics Today.* Downers Grove: InterVarsity, 1983.

———. *God's People in God's Land: Family, Land, and Property in the Old Testament.* Grand Rapids: Eerdmans, 1990.

———. "Jubilee, Year of." In vol. 3 of the *Anchor Bible Dictionary*, ed. David Noel Freedman et al., 1025-30. New York: Doubleday, 1992.

Wright, N. T. *Jesus and the Victory of God*, vol. 2 of *Christian Origins and the Question of God.* Minneapolis: Fortress, 1996.

———. *The New Testament and the People of God*, vol. 1 of Christian Origins and the Question of God. Minneapolis: Fortress, 1992.

———. "One God, One Lord, One People: Incarnational Christology for a Church in a Pagan Environment." *Ex Auditu* 7 (1991): 45-58.

Wuthnow, Robert. *Loose Connections: Joining Together in America's Fragmented Communities.* Cambridge: Harvard University Press, 1998.

Yoder, John Howard. *For the Nations: Essays Public and Evangelical.* Grand Rapids: Eerdmans, 1997.

———. *The Politics of Jesus: Vicit Agnus Noster*, 2d ed. Grand Rapids: Eerdmans, 1994.

Young, Iris Marion. *Justice and the Politics of Difference.* Princeton: Princeton University Press, 1990.

Zukin, Sharon. "How 'Bad' Is It? Institutions and Intentions in the Study of the American Ghetto." *International Journal of Urban and Regional Research* 22, no. 3 (1998): 511-20.

Acknowledgments

This book was born out of life in the community of Sandtown. I am grateful for having lived in Sandtown for many reasons, not least of which is that my neighbors taught me about grace and faith, hope and love. I am especially thankful for the following people: Jermaine Alexander, Nina Anderson, Fitt Bennett, Ulysses Carter, Lucky Crosby, Mack Daniels, William "Tick" Eades, William Earl "Shocky" Green, Elder C. W. Harris, Amelia Harris, Antoine Holly, Janice Jamison, Ella Johnson, Gary Mitchell, Arteze Montgomery, Linda Paige, Frank Ross, Mamie Shaw, Richard Shaw, Raymond Shaw, Thomas Shedrick, Sylvia Simmons, Elnora Smith, Sonia Street, Al Stokes, LaVerne Stokes, and Reginald "Man" Williams. The value of Isaac Newman's friendship can hardly be calculated.

In making connections between faith and urban practice, I am indebted to many writers, teachers, and practitioners. I mention but three here who played a particularly important role in the shaping of my thinking and my ministry. The late Dr. Harvie Conn of Westminster Theological Seminary (Philadelphia) schooled me in reading Scripture as the story of God's love in Christ for the city. Dr. Stephen Fowl at Loyola College in Baltimore has been an invaluable sounding board and teacher. Having his friendship is a gift and a privilege. And Dr. John Perkins provided the core model of church and community development that has guided much of my journey and served in a foundational way for New Song.

New Song Community Church in Sandtown provided me with the opportunity to be a pastor and share in Christ's call in the city, for which I will always be thankful to God. Additionally, I want to express my immense respect for and gratitude to the staff and boards of the ministries associated with New Song in Sandtown, and indeed the larger community of faith that helps bring it all together. Here in New York, where I moved to be a part of starting the New Song Community Church in Harlem, I wish to thank the church community, and in particular Johnny Acevedo and Jeff White. Also, Tim Keller and Terry Gyger have long been enthusiastic supporters of New Song and my own ministry, and for this I am profoundly grateful.

My life has been graced by the friendship and influence of many, and I can express my gratitude to only a handful of them here. From "across the pond," Bishop Peter Price has provided seasoned pastoral direction and considerable encouragement. Such a friendship, one shared with Dee Price, has always been a timely grace. Manuel Ortiz has provided me with steady encouragement and modeled urban pastoral care. Sister Grace has helped me understand and stay faithful to my journey. For pointing me in new and formative directions still unfolding, I am profoundly thankful to Andrew F. Walls. For sharing with me a new way of being church, I remember with gratitude Guillermo Cook. I am also thankful for the providential influence of Charles Anderson, Bob Aronson, Susan Baker, Carl Ellis, Roger and Edna Greenway, Bill Krispin, Tom Lutz, Gray Matthews, Reginald McLelland, Randy Nabors, and Christine Pohl. All who know me will know that the music and vision of Bruce Cockburn has been a source of sustenance for many years.

As the writing of this book proceeded, Charles Marsh at the University of Virginia and the director of the Project on Lived Theology provided me with many opportunities for learning and interaction. I am grateful for the many ways he has supported and encouraged my work, not least of which was his invitation to be part of the Project's work group on community building, a unique privilege. Together, Charles and Karen Marsh host the wonderful Bonhoeffer House.

At a crucial stage in the preparation of this book, I was awarded a grant by the Louisville Institute, a Lilly Endowment Program for the Study of American Religion. I take great pleasure in thanking the Louisville Institute and Dr. James W. Lewis, the Executive Director, for his interest and encouragement. A fellowship for study at the H. Henry Meeter Center at Calvin College and Seminary afforded me a key research opportunity.

Sam Eerdmans took on my book with enthusiasm and commitment, and I have enjoyed the privilege of working with him. In fact, it has been a joy to work with everyone at Eerdmans, including James Chiampas and Michael Thomson. I especially wish to offer my deep thanks to Mary Hietbrink, who brought great skill and patience to the editorial process. She made this a better book.

I am especially honored that LaVerne Stokes agreed to write the preface and Miroslav Volf the foreword. The reader will see my significant debt to each of them, especially in my understanding of community, theology, and the ministry of reconciliation.

Stephen Fowl, Susan Massey, Omar McRoberts, LaVerne Stokes, Allan Tibbels, and Jeff White all read and commented on all or part of the manuscript in one of its various stages. Stephen Lutz helped see this book off on its formal journey. Of course, any mistakes that may remain are mine. The reader should also know that I do not presume to officially represent New Song in the views I express in this book, but I am honored to be able to tell something of the story — and, I hope, tell it faithfully.

For over twenty-five years, I have been blessed to call Allan Tibbels a friend. During the past fifteen of these years, we have carried on an almost daily conversation about the church, discipleship, culture, politics, sports, and the challenges of the city. In countless ways, this conversation is the substructure of this book, and I am indebted to him at every level. Allan is an exemplar of self-giving Christian leadership, and his practice of it has been to my eternal benefit. My immense respect and gratitude extends to his wife, Susan Tibbels, and their daughters, Jennifer and Jessica, who have shared the call.

My parents, Raymond and Sally Gornik, have been unfailing in their encouragement, support, and love throughout my life. They provided me with everything I ever needed, not least of which is the foundation of faith. There is simply no way to fully express my gratitude to my parents for their love and godly influence. My sisters, Susan and Karen, have made being a brother a privilege. It is a great sadness for me that my father did not live to see the completion of this book (and a number of other important events in my life as well). In the making of this book, no one watched over every page more closely than Tungba, a shadow who is greatly missed.

This book is dedicated to my wife, Rita Aszalos, who shares the journey and whose love and friendship fill my days. That Rita loves me so much is a grace that I have not language to describe. With Rita has come her "home" of Hungary, and my life is considerably richer because of my new extended family and adopted city of Budapest. Through her work as a physician, Rita faithfully pursues the peace of the city. She is a blessing to those she serves and a daily example to me. Together we share the gift of our son, Peter, a source of endless wonder and laughter. It is my prayer that God's promised peace will extend over his life and the city in which he was born and dwells.